VICTORIAN
PRINT MEDIA

A READER

EDITED BY

Andrew King and John Plunkett

OXFORD
UNIVERSITY PRESS

OXFORD
UNIVERSITY PRESS

Great Clarendon Street, Oxford OX2 6DP

Oxford University Press is a department of the University of Oxford.
It furthers the University's objective of excellence in research, scholarship,
and education by publishing worldwide in

Oxford New York

Auckland Cape Town Dar es Salaam Hong Kong Karachi
Kuala Lumpur Madrid Melbourne Mexico City Nairobi
New Delhi Shanghai Taipei Toronto

With offices in

Argentina Austria Brazil Chile Czech Republic France Greece
Guatemala Hungary Italy Japan Poland Portugal Singapore
South Korea Switzerland Thailand Turkey Ukraine Vietnam

Oxford is a registered trade mark of Oxford University Press
in the UK and in certain other countries

Published in the United States
by Oxford University Press Inc., New York

© Andrew King and John Plunkett 2005

The moral rights of the authors have been asserted
Database right Oxford University Press (maker)

First published 2005

British Library Cataloguing in Publication Data

Data available

Library of Congress Cataloging in Publication Data
Victorian print media: a reader / edited by Andrew King and John Plunkett
P. cm

ISBN 0-19-927037-6 (hbk. : alk. paper) – ISBN 0-19-927038-4 (pbk. :
alk. paper)

1. Press–Great Britain–History–19th century. 2. Popular literature –
Great Britain–History and criticism. I. King, Andrew, 1957- .
II. Plunkett, John, 1974-.

PN5117V53 2005 070. 1 '7' 094109034–dc22   2005024338

Typeset by SPI Publisher Services, Pondicherry, India
Printed in Great Britain on acid-free paper by
Biddles Ltd., King's Lynn, Norfolk

ISBN 0-19-927038-4   978-0-19-927038-5 (Pbk.)
ISBN 0-19-927037-6   978-0-19-927037-8 (Hbk.)

1 3 5 7 9 10 8 6 4 2

ACKNOWLEDGEMENTS

WE should like to thank the librarians at the University of Exeter, the British Library at St Pancras and at Colindale, and the Senate House Library of the University of London, for all their assistance. Particular thanks go to Jessica Gardner at Exeter for dealing with many and various requests. We are also grateful to those students who helped us trial early versions of the following.

John would like to thank Kyriaki Hadjiafxendi for her advice and support; Andrew would like to thank the VICTORIA discussion list for generously sharing their collective knowledge and Lesley Hayman for her patience.

This book records the memory of our friend and colleague Chris Willis, in whose lively and much missed presence we first mooted a book such as this.

Figs. 1, 2 (the *Poor Man's Guardian*), and 17 are reproduced courtesy of the British Library; Figs. 3, 9, 10, 11, 12, 18, 19, 20, 21, 22, courtesy of University of Exeter Library; Figs. 4, 13, 14, 15, 16, courtesy of Special Collections, University of Exeter Library; Fig. 5, by permission of Andrew King; Figs. 6, 7, 8, courtesy of Bill Douglas Centre, University of Exeter Library; Fig. 2 (the newspaper stamp), from John Chandler and Henry Dagnall's *Newspaper and Almanac Stamps of Great Britain and Ireland* (1981: 208), courtesy of the Great Britain Philatelic Society.

CONTENTS

III: THE WORD OF LAW/THE LAW OF THE WORD

VI: READING SPACES

VII: AUTHORS, JOURNALISTS, REVIEWERS

VIII: NEWSPAPERS

IX: GRAPHIC MEDIA

LIST OF ILLUSTRATIONS

EDITORS' NOTE

OMISSIONS from material as originally published are marked by ellipses within square brackets; thus [...]. Where passages have been omitted from periodical articles, the pages we quote from are shown in square brackets at the end of the bibliographic details of each headnote. Extracts from articles without square brackets indicate that no whole pages have been excised. Extracts from books, on the other hand, follow the usual referencing procedure, indicating the pages quoted without brackets.

All endnotes, unless otherwise indicated, are by the editors.

Original spelling and punctuation have been retained in the extracts, even where this has meant reproducing incomplete sentences, inconsistent spellings, or typographical errors. To correct or systematize these varied signs of the mode of production was, we felt, inappropriate to our aims; on occasion we have felt it necessary to add an explanatory note where the sense was confused by typography. However, there is a major exception to our resistance to silent regularization: the double quotation marks preferred by our sources have been converted to single in accordance with OUP house style.

While we both contributed to all sections, John Plunkett was primarily responsible for Sections IV, VI, VII, VIII, and IX, and Andrew King for Sections I, II, III, and V.

INTRODUCTION

we live and move and have our being in print.
[Abraham Hayward], 'Advertising',
Edinburgh Review, 77 (1843), 2.

A SCEPTIC might remark that our epigraph is nothing but a hyper-
bolic marketing ploy: of course Hayward would make such a grandi-
ose claim; he was a prolific writer who moved in London's elite
literary circles, and we are merely using his words to puff our own
book. For all the validity of those assertions, it is also true that, during
the period in which Hayward was in business, print came to dominate
British society to such an extent that oral forms of culture lost much of
their status. The essence of nineteenth-century Britain might indeed
be defined as a move towards a society's 'Being-in-Print'. The media-
saturated society we experience today emerged from this nineteenth-
century mediamorphosis, and one of our aims is to provide a partial
genealogy of the present, noting differences as well as similarities.[1]
This Reader gathers heterogeneous material so as to facilitate new
understandings of the way print media operated in relation not only to
the expected literary categories of authors and readers, but to society
more generally. In so doing it aims to problematize the concepts of
'author' and 'reader', and indeed, 'print media', 'literature', and
'society', too.

It is a commonplace that the expansion of interest in book and print
history has been encouraged by the growth of electronic media during
the last thirty years. The doxa goes that such a confrontation with new
media has alerted us to the material and phenomenological boundaries of the old: we are more attentive now to the specificities and limits
of 'Being-in-Print' because it no longer seems to apply as comprehen-
sively to us. Rather than simply sealing the limits of print, however,
electronic media have also dramatically opened them up. As Jerome
McGann and others have argued, modern technologies have transformed the scope as well as the methodology of research: they have

made possible new histories, allowed once invisible cultural forma-
tions to emerge.[2] The same technologies have also reinvigorated the
burden of proliferation that nineteenth-century commentators themselves felt long before Virginia Woolf's *Orlando* observed that in the
nineteenth century 'sentences swelled, adjectives multiplied, lyrics
became epics, and little trifles that had been essays a column long
were now encyclopaedias in ten or twenty volumes.'[3] If between 1840
and 1870 the British population rose by 40 per cent, the number of
books published annually rose by about 400 per cent.[4] In 1864
Mitchell's *Newspaper Press Directory* already listed 1,764 periodical
titles; by 1887 it listed 3,597.[5] Individuals were often shockingly
prolific. G. W. M. Reynolds (1814–79) published *The Mysteries of
London* and its continuation *The Mysteries of the Court of London*
between 1844 and 1856 in 624 weekly penny numbers. This serial
alone comprises around 4.5 million words. Simultaneously, Reynolds
edited several periodicals and a weekly newspaper besides writing
innumerable other fiction texts and non-fiction articles. A standard
captatio benevolentiae expressed by students of Victorian print media
is an amazed apology for such proliferation. As all of us find, new
media notwithstanding, strict selection is essential.

Hand-in-hand with selection walk recontextualization and remediation. Whereas once an article may have been used for entertainment,
alluding effortlessly to current events, now it forms part of a university
syllabus, its references requiring painstaking elucidation. Given the
fragility and rarity of the relevant material, it almost always needs to be
transmuted into different media forms: a periodical becomes a series
of web-pages, or, as here, extracts assembled into a book. In a sense
this double displacement, of new context and new media, misrepre-
sents the primary sources. While not believing one can recover the
purity of any first reception (or even that such purity existed),
nonetheless we feel we can negotiate with this recontextualization
and remediation by deliberately exploiting the constraints and possibilities of the book format; in fact, this book.

One of the problems with anthologies is that issues that emerge
from specific contexts are often too hastily universalized. The tendency to generalize downplays not only why articles were published
but where and when (Laswell's famous questions spring to mind:
'Who says What in Which channel to Whom with What Effect').[6]

While not dismissing the possibility or value of generalization, we have sought to counter its centrifugal force by anchoring each piece in its context with a short headnote and liberal annotation, as well as with an introduction to each section that seeks to place the individual piece in a wider narrative. By these means we are seeking to work with, not against, the remediation and recontextualization that this book involves.

We feel that there is a need for a Reader in book form that can be used to introduce students to the key features of nineteenth-century print media, while providing a manageable historical and conceptual map for those already working in this field. Our choices are intended as much to provoke further questions and research as much as to establish an overview. Indeed, there are many contradictions between the extracts that we have been unable to comment on (several extracts disagree over the uses and status of the Bible, for instance).

The Reader consists of nine themed sections, each addressing a specific conceptual and/or historical issue, such as the different modes of authorship. Articles within each section are usually in chrono-logical order, except in one or two cases where we felt another arrangement led to greater clarity. It will soon be discovered that similar issues recur in different sections. Thus, Section II, on the perceived influence of print media, is closely linked to Section III, on judicial attempts to restrict the circulation of certain kinds of publi-cation. Similarly, the belief in the improving educational effect of literature expressed in Sections I and II is directly connected to the growth of institutions like free public libraries and mechanics' insti-tutes, which are examined in the section on 'Reading Spaces'. Such cross-relations are inevitable and welcome, indicative of the overde-termination of any media text or institution and the arbitrary but necessary artificiality of our division of the field.

Unsurprising, given our earlier stress on proliferation, will be our claim that each section could easily have been the subject of an individual Reader. We have not only had to select our sources: some have had to be substantially cut, principally because of the space limitations that are part of the essence of the book as a media form. It is fair to say that at least some of the pieces were written by authors who had pages to fill and deadlines to meet: the swollen sentences Orlando noted were partly a consequence of mode of production. As Thackeray memorably declared in the semi-autobiographical *Pendennis*, '[a] literary man has often to work for his bread against time, or against his will, or in spite of his health, or of his indolence, or of his repugnance to the subject on which he is called to exert himself, just like any other daily toiler.'[7] The effects of this industrial labour are often apparent in the extracts we have chosen. While our editing has inevitably sacrificed the fulsomeness of some pieces, it has not, we hope, falsely represented their general tenor or style.

Most extracts in the Reader are drawn from the periodical press, rather than from, say, authors' letters or publishers' records. There are several reasons for this. Nineteenth-century periodicals, out of self-interest as well as critical concern, frequently discoursed upon their own practices, status, and roles, as well as upon the industry in general. Thus, W. T. Stead's famous articles 'Government by Journalism' and 'The Future of Journalism' were not published in the evening daily newspaper, the *Pall Mall Gazette*, which Stead edited. Rather he chose the more discursive, reflective, less transitory, and more authoritative space provided by a monthly periodical, the *Contemporary Review*. The predominance of periodical articles here is therefore a telling index of the importance of the periodical press as a media form.

Articles from the periodical press also have the advantage of being public documents that were often intended to be interventions in specific debates over the politics or ethics of particular texts or print media forms. Such articles have a topicality and social embeddedness that link the public and private in intricate and often arcane ways. Wilkie Collins's famous essay on the 'Unknown Public' is a good example of this, its public and private meanings rendered visible here by annotation and comparison with pieces on similar topics.

It is no accident that our coverage of print media has a substantial number of articles that examine 'popular' media forms. Charles Knight, the nineteenth-century publisher who worked hardest to disseminate low-cost reading matter in the name of progress, once shrewdly observed that the process of printing was 'unquestionably a cheap process, provided a sufficient number of copies of any particular book are printed, so as to render the proportion of the first expense upon a single copy inconsiderable.'[8] Victorian print media, encouraged by population growth, rising living standards, and educational change and reform, were driven largely by the economic logic Knight identifies. Increasing numbers of readers created economies of scale for publishers, which overall favoured lower prices and more production, which attracted more readers, and so on and so forth in a continuously widening gyre. Indeed, one of the underlying models for the organization of this Reader comprises Robert Darnton's notion of a communications circuit. Darnton argued that the existence of a text can be understood through a process of cultural transmission, 'that runs from the author to the publisher (if the bookseller does not assume that role), the printer, the shipper, the bookseller, and the reader'.[9] One of the strengths of Darnton's circular model is that it can start at different points. Readers, for example, may either end or begin the circuit depending on whether they influence authors before or after the composition of a text. We consider stages of the communications circuit in three sections in particular: Printing, Publishing, Communication; Reading Spaces; and Authors, Journalists, Reviewers. The section on law scrutinizes some of the legal factors—taxation, copyright, obscenity—that regulated the circuit, and some pieces in Section II ponder whether 'influence' flows from producer to consumer or vice versa.

Section I, Setting the Scene, suggests that it was in the 1820s and 1830s that the main paradigms were laid down for the description of print media split into mass and restricted markets. Subsequent sections demonstrate this genealogical inheritance by exemplifying how versions of these competing visions underpinned many of the arguments that took place later in the century. The section called The Influence of Print is more conceptual, comprising articles that offer different models of the way that print media were believed to impinge on individual, class, and gender subjectivity. Sections on Newspapers and Graphic Media are self-explanatory, while Investigating the Popular examines the explosion of mass-market fiction from the 1840s to the 1860s. It also provides examples of the conflicting attempts to define and taxonomize 'popular literature'.

The interrelationship between the different sections reveals certain recurrent concerns. Gender, for example, runs through all the sections. We include a significant number of articles by women that describe their roles as authors and readers, from Sarah Stickney Ellis extolling the virtues of domestic reading to Charlotte O'Conor Eccles describing her frustrations as a professional journalist competing with her male colleagues in the 1890s. There is also abundant material that exemplifies patriarchal anxieties over the relationship between women and print media. Even extracts that do not directly address the issue of gender often implicitly emphasize the gendered space of print media through their reliance on gendered tropes or models. Thus, for example, the mass market is frequently feminized in contrast to masculine, high-status, literary production.

A note on our title to end with. This is a Reader in Victorian *Print Media* rather than in book history, the periodical press, or even print culture. We did not settle on this title lightly. We began by rejecting the terms 'book history' and 'periodical press' as we felt it essential to deal with a variety of print forms: books, periodicals, pamphlets, newspapers, sheet music, and so on, all existed in symbiotic relations with one another. We wanted to highlight this connectivity. 'Print culture' lasted longer in our thoughts and our non-use of the term is based less on rejection than on a preference for the term 'media'. Although usage of 'media' in the modern sense arose only in the 1920s, and our title may therefore be regarded in some quarters as anachronistic, we feel it justified not least because to exclude the term would problematically elevate the emic above the etic, the past above the present, the researched above the researcher. We do not pretend to be offering a transparent view of the past but a remediated one. What we have preferred is to oscillate between insiders' and outsiders' perspectives, between the early twenty-first century and the nineteenth: we are indeed mediating between them. Our use of the term 'media' also reflects the way our research is related not only to the disciplines of Literature and History, but to Media and Cultural Studies, whose insights, derived from textual theory and from sociology, inflect the organization of this book just as much as those of its older siblings. The title also embodies our desire to stress the transactional and transitive nature of the primary sources even within their own time. The extracts we have chosen were communications between people about communications between people: in other words, they were public mediations not solitary meditations. 'Media', then, we prefer for its stress on activity and movement. Whereas 'print culture' risks systematization, 'print media' emphasizes process.

Finally, we feel we need to explain our use of the adjective 'Victorian'. That its periodization is problematic is generally acknowledged now, and indeed several of the extracts below were not published in Britain or while Victoria was queen. 'Nineteenth-century' was the best alternative we considered. However, besides being clumsier than 'Victorian', this seemingly neutral replacement would have too easily excised the global—often imperialist—element of the expansion of print media. Our selection shows this to be key in areas as diverse and unexpected as copyright law, paper production, popular narrative, the export of stereotypes (in all senses), and even the longevity of the three-volume novel. The embeddedness of print media in imperial expansion is signalled by the image on the Reader's cover. In Tissot's 1870 portrait of Colonel Burnaby, a variety of print media forms—map, book, perhaps periodical—are taken-for-granted accessories of a fashionable society lion, narcissistic, glamorous, who himself published accounts of his imperial exploits, and who died while trying to relieve Khartoum in 1885. In the end, then, it was precisely for the fraught, troubling nature of 'Victorian' that we chose to retain it. In so doing, we embrace the abundance and heterogeneity of a field and time that is both our problem, like Orlando's, and yet our delight.

NOTES TO INTRODUCTION

1. Roger Fidler uses the term 'mediamorphosis' to name the process of media transformation: see his *Mediamorphosis: Understanding New Media* (London: Sage, 1999).
2. Jerome McGann, *Radiant Textuality: Literature after the World Wide Web* (New York: Palgrave, 2001).
3. Virginia Woolf, *Orlando* (1928; London: Vintage, 2000), 148.
4. Philip Davis, *The Oxford English Literary History, viii., 1830–1880, The Victorians* (Oxford: Oxford University Press, 2002), 202.
5. Simon Eliot, *Some Patterns and Trends in British Publishing, 1800–1919* (London: Bibliographical Society, 1993), 148.
6. Harold Lasswell, 'The Structure and Function of Communication in Society', in Lyman Bryson (ed.), *The Communication of Ideas* (New York: Institute for Religious and Social Studies, 1948), 37–51.

7. William Thackeray, *The History of Pendennis* (London: Smith, Elder & Co., 1910), 459–60.

8. Charles Knight, 'The Commercial History of a Penny Magazine', *Penny Magazine*, 2 (1833), 377.

9. Robert Darnton, 'What is the History of Books?', in David Finkelstein and Alistair McCleery (eds.), *The Book History Reader* (London: Routledge, 2002), 11.

I

SETTING THE SCENE

INTRODUCTION

Although this Reader is concerned mainly with the period from 1830 to 1900, it was in the previous two decades that many of the tropes used to describe the media assumed forms we are familiar with today. Discursive positions began to crystallize around two issues in particular: the significance of the spread of cheap printed matter and the peculiarly 'modern' phenomenon of the periodical press. This section examines contrasting visions of the role of the periodical press in the fifteen years prior to Queen Victoria's accession in 1837.

Debates over the influence of cheap literature, especially its ability to reform or corrupt readers, dominated those years. The spectre of the French Revolution, coupled with the vigorous production of radical journals and the battle over the unstamped press in the run-up to the 1832 Reform Bill, led to denunciations of mass-market reading as socially inflammatory. This aversion was predominantly a Tory discourse, here exemplified by Archibald Alison's essay from the fiercely conservative *Blackwood's Edinburgh Magazine*. As the articles by James Mill and Henry Brougham make clear, Whigs and Radicals opposed this view. They argued instead for the democratic and progressive role of print media; that cheap print had the potential to 'raise' the mental level of the nation as a whole and so prevent, not cause, revolution. Mutant forms of these differing but equally anxious visions underpinned many of the arguments that took place later in the century, though their attachment to party politics gradually dissolved.

The extracts in this section indicate the prestige of the 'Review' in the first half of the nineteenth century. The Whig *Edinburgh Review* was founded in 1802 and the Tory *Quarterly Review* opened seven years later in deliberate opposition. In 1817 *Blackwood's Edinburgh Review*, a monthly, was founded to undercut both, while the Radical quarterly and youngest member of the dominant quadrumvirate, the *Westminster Review*, was launched in 1824. These expensive six-shilling periodicals had circulations only in the thousands, but their importance stems from the social positions of their readers, not the numbers printed. At a time when literacy was comparatively circum- scribed and the technology for mass-reproduction of print limited, quarterlies operated as the connecting threads of a network amongst cultural and political decision-makers, who, in turn, consolidated their own positions by grouping themselves around specific period- icals. This is the significance not only of the Reviews' explicit party- political alliances but also of their cliquish attitudes to the arts, such as the *Edinburgh*'s 1807 attack on the 'Lake poets' (a coinage of its own). The role of the periodical in sustaining social networks can also be observed in the practice of anonymity. The Reviews did not append names to their 'reviews', preferring instead a magisterial 'we', the persona of the periodical as a whole. Nonetheless, such anonymity also invited a game of guess-the-author for members of the circle. Brougham's authorship of the *Edinburgh* piece below, for example, would surely have been inferred by many of the small group that comprised that quarterly's readers.

One reason for the significance of these periodicals was that they reinvented the scope of a 'review' so that it became an extended dissertation upon important political, religious, or social issues, in- cluding those concerned with print media themselves. William Hazlitt, John Stuart Mill, and James Mill all contributed famous articles about the media.[1] James Mill's piece, with which we open, offers remarkable insights into the operation of cultural hegemony. Its general points need to be seen as partly the effects of its immediate context, however. It was the manifesto of the *Westminster*: it was designed to generate notoriety and succeeded.[2] By exposing the conditions of the media market, and in particular the hidden political machinations of its rivals, the *Westminster* was making a bid for its own cultural and political legitimation. And yet, as Mill himself remarks while admitting his own implication in the 'seducements' of periodical publication, it is also possible *to some extent* to escape the immediate and local into the realms of abstract justice and truth.

Both the Mill and Brougham pieces are founded on an enlighten- ment ideal co-opted by Whigs and Radicals. The idea was that human improvement might be achieved by the diffusion of print media through the social body. Brougham, a prominent Whig writing in the major intellectual organ of the party, argues for the democratic benefits of popular reading and against the 'taxes on knowledge' designed to restrict the spread of political information. The Whig and Radical opposition to these restrictions stemmed, in part, from a faith in human rationality: they believed that a free market in print media (as in all commodities) would 'purify the public taste even upon topics which too naturally excite the worser feelings of our nature.'[3]

In contrast to Mill and Brougham, the Tory Alison relies on an essentially pessimistic and religious conception of the human subject as fallen and all too liable to sin. Alison explicitly genders the relationship between reader and producer: in a narrative founded on Christian mythology, the consuming masses are feminized, Eve-like, and only the Coming of the (presumably male) Genius can save them from seduction by the demagogic snake. But meanwhile, since, like Christ, Genius can neither be bought nor predicted, lesser writers must be paid in order to keep the populace on the straight and narrow.[4]

Although politically opposed, the extracts from Mill and Alison share one important similarity: they both think that, fundamentally, readers love texts because texts flatter them. Many of the ways media can be conceptualized have existed since classical times and, in drawing on the pre-industrial notion of the poet flattering his patron, Mill and Alison show the way long-standing tropes can be given new meanings to describe a society undergoing profound mediamorphosis.

FURTHER READING:

Keen; Klancher; Mill; Parker; Rauch; St Clair; Shattock, *Politics*; Sullivan, vol. ii; Wheatley.

[James Mill], 'Periodical Literature I. Edinburgh Review. Vol 1, 2, &c.', *Westminster Review*, 1 (January 1824), 206–68 [206–11, 212, 215, 219–22]

This article was a manifesto for the new London-based quarterly, the *Westminster Review*. The periodical was established as the organ of the Philosophical Radicals, a group of Utilitarians, led by James Mill (1773–1835) and Jeremy Bentham (1748–1832), who believed in the value of education and science as bringers of happiness. Never commercially viable in its first years, despite a circulation of around 2,000, the *Westminster* was heavily subvented by Bentham. While the extract provides a ruthlessly materialist analysis of the hegemony of the *Edinburgh* and *Quarterly*, its very critique only contributed to the prestige of the Reviews as media forms appropriate for intellectual debate.

If periodical criticism is good for any thing, it cannot be less needed in the case of periodical literature, than of any other class of the productions of the press. It is indeed a subject of wonder, that periodical publications should have existed so long, and have come at last to occupy so great a portion of the time and attention of the largest class of readers, without having become subject to a regular and systematic course of criticism. We trust it will appear that we shall have rendered an important service to the progress of the human mind, in setting at least an example of this species of control [. . .]

For a considerable number of years this field has been to such a degree occupied by two rival, celebrated, and successful publications, that the old have sunk into insignificance: the attempt to elevate new ones, has hitherto proved abortive [. . .]

Another circumstance renders criticism peculiarly necessary in the case of the publications to which we have alluded; we mean, the Edinburgh and Quarterly Reviews: under the guise of reviewing books, these publications have introduced the practice of publishing dissertations, not only upon the topics of the day, but upon all the most important questions of morals and legislation, in the most extensive acceptation of these terms. Whatever occasion, therefore, there can be for that species of censorship which criticism exercises over those who assume the task of supplying nourishment to the human mind, it is presented by the publications in question, and with peculiar circumstances of aggravation.

Of these circumstances, some they have in common with other periodical publications; some are peculiar to themselves. One law to which periodical literature is subject is attended with consequences, the good and evil of which have never yet been sufficiently analysed, though it is of the highest importance that they should be familiarised to the public mind. If a work is published, not periodical, and possesses real merit, it can afford to be overlooked for a time; and though it may be little noticed for the first year, or years, may count with tolerable certainty upon that degree of ultimate fame to which it is entitled. Not so with periodical literature. That must have immediate success, to secure so much as existence. A periodical production must sell immediately, at least to a certain extent, otherwise it cannot be carried on. A periodical production must be read the next day, or month, or quarter, otherwise it will not be read at all. Every motive, therefore, which prompts to the production of any thing periodical, prompts to the study of immediate effect, of unpostponed popularity, of the applause of the moment. [...]

On the favourable side it may be affirmed, that as the diffusion of all the good which is derived from reading, must be in proportion to the diffusion of this which is its instrument, this peculiarity in periodical literature is an eminent advantage. By consulting the public taste with continual anxiety, the pleasures of reading are perpetually supplied to the greatest possible number. [...]

The most effectual mode of doing good to mankind by reading, is, to correct their errors; to expose their prejudices; to refute opinions which are generated only by partial interests, but to which men are, for that reason, so much the more attached; to censure whatever is mean and selfish in their behaviour, and attach honour to actions solely in proportion to their tendency to increase the sum of happiness, lessen the sum of misery.

But this is a course which periodical literature cannot pursue. To please the great body of men, which is the object of the periodical writer, he must flatter their prejudices. Instead of calling in question the opinions to which they are wedded, he must applaud them; and the more he can furnish such men with reasons for being more in love with their opinions than before, the more he is sure of commanding their approbation, and of increasing their zeal to promote the reputation of his work.

The most mischievous of all erroneous opinions are those which lead to the injury of the great number of mankind, for the benefit of the small number; which tend to make it the interest of the small number, by giving them the power, to oppress the great number in all practicable ways, and to brutalise them for the purpose of rendering the oppression more easy, and more secure. [...]

The opinions, on the propagation of which the success of periodical writing depends,—immediate success, that success which is essential to their existence,—are the opinions in vogue; the opinions of those whose influence is the most extensive, who can go farthest in creating or hindering a reputation. But what is the class most instrumental in setting the fashion, which exercises the greatest control over the opinions of other men? The answer is not uncertain. The people of power compose it. The favourite opinions of people in power are the opinions which favour their own power; those opinions which we have already characterised as being the grand instruments of evil in this world, the ultimate and real cause of the degradation and misery of the great mass of mankind. To these opinions periodical literature is under a sort of necessity, under an inducement which generally operates as necessity, of serving as a pandar.

It is a common observation, that notwithstanding the influence of error in the world, arising partly from ignorance, partly from the influence of interested opinions in high quarters, the opinion of the wise and disinterested, though they are small in number, always, or at least generally, prevails at last, and becomes the opinion of the world. That there is this tendency in the opinions of the wise, is certain; and it is the ground of all our hopes for the amelioration of mankind. When an opinion, founded on truth, and tending to good, is once declared, and when there is the means of making it generally known, and of calling to it continually the attention of mankind, it is sure to make its way, and by degrees to bear down all that opposes it.

Here, however, the characteristic malady of periodical literature is most clearly seen. Instead of aiding this beneficent progress, it is opposed to it. The success of those important opinions, the progress of which involves the overthrow of opinions which are dearest to the classes by whom power is exercised for their own benefit over the rest of the community, and dear to them for this reason, that they tend to the support of the power which they so employ, is *slow*. Periodical literature depends upon *immediate* success. It must, therefore, patronise the opinions which are now in vogue, the opinions of those who are now in power. It will obtain applause, and will receive reward, in proportion as it is successful in finding plausible reasons for the maintenance of the favourite opinions of the powerful classes, and plausible reasons for the discountenance and rejection of the opinions which tend to rescue the interests of the greater number from the subjection under which they lie to the interests of the small number. In this view, it is evident, that, so long as the interest of the smaller number is the predominating interest in any community; so long periodical literature is the natural enemy of the most important and beneficent class of opinions, and so long may the balance of its effects be expected to be decidedly in opposition to them. We say the balance of its effects, because there is no doubt that occasionally, from various motives, the more important of which we shall think it expedient to describe, the periodical press displays exertions both in opposition to the opinions which tend to confirm abusive powers in the hands of the few, and in favour of the opinions which tend to rescue from these powers the interests of the greater number.

After the mass of the people have become a reading people, a reward is held out for writings addressed peculiarly to them. The opinions of the people will, of course, be consulted in such writings; and those opinions which are peculiarly recommended to the powerful classes by the circumstance of their favouring the existence of those powers of theirs, which may be used for their personal purposes, will not be the peculiar objects of applause. But it is with the more numerous, as it is with the less numerous classes; they have some opinions which are just as well as important, and they have others which are erroneous. [...]

We have seen, during some late years, in this country, since the talent of reading has become more general, periodical publications, addressed in a particular manner to the more numerous class. They are cheap publications, from the circumstances of the purchasers; and they have been worse than they otherwise might have been, from the characters of those who have been the principal instruments in their production, and who, had they been wiser and better men (for, with little exception, they have been very defective in one or other, or both, of these requisites), might have obtained as much success, with less subservience to the errors of those to whom they have addressed. It is abundantly apparent, however, even on a cursory inspection of the writings to which we have thus alluded, that the principal influence to which they bend is that of the favourite opinions, right or wrong, of those to whom they look for their reward. That writings produced under this influence can hardly fail, where men are as ill instructed as they still are in this country, and where partial and sinister interests so greatly preponderate, to have a greater tendency to evil than good, we imagine cannot, after what we have stated, be regarded as a matter of doubt.

The two publications which we have already pointed out as destined to be the principal objects of our attention in this department, are addressed to the aristocratical classes. From the circumstances belonging to them it will appear that they may be regarded as almost exclusively addressed to those classes. To what degree they have been subservient to the interests of those classes, in other words, hostile to the interests of the more numerous class, it would be premature in us, and perhaps hardly fair, as yet, to pronounce. That can be properly determined only by evidence adduced [...]

Assuming that they agree in this main and characteristic circumstance, of being addressed to the aristocratical classes, upon what principle, we may be asked, do we account for the great diversity which appears in their tone and character; a diversity so remarkable, that they are not regarded as competitors, but as enemies, as tending not to the same, but to opposite ends; as promoting irreconcilable opinions, the one upholding what the other endeavours to destroy ? [...]

In our own country, the aristocracy is a motley body; and it imports us to be familiarly acquainted with the ingredients of the compound. [...]

The more efficient part of it is undoubtedly that small number of leading families, probably not two hundred in all, which returns a majority of the members of the House of Commons. [...]

The aristocracy of this country are naturally, in their political proceedings, divided, under the guidance of their interests, into two sections. The Quarterly Review follows the one section: the Edinburgh Review follows the other. The one of these sections is commonly known under the title of the ministerial party. The other is known under that of the opposition party.[5] [...]

From this development of the interests and views of the two sections of the aristocracy in this country, it is clearly seen what may be expected to be the aim and tendency of the publications, particularly periodical, which look for success to the favour and applause of the one or the other. Those on the ministerial side have, as far as the interests of the aristocracy are concerned, a more simple course to pursue. They advocate them directly, and with enthusiasm, affected, or real. The aristocracy are spoken of as the country. Whenever the interests of the country are named, it is the interests of the aristocracy that are meant. [...]

The course which is necessary to be pursued, by such periodical publications as adopt the vocation of promoting the cause of the opposition section of the aristocracy, will be easily understood, after what has been already said, without many words for its elucidation. The seesaw of the party must be recommended [between the aristocracy and the people]. It is called the middle course. Every art is used to gain it reputation, under the title of moderation, and by the application of bad names to the two sets of opinions, between which the party oscillates, and which it is in reality putting forward by turns. The set of opinions, purely on the side of aristocratical power, are called despotical. Those which support the demand of effectual securities in favour of the people are declared anarchical, and are commonly stigmatised by some nickname in the slang of the day; jacobinical, for instance, at one time; radical, at another. [...]

It is essential, in writing upon this plan, to deal as much as possible in vague language, and cultivate the skilful use of it. Words which appear to mean much, and may by those to whom they are addressed be interpreted to mean much, but which may also, when it suits the convenience of those who have used them, be shown to mean little or nothing, are of singular importance to those whose business it is to play the game of compromise, to trim between irreconcilable interests, to seesaw between contradictory opinions.

Language of this description is peculiarly needed in making declarations which are meant to gain favour with the people. A party which is itself a section of the aristocracy, which desires to please the aristocracy, and by means of pleasing them to become the distributors of the good things which the possession of the powers of the government bestows upon the aristocracy, risk nothing by speaking explicitly in favour of their privileges. What is requisite is to have vague terms at command, when it is necessary to speak in opposition to these privileges. Aristocratical domination, in the abstract, may be spoken of as something exceedingly hateful, or pregnant with the worst of consequences. The people may be exhorted to be on their guard against it. [...] In the meantime, great care must be used not to remove any part of the veil which conceals from the view of the people, the real amount of aristocratical power in this country. When any specific measure is proposed, which would really operate to the diminution of that power,—choosing the members of parliament by ballot, for instance,—it must be loudly decried, and every thing must be done to attach to it, if possible, the apprehension of evil consequences. [...]

One word of a personal nature seems to be required. We have described the interests which operate to withdraw periodical writers from the line of utility, and we have represented it as nearly impossible for them to keep true to it. What! Are we, it may be asked, superior to seducements to which all other men succumb? If periodical writing is by its nature so imbued with evil, why is it that we propose to add to the supply of a noxious commodity? Do we promise to keep out the poison which all other men yield to the temptation of putting in? If we made such a pretension, our countrymen would do right in laughing it to scorn; and we hope they would not fail to adopt so proper a course. We have no claim to be trusted, any more than anyone among our contemporaries: but we have a claim to be tried. Men have diversities of taste; and it is not impossible that a man should exist who really has a taste for the establishment of the securities for good government, and would derive more pleasure from the success of this pursuit, than of any other pursuit in which he could engage, wealth or power not excepted. All that we desire is, that it may not be reckoned impossible that we may belong to a class of this description.

There is another motive, as selfish as that which we ascribe to any body, by which we may be actuated. We may be sanguine enough, or silly enough, or clear-sighted enough, to believe, that intellectual and moral qualities have made a great progress among the people of this country; and that the class who will really approve endeavours, in favour of good government, and of the happiness and intelligence of men, are a class sufficiently numerous to reward our endeavours. No matter what our motives may be, the public will soon see whether our actions continue true to the ends which we profess; and that is all by which their interests can be affected; all, therefore, about which they need to care. [...]

[Henry Brougham], 'Progress of the People—The Periodical Press', *Edinburgh Review*, 57 (April 1833), 239-48 [240-2]

Brougham (1778–1868) had co-founded the *Edinburgh Review* in 1802. He was instrumental in setting up the Society for the Diffusion of Useful Knowledge in 1827 and, as a radical Whig MP, repeatedly put before Parliament bills for state-funded education (all defeated). In 1830 he had been made Chancellor and strongly supported the 1832 Reform Act that extended the franchise. The extract is from a 'review' of the new penny weeklies, just out in bound annual format: the *Penny Magazine*, founded by the SDUK in the year of the Reform Act, the rival 'High Church' *Saturday Magazine of the Society for Propagating Christian Knowledge*, and the commercial—and eminently respectable—1½d. *Chambers's Edinburgh Journal*.

It is a most delightful reflection for the friend of human improvement, to think, that at the low price of a few shillings, the poor may obtain, and with all the accommodation which periodical publication affords, a volume of five or six hundred pages, in small folio, and upwards of three hundred excellent engravings. But it is far more delightful to reflect, that hundreds of thousands crowd round the sources whence the streams of pure and useful knowledge flow; and that the numbers who thirst for it, and can thus slake that thirst, may be reckoned by the million.[6]

The growing taste for such works will not indeed deprive politics and polemics of their peculiar interest; but they will surely make the people more capable of judging soundly and charitably upon matters of controversy, whether civil or religious—and will, we confidently expect, purify the public taste even upon topics which too naturally excite the worser feelings of our nature. A reduction of the taxes upon one species of knowledge (the news of the day) will further this important amendment;—especially by encouraging provincial papers, perhaps the most important part of the periodical press; and by enabling those who are bent upon instructing all classes of the community to combine matter of ordinary intelligence with other less ephemeral information.

The success attending such works as we are now speaking of, is a triumphant answer to those who, in disparagement at once of the People and the Press, are so fond of repeating, that nothing will sell which is not seasoned with ribaldry and libel. The taste for these has been, we admit, most deplorable—such as reflects deep and lasting disgrace on its contemptible victims. Who are they? Not the middle—and certainly not the lower classes, with the exception perhaps of a few hundreds in the greater towns—an exception not worth mentioning. But the part of the community which is a prey to the passion for slander,—which furnishes the whole demand for this vile produce of falsehood and spite,—which, indeed, can hardly drag on its existence without a periodical supply of the hateful debasing stimulus—is that which, 'clerical as well as lay,'[7] arrogates to itself the name of 'higher classes,' and the right (monstrous inconsistency!) of unceasing invective against the licentiousness of the press. That they should grudge the poor man his cheap book of wholesome information, and complain of those who provide him with it, is about as reasonable as it would be for a sot, whose vitiated palate can bear nothing weaker than brandy, to accuse the brewer of encouraging dram-drinking, or to denounce the water-drinker as intemperate.

In another point of view, and at the present crisis,[8] we hold all these indications of popular improvement extremely important. They afford the most solid hopes of information and regular habits becoming so prevalent as to give the bulk of the people—even the poorest—a perceptible influence upon the conduct of public affairs; and their admission to a more direct share in the operations of representative government, cannot fail to follow in the course of a short time, not only with safety, but with benefit, to the security of all our institutions. We now see the leaders of the High Church party occupied in making secular knowledge so cheap, that every one above the lot of beggary may acquire it. Was this, could this have been, their vocation half a century ago? Was it forty years ago, at the breaking out of the French Revolution and War? Was it thirty years ago, when that war was renewed?[9] Then who shall presume to say, that the same party may not, moving onward in their own improvement with an accelerated pace, in ten or twelve years more, have discovered that the best means of fixing our institutions upon an imperishable foundation, is making those love them for whom they exist,—the body of the people; and to the body of the people intrusting their defence? [...]

[Archibald Alison], 'The Influence of the Press', *Blackwood's Edinburgh Magazine*, 36 (September 1834), 373-91 [373-4, 376-7, 379-81]

In 1817 William Blackwood started his *Magazine* as Tory opposition to the *Edinburgh Review*. 'Maga' (as *Blackwood's* was affectionately called) cost the same as the quarterlies but came out every month. Lighter and often more personal in tone, it quickly built up a larger readership. Alison (1792–1867) was a well-known Scottish Tory and a regular Blackwood's author: from 1831 he wrote extensively for Maga and in 1833 the firm published the first two volumes of his best-known work, the *History of Europe*. A section of the article not reproduced here attributes Maga's 9,000 circulation to its unwavering opposition to free trade.

Every one gifted with powers of foresight or historical information, is sensible of the influence of the press, and deplores its present pernicious tendency. Every one sees that it has effected a greater change in human affairs, than either gunpowder or the compass. Every wise man trembles at the perilous ascendency of democratic ambition which the extension of political reading, with which it is attended, to the lower orders has given, and every good man laments the ruinous vigour with which the depraved principles of our nature have shot up under its fostering influence; but no one thinks of considering how this new and terrible power is to be mastered, and the dissolving principles with which it is invested, again brought under the dominion of virtue and religion. [. . .]

The features by which the press,—meaning by that term, not the great works which are destined permanently to delight and instruct mankind, but those lighter productions which attract and are alone read by the multitude—newspapers, magazines, reviews, novels, superficial travels—is now distinguished, are a general democratic, and an increasing licentious character. [. . .] Generally speaking, the press is decidedly democratic; and this is proved to demonstration, by the immense circulation which the leading papers which have adopted the side of politics have obtained. That it is daily, too, becoming more licentious, that strong and vivid pictures addressed to the passions and the imagination, incitements to sensual indulgence, and that fatal union of genius with voluptuousness which is the well-known sign of a declining age, have of late become prevalent, is a matter of universal observation. Works of an opposite character, indeed, are able and numerous; [...] but the immense circulation of the productions which stimulate the political or the private passions, sufficiently proves that it is they which fall in with the spirit of the age.

It is not less observable, that the influence of property, and the higher classes, as hitherto exerted, is obviously and totally unable, in determining the character of reading at least, to counteract this tendency. This is a very remarkable circumstance, which lies at the bottom of all really useful discussion on this subject, but to which by no means sufficient attention has yet been paid. In every other department, wealth can counterbalance, and more than counterbalance, the influence of numbers; but in determining the character of the daily or periodical press, it has no such power. The great bulk of the labour of the manufacturer is made for the higher ranks; they command all the genius and industry of artists and artisans of every description; but in that highest of all departments of exertion, human thought, at least in that portion of it which is addressed to the multitude, the overbearing influence of numbers is at once apparent. [...] The greatest genius, the noblest talents, indeed, are exerted on the Conservative side; but their sphere of operation is comparatively limited: it is chiefly confined to those who, from their education or habits, are already inclined to that way of thinking; and the immense multitude of the middling and lower orders continue to brood incessantly over the democratic press—over those who laud their wisdom, and magnify their capacity, and flatter their vanity— who tell them, that their opinion cannot err, and that, in the increase of their influence, is to be found the only effectual antidote to all the evils of society. [...]

The democratic character of the press is obviously owing to the fact, that nothing is so acceptable to the human heart as flattery. The immense majority of mankind, totally incapable, from their habits, capacity, and acquirements, of taking any useful part in public affairs, like nothing so much as to be told that they are perfectly qualified to take the lead. The less that they are so qualified, the more are they gratified by being told so; just as a woman who has long been accustomed to the sway of beauty, is less liable to intoxication from its praises, than one who, from a homelier appearance, has been less habituated to resist the insinuating poison. A man who has spent twenty years in the study of history or politics, will probably feel great difficulty in deciding on many of the questions which now agitate society, and willingly withdraw from the responsibility of taking any share in directing public affairs; but a ten-pounder, who has read the Radical journals for a few months, will experience no such hesitation, and determine at once on the weightiest interests of society, without any other instructors but his favourite political flatterers. It is not in human nature for ignorance to resist flattery, or ambition the possession of power; and therefore it is, that the democratic press ever is the most acceptable to the lower orders, because it is there, and there only, that they find the continued praises, which are the most grateful of all music to their ears, and the incitements to power, which are the most powerful of all allurements to their ambition.

The licentious and depraved character of so large a portion, at least of the lower strata, of the press, is the natural consequence of the inherent corruption of our nature; and of the fatal truth, that the human mind, when left to itself, will take to wickedness as the sparks fly upwards. This truth, long ago revealed to our first parents, and incessantly inculcated in religion, is now receiving its clearest illustration, in the character of a large portion of the democratic press, and the rapid dissolution of all the bonds of society, under the influence of an unrestrained discussion of public affairs. It is here that the enormous, the irreparable error of the present times is to be found. The advocates of education, overlooking all the dictates of experience, deaf to all the revelations of religion, insensible to all the conclusions of reason, uniformly asserted, that to make the human mind virtuous, it was sufficient to render it enlightened; and that if the people were only taught to read, there could be no doubt that they would select only what would improve and elevate their minds. But the inherent depravity of our nature has speedily shewn itself, amidst these dreams of political enthusiasts. [...] Paris and London, the two leaders of what is called civilisation, are now the great marts of profligacy, obscenity, and irreligion; and amidst the rapture of the educationists, and incessant eulogies on the growing lights of the age, enough of wickedness, clothed in seductive forms, is daily issuing from these great fountains of corruption, as is sufficient, if continued for half a century, to overturn the whole civilisation and liberties of Europe.

The inability of property and education to counteract or check this downward progress, is owing to a peculiarity in the form in which knowledge is transmitted, which has hitherto met with but little attention, but is nevertheless attended with most important consequences, and lies at the foundation of all the important consequence of the press in public affairs. This is the fact, that the daily press, from which nine-tenths of mankind implicitly adopt their opinions, *is not, and cannot be, encouraged by wealth, education, or virtue, in any degree at all proportioned to their resources or importance*, and, consequently, the superior number of the lower orders gives them a decided preponderance over all the better classes of society. A great Conservative noblemen takes in, perhaps, three or four daily papers, and that is the whole encouragement which his L.100,000 a-year gives to the Conservative Journals. Sir Walter Scott took in one, and that was the limit to his influence over the daily press. Ten Radicals, subscribing together [...] neutralize one Conservative whose income is two hundred times as great as all theirs put together, and exceed fourfold that of the greatest genius of modern times. [...]

We do not by any means assert that the rich and the great have not their weaknesses and their depravities as well as the poor and the indigent; we know perfectly that they have, and are clearly of opinion, that a press exclusively addressed to them would speedily become as depraved, corrupted, and disgraceful, as that chiefly intended for the working classes. It is in the due intermixture of both that any thing like an antidote to the common depravity of all is to be found; and without the perpetual superintendence and efforts of religion, all attempts to stem the torrent of evil, even in this way, will prove ineffectual. [...]

What, then, is to be done, in combating so subtle and penetrating a poison? [...] Is man inevitably expelled from Paradise by eating of the Tree of Knowledge? [...] [I]f a remedy exists, it is to be found in the principles we are now about to develope.

The editors and journalists who conduct the public press, are, for the most part, not inclined from conviction, or a sense of public duty, to revolutionary principles. [...] [T]he motive which originally influences them is a desire of gain. Doubtless, there are many sincere and honest Republicans in this as in every other class; but this is not the case with the whole. Many of them espouse the democratic side in politics, and the licentious in morals, because they find it the most popular, and because they would rather sell thousands of their paper or periodical, than hundreds. This being the ruling principle, the remedy for the evil is to be found in the discovery of a countervailing motive, equally strong and equally general in its operation. This is to be found only in the love of gain.[...]

It is in vain to talk of coercing the press by fetters, or prosecutions. These brutal remedies, fit only for a savage age, are in the end totally inadequate to coerce its excesses. [...]

But how, it will be asked, is opinion to be brought round to the real and ultimate interests of society? How are the many to be induced to read works or journals which cease to flatter their vanity, and discard those which do? Who is to persuade the multitude, that property should be the moving, and numbers only the restraining power? [...]

The success of all attempts, indeed, to withstand the allurements of democracy to society, just as of all attempts to resist the seduction of the senses in the individual, is doubtful, but it is not hopeless. The great point is to organize a Conservative militia to combat the force of anarchy with its own weapons; to fight the demons of hell, not with the coarse and vulgar instruments of prosecutions and dungeons, but the diamond of genius and the sword of truth. The popular, not less than the female heart, may be won by genius, when wealth sues in vain. Hitherto the press has proved so formidable, because its powers, from the cause we have mentioned, have been exerted chiefly on the side of anarchy, and no adequate counteracting defences have been set up to resist its assaults. It was the same when gunpowder was first invented: the old battlements, impregnable to the array of feudal power, were found to be wholly defenceless against this new method of attack; and down went tower and town before the terrible tempest of the breaching batteries. By degrees, however, it was discovered that the same power might be applied to the defence of bulwarks; and the genius of Vauban restored the balance of attack and defence, and enabled the besieged, behind their green mounds and sloping glacis, long to defy the attacks of the greatest beleaguering force.[10] WHAT WE WANT IS A VAUBAN OF THE PRESS; some mighty genius, which, measuring the whole extent of the power to be resisted, and the immeasurable perils consequent on its triumph, shall devise the means of organizing the powers of thought in an effective and systematic manner, in defence of justice, order, and truth, and counterbalancing, by the concentrated influence of government and property, the present overwhelming ascendency of numbers. [...]

All the great efforts of genius, from the beginning of the world, have been the result of inward inspiration, ebullitions of the *feu sacré*;[11] and, however much [financial] interest may be an additional or secondary inducement, it never yet, to such men, was the primary object. But, admitting all this to be true,—conceding that by no efforts of property you will ever be able to summon up at will a Milton, a Newton, a Scott, a Chateaubriand,—still the question remains, may you not by such methods command the ruder and humbler, perhaps, but not less effective powers, of such men as are qualified, and perhaps better qualified than their superiors in genius, to arrest the attention of the multitude,—of a Wilkes, a Horne Tooke, or a Cobbett?[12] [...]

NOTES TO SECTION I

1. [William Hazlitt], 'The Periodical Press', *Edinburgh Review*, 38 (May 1823) 349–78. [John Stuart Mill], 'Periodical Literature: Edinburgh Review', *Westminster Review*, 1 (April 1824), 505–41.

2. John Stuart Mill, *Autobiography*, ed. Harold J. Laski (London: Oxford University Press, 1924), 78.

3. Brougham, 'Progress of the People', 241.

4. See also Aled Jones, *Powers of the Press: Newspapers, Power and the Public in Nineteenth-Century England* (Aldershot: Scolar Press, 1996), 157–9.

5. i.e. Tory and Whig respectively.

6. *Original note*: The preface [to the *Penny Magazine*] [...] calculates the readers of the Penny Magazine at one million, and the three works most probably are circulated among different parts of the community.

7. *Original note*: There is but one opinion entertained, we find, among our southern neighbours, as to the encouragement given to slanderous newspapers by the High Church party. From this reproach our Church is happily free.

8. The precise referent is not clear: it may perhaps concern disturbances in Ireland around the recent elections.

9. France declared war on Britain on 1 February 1793 (–1802) and again in May 1803 (–1815).

10. Sébastien Le Prestre de Vauban (1633–1707), French military engineer famous for his innovations. A 'glacis' is a slope outside a fort designed to expose attackers to the weapons of the defenders.

11. Sacred flame, i.e. the Holy Ghost. The reference is to the Pentecost.

12. John Wilkes (1725–97), radical politician who campaigned for political reform and press freedom. John Horne Tooke (1736–1812), radical politician who fought for political reform, charged with treason in 1794 but found not guilty. William Cobbet (1763–1835), widely-read radical writer.

II

THE INFLUENCE OF PRINT

INTRODUCTION

What happens when we engage with a media text? Does it influence us, and if so, how? There are no simple, pure answers to these questions, and the extracts below all mix assumptions and models at a sometimes dizzying pace and in often oblique ways. This introduction seeks to separate out some of the models and assumptions from the mix, and to trace a few of the connections between them.

Interaction of media and audience is usually conceptualized in metaphorical terms: indeed, the term 'influence' is itself metaphorical. Literally it means 'a flowing in'; during the Renaissance the word was used to denominate mysterious astrological fluids that flow into us from the stars and make us act as we do. When applied to the media, the term even now retains something of inexplicable magic. 'Influence' often refers to flow of information and, as will be plain in the subsequent section on the law, power is often maintained through control of this flow. A hydraulic notion can be discerned in talk of the media as 'safety-valves' that keep the machinery of society working properly (Greg). Even more common is the stop-cock model, a conception of influence that much media regulation is based on. The French Revolutions of 1789, 1830, and 1848 were all perceived as caused by unchecked floods of print through the social body: flow of media into the lower classes was considered a major problem. As we saw in the first section, the Tories preferred to restrict that flow while the Whigs promoted improving literature to flush out the seditious. In both cases there was an underlying anxiety about class warfare: hence the hydraulic model may slide into the idea of the media as weapons (as in Fanny Mayne).

Formal regulation is only one result of worries about influence. Informal regulation is even more pervasive. In nineteenth-century Britain this was often based on 'bowdlerization' whereby texts were expurgated of matter deemed inappropriate for the 'impressionable'. Gender control was often at stake: what was to flow into the non-patriarchal was only the pure, since one of the major roles of the media was to teach and maintain appropriate gender roles and identities. This might entail keeping the non-patriarchal ignorant, an action legitimated by the notion that the imagination, especially of females, was all too liable to error. However different they are in tone, the piece from the *Wesleyan Magazine* and Greg (1859) share this idea. Edward Salmon inserts it into the context of imperial racial theories, presenting orthodox gender roles as necessary to the raising of a master race.

Ways we discuss media influence today are often developments of nineteenth-century models, however different their contexts and finer meanings. The 1830 piece from the *Penny Satirist*, like Fanny Mayne's and Salmon's essays, is based on notions of what today many newspapers would call 'copy-cat' crimes: audiences translate the symbolic—what they perceive in the media—into material life. Then again, several extracts in various sections of this Reader treat audiences as a single 'mass' whereby messages can be injected into a passive social body, prefiguring 1930s propaganda theory and much Frankfurt school writing. The articles by Salmon and the *Wesleyan Magazine* propose the idea that the media seduce through offering idealized images of audiences, which resonates with Lacan-inspired notions of the media as flattering mirrors (as in Williamson). The extract in Section VIII by 'A Journeyman Engineer' even anticipates Althusser's notion of 'interpellation'.

Janice Radway reminded us that 'reading is not eating', but we continue to talk of the 'consumption' of media texts, sliding together bodily ingestion and the capitalist commodification of representation. Many discussions of influence in the nineteenth century treated texts as food. Reading nourished or poisoned bodies like victuals or drink (the latter always carrying a hint of substance abuse, whether referring explicitly to alcohol or to an all-too-easily digested soup). But reading affected bodies in other ways too, causing shocks like electricity, explosions, wounding us like weapons—or sticking to our skins like pitch. Sometimes these tropes were linked to specific genres: sensation fiction, for example, was often described as generating extreme bodily effects.

While texts and bodies were often related, reading was also and more importantly perceived as influencing the soul, with all the religious and moral implications that involved. Reading was compared to listening to sermons or to being taught, and the spirit might be cultivated or tended like a garden or, conversely, allowed to lie fallow or grow weeds (Salmon; Greg, 1859; Mansel; *Medical Critic*). The Alison piece from Section I is especially rich in metaphor and worth considering in this light.

That there were cases of resistance to the overt ways texts tried to influence readers is evident in many extracts in this Reader. Cooper beautifully shows how a poor autodidact might appropriate the Whig model to integrate himself into the established hierarchy, and then to attempt to modify that hierarchy by turning cultural skills into political ones. A much more overt example of resistance can be observed in the amusing extract from Netta Syrett's novel. Its balletic lightness contrasts not only with the opening extract from the *Penny Satirist* (which concerns influence on boys), but also with the serious resistance of those women, such as Evadne in Sarah Grand's *Heavenly Twins* (1893), who, for all their efforts to escape, remain trapped within the weightiness they learned from their forefathers.

FURTHER READING:

Althusser; Ang, 'Nature of the Audience', *Living Room Wars*; Brantlinger; Fetterly; Flint; Gilbert; Habermas; Radway; Rose; Vincent, *Bread*; Williams; Williamson.

'The March of Knowledge: or Just Come from Seeing "Jack Sheppard"', *Penny Satirist: A Cheap Substitute for a Weekly Newspaper*, 3 (14 December 1839), 1

'The March of Knowledge', an insulting term associated primarily with the early 1830s and Brougham's drive to educate the masses, was revived again over 1839–40 by the publication of *Jack Sheppard*, a three-volume Newgate novel by Harrison Ainsworth, which had a thief and gaol-breaker as hero. It spawned many imitations and theatrical versions.[1] The *Penny Satirist* (1837–46) was a Radical/Whig illustrated paper that tended to court whatever it perceived as the dominant opinion, as here. Its woodcuts were by C. J. Grant, well-known for his vigorous style.

FIG. 1. [C. J. Grant], 'The March of Knowledge: or Just Come from Seeing "Jack Sheppard" ', *Penny Satirist*, 14 December 1839, 1.

FIRST JUVENILE.—I say, wasn't it well acted?

SECOND JUV.—I believe you. I do likes to see them sort o-robber pieces. I wouldn't give a tizzy to see wot is call'd a moral play—they ar' so precious dull. This Jack Sheppard is worth the whole on 'em.

THIRD JUV.—How I should like to be among the jolly cocks; plenty to eat, drink and spend—and everyone has his *mott* too![2]

FOURTH JUV.—Ar; shouldn't I like to be among 'em in real arnest. Wot jovial lives they seem to lead! and wot's the odds, so long as you ar' happy? Only see how such coves are handled down to posterity, I thinks it's call'd, by means of books, and plays, and pictures!

FIFTH JUV.—Blow'd if I shouldn't just like to be another *Jack Sheppard*—it only wants a little pluck to begin with.—ALL FIVE.—That's all.

F.[anny] M.[ayne], 'The Literature of the Working Classes', *Englishwoman's Magazine, and Christian Mother's Miscellany*, NS 5 (October 1850), 619-22

The Englishwoman's Magazine started life as the *Christian Mother's Magazine* in 1844 and ran until 1857. Its shilling monthly mission to cultivate Christian values through the printed word is visible not only in this article but in several other pieces it printed on the same topic around this time. Fanny Mayne, novelist and biographer, subsequently produced a version of this article as pamphlet 'for private circulation', *The Perilous Nature of the Penny Periodical Press* (1851), and went on to edit her own improving periodical, *The True Briton: A Home Friend and Evening Companion* (1851-4).

I believe, that the dulness and apathy—sometimes real, oftener assumed—the infidelity, negative or actual, that the minister meets with in persons in old age, or on their death-bed, are not the careless weeds that have sprung up naturally in the soil of a sinful heart, but that they are tares, sown by Satan and his agents on earth, which tares have choked the good seed of early training. I think, that it will be found on inquiry, that in most cases, the minds of the working-classes are by no means allowed to lie fallow after the period of quitting school. Nay, I know for certain, that the working-classes of the country, both in agricultural and manufacturing districts, are, to a great extent, a *reading people*; *a reading* and a *thinking people!*

The question will be asked, What do they read? Where can they get books? It will be said, they have none; they cannot afford to buy them. This is by no means the case. The working-classes of the country have a press of their own; books,—if so they may be called—of their own; newspapers, magazines, periodicals, novels, of their own. They can, and will, and do afford to buy them. They will deprive themselves of their luxuries,—yes! more than that,—they will deprive themselves of their necessary food, and spend their last halfpenny in the indulgence of their literary propensities. So true is the saying, that, *reading is a sensual gratification*; though not always the most refined of sensual gratifications.

It is a lamentable fact, that the poor, having almost universally acquired the power of reading,—this power having been in most cases supplied gratis, or nearly so, by the wisdom and right feeling of the higher classes,—have been left almost entirely alone as to the employment of this power. It is true, that in some parishes, there are *lending libraries*; but the books supplied by these are very often not to be had at a moment's notice; and when had, are not such as to attract the attention of a wearied labourer. Giving all credit to the immense amount of good done by the works published by the Christian Knowledge Society in both its branches, and more especially by the Religious Tract Society, still both these Societies are behind the times, in the supply of suitable and attractive reading for the working classes.³ Their scientific works are too learned; that is, they are not simple or lucid enough in their style, or *English* enough in their diction: their tales are not, in general, sufficiently imaginative: and above all, the books are still in price above the means of the generality of the working classes. Halfpenny, penny, and three-halfpenny works are what they buy. Brought to their doors by itinerant vendors, thousands, not to say millions of such works are dispersed weekly through the country. If my authority for this statement be asked, I turn to one of the letters published in the *Morning Chronicle*, on 'Labour and the Poor.' There it is stated, that above 62,000 decidedly pernicious penny or three-halfpenny works are sold weekly, from *one* shop in Liverpool. Again, it is stated in *The Ragged School Union Magazine* for August 1850, that the average sale in London of such works is 400,000 weekly; or 20,800,000 yearly.⁴ It is difficult to devise means for ascertaining the sale throughout the kingdom, but the extent thereof must be incredible, if not incalculable.

Can a man touch pitch, and his hands not be defiled? Can he take fire in his bosom, and his clothes not be burned? Surely not. As certainly as we read a glowing description of any transaction—be it what it may—we throw ourselves into the situation of the describers or of the actors in that transaction. Man, by nature, is a being of imitative sympathy. Facts testify to this; witness the well-known truth, that when one person had, not long ago, thrown himself from the monument, others tried to do the same; that poisoning, begets poisoners; a murder, murderers; down to the fact of our every-day experience, that one *yawner* in a company will produce several.

Tales of imagination then, that deal in murders, and in other species of iniquity, lead to the actual commission of similar sins. The history of a sceptic will lead others to scepticism. We cannot help being drawn, as it were, into the mind of the narrator, whether he narrate actions or feelings. Are the *million* then fed with the moral poison of tales of crime, and of open or insinuated infidelity? The result must be a callousness to crime, and a doubting of revealed truth, going on to the actual commission of the one, and to the absolute denial of the other.

Can no steps be taken to remedy this crying evil?

The first great step is, to promote by every means in our power, the circulation of a better description of cheap literature. The two societies above-mentioned should begin by issuing all their instructive and larger works, in penny numbers, as well as their religious tracts and magazines. But this will not be enough. It is an acknowledged fact, that the public mind is most chiefly attracted by periodical works, containing tales of imagination, and other articles, some descriptive, some very instructive, running on from week to week. Advantage should be taken of this, to get out periodical works of a higher stamp as to religion and morals; of a really good Christian spirit, though not, necessarily, entirely religious. The highest religious truths,—ay, and the most serious heresies, too,—have been inculcated and learned among the higher classes, by means of works of imagination. Such works are acknowledged by all parties to be lawful weapons. Why may not such be adapted in their style and form to the working classes? Why may not tales of imagination for the working classes be written in such a style as to lead to good, rather than to evil? Let them be as exciting as they can be,—but exciting to horror at sin, and to a love and esteem for that which is true, lovely, pure, and of good report.

It would, in short, be endless to describe all the means that might be taken, and that ought to be taken, to provide the *working classes* with a species of literature superior to that which is now offered to them. Be it remembered, that this cannot be done solely by the regular sale at shops; but must be effected, as the lower description of works are sold, by itinerant venders from door to door. Those who *love their country*, will try to assist in this work; for the lawlessness and chartism disseminated by the penny press, is undermining the foundations of our tranquillity. Those *who love the souls* of their fellow-creatures will be up and doing in providing a substitute for the atrocities and impurities described and rendered attractive in this pernicious litera- ture. Above all, those who desire *the glory of their God* will do all that in them lies to hinder the circulation of blasphemous and shocking works against the Most High and his Word. [...]

[William Rathbone Greg], 'The Newspaper Press', *Edinburgh Review*, 102 (October 1855), 470-98 [470, 477-83]

Greg (1809–81), Manchester mill owner, writer, and civil servant (in that order), was reputed for his commitment to politics, lack of interest in party politics, and faith in the idea of enlightened oligarchy. Greg wrote this review while earning his living as a writer after the failure of his mill. It was inspired by the first volume-length history of the press, F. K. Hunt's *The Fourth Estate* (1850), R. Blakey's just-published *History of Political Literature*, and an account of George III. The press in late 1855 was particularly confident. William Howard Russell of *The Times* was perceived as having brought down the government through his reportage of the incompetent conduct of the Crimean War, and the Stamp Tax had recently been made optional (see next section). The *Edinburgh Review*'s longstanding support for a free market in the press seemed now vindicated.

In common with everything of signal strength, Journalism is a plant of slow and gradual growth. The Fourth Estate, like the Third Estate, has reached its present dimensions and its actual power from slight beginnings, by continuous accretions, and through a long course of systematic and unremitting encroachments. Of far more modern date than the other estates of the realm, it has overshadowed and surpassed them all. It has created the want which it supplies. It has obtained paramount influence and authority partly by assuming them, but still more by deserving them. Of all *puissances*[5] in the political world, it is at once the mightiest, the most irresponsible, the best administered, and the least misused. [. . .]

Thus by gradual steps, and through much tribulation, the newspaper press of England has attained to the mighty influence which it now exercises. That influence it is scarcely possible to exaggerate. Journalism is now truly an estate of the realm; more powerful than any of the other estates; more powerful than all of them combined if it could ever be brought to act as a united and concentrated whole. Nor need we wonder at its sway. It furnishes the daily reading of millions.

It furnishes the exclusive reading of hundreds of thousands. Not only does it supply the nation with nearly all the information on public topics which it possesses, but it supplies it with its notions and opinions in addition. It furnishes not only the materials on which our conclusions must be founded: it furnishes the conclusions themselves, cut and dried—coined, stamped, and polished. It inquires, reflects, decides for us. For five pence or a penny (as the case may be) it *does all the thinking* of the nation; saves us the trouble of weighing and perpending, of comparing and deliberating; and presents us with ready-made opinions clearly and forcibly expressed. For the number of those who form their own conclusions on public matters independently of their newspapers, or who take the trouble or risk perplexity of reading more newspapers than one, are few indeed, and are chiefly to be found in the metropolis. [...]

The newspaper press owes its influence to three causes,—to the special value of the functions which it exercises; to the remarkable talent with which it is habitually conducted; and to the generally high and pure character which it maintains.

In the first place, it is a necessary portion, complement, and guardian of free institutions. In a country where the people—*i.e.* the great mass of the educated classes—govern, where they take that ceaseless and paramount interest in public affairs which is at once the inseparable symptom and the surest safeguard of political and civil liberty, where, in a word, they are participating citizens, not passive subjects, of the State,—it is of the most essential consequence that they should be furnished from day to day with the materials requisite for informing their minds and enlightening their judgment. If they are in any degree to control, to guide, to stimulate the administration, they must, as far as possible, become qualified to do so. They need, therefore, to be kept *au courant*[6] of all transactions and events which bear upon the interests or credit of their country. [...]

Again: Journalism is needed as part and parcel of the *representation* of the country. The House of Commons is not, and perhaps never can be made, a complete and perfect representative of all classes, all interests, all shades of opinion. Certainly it has not yet realised that bright ideal. Non-electors are more numerous than electors. Thousands of Englishman of nearly every rank—dwellers in towns that are not boroughs, dwellers in counties who are not freeholders nor large tenants, residents in cities who are not householders—have no members of Parliament to listen to them and to speak for them. [...] We all feel that we could not do without the vent for expression which the Newspaper Press affords us. We should explode were it not for such an immediate and ample safety-valve. We could not possibly wait for the slow expression, the inadequate and inaccurate exposition of our sentiments and opinions which only could be furnished to us by our senators in St. Stephens![7] It is not too much to say that if by any accident journalism were to become suddenly extinct, such a Parliamentary Reform as the wildest of us have never dreamed of, would become an instant and paramount necessity. Those who have no share in the choice of members, those who feel themselves inadequately represented or misrepresented, those who find in Parliament none who hold their peculiar doctrines or who are qualified to give them effective utterance,—would all join to insist upon such an entire renovation and reconstitution of the representative assembly as would throw all previous 'organic changes' into the shade.

But perhaps one of the most necessary and practically important functions of the Daily Press is the opening it affords for the exposition of individual grievances and wrongs. It is a surer guarantee against injustice and oppression than any institutions or any forms of government could be. Even the freest and most popular executive wields fearful instruments of quiet and insensible tyranny which the victims of them could neither escape nor resist, but which they may expose. [...]

The services rendered by the 'fourth estate' to the Government are scarcely less necessary or important than those which it renders to the People. It supplies the latter with a safe channel for the expression of those feelings which might else find a vent in overt acts of discontent and insubordination, and it keeps the former cognisant of popular sentiments and passions which it is most essential it should understand and be early made acquainted with. It would be very difficult for even the best intentioned administration to be thoroughly well informed as to the state of feeling and opinion in the nation, except through the medium of the various and discrepant organs of the daily and weekly press. The House of Commons can only most imperfectly supply this information; often its members themselves learn the wishes of their constituents principally or exclusively through this unrecognised channel. [...]

The value of Journalism as a safety-valve in moderating discontent by allowing it a vent, in expending the energies and exposing the weaknesses and fallacies of demagogues, and in thus preserving the peace and order of society through the joint securities of freedom and of justice, can only be fully estimated by governments which have tried the opposite scheme, or observers who have closely watched its operation. [...]

But the Periodical Press is invaluable to the Government in another way. Through it ministers can instruct and inoculate the nation. They, as well as their critics and antagonists, have access to its columns. It is an engine which they or their friends can use as effectually as it can be used against them. By its means they may prepare the public mind for a great measure, educate it to the understanding of a complicated subject, penetrate it to the core with some healing or prolific principle, clear up misconceptions, defend themselves against slanderous accusations, insinuate needful elucidations and explanations which yet could not well have been officially supplied. In those few cases in which the Government has been in advance of the people (the new Poor Law was one), by using the Press as an instrument of education, it has made that possible which might otherwise have been attempted in vain.

Finally, newspapers are of the utmost service to Government in completing and correcting its official information. They have now reached a pitch of wealth and talent which enables them to command wider, abler, and more numerous channels in every quarter of the world than are often open to the agents of Government. It may seem strange and scarcely creditable that it should be so, but the fact is undeniable that the leading journals for many years past have communicated tidings of important events to the public before those tidings had reached ministers through their ordinary official correspondence. The more agitating the crisis, and the more momentous the news, the more likely is it to be early received by those whose profession, pride, and interest it is to obtain it and publish it with marvellous rapidity. [...]

'S.', 'What is the Harm of Novel-Reading?' *Wesleyan-Methodist Magazine*, 78, 2, 5th series (October 1855), 932-4 [933-4]

The shilling monthly *Wesleyan-Methodist Magazine* (1778–1969) was the organ of a vigorous Protestant sect who tolerated no images of any kind in their chapels and who stressed the religious aspects of the printed word. The following is typical of a much wider social sector than Methodists, however: Flaubert's *Madame Bovary*, published in 1856, is but one—if more famous—example of the notion that novel-reading was dangerous for young women. The following comprises the end of a sensational story about a girl who was allowed by her father to read whatever she wanted.

Writers of fiction absorbed all her hours. Circulating libraries were ransacked, that she might find the most stimulating novels.

The influence of this trashy reading was soon apparent in her looks, tempers, language, and manners. Impatient of all restraint, she wandered in the paths of the tempter. The love-tales of her favourite authors inflamed her imagination. She dreamed and spoke of splendid matches, till she became quite unfitted of the matter-of-fact world in which her lot was cast. As for domestic duties, they were too common-place for so gay a young lady. These she would leave to the home-spun Marthas, whose genius was formed to superintend them. She possessed no fortune, but was fully prepared to spend one, should it ever come into her possession. Her course downward was fearfully rapid. Erelong she told a confidant that she would rather become the mistress of a gentleman than the wife of a tradesman!— words, alas! but premonitory. A 'gentleman' appeared as a suitor, promised marriage, abused her credulity, kept her in suspense, and then abandoned her. She was forsaken of all her friends. Misery stared her in the face. Golden dreams of sinful pleasure—the creation of novel-reading—ended in disgrace, ruin, disease, a broken heart, and an untimely grave! She passed into eternity without hope, in what might have been the very bloom of her days, leaving behind her two unhappy infants, to perpetuate her shame. [...]

The press teems with fiction, set forth in the most fascinating style, the tendency of which is to allure into forbidden paths. Ought we not be as careful about the food of the mind, as we are about the food of the body? In either case poison, however sweet, will destroy life. The difference is, that in the one case the body is killed, in the other the soul!

[William Rathbone Greg], 'False Morality of Lady Novelists', *National Review*, 8 (January 1859), 144–67 [144–9]

Despite lasting only nine years, the *National Review* (1855–64) was one of the most prestigious quarterlies of mid-century, edited by the notable economists and journalists Walter Bagehot (1826–77) and Richard Holt Hutton (1826–97). In 1856 Greg had been made a commissioner at the board of customs and became financially independent of writing, but as a member of the coterie that ran the *National* he continued to contribute a large number of articles. The piece below is ostensibly a review of five novels, including *Ruth* 'By the Author of "Mary Barton" ' (Elizabeth Gaskell), and three pseudonymous novels, one by 'Holme Lee' and two by 'Hamilton Murray' (the fifth novel, *Framleigh Hall*, is anonymous and its authorship untraced). Despite their pseudonyms, Greg recognizes the hand of 'ladies': Holme Lee was Harriet Parr, an author favoured by Mudie's lending library for her moral purity, and 'Hamilton Murray' was Baroness Marie Pauline Rose Blaze de Bury.

It is not easy to over-estimate the importance of novels, whether we regard the influence they exercise upon an age, or the indications they afford of its characteristic tendencies and features. [. . .] We are by no means sure that, with reference to the sphere and nature of the impressions they produce, prose works of fiction do not constitute precisely that branch of the intellectual activity of a nation which a far-seeing moralist would watch with the most vigilant concern. [. . .]

There are many reasons why we should look upon novels in this serious point of view. They are the sole or chief reading of numbers; and these numbers are mainly to be found among the rich and idle, whose wealth, leisure, and social position combine to give to their tastes and example an influence wholly out of proportion either to their mental activity or to their mental powers. They are the reading of most men in their idler and more impressionable hours, when the fatigued mind requires rest and recreation; when the brain, therefore, is comparatively passive; and when, the critical and combative faculties being laid to sleep, the pabulum offered is imbibed without being judged or sifted. They form, too, an unfortunately large proportion of the habitual reading of the young at the exact crisis of life when the spirit is at once most susceptible and most tenacious—

'Wax to receive, and marble to retain;'[8]

when the memory is fresh, and has a greedy and by no means discriminating appetite; when the moral standard is for the most part fluctuating or unformed; when experience affords no criterion whereby to separate the true from the false in the delineations of life, and the degree of culture is as yet insufficient to distinguish the pure from the meretricious, the sound from the unsound, in taste. [...] Finally, novels constitute a principal part of the reading of women, who are always impressionable, in whom at all times the emotional element is more awake and more powerful than the critical, whose feelings are more easily aroused and whose estimates are more easily influenced than ours, while at the same time the correctness of their feelings and the justice of their estimates are matters of the most special and preëminent concern.

There are peculiarities, again, in works of fiction which must always secure them a vast influence on all classes of societies and all sorts of minds. They are read without effort, and remembered without trouble. We have to chain down our attention to read other books with profit; these enchain our attention of themselves. Other books often leave no impression on the mind at all; these, for good or evil, for a while or for long, always produce *some* impression. Other books are effective only when digested and assimilated; novels either need no digestion, or rather present their matter to us in an already digested form. Histories, philosophies, political treatises, to a certain extent even first-class poetry, are solid and often tough food, which requires laborious and slow mastication. Novels are like soup or jelly; they may be drunk off at a draught or swallowed whole, certain of being easily and rapidly absorbed into the system.

[...] We incline to think that a far larger number of persons receive the bias of their course and the complexion of their character from reading novels than from hearing sermons. We do not, indeed, hear of sudden conversions and entire and enduring changes of life and temper consequent on the perusal of romances, such as are occasionally said to follow the stirring eloquence of some great divine; though we believe that more analogous cases might be found than is usually supposed, were there any missionary enthusiasts to chronicle them, and were the recipients of the new spirit skilful and careful to trace back the healing influence to its source. But we are convinced that the instances are numerous beyond conception in which souls trembling and hesitating on the verge of good and evil have been determined towards the former by some scene of fiction falling in their way at the critical moment of their mental history; in which minds have been sustained in hours of weakness and strengthened in hours of temptation by lifelike pictures of sorrows endured and trials surmounted in virtue of some great principle or some true sentiment; and in which sinners, fallen indeed, but not lost, have been induced to pause, to recoil, and to recover, by seeing in some work which they had opened only for amusement the hideousness of a crime whose revolting features they could not recognise except when reflected in a mirror. Numbers have first, not *learned* perhaps, but been actually brought to perceive and realise with practical result, the attractions of 'whatsoever things are pure, holy, lovely, and of good report,' by seeing their vivid delineations in the pages of 'an owre true tale.'[9] Numbers who *might* no doubt have acquired their estimates of the relative gravity or excellence of favourite faults or difficult virtues from authorised Bibles or accredited moralists, have in reality learned them—often, alas, blended with a fearful degree of error—from fictitious histories; and seek their personal code of laws in Scott, or Bulwer, or Victor Hugo, or George Sand, or the Countess Hahn-Hahn, or Manzoni, in place of drawing it direct and pure from the Catechism or the Gospel.[10] And far larger numbers still, as we may all of us be conscious from our own experience, owe it to the novels with which they occasionally refresh their wayworn spirits along the world's hot and dusty thoroughfare, that the perception of the beautiful, the enthusiasm for the grand, and all the finer sentiments and gentler and tenderer emotions which soften and embellish life, are not utterly dried up, or crusted over, or trodden out, amid the fatigues and conflicts and turmoil of this arid and weary existence.

There is yet another consideration which points in the same direction. Prose fiction furnishes not only the favourite reading of the young; it is also the line in which young writers most incline to try their powers. A few of the more enthusiastic make their first essay in verse, but the large majority prefer novels. These are easier, they require less sustained effort, and they are incomparably more certain of an audience. Again, women, as we have said above, are the chief readers of novels; they are also, of late at least, the chief writers of them. A great proportion of these authoresses too are *young* ladies. There are vast numbers of lady novelists, for much the same reason that there are vast numbers of sempstresses. Thousands of women have nothing to do, and yet are under the necessity of doing something. Every woman can handle a needle *tant bien que mal*:[11] every unemployed woman, therefore, takes to sewing. Hundreds of educated ladies have nothing to do, and yet are tormented with a most natural desire, nay are often under a positive obligation, to do something. Every educated lady can handle a pen *tant bien que mal*: all such, therefore, take to writing—and to novel-writing, both as the kind of which requires the least special qualification and the least severe study, and also as the only kind which will sell. [...] [T]he supply of the fiction market has mainly fallen into their hands; and it speaks well for the general taste and cultivation of the age, that, under such circumstances, so many of the new novels that pour forth weekly from the press should be really interesting and clever, and that so few should be utterly poor or bad. But it is in the nature of things impossible that productions of such a character, from such a source, however able or however captivating, should not be radically and inherently defective. The plot may be exciting, the style may be flowing, the sentiments may be pleasing and even stirring, and the characters may be natural, interesting, and well sustained; but the views of life and the judgments of conduct must be imperfect and superficial, and will often be thoroughly unsound. These things cannot be surely deduced, as is too often fancied, from certain fixed rules and principles which may be learned *à priori*; they depend in a great measure on observation and experience, on knowledge of the world and of the characters that move and act there, and on the ascertained consequences of actions and influences of qualities. Now here the young are necessarily wanting. If the writer be a young man, his experience of life must be brief, imperfect, and inadequate. If the writer be a young lady, her experience must be not only all this, but must be partial in addition. Whole spheres of observation, whole branches of character and conduct, are almost inevitably closed to her. Nay, even with respect to the one topic that forms the staple of most novels, and a main ingredient in all, viz. love, [...] many of the saddest and deepest truths in the strange science of sexual affection are to her mysteriously and mercifully veiled; and the knowledge of them can only be purchased at such a fearful cost, that we cannot wish it otherwise. [...]

In short—and to sum up in a single sentence the gist of all that we have said—that branch of the literature of our day which exercises the widest and most penetrating influence on the age,—from which the young and impressible (nearly all of us, in short, at one period or other) chiefly draw their notions of life, their canons of judgement, their habitual sentiments and feelings (so far as these are drawn from literature at all), and their impressions as to what is admirable and right and what is detestable and wrong,—is in the hands of writers whose experience of life is seldom wide and never deep, whose sympathies have not yet been chastened or corrected, whose philosophy is inevitably superficial, whose judgement cannot possibly be matured, and is not very likely to be sound. The result is, that we are constantly gazing on inaccurate pictures, constantly sympathising with artificial or reprehensible emotions, constantly admiring culpable conduct, constantly imbibing false morality.

admirable organization of the literary market, that a supply of acceptable fiction has so closely followed, or has even in some degree anticipated and created the demand. If this be so, [...] it follows that the craving for excitement itself is the only element in the matter that presents much interest to the psychologist, or requires much examination at his hands. Is this craving then in any sense a novelty, either in its essential nature, or in its direction, or in its extent? and if so, of what nature are the evils it produces, and where are we to seek their remedy.

In reply to these questions, it appears to us that the love of excitement incidental to the idle members of prosperous communities is showing itself, to some degree, in a direction new to the present generation, and in an extent which, although vastly exceeding anything ever before witnessed, is only commensurate with the immense increase and wonderful diffusion of wealth and superficial knowledge. People with nothing to do, and with sufficient money to live in luxury, have always had, and from the nature of the human mind always must have, a strong desire for 'sensations'—a desire that has invariably found gratification in the acts and sayings of conspicuous criminals. When ladies and gentlemen escorted renowned highwaymen to Tyburn, and when gambling and drinking were the universal customs of polite society, this desire was at least as glaringly shown as it is in the present day, even although it did not extend so far, or spread so deeply, on account of the different social conditions of the time. [...] Our traders and manufacturers, collectively growing rich with un-exampled rapidity, have, by their families, enormously swelled the number of the wealthy unemployed, to whom the craving for sensation comes with a force intensified by the absence, or by the general condemnation, of many of the most stimulating resources of an earlier period. The pattern set by an exemplary court and a decorous nobility leading to the almost universal abandonment of gambling and drinking, has added to the natural consequences of those vices the absolute demoralisation that attends upon practices held in universal disrepute, and has left them as the uninvaded and unenvied privileges of some of the vilest of mankind. [...]

For a certain time the want of sensation impressed itself upon literature and the stage [...] The males thus suffering have found resources in muscular Christianity and the rifle movement; the females, in the fabrication and perusal of sensation literature. [...]

There have been times, not very remote, in English history, when immorality was uninteresting and prosaic, simply by reason of its universality. In the present day, ladies of station who offend, place themselves by a single effort in the position of distinguished criminals, and excite a share in the concern felt about the conduct and welfare of such persons as Mr. Leopold Redpath or the late Mrs Manning.[15] We see no reason to fear that this concern will in the least degree tend to increase the crimes of swindling or homicide; and we do not fear either, that the eager perusal of the unsavoury revelations made before Sir Creswell Creswell[16] will, as a rule, in any appreciable degree undermine the virtue of our wives and daughters [...] [A]mong other things they will at least learn the unerring action of the Nemesis that awaits upon sin [...]

And if such be the lesson taught by the current realities of life around us, such will also, in the main, be the lesson taught by the fiction that reflects that life, and that must reflect it faithfully, in order to attract and maintain an audience. [...] [A]lthough a sensation novelist must step a little over the bounds of probability, although clandestine marriages with grooms are unfrequent and although, when contracted, they usually involve a totally different chain of consequences from those imagined by Miss Braddon—still, young ladies who read newspapers will not, on the whole, learn much previously unknown evil from the romance;[17] and they will be furnished with an additional incentive to the exercise of caution and prudence with regard to the degree in which their fancies are to be indulged. The world, it is trite to say, moves fast, evil of every sort is rampant and unconcealed around us; and it is possible that 'Sensation literature' may become a substitute, not altogether to be despised, for the didactic teaching that was in vogue with an earlier generation.

'Reading as a Means of Culture', *Sharpe's London Magazine*, NS 31 (December 1867), 316-23 [316, 323]

Sharpe's (1845-70) underwent various transformations. It started as a penny-halfpenny illustrated weekly aimed at respectable family reading and, in 1848, became a shilling monthly. In common with many periodicals that targeted domestic readerships, it gradually metamorphosed into a women's magazine. It is from this latter period that this article is taken, a collage of commonplaces aimed at the respectable 'lady'.

In the early stages of the world, before the art of writing was invented, men had to depend, for the acquisition of knowledge, chiefly upon oral instruction [...] And as the family bond was then a strong one, each child was in a pre-eminent sense the pupil of his parent, and each patriarch the teacher of his child [...]

But since the art of paper-making was invented, and, as related to this, the art of printing, a mighty change has taken place [...] In our own country, where all may, if they choose, enjoy the advantages of popular education, the majority are readers. [...]

WHAT, THEN, IS THE END TO BE AIMED AT IN READING?

Now, a large class of readers propose to themselves no end at all in their reading. They feel attracted to the page of a book or to the column of a newspaper, just as they are to a garden of flowers, or to a winding river. They have no purpose in view; they have no object to be accomplished. The act of reading terminates in itself, so far as any end is concerned. It is just a matter of present gratification, of present amusement.

Another class read only to kill time, which otherwise would hang heavily on their hands. Their minds are listless, or they are tormented with sad thoughts, or inward upbraidings, or remorse, or shame, from which they wish to escape; and by killing time in this escape from themselves, so far forth, they commit suicide.

Another class read in order to make a show of learning. They read incessantly, and incessantly boast of what they have read. They are ostentatious; they are vain in their knowledge, and pedantic.

The true end of reading, as the means of self-culture, is evidently, in the very statement of the terms of the proposition, self-culture. Now, self-culture aims at the improvement of all the higher powers of our nature. [...] By holding intercourse with the great minds of the world as they still live in their works, we can become like them. Our memories can be stored with the treasures of knowledge gathered by them. Our imaginations can rove freely among the forms of thought among which they expatiated with delight. Our judgment can decide correctly in view of the facts which they have collected, and the principles which they have evolved, and the reasonings they have elaborated. Our wills can be confirmed by the motives they administer. Our hearts can be brought into harmony with their hearts by contemplating what awakened their emotional nature. Our moral feelings can become assimilated to theirs by inhaling their spirit.

In books we have the concentrated wisdom of past ages and of the present, which we can appropriate to ourselves, for our own improvement and that of others. The true end of reading is to make this appropriation. Lord Bacon's rule is the best: 'Read, not to contradict and confute, nor to believe and take for granted, nor to find talk and discourse, but to weigh and consider.'[18]

[...] In good books, we hold converse with the great minds which composed them. We contract an undying friendship for those great minds that have ministered to our happiness and our improvement. As we advance in years, other friends fall off, or prove treacherous, or die; but those minds continue the same, and we turn to them, from a frowning or a smiling world, with increasing confidence and delight, as to old friends and tried friends that will ever be dear to us.

Thomas Cooper, *The Life of Thomas Cooper. Written by Himself* (London: Hodder & Stoughton, 1872), 53, 55-60, 62-4

Cooper (1805-92), autodidact poet, political activist, novelist, was the model for Charles Kingsley's *Alton Locke* (1850)—though the passage below might also resonate uncomfortably with Hardy's *Jude the Obscure* (1896). Cooper's autobiography is fascinating not only for his account of Chartism but for the details of his self-education. As will be clear, he is less interested in interpreting texts than using them to integrate himself into an imagined high-status society. In the passage below he is 19, an apprentice shoemaker in Gainsborough, Lincolnshire. He has just joined a cheap private circulating library and started borrowing from a free one.

From Chapter VI. Student-Life: Its Enjoyments: 1824-1828

How rich I was, with ten shillings per week, to buy food and clothes— now all this intellectual food was glutting me on every side! And how resolute I was on becoming solitary, and also on becoming a scholar! What though I could not get to Cambridge, like Kirke White, could I not study as hard as he studied, and learn as fast?[19] Friends and acquaintances had left the little old town, one after another; but I would not leave it. I would learn enough in that corner to enable myself to enter on mature life with success; and I would have no friend in addition to my new friend John Hough, with whom I had promised to spend a couple of hours or more, every Saturday night, in intellectual converse. [...]

One of the greatest incentives I had to solid study was the reading, in Drew's 'Imperial Magazine,' an account of the life of Dr. Samuel Lee, Professor of Hebrew in the University of Cambridge, and a scholar, it was said, in more than a dozen languages.[20] He had been apprenticed to a carpenter at eleven years old, had bought Ruddiman's Latin Rudiments on an old book-stall for a trifle, and learnt the whole book by heart; and had stepped on, from Corderius's

Colloquies to Caesar,[21] and from Caesar to Virgil, and so on; and had learnt to read Greek, Hebrew, and Syriac, all from self-tuition, by the time he was five or six and twenty. Yet he was ignorant of English Grammar and Arithmetic!

I said in my heart, if one man can teach himself a language, another can. But there seemed such a wealth of means of learning now around me, that I felt as if I must attempt to accomplish a broader triumph of self-education than Lee accomplished. I must try if I could not combine the study of languages with that of mathematics; complete a full course of reading in ancient and modern history, and get an accurate and ample acquaintance with the literature of the day [...]

I must add, that there was some sadness mingled with these buoyant resolves. The thought of dear Henry Whillock's death would bring serious fears about his spiritual state and my own fitness for death.[22] My new friend Hough carefully reminded me of the true wisdom there was in being prepared to die; and when I told him, without any concealment, of the doubts we had gathered from reading those sceptical books, he solemnly advised me to enter on a course of reading of the Evidences of Christianity. I promised to do so; and I gradually drew up my plans for study and the employment of time into a written form. To this I added written resolves of a very necessary kind: that I would speak grammatically, and pronounce with propriety; and I would do these always. [...]

I thought it possible that by the time I reached the age of twenty-four I might be able to master the elements of Latin, Greek, Hebrew, and French; might get well through Euclid, and through a course of Algebra; might commit the entire 'Paradise Lost,' and seven of the best plays of Shakespeare, to memory; and might read a large and solid course of history, and of religious evidences; and be well acquainted also with the current literature of the day.

I failed considerably, but I sped on joyfully while health and strength lasted. I was between nineteen and twenty when I began to commit Ruddiman's Rudiments to memory—thinking it was better of begin to learn Latin with the book that Lee used—though I found afterwards I might have done better. I committed almost the entire volume to memory—notes and all. Afterwards, I found Israel Lyon's small Hebrew Grammar, on a stall, bought it for a shilling, and practised Hebrew *writing* as the surest means of beginning to learn, every Sunday evening. I got hold of a Greek Grammar about a year after; but did not master it earnestly, because I thought it better to keep close to the Latin for some time. I also picked up a small French Grammar; but *that* seemed so easy, that I thought I could master it without care or trouble.

On Sunday mornings, whether I walked, or had to stay indoors on account of the weather, my first task was to commit a portion of the 'Paradise Lost' to memory. I usually spent the remainder of Sunday, save the evening, whether I walked or remained at home, in reading something that bore on the Evidences. Thus I not only read through the well-known 'Natural Theology' and 'Horæ Paulinæ,' and 'Evidences' of Paley, and the equally popular 'Apologies for the Bible and Christianity' of Bishop Watson, Soame Jenyns' 'Internal Evidences,' Lord Lyttelton's 'Conversion of St. Paul,' and Sherlock's 'Trial of the Witnesses,'—but I diligently read books that required deeper thinking, and some that were filled with profound learning—such as Butler's 'Analogy,' Bentley's 'Folly of Atheism,' Dr. Samuel Clarke's 'Demonstrations of the Being and Attributes of God,' Stillingfleet's 'Origines Sacræ,' and Warburton's 'Divine Legation of Moses.'

Historical reading, or the grammar of some language, or translation, was my first employment on week-day mornings, whether I rose at three or four, until seven o'clock, when I sat down to the stall.

A book or a periodical in my hand while I breakfasted, gave me another half-hour's reading. I had another half-hour, and sometimes an hour's reading, or study of language, at from one to two o'clock, the time of dinner—usually eating my food with a spoon, after I had cut it in pieces, and having my eyes on a book all the time.

I sat at work till eight, and sometimes nine, at night; and, then, either read, or walked about our little room and committed 'Hamlet' to memory, or the rhymes of some modern poet, until compelled to go to bed from sheer exhaustion—for it must be remembered that I was repeating something, audibly, as I sat at work, the greater part of the day—either declensions and conjugations, or rules of syntax, or propositions of Euclid, or the 'Paradise Lost,' or 'Hamlet,' or poetry of some modern or living author.

In the spring of 1826, after getting through Valpy's Delectus, and a part of Stewart's 'Cornelius Nepos,' and also a part of Justin, but somewhat clumsily, with the help of Ainsworth's Dictionary,

I commenced Cæsar, and sped on well, so that by the time I had reached the third book, 'De Bello Gallico,' I found myself able to read page after page, with scarcely more than a glance, now and then, at the dictionary. I remember well my first triumphant feeling of this kind. I sat on Pingle Hill; it was about five in the morning, the sun shone brightly; and as I lifted my eyes from the classic page of the great conqueror of the Gauls and Helvetians, and they fell on the mouldering pile called the 'Old Hall'—part of which had been a stronghold of John of Gaunt, and of one of the barons in the reign of Stephen—I said to myself, 'I have made a greater conquest, without the aid of a living teacher, than the proudest warrior ever made—for I have conquered and entered into the possession of a new mind.' And *that* seems to me the truest expression, when you find you can read a language you could not read before.

When I had finished Cæsar's Commentaries on the Gallic War, I took up the Eneid, and soon grew in love with Virgil: a love which has lasted—for, notwithstanding the protest some people make against the 'tameness' of Virgil, as compared with Homer, the graceful Mantuan always affords me high intellectual pleasure. [...]

My friend Hough's conversation, on the Saturday nights, was both a relief and an inspiration to me. He was not only well read in standard old English literature, more especially divinity, but he was passionately attached to metaphysics,—had read Locke, and Berkeley, and Hobbes, and Dugald Stewart; and during the first year of our acquaintance took to the enthusiastic perusal of Cudworth. The grand expanse of his forehead showed the strength of his reasoning faculties as well as of his ideality; and he kindled into warmth as we entered into debate. With him I discussed questions relating to mind, to religion, to history, and general literature; and these weekly conversations, as I returned to my reading and studies, gave a new impulse to thought and inquiry. He also used to say, 'You do me good. You freshen my mind, weekly.' [...]

In the hurry and whirl of my changeful life, I have lost the journal that I kept so strictly in those years, and all written records of my reading; but I can recal the feeling of pleasure, or profound interest, I experienced in reading many a volume; and the feeling is often associated with some feature of a landscape, or turn of the woods, or appearance of the hills or lanes where I walked. Thus the dear old remembrances often flash upon me, after all these years; and I seem to see the page, and the rural spot where I read it, as clearly as if it had happened only an hour ago. How strange it seems—seeing that I, often, cannot call to mind whether I wrote to such a person last week; and, most commonly, forget the names and features of persons with whom I have but lately become acquainted,—nay, often forget, utterly, some things I saw, or some actions I performed, not a month ago!

Blair's 'Lectures on Rhetoric and the Belles Lettres' was another book that I analysed very closely and laboriously, being determined on acquiring a thorough judgment of style and literary excellence. All this practice seemed to destroy the desire of composing poetry of my own. Milton's verse seemed to overawe me, as I committed it to memory, and repeated it daily; and the perfection of his music, as well as the gigantic stature of his intellect, were fully perceived by my mind. The wondrous knowledge of the heart unfolded by Shakespeare, made me shrink into insignificance; while the sweetness, the marvellous power of expression and grandeur of his poetry seemed to transport me, at times, out of the vulgar world of circumstances in which I lived bodily. Besides the two great poets, I made myself familiar with others; and committed to memory thousands of lines by Burns, and Coleridge, and Wordsworth, and Scott, and Byron, and Moore, and Campbell, and Southey, and Keats. And the repetition, daily, of poetry displaying all the harmonies of rhythm—all the opulence of the stores of expressing thought—repressed all desire of composing poetry myself. I said to myself, daily—'I am educating my ear and my mind, and I shall be ripe for my true work in time.'

Edward G. Salmon, 'What Girls Read', *Nineteenth Century*, 20 (November 1886), 515-29 [515-16, 521-3, 526, 527]

The *Nineteenth Century* (1877-1972, with changes of title) was a high-status, male-centred monthly whose contributors included Matthew Arnold, Trollope, Tennyson, the scientists Huxley and Galton, and the historian Froude. Salmon (1865-1955) was at the very beginning of his career as an editor and writer when he composed three pieces on the reading habits of boys, girls, and the working class. The first he placed in the prestigious *Fortnightly Review* (1865-1954, with change of title), but the latter two he managed to get into the even more exalted *Nineteenth Century*.

Girls, like boys, in recent years have been remarkably favoured in the matter of their reading. They cannot complain, with any justice, that they are ignored in the piles of juvenile literature laid annually upon the booksellers' shelves. [...] Girls' literature would be much more successful than it is [, however,] if it were less goody-goody. Girls will tolerate preaching just as little as boys, and to hit the happy medium between the story of philistine purity and the novel of Pandæmoniacal vice is not apparently always easy. Girls' literature, properly so called, contains much really good writing, much that is beautiful and ennobling. It appeals in the main to the highest instincts of honour and truth of which humanity is capable. But with all its merits, it frequently lacks the peculiar qualities which can alone make girls' books as palatable to girls as boys' books are to boys.

This deficiency is not quite the fault of those who aspire to write for girls, but is of the essence of the subjects which offer themselves for treatment. 'Go'—a monosyllable signifying startling situations and unflagging movement—characterises boys' books, and girls' books will never be as successful as are boys' books until the characteristic is imported into them. 'Slow and sure' is not the motto of either reader or writer in these days. Public and publicist are acceptable to each other in proportion as they are ready to conform to the electric influences of the times. When books were few and far between, an author might indulge in long-winded dissertations almost to his heart's content. Now, if he has a moral to point, he must point it in the facts of his narrative: not in a sermon, which plays the part of rearguard to every incident. Girl-life does not lend itself to vigorous and stirring treatment in the manner that boy-life does. It is far more difficult to enlist the reader's interest in domestic *contretemps* and daily affairs than in fierce combats between nations, or in the accidents of all kinds into which boys and men, by the very nature of their callings, are for ever being led. In the ranks of girls and women it may be conceded are centred the greatest heroism, the noblest devotion, the highest purpose, the longest suffering, the harshest and cruellest of human trials. The courage which meets privation or ignores self for the sake of those near and dear is woman's. It is courage of the first order. The courage which makes a man face boldly an enemy on the field of battle or fling himself into the boiling surf to rescue a fellow-creature is, too, deserving of all honour, but it is, nevertheless, courage of a secondary order and is primarily man's. Heroines like Grace Darling are few. Heroes like Robert Clive are many.[23] It requires to face fever in a loathsome alley, or to minister to the needs of the wounded soldier, a courage dissimilar in all respects to that called forth by the necessity of spiking a gun or swimming out to a wreck. The one is devotion, human, spiritual, Christian; the other is pluck, animal-like in its character, desperate in its instincts. The former is noted by God and lauded by man, but requires an uncommon power to treat adequately from the point of view of the story reader; the latter is easily susceptible of a treatment, feverish and romantic, which may be expected to appeal to the dullest of imaginations. The gore of the battle-field and the flames of the burning building are facts more readily grasped by, and hence more interesting to, the majority of youthful readers than the sick room and injured heart. [...]

As it is, the teaching which comes of girls' books practically amounts to this. If you are wicked you must reform, and when you have reformed you will die! Good young people are not allowed to see many years of life. It is an uncompromisingly severe rendering of the classic axiom 'whom the gods love die young.' I cannot indicate what I mean better than by reference to a story which everyone knows, *The Old Curiosity Shop*. Why did Little Nell die? If she was too good for the world, why was she ever brought into it; if she was not, why, in the midst of the sin, the misery, the suffering of mankind, were her sunny presence and beneficent influence removed so soon? The question might be asked with tenfold force of half the works written for girls. [. . .]

Girls' literature performs one very useful function. It enables girls to read something above mere baby tales, and yet keeps them from the influence of novels of a sort which should be read only by persons capable of forming a discreet judgement. It is a long jump from Æsop to 'Ouida', and to place Miss Sarah Doudney or Miss Anna Beale between Æsop and 'Ouida' may at least prevent a disastrous moral fall.[24] It is just as appropriate and necessary that girls should read books suitable to their age as that they should wear suitable dresses. The chief end served by 'girls' literature' is that, whilst it advances beyond the nursery, it stops short of the full blaze of the drawing-room.

As with boys' literature, so with girls'. That which the working-class lads read is generally of the lowest and most vicious character: that which their sisters read is in no way superior. The boy takes in the penny dreadful; the girl secures the penny novelette, which is equally deserving of the adjective. Because the influence of these love and murder concoctions among girls is not so apparent to the public eye as the influence of the burglar and bushranging fiction among boys, it must not be supposed that the influence is less real. It is, in fact, in many ways not only more real, but more painful. Boys may be driven to sea or to break into houses by the stories they read; their actions are at once recorded in the columns of the daily papers. With girls the injury is more invidious and subtle. It is almost exclusively domestic. We do not often see an account of a girl committing any very serious fault through her reading. But let us go into the houses of the poor, and try to discover what is the effect on the maiden mind of the trash which maidens buy. If we were to trace the matter to its source, we should probably find that the high-flown conceits and pretensions of the poorer girls of the period,[25] their dislike of manual work and love of freedom, spring largely from notions imbibed in the course of a perusal of their penny fictions. Their conduct towards their friends, their parents, their husbands, their employers, is coloured by what they then gather. They obtain distorted views of life, and the bad influence of these works on themselves is handed down to their children and scattered broadcast throughout the family. Where all is so decidedly unwholesome it is unnecessary to mention names. With the exception of the *Girls' Own Paper* and *Every Girl's Magazine*, which are not largely purchased by working-class girls, there is hardly a magazine read by them which it would not be a moral benefit to have swept off the face of the earth.[26] It would be well for philanthropists to bear this fact in mind. There is a wide and splendid field for the display of a humanising and elevating literature among girls. Such a literature ought not to be beyond our reach. Girls can hardly be much blamed for reading the hideous nonsense they do, when so little that is interesting and stirring in plot, and bright and suggestive in character, is to be had. [...]

The young mind is a virgin soil, and whether weeds or rare flowers and beautiful trees are to spring up in it will, of course, depend upon the character of the seeds sown. You cannot scatter literary tares and reap mental corn. A good book is the consecrated essence of a holy genius, bringing new light to the brain and cultivating the heart for the inception of noble motives. Boys' literature of a sound kind ought to help build up men. Girls' literature ought to help to build up women. If in choosing the books that boys shall read it is necessary to remember that we are choosing mental food for future chiefs of a great race, it is equally important not to forget in choosing books for girls that we are choosing mental food for the future wives and mothers of that race. When Mr. Ruskin says that man's work is public and woman's private, he seems for the moment insensible to the public work of women as exercised through their influence on their husbands, brothers, and fathers.[27] Woman's work in the ordering, beautifying, and elevating of the commonweal is hardly second to man's; and it is this which ought to be borne in mind in rearing girls. [...]

Perhaps the best reading which girls can possibly have is biography, especially female biography, of which many excellent works have been published. One cannot help as one reads the biographies of great women—whether of Miss Florence Nightingale, Mrs. Fry, or Lady Russell—being struck by the purity of purpose and God-fearing zeal which moved most of their subjects.[28] There are few women who have made themselves famous who have not been in the habit, in all their trials and tribulations, of turning to their Bibles for comfort with a touching simplicity of faith. Young people cannot read too much biography, and, however addicted to fiction they may be, parents will find record of fact an admirable method of balancing their children's mind. Fiction should lend relief to girl-life, biography should impart right principle, and poetry grace. To feast too much on any one of these is unwise, and though probably fiction will always be most popular, girls should be encouraged to read more poetry and much more biography than they are, I think, accustomed to.

Netta Syrett, *The Victorians* (London, T. Fisher Unwin, 1915), 45-7

Netta Syrett (1865–1945), a teacher who wrote children's books as well as thirty-eight novels and numerous short stories, is most famous today as a 'New Woman' writer of the 1890s. Syrett's publisher, Fisher Unwin, was known for its new and 'advanced' writing and *The Victorians*, a largely autobiographical novel centring on the changing roles of women at the end the century, shows Syrett's resistance to dominant stereotypes on many levels. The following extract is set in the early 1880s when the heroine, Rose, is 9 years old. *The Play Grammar* was a real book, by the children's author Julia Corner, published in 1848. The extract is an example of Syrett's own resistance as a real reader: if the clown and plum pudding illustrations are more or less accurately described, the maternal disquisition on interjections is by no means as ridiculously cruel in the original, even if most of its elements do occur there.

Miss Piddock [Rose's governess] now took up 'The Play Grammar', and 'heard' her pupil repeat the prepared task. It concerned the degrees of comparison of adjectives, and was illustrated by woodcuts showing three plum-puddings in various stages of heated activity. From the 'positive' pudding a small puff of smoke ascended, the 'comparative' one steamed with praiseworthy energy, while the 'superlative' delicacy was a veritable Vesuvius. Three clowns beneath the puddings were intended to portray the relative meaning of 'funny, funnier, funniest,' but the artist's instructive intent to fix attention on the rules of grammar, was frustrated by the human interest evoked by his clowns in the annoying brain of Rose.

She studied their faces attentively, and despite the broader grin on the countenance of the 'comparative' comedian, she considered the 'positive' entertainer much more amusing, and insisted on debating the question with Miss Piddock, consulting her also on his patronymic and private history [...]

Rose stumbled through her repetition of the next page—a dull page unenlivened by pictures, and was bidden to read aloud the chapter that followed. She demurred, declaring in favour of another chapter setting forth the nature and purpose of the interjection. This was headed by a picture of a little girl with ringlets and long trousers limping into an Early Victorian room, where 'Mamma,' brimming over with useful knowledge, awaited her daughter.

Miss Piddock as usual gave in after the customary wrangle, and in defiance of all sequence Rose began to read the paragraph which interested her solely on account of the trousered little girl known in 'The Play Grammar' as 'Fanny'. Her reading was punctuated with delighted giggles.

' "La, Mamma!" cried Fanny, "I have twisted my ankle."

' "There, Fanny!" returned Mamma, plunging without a word of sympathy into English grammar.

' "You have uttered an interjection." '

Rose, who had been many times through 'The Play Grammar,' never ceased to be amused by this conversational opening. She laughed till Lucie, hitherto industriously and without the smallest comprehension insisting in a copybook that 'the whale is a mammal,' joined in her mirth and began carelessly to smudge the record of that mysterious fact.

' "La!" ' repeated Rose mockingly. 'Nobody says "la" now. And nobody wears trousers like Fanny. This book must have been written ages ago. And do you believe Fanny was interested, like they make out here, in adverbs and adjectives and things? I don't. [...]

NOTES TO SECTION II

1. At least seven adaptations were staged in 1839 alone, the most successful being John Buckstone's at the Adelphi Theatre, reviewed by *The Times* on 29 October.
2. A play on *bon mot* (witty expression).
3. The Society for the Promotion of Christian Knowledge (1698–   ) was begun to spread the Anglican word to the poor, and to that end set up thousands of schools in the eighteenth century. By the middle of the following century it had become famous for its cheap publications. The Religious Tract Society (1799–   ) was Evangelical and the largest distributor of Bibles and other religious material.

4. The figure given in 'Immorality of the London Press', *Ragged School Union Magazine* (August 1850), 194, is actually 28,862,000 for the year 1845. These figures became iconic, repeated later in the century: see e.g. John Pownall Harrison, 'Cheap Literature—Past and Present', *Companion to the British Almanac* (1873), 65.
5. Powers.
6. Up-to-date.
7. Members of Parliament (St Stephen's was the Royal Chapel in the Palace of Westminster, before the latter burned down in 1834. Remnants of the chapel were incorporated in the new Houses of Parliament).
8. Byron, *Beppo*, stanza 34, line 6.
9. Hector McNeill's *Scotland's skaith; or, the History o' Will and Jean: owre true a tale!* (Edinburgh: Mundell and Son, 1795) was a poem intended to show the evils of whisky.
10. For more on Walter Scott, see p. 173-4; on Edward Bulwer (-Lytton), see p. 116. The non-British writers were all renowned for their didacticism and activism. Victor (Marie) Hugo (1802-85), French poet, dramatist, and novelist was heavily involved in politics in the 1830s and 1840s, in exile from France since 1851; George Sand (1804-76), French novelist with strong proto–feminist and later Christian and socialist intent; Ida Countess of Hahn–Hahn (1805-80), prolific German novelist who specialized in independent aristocratic heroines; Alessandro Manzoni (1785-1873), Italian nationalist poet and novelist, famous mainly for his historical novel *I Promessi sposi* (1825-7). All were well published in English translations.
11. 'For better or worse'.
12. 'Man comprises nerves alone.' Pierre Jean George Cabanis (1757-1808) was a French doctor notable for his materialist views, as expressed in his *Rapports du physique et du moral de l'homme* (1802).
13. 'If you can, [do it] well; if [you can] not, [do it] somehow or other.'
14. The idea of 'spasmodic poetry' was associated mainly with Philip Bailey (1816-1902) and Sidney Dobell (1824-74) in the 1840s and 1850s. It was marked by extremely emotive language developed partly from the work of Keats and Shelley.
15. Redpath, the registrar of the Great Northern Railway, forged share certificates, and sold them at a profit of about £240,000. He was eventually caught, found guilty, and transported for life. In 1849 Maria Manning, with the aid of her husband, had killed her lover for his money and buried him under the kitchen floor: the body was discovered, and the Mannings were caught, tried, and executed.

16. Cresswell (1794–1863) was the first judge of the new court for probate, divorce, and matrimonial causes (established in 1858).

17. A reference to Mary Braddon's *Aurora Floyd* (serialized in *Temple Bar*, January 1862–January 1863; published in 3 volumes by Tinsley, January 1863). The novel is discussed in parts of the article not reproduced here.

18. From Francis Bacon, 'Of Studies' in *Essays* (orig. 1597, often reprinted).

19. Henry Kirke White (1785–1806), an autodidact poet favoured by Southey and others, was the son of a butcher. He eventually obtained work in a lawyer's office and, through his employer's connections, entered Cambridge University. He died a year later.

20. *The Imperial Magazine* (1819–34), a 2s. illustrated monthly with a lower-middle-class Dissenting readership edited by Samuel Drew, gave especial importance to the biographies of famous men. Dr Lee (1783–52) was exactly as Cooper says.

21. We have chosen not to explain all the references in this extract: readers may draw conclusions without knowing the detailed publication histories of these texts.

22. Whillock was a friend mentioned in a previous chapter.

23. Grace Darling (1815–42), famous for helping save passengers from a sinking ship off the Northumberland coast in 1838. Robert Clive (1725–74), solder-statesman whose military heroics helped secure British control over India.

24. The *Fables* of the classical moralist Aesop were standard reading for children. Ouida: Marie Louise (de la) Ramé (1839–1908), author of many works with a 'fast' reputation; Sarah Doudney (1843–1926) and Anne [*sic*] Beale (?–1900), both authors of pious works treated as void of 'go' in sections of the article not printed here.

25. The 'girl of the period' was a media creation originating in an article (by Eliza Lynne Linton) in the *Saturday Review* (14 March 1868: 339–40). Rather than through work or virtue, 'girls of the period' tried to find rich husbands through fashion and their bodies.

26. *Girls' Own Paper* (1880–1965) was produced by the Religious Tract Society, like its brother *Boys' Own Paper* (1879–1967), explicitly to counteract reading with pernicious tendencies. *Every Girl's Magazine* (1878–88), despite its title, was actually aimed at the general family reader.

27. If this is a reference to Ruskin's famous essays on gender relations in *Sesame and Lilies* (1865), it is unfair, since Ruskin makes exactly the points Salmon does.

28. Florence Nightingale (1820–1910), famous for her reforms in nursing; Elizabeth Fry (1780–1845), prison reformer and philanthropist. Lady Rachel Russell (1636–1723) was a model of conjugal devotion. All were the subject of numerous biographies.

III

THE WORD OF LAW/THE LAW OF THE WORD

INTRODUCTION

The legal regulation of the media was and still is a wide-ranging, complex, and confusing matter. As remarked in the general Introduction, selection is essential: the changes in libel laws can only be hinted at here, and the Official Secrets Act (1889), laws covering the conditions of workers in the printing trade, and the relations of consumer and retailer are not covered at all.[1] Rather, what we have chosen to do is to select material on three topics: the 'Taxes on Knowledge', obscenity, and copyright. The first and last affected the availability of texts through pricing (see the extracts from the *Newspaper Press Directory*, Collet, *The Times*, Arnold); the second regulated the sale of material considered threatening to the social order (see below, '*The Queen* v. *Benjamin Hicklin*', 'Prosecution for Publishing an Alleged Obscene Book').

Our overall narrative, uniting all three topics, entails a transformation from regulation tied in with government of the social and political body to that concerned with the individual sexualized body: a move of regulation from the public to the private. The narrative relates to copyright insofar as the rights of the individual author became increasingly stressed in an area that had originally been concerned with promoting and protecting the *national* production of texts.[2] Linking obscenity with the Taxes on Knowledge is the idea that government should control representation. Earlier in the century representation in the media and in parliament through the vote were closely connected (a point picked up by Greg in Section II). Later in the century media representation became more of an aesthetic and ethical concern. Thus, whereas in the 1830s Henry Hetherington went to gaol for printing his criticisms of the government and demanding the vote (see the extract from the *Poor Man's Guardian*), the publisher Henry Vizetelly was imprisoned in 1889 for publishing 'obscene' translations of Zola's naturalist novels.[3]

The section opens with two pieces on the 'Taxes on Knowledge'. A tax, whereby each copy of a newspaper had to be stamped and the stamp paid for, was first imposed in 1712. Its purpose was less to regulate the press, however, than to fund the War of the Spanish Succession. At the same time, a shilling duty on each advertisement became obligatory, payable by the advertiser. The taxes were found too useful to stop after the war ended, and indeed were gradually raised until in 1815 the stamp tax reached 4d. and the advertisement duty 3s. 6d. (punitive at a time when the unemployed advertised to get work). Paper itself was additionally taxed at a variable rate depending on its quality. In 1819, in response to social unrest, the government passed the infamous 'Six Acts', one of which attempted to tighten the legal classification of a newspaper. The aim now was to make oppositional journals liable for Stamp Duty and thus too expensive for poor readers. That same year it was decreed that newspaper proprietors had to give a £300 bond on start-up as surety against any possible fines or convictions for libel. In addition, in the second quarter of the century, there were various other taxes on print media, such as one on pamphlets. It was indeed, as numerous publications repeatedly lamented, prohibitively expensive for all but the wealthy to gain direct access to media representation either as users or as producers. Such restrictions effectively favoured certain segments of the print media market: the pro-establishment *Times*, for example, had a huge rise in its circulation between 1837 and 1850 at the expense of other papers. The 'Taxes on Knowledge' had changed from being just another way to raise government revenue to an attempt at social control. Protest against these restrictions was widespread. The high point of unstamped, illegal newspapers occurred between 1830 and 1836; the government responded by prosecuting over seven hundred printers, publishers, and vendors. The extract from the *Poor Man's Guardian* exemplifies the persecutions suffered.

One way the government maintained control was by generating confusion and complexity (cf. Mill in Section I on the usefulness of ambiguity). As the extract from Mitchell's *Newspaper Press Directory* ironically queried, what, after all, is the 'news' that defines a 'newspaper'? What is an 'advertisement'? In absolute terms these questions are unanswerable, but when backed by the brute force of the police and prison, the answers are clear enough—whatever the controllers of these forces say they are.

Section I outlined the Whig method of controlling the media. In 1833 they had their way when the advertisement duty was reduced to 1s. 6d. Three years later the Stamp came down a penny at the same time as the paper duty was reduced. The resultant opening of the market caused a massive decline in the numbers of unstamped newspapers. It was not until 1855, however, that the Stamp Duty was made optional, as the Collet extract describes (see also Section VII below). The Collet is interesting because it contradicts the common idea of the universal struggle of 'the people' against an oppressive minority; the number of warriors for press freedom in fact comprised only a small network which lasted in various combinations throughout the century. For instance, the erstwhile Chartist George Jacob Holyoake (1817–1906), friend of Collet and Hetherington, was closely connected to later challengers of the obscenity laws, Charles Bradlaugh and Annie Besant, through the atheist Secularist Society.

The two extracts on the obscenity laws, while calling attention to the policing of moral boundaries, pivot on the notion of textual intention, so much discussed in literary theory over recent decades. In both extracts the intention of the defendant/appellant—the cause— is retrospectively imagined from the presumed effect. The actual intentions of the accused were deemed honest in both cases; nevertheless the 'tendency' of the texts was still deemed 'to deprave and corrupt'. In the law (acknowledged openly as a fiction) this logically meant that the intentions of the sellers and producers of the texts were to deprave as well. What might seem a bizarre logic to us was, to the classically trained lawyer of Victorian Britain, self-evident: the link between 'intention' and 'tendency', cause and effect, lay in the etymology of the words themselves, since both derived from the Latin verb 'tendere' ('to aim'). To make such a link it was necessary to think that meaning lay 'in' words, independent of context and 'intended' by the producer (or seller) of the words. But the law was also based on a contradictory insistence on how meaning was dependent upon context. As one of the judges says in the Hicklin case, a picture in a gallery would not be obscene, but reproduced in a photograph and sold on the street so that children could see it, it might be. While intention and context are often debated in abstract philosophical terms, in the extracts below they are employed in two very concrete attempts to keep information in the hands of a small number of men.

Copyright in Britain dates from 1710, when the rights of reproduction of a printed text were assigned to authors or their assignees for fourteen years. An 1814 Act lengthened this to twenty-eight years. Another in 1842, agitated for by Dickens, Wordsworth, and Carlyle, amongst others, extended it to forty-two years from publication or the author's life plus seven years, whichever was longer. But while authorial copyright seems natural to us, there was considerable opposition to it from publishers and even from professional writers. Copyright certainly benefited figures such as Dickens, but most writers in the first half of the century and beyond needed ready cash and sold their copyright to publishers. Matthew Arnold's essay on copyright, provoked by an 1878 Royal Commission report, attempts to balance the need to protect authors' incomes (such as his own) with the desire to ensure that copyright restrictions did not prevent the spread of cheap literature. The extracts from *The Times*, originating in an important sector of print media often forgotten in histories of print culture, the music publishing industry, focus on a key moment in the history of international copyright, connecting it, as was common, not simply to private property but to national identity, a theme that emerges several times in this Reader.

FURTHER READING:

Barnes, *Free Trade*; Annie Besant; Chandler and Dagnall; Feather; Hyland and Sammells; Myers and Harris; Nowell-Smith; Parson; Patten; Saunders; Seville; Sherman and Strowel.

[James Bronterre O'Brien], 'Persecution and Imprisonment of Mr. Hetherington', *Poor Man's Guardian*, 12 January 1833, 1–2

The *Poor Man's Guardian*, begun by Henry Hetherington in 1831, was one of the most widely known of the unstamped publications of the 1830s. These sought to provide political news at a price appropriate for the poor, a penny. In place of the government's red stamp that signified that a newspaper had paid the requisite tax, the *Poor Man's Guardian* printed the logo in Figure 2, linking in one image both political and media 'representation', universal suffrage and universal media access. Like many of his sales agents, Hetherington was imprisoned. The following, written by the paper's editor from November 1832, refers to his second arrest. It also mentions the advantages the tax gave *The Times* (stamped newspapers were able to travel post-free throughout the country and so appeal to non-local audiences).

FIG. 2. Official Stamp (*right*) and Mock Stamp (*left*), from *Poor Man's Guardian*, 1 November 1834.

PERSECUTION AND IMPRISONMENT OF
Mr. HETHERINGTON.

Editor's Remarks on the iniquitous spirit and administration of the Newspaper Stamp Laws.—The Whigs shewn up, &c. &c.

Friends, Brethren, and Fellow-countrymen,

In the two numbers of the *Guardian* preceding the last, we apprised you of the new persecution instituted against Mr. Hetherington, by the Commissioners of Stamps, acting, of course, under the instruction of his Majesty's Whig ministers. Two informations charged him with selling certain copies of that 'Great Unstamped,' the *Poor Man's Guardian*.[4] The fact (which nobody denied, and which Mr. Hetherington would glory in proclaiming from the house-tops of all England) was *legally* proved by the evidence of two agents in the employ of the Stamp Commissioners, and Mr. H. not appearing, and his name having been three times called at the door of the office—he was convicted on the two informations, and sentenced to pay a fine of *forty pounds*, or in default to be committed for twelve months to the new prison in Clerkenwell. The latter part of this sentence is now being executed. Three warrants were issued for his apprehension, and Stephens, a Bow Street officer, made good his capture on Saturday last; Mr. Hetherington was apprehended on his way from Birmingham to Coventry, and is now (to use the language of the *True Sun*) 'in the keeping of that only 'Poor Man's Guardian' which the modern system of law recognises—THE GAOLER.'[5]

Poor men of England!—there is no law for you in this country—no law, we mean, for your protection. There are plenty of laws to plunder you, to pauperise you, to overwork you, to starve you, to whip you, to transport you, to hang you; but—we repeat it emphatically—there is no law for your protection. The rulers of this country are a band of villains, whose actions prove them to be leagued together for your and our destruction. Not only are all their 'laws' levelled at our happiness—nay, at our very means of existence—but the *administration* of these laws is, if possible, still more iniquitous than the *principle* of their enactment. Not content with framing the law in such a shape and spirit as to give the *rich* all its benefits, and the *poor* all its penalties, they deny us even the consolation of seeing an iniquitous law equitably administered. Take for instance the law under which Mr. Hetherington has been convicted. First look to the injustice of the law itself, and then to the iniquity of its administration.

The newspaper stamp law was notoriously enacted to prevent the poor from acquiring cheap political knowledge, or, in plain English, to prevent the poor from finding out the crimes of the rich, as illustrated by the acts of government, that government being exclusively a government of the rich. The effect of the fourpenny stamp, combined with the advertisement duty and required *sureties*, is to create for the rich a complete monopoly of the stamped press. No poor man can establish a stamped paper, nor could any rich man conduct such a paper, *upon honest principles*, without loss or ruin. The consequence is, that without the unstamped papers, the poor must be driven for political information to the journals of the rich, that is to say, to those literary assassins who, as sharers of the spoil, are necessarily the accomplices of government, in all schemes for deceiving, plundering, brutalizing, and (in a moral sense) Burking the people.[6]

The 'bloody old *Times*,' for instance, is enabled by this monopoly to nett a clear income of £50,000 a-year from its sale and advertisements, not to speak of what it may derive in bribes from the government, the stock-jobbers, and the aristocracy. The whole of this enormous revenue comes, directly or indirectly, out of the pockets of the people; directly as where it is paid for the insertion of advertisements by poor people out of place,[7] and indirectly where the advances are made by aristocrats, out of the plunderings of the people. In either case the people are as effectually robbed by the operation of the law, as if the money were taken from them by highwaymen, holding pistols to their throats. Why should a poor man be compelled to pay *seven-pence* for a paper full of lies, when he desires to pay only a *penny* or *two-pence* for a paper full of truth? and why should an unfortunate servant or needy governess be obliged to part with, perhaps, her last half sovereign—for the insertion of an advertisement, which an unstamped New York paper would publish for a sixth part of the sum? Is it right, fellow-countrymen, that a crew of fellows in Printing-house Square, who are afraid to have their names known to the public, and who meet together at midnight like conspirators, should be enabled by their accomplices in the government, to fleece the unfortunate, whom they are everlastingly calumniating under the names of '*destructives*,' '*rabble unions*,' '*revolutionary fiends*,' &c. And are you and we to be thus insulted and robbed, in order that Walter, of the *Times*, may buy a broad estate at Bearwood, in Berkshire, and present Mrs. Barnes, of Nelson Square, with a splendid coach equipage upon her marriage to one of the Editors?[8] And while these monstrous exactions and plunderings are going on for the benefit of hypocrites, is an honest man like Hetherington not only to lose his liberty and health, but must himself and his editor be deprived of a *scant* subsistence? [...]

Charles Mitchell, 'Law of Newspapers', in *The Newspaper Press Directory, Containing Full Particulars Relative to Each Journal Published in the United Kingdom and British Isles* (London: C. Mitchell, 1851), 39-69 [40-5]

Mitchell's *Newspaper Press Directory* (still published, now under the name of *Benn's Media Directory*) was explicitly intended to help commercial traders place advertisements in the publications most suitable for their products. To that end the *Directory* also addressed the newspaper proprietors whose publications would carry the adverts. A detailed and spirited account of libel law as it affected newspapers and their proprietors had been given in the second edition (1847); the following is extracted from an additional section inserted at the request of users.

Restrictions and Regulations imposed by the Government upon Proprietors of Newspapers for Revenue Purposes.

SECT. I. Here we must consider the *legal definition* of a newspaper, which, strange to say, is involved in some difficulty; as all matters are which are questions of *degree*, as this is. For 'news' are events of recent recurrence, as what is *recent* is *relative*: *i.e.* relates to people's means of information; so that without going so far as to suggest, with some wag, that to ignorant persons Rollin's Ancient History[9] might be news—it is obvious that the idea of what is *recent* is *uncertain*, and the definition of it must be arbitrary. So we must come to the *legislative* definition of it, which appears to be the limitation of a lunar month, or at least twenty-six days, within which any matters are legally 'news;' and if this limitation appear arbitrary and absurd, it must be remembered that, in a sense, so are all arbitrary limitations (as that of legal infancy, for instance) where we are unable to dispense with some limitation, and cannot arrive at absolute certainty. So that, as the barber in Boz says, 'We must draw the line *somewhere*.'[10]

By the 6 & 7 Will. IV. c. 76, a newspaper is defined to be any paper containing public news, intelligence, or occurrences, to be dispersed and made public, however old the 'news' may be, unless the 'intelligence' consist only or principally of advertisements, in which case they cease to be 'news' after twenty-six days: but on the other hand, if there be, without any news at all, any remarks or observations thereon, or on any public intelligence or occurrences, the paper is a 'newspaper', unless twenty-six days shall elapse between each number, or unless the size exceed two sheets, or the price exceed sixpence. So much for *what is* a newspaper.

SECT. II. Next, what is *requisite for* a newspaper, so far as respects the State. Our readers are well aware, of course, of the *declaration* required to be delivered either to the Commissioner of Stamps at their head office, or distributor of stamps, or other proper officer appointed by them for that purpose. We shall only observe here, that [...] the declaration must specify the names, &c., of at least two proprietors, (whose shares shall not be less than any others') resident in this country [...]

It is very important to observe, that the declaration as last filed, will be evidence in a court of law on proceedings civil or criminal [...]

2. So, *secondly*, our readers are, of course, equally aware of the libel and *advertisement bonds* [...]

3. Then, *thirdly*, as to *stamping*, we need scarcely say that the commissioners or their officers may sell stamped paper, or stamp paper supplied to them. [...]

4. Then, *fourthly*, as to the *printing* or publishing. If any person knowingly print or publish, or cause to be printed or published any newspaper, on paper not duly stamped, or knowingly sell, *dispose of*, or *distribute*, or even have in his possession such newspaper he is liable for every *single copy* to forfeit 50*l*.! the officer of stamp duties, or any person authorized by the commissioners, having power to *apprehend* him and take him before a justice, who may *commit him for three months* in default! There is also a penalty for sending abroad any newspaper not duly stamped. [...]

5. Then, *fifthly*, as to the *publishing*. Within three days next following the day of publication (unless within twenty miles of London, Edinburgh, or Dublin, when it must be the same day), there must be two copies of each number, and of every edition thereof, delivered to the proper officer, who at any time within two years is

bound to produce it as evidence in any legal proceedings. The penalty for neglect is 20*l.*

6. Then, *sixthly,* as to what *follows* publishing. The advertisement duty is to be paid within twenty-eight days *after the last day* of every calendar month, *for* such calendar month. It is important to observe that stamps will not be supplied if advertisement duty be in arrear [...]

SECT. III. OF ADVERTISEMENTS.—First, as to the *definition* of an 'advertisement,' which, like that of 'newspaper,' is necessarily *uncertain,* and so somewhat arbitrary. We have seen that advertisements are 'news;' so that a paper composed wholly of them will legally be a newspaper. The reverse would not hold, viz., that whatever is *news* must be *an advertisement.* It is much easier to say when it is *not*; a definition should state what *is.* That the information is intended to be *prospectively useful* to certain parties would not do; for so it is of a large portion of the news. That it is intended to benefit or interest the *advertiser* would do better; but then some advertisements, (as to relatives who have quarrelled, &c.) could scarcely be included in *this* definition; at all events, if it went upon pecuniary, and not on the larger idea of a personal interest. That the insertion is *paid for* would not, of course, be in itself decisive as a definition, though a good practical test applied to eke out some more doubtful one. Probably the best definition is, some notice inserted exclusively for the purposes, advantage, or interest of the party concerned therein, by means of information to third parties: this, it will be seen, gets reviews of books out of danger, for they are inserted not exclusively for the advantage of the bookseller, but for the sake of the readers. A common idea is, that the insertion of the *price* would make the review an advertisement, and doubtless, as Stamp Office law, this would be *decisive*; but it is a hard thing to 'draw the line,' and one of a large class of cases in which it is next to impossible to give a correct definition. [...]

'The Copyright Question', *The Times*, 3 July 1851, 8

Music publishing was big business in the nineteenth century: the only form of the mass distribution of music was through print until the widespread use of radio and recordings in the twentieth century. Given the dominance of Italians, Germans, and French in high-status music production, it is hardly surprising that international copyright early came to the fore in this area. The meeting described below was stimulated by what was to become one of the most cited cases in nineteenth-century copyright trials. In 1851 the famous music publisher Boosey prosecuted his much less prestigious rival, Jefferys, for breach of copyright. Jefferys had published an extract from Bellini's opera *La Sonnambula*, which Boosey had registered for copyright in Britain twenty years previously. Jefferys won, however, because copyright was deemed to exist only for 'aliens' who resided in Britain and Bellini had been resident in Milan in 1831. Boosey appealed and the initial verdict was overturned at the Court of Error. As the following article demonstrates, this caused great anxiety amongst diverse sectors of print media. Eventually, however, Jefferys, supported by many colleagues, took the case to the Lords where the original judgment was confirmed.

A very numerous meeting of British authors, publishers, stationers, printers, and others interested in the subject of copyright, was held on Tuesday afternoon at the Hanover-square Rooms, to take into consideration the present anomalous state of the laws relating thereto, as recently interpreted in the Court of Error. The circular convening the meeting stated, that by this interpretation, which reversed several recent decisions, the claim of a non-resident foreign author to copyright was allowed, although the English author was strictly excluded from the benefit in foreign countries. The unreciprocated privilege thus conferred on foreigners, if finally established, would prove extremely prejudicial to the interests of British literature in all its departments, while it removed every inducement to the acceptance of their proposed International Copyright Act. The chair was taken by Sir Edward Bulwer Lytton, who was supported by Mr. Henry Bohn as vice-chairman. Among those on the platform we observed

Messrs. George Cruikshank, William Howitt, John Britton, Henry Colburn, R. H. Horne, and William Macfarlane, &c.[11]

Sir E. BULWER LYTTON opened the proceedings by an able speech, in which he observed, that he had been requested to take the chair, to bring before the public a question which was exciting a great deal of interest among all those who were connected with literary property. [...] An act of Parliament, entitled the 8th of Anne, was cited as an act for the encouragement of learning by vesting the copies of printed books in the authors and purchasers of such copies during the time mentioned therein [...] It was true that at first foreign works had very little interest here; they were naturally more sought after in the land where the language in which they were written was used. But more lately [foreign publishers] had begun to publish works in countries other than their own, and in some cases political and theological works, which were contrary to the opinions of their own country, were published in other countries. This was the case both with French and Italian authors. [...] He would pass at once to a case which occurred two years back [...] In the case of 'Boosey v. Purday' it was declared that the right was only intended for the benefit of English authors and that foreigners could not obtain a copyright here.[12] All this had been reversed by Lord Campbell, who had decided that the foreigner, by sending his work here for first or simultaneous publication, and the publisher in this country, have the same privileges as an English author. [...] It was only since the peace that our literature had been published abroad.[13] [...] Since the peace a large reading public was formed [outside Britain] who obtained the works of authors without their getting one shilling remuneration for it. He would appeal to any author or bookseller present to say if there was not a considerable diminution in the demand for works. In lighter literature, it was true, the one in which he himself was engaged (applause), there was more demand; but, when they looked to the severe learning which the act of Anne was intended to protect, he would ask whether 200 or 300 copies would not make all the distinction between profit and loss? and, further, was not this difference in the demand created by the foreign reprints abroad used in Canada and the colonies? And this made so much difference that our *Belles Lettres* were daily becoming extinct. When he had the honours of being in Parliament he had placed on the table a motion for an international copyright act. (Applause.) They had recently passed an act by which copyright was given to the authors of those countries that would reciprocate the same. Some of the German States had entered into this arrangement. France and America still held back[14] [...] In light literature alone, in his own case, if this law had been established when he began to write, he should have been 60,000*l.* richer. He had no doubt the same results would have been observed in every other branch, and moreover that America would become a contributor to them instead of their chief despoiler. [...] By not joining in international copyright the Americans were not protecting their own authors. The publishers could tell any of their historians that he could get the best history of England (Macauley's) for nothing, and therefore would not give him his price; or to the novelist, that he could obtain the last work of Dickens; and so, when all these works were selling for a few cents throughout the country, the effect on the composition of their own authors must be very bad, as it would make them merely copyists of these works, instead of producing a spontaneous and distinct literature, as inhabitants of a totally different country. [...]

Mr. H. G. BOHN said [... h]e would first mention the case of 'Boosey v. Jefferys,' which, as the most recent decision, was more immediately before them. He considered the judgement in that case as directly opposed to the commercial spirit of the age, inasmuch as it promoted foreign monopoly in this country, imposed foreign restrictions on a large ingredient of their cheap literature, and by removing all inducements towards international copyright, put a *veto* on the beneficial extension of their own literature abroad. It held out a premium to foreign countries to plunder them more extensively than ever, their hands being more securely tied from self-defence. [...] He concluded by moving the following resolution:—

'That this meeting views with apprehension the recent decisions of the Court of Error, reversing the previous decision of the Court of Exchequer, and thereby declaring that foreign residents abroad are entitled to British copyright, although subjects of a State which declines to avail itself of the International Copyright Act; that such decision, if finally established, must prove extremely prejudicial to the interests of British literature in all its departments, while it removes a material inducement to the acceptance by foreign States of the International Copyright Act.' [...]

ERNEST JONES (the Chartist),[15] moved an amendment to the effect—that the meeting viewed with satisfaction the recent judgment of Lord Campbell as one of the preparatory steps, and as being most conducive to that which justice required, an international law of copyright—which was seconded by MR. WILKES, bookseller, of Craven-street.[16]

Mr. FOGGLE spoke in support of the resolution.

Mr. COLBURN said, that until some law was passed to protect copyright the interests of authors were much endangered. They would not write unless they were protected. He had given 800*l.* or 1,000*l.* for books which at the present time, owing to the state of the law he would not give 100*l.* for. There was a novel he had lately brought out which had been taken over and reprinted in America, and not only this, but published in a newspaper there; and this newspaper would be sent all over the country free of expense by Government.

Mr. JEFFERYS spoke of the piracy used with respect to musical publications.

Mr. NOVELLO supported the amendment.[17]

[. . .] [T]he chairman put the amendment, which was lost, and the original resolution was carried.

Collet Dobson Collet, *History of the Taxes on Knowledge: their Origin and Repeal*, vol. ii (London: T. Fisher Unwin, 1899), 4–8, 16–19, 24–5

The newspaper stamp tax was made optional in 1855 partly through the efforts of the Association of the Repeal of the Stamp Tax (founded in 1851, its president T. Milner-Gibson, a Liberal MP), partly through the commitment of the Whig Chancellor Gladstone in a coalition government led by Tories, and partly because of a massive increase in demand for news caused by the Crimean War (1854–6). Another reason was revenge on *The Times*. The Stamp had secured the supremacy of *The Times* in exchange for general support of the government. However, *The Times* provoked the Roebuck enquiry by exposing military and administrative incompetence in the Crimea. This undermined the trust the government had held in the paper. Collet (1813–98) was a newspaper editor and activist in the Association, and a friend of Karl Marx.

The outbreak of the Crimean War, and the great demand for news following on the victory of the Alma, brought fresh difficulties on the Stamp Office. The first to meet this demand was the Lord Mayor of London, who, on September 30, 1854, issued a placard informing the public of the battle. We promptly sent him a warning that a similar sheet published by him before the expiration of twenty-six days would be a breach of the Newspaper Act. On the day that this letter was dated, the Lord Mayor issued another placard, and thereby incurred the charge from which we had sought to guard him. However, he did not repeat the experiment, his journalistic zeal being probably damped when he found that the capture of Sebastopol, announced in his second effort, had been postponed indefinitely.[18] In the course of the week many unstamped narratives of the battle of the Alma were published and several new publications were set up on the spur of the moment, including *Capture of Sebastopol, a Supplement*, published October 2nd; *Sebastopol Fly Sheet, No.* 1, October 3rd; *Sebastopol Chronicle No.* 1, October 4th—all by Mr. Hobson, an enterprising publisher at Ashton-under-Lyne.

It was before this patriotic demonstration of the Lord Mayor that Mr. James Watson Finlay, editor, but not proprietor, of the *Edinburgh Guardian*, a paper of similar rank to the London *Spectator* or *Examiner*, called at our office.[19] Mr. Finlay felt as indignant as we did at the fetters of the Press, and saw in existing circumstances a favourable opportunity of breaking them down. A daily war newspaper would be the surest means of exciting attention, and was sufficiently in accordance with the practice of the Board of Inland Revenue to make it possible thus to gratify the public curiosity without the certainty of suppression by authority. The plan was quite in accordance with our system of making new assaults on the practices of Somerset House; making only one at a time, but making a fresh move whenever there was a good opportunity. *Holt's Army and Navy Despatch* was brought out a little while before Great Britain took part in the war. It was registered as a newspaper, but was stamped only for postal circulation. Like the *Athenæum* and the *Builder* it came out only once a week. It was confined to one subject—the war—and professed, on this ground, to be legal.[20] Mr. Finlay planned a newspaper that should come out every day. In fact, soon after its commencement, about October 8th, it came out three times a day, each edition bringing down the news to a later date than before. It therefore was not purchased only by those who were not in the habit of buying a newspaper at all. It competed with the Weekly Press. Under the anxiety about the war people left off buying the weekly papers at fourpence half-penny each, and paid a penny a day for the *War Telegraph*. They got more in proportion for the money and they had only one day instead of seven to wait for their news. The daily *War Telegraph* was not more illegal than the weekly *Army and Navy Despatch*. The law discriminated a weekly paper from a monthly paper in favour of the latter, but it gave no privilege to a weekly paper over a daily one. Nor did the law or the practice of the Stamp Office give any preference to literature or to architecture over military affairs.

Mr. Finlay's exploit was the first and the most important assault on the system, but on October 20th two penny papers came out at Manchester, a daily *War Express* and a daily *War Telegraph*. Mr. Barstow had for some time published at Manchester a weekly war paper. If the readers of the high price stamped papers did buy this penny paper, they would buy it in addition to the stamped one. But when fresh news of the war was offered every day, the temptation to pay a penny a day involved the economy of giving up the dear weekly paper. The provincial newspapers began to be alarmed lest they should be destroyed by this growing hailstorm of unstamped rivals, and not only at Edinburgh and Manchester, but at Birmingham and other places, the proprietors began to use strong language, not in leading articles, but in letters to the Chancellor of the Exchequer and to the officers of Inland Revenue, threatening that they too would publish their newspapers unstamped.

The result was a shower of Exchequer writs from Mr. Timm,[21] beginning with the *War Chronicle* and *Holt's Army and Navy Despatch*. A week later he descended on the *Edinburgh War Telegraph*, and from day to day the reign of terror continued. In most cases the journals were frightened into surrender: thus on November 22nd both the *Edinburgh War Telegraph* and the *Manchester War Express* came out with the stamp. But the new publisher of the *War Chronicle* having grown wary, Messrs. Holyoake undertook the publication in order to try the question, and sent word through our solicitors to the Stamp Office.[22] They immediately threatened summary proceedings. December 6th accordingly witnessed the publication of *Collet's First (Monthly) War Chronicle*, which was followed at weekly intervals by *Moore's War Chronicle*, *Hoppey's War Chronicle*, and *The War Chronicle*. Further, a deputation, introduced by Mr. Milner-Gibson, waited on Mr. Gladstone, to ask him not to allow any proceedings to be taken in the Court of Exchequer until after a verdict in that Court against *Holt's Army and Navy Gazette*. The Chancellor of the Exchequer was kindly, but uncommunicative; 'all that I have to do,' said he, 'is to see that the revenue is protected.' After he had withdrawn, the Attorney-General remarked 'God forbid that my name should be connected with the prosecution of any newspaper.' [...]

Fortified by the usual resolutions passed at our annual meeting, Mr. Milner-Gibson rose in the House on the 12th of December and questioned Mr. Gladstone as to his intentions, dwelling especially on the case of the war papers. The Chancellor of the Exchequer declined to be led into controversy, but promised that his Bill should be laid on the table after Christmas. [...]

Mr. Gladstone gave notice of his resolution for Monday, the 29th of January [...]

The battle seemed practically over. But on that very day Mr. Roebuck carried his motion for a Committee on the Army before Sebastopol by 305 to 148.[23] On the 21st Lord Aberdeen resigned, and on February 8th Lord Palmerston became Prime Minister. On Friday, February 2nd, Mr. Gladstone brought forward his resolutions, but having been threatened with an amendment to insert 3 oz. instead of four, he altered his resolution into an abstract one that the postage of printed matter should be regulated by weight.

Mr. Gladstone's Bill was read a first time on the 20th. It abolished—

1. The compulsory Stamp, and
2. The Security System.
3. All postal matter was admitted to a postage of one penny per 4 oz., or for any portion of 4 oz.
4. All newspapers now existing, or henceforth to exist, may stamp a portion of their impression for the post; such portion to have the privilege of re-transmission for seven days from the date of publication, and such papers, if over 4 oz. and under 6 oz., will require only a three-halfpenny stamp.
5. All existing newspapers—though exceeding 4 oz. in weight, but not exceeding 2,295 square inches, and not published on more than two pieces of paper—may (during ten years) go by post for seven days for a penny, if stamped, but cannot go at that rate for a stamped envelope.

As we explained in our *Gazette*, we felt deeply grateful to Mr. Gladstone and to Sir Alexander Cockburn, the Attorney-General,[24] for the first three provisions, though we regretted the fourth and fifth as concessions to a powerful interest that would keep things as they were. Our annual meeting held on the following night broke up in high spirits. We could not foresee that the full liberty offered by Mr. Gladstone's Bill would be withheld for fourteen years longer.

The acceptance of Mr. Roebuck's Committee by Lord Palmerston necessitated, as the world knows, Mr. Gladstone's resignation. He was succeeded by Sir George Cornewall Lewis, the editor of the *Edinburgh Review*, which had upheld the stamp. All our difficulties began over again, since we had to convert the new Chancellor of the Exchequer. [...]

In the end, [... he] extended the seven days for re-transmission to fourteen, and accepted the rate of four ounces a penny for any printed matter, reserving the impressed stamp as a privilege for registered periodicals published at intervals not greater than thirty-one days, and giving the old securities.

At the present time (1895) any newspaper can go through the post *once* for a half-penny, and at the same rate only two ounces of printed matter obtain the same convenience. The *Times* with twelve pages weighs a very little under four ounces. It generally contains sixteen pages, weighing five ounces. If it were not a newspaper it would pay three-halfpence, three rates instead of one. Well, a preference of three to one is not so unfair as one of ninety-six to one. We never claimed the right to dictate what the postal rate should be. What we did claim was the right to print and publish without any previous restraint, and, above all, without paying a tax.

'The Queen v. Benjamin Hicklin', 29 April 1868, *Law Reports: Queen's Bench*, III, 1867-68 (London: William Clowes, 1868), 360-79 [360-3, 365-7, 370-1, 373]

The following extract concerns one of the most famous cases in British publishing history, for it defined the concept of 'obscenity' for the next hundred years. The first paragraph summarizes the Obscene Publications Act of April 1857, while the rest outlines the case, giving the remarks and the later commentaries (in the square brackets conventional to this genre) of the Judges on the Queen's Bench, before whom this case was brought on appeal. The Lord Chief Justice of the Queen's Bench was a notable Liberal, the Rt. Hon. Sir Alexander Cockburn (1802-80), mentioned in the previous extract. Two lengthy and detailed footnotes have been silently deleted from this extract.

By 20 & 21 Vict. c. 83, s. 1, if upon complaint that there is reason to believe that any obscene books, &c. are kept in any house or other place, for the purpose of sale or distribution, and upon proof that one or more of such articles has been sold or distributed in connection with such place, justices may, upon being satisfied that such articles are of such a character and description that the publication of them would be a misdemeanor and proper to be prosecuted as such, order by special warrant that such articles shall be seized, and after summoning the occupier of the house, the same or other justices may, if they are satisfied that the articles seized are of the character stated in the warrant, and have been kept for the purposes aforesaid, order them to be destroyed. [. . .]

At the quarter-sessions for the borough of Wolverhampton on the 27th of May, 1867, Henry Scott appealed against an order made by two justices of the borough under 20 & 21 Vict. c. 83 whereby the justices ordered certain books which had been seized in the dwelling-house of the appellant, within their jurisdiction, to be destroyed, as being obscene books within the meaning of the statute.

The appellant is a metal broker, residing in the town of Wolverhampton, and a person of respectable position and character. He is a member of a body styled 'The Protestant Electoral Union,' whose objects are, inter alia, 'to protest against those teachings and practices which are un-English, immoral, and blasphemous, to maintain the Protestantism of the Bible and the liberty of England,' and 'to promote the return to Parliament of men who will assist them in these objects, and particularly will expose and defeat the deep-laid machinations of the Jesuits, and resist grants of money for Romish purposes.' In order to promote the objects and principles of this society, the appellant purchased from time to time, at the central office of the society in London, copies of a pamphlet, entitled 'The Confessional Unmasked; shewing the depravity of the Romish priesthood, the iniquity of the Confessional, and the questions put to females in confession;' of which pamphlets he sold between two and three thousand copies at the price he gave for them, viz., 1s. each, to any person who applied for them.[25]

A complaint was thereupon made before two justices of the borough, by a police officer acting under the direction of the Watch Committee of the borough, and the justices issued their warrant under the above statute, by virtue of which warrant 252 of the pamphlets were seized on the premises of the appellant, and ordered by the justices to be destroyed.

The pamphlet consists of extracts taken from the works of certain theologians who have written at various times on the doctrines and discipline of the Church of Rome, and particularly on the practice of auricular confession. On one side of the page are printed passages in the original Latin, correctly extracted from the works of those writers, and opposite to each extract is placed a free translation of such extract into English. The pamphlet also contains a preface and notes and comments, condemnatory of the tracts and principles laid down by the authors from whose works the extracts are taken. About one half of the pamphlet relates to casuistical and controversial questions which are not obscene, but the remainder of the pamphlet is obscene in fact as relating to impure and filthy acts, words, and ideas. The appellant did not keep or sell the pamphlets for purposes of gain, nor to prejudice good morals, though the indiscriminate sale and circulation of them is calculated to have that effect; but he kept and sold the pamphlets, as a member of the Protestant Electoral Union, to promote the objects of that society, and to expose what he deems to be errors of the Church of Rome, and particularly the immorality of the Confessional.

The recorder[26] was of opinion that, under these circumstances, the sale and distribution of the pamphlets would not be a misdemeanor, nor, consequently, be proper to be prosecuted as such, and that the possession of them by the appellant was not unlawful within the meaning of the statute. He therefore quashed the order of the justices, and directed the pamphlets seized to be returned to the appellant, subject to the opinion of the Court of Queen's Bench.

If the Court should be of opinion, upon the facts stated, that the sale and distribution of the pamphlets by the appellant would be a misdemeanor, and proper to be prosecuted as such, the order of the justices for destroying the pamphlets so seized was to be enforced; if not, the order was to be quashed [...]

COCKBURN, C. J.: [...] The mere use of obscene words, or the occurrence of obscene passages, does not make the work obscene. Thus Milton, in his celebrated defence of himself,[27] justifies by examples the use of language adequate to the occasion, though it may be obscene. [...] What can be more obscene than many pictures publicly exhibited, as the Venus in the Dulwich gallery?

[LUSH, J. It does not follow that because such a picture is exhibited in a public gallery, that photographs of it might be sold in the streets with impunity.]

What can be more obscene than Bayle's Dictionary,[28] or many of the works of the standard authors in English poetry, from Chaucer to Byron? [...]

[A medical treatise, with illustrations necessary for the information of those for whose education or information the work is intended, may, in a certain sense, be obscene, and yet not the subject for indictment; but it can never be that these prints may be exhibited for any one, boys and girls, to see as they pass. The immunity must depend upon the circumstances of the publication.] [...]

I think that if there be an infraction of the law the intention to break the law must be inferred, and the criminal character of the publication is not affected or qualified by there being some ulterior object in view (which is the immediate and primary object of the parties) of a different and honest character. [...] I think the test of obscenity is to deprave and corrupt those whose minds are open to such immoral influences, and into whose hands a publication of this sort may fall. Now, with regard to this work, it is quite certain that it would suggest to the minds of the young of either sex, or even to persons of more advanced years, thoughts of a most impure and libidinous character. The very reason why this work is put forward to expose the practices of the Roman Catholic confessional is the tendency of questions, involving practices and propensities of a certain description, to do mischief to the minds of those to whom such questions are addressed, by suggesting thoughts and desires which otherwise would not have occurred to their minds. If that be the case as between the priest and the person confessing, it manifestly must equally be so when the whole is put into the shape of a series of paragraphs, one following upon another, each involving some impure practices, some of them of the most filthy and disgusting and unnatural description it is possible to imagine. I take it therefore, that, apart from the ulterior object which the publisher of this work had in view, the work itself is, in every sense of the term, an obscene publication, and that, consequently, as the law of England does not allow of any obscene publication, such publication is indictable. [...]

I hold that, where a man publishes a work manifestly obscene, he must be taken to have had the intention which is implied from that act; and that, as soon as you have an illegal act thus established, quoad the intention and quoad the act,[29] it does not lie in the mouth of the man who does it to say, 'Well, I was breaking the law, but I was breaking it for some wholesome and salutary purpose.' The law does not allow that; you must abide by the law, and if you would accomplish your object, you must do it in a legal manner, or let it alone; you must not do it in a manner which is illegal.

'Prosecution for Publishing an Alleged Obscene Book', *The Weekly Times: A London Newspaper of History, Politics, Literature, Science and Art*, 24 June 1877, 2

It is still not clear who was behind the prosecution of the two untiring freethinkers Charles Bradlaugh (1833–91) and Annie Besant (1847–1933) for publishing material on birth control methods. No government or public body was involved; it may have been the Society for the Suppression of Vice (founded in 1802). We have chosen to quote from one of the best selling weekly penny newspapers (circulation about 200,000). Its account is tame compared to some such as *Reynolds's Newspaper*, but typical for that reason. The guilty verdict recorded below was later quashed (for technical reasons, not ethical). Note that the Lord Chief Justice was again Sir Alexander Cockburn.

Charles Bradlaugh and Annie Besant surrendered to their recognisances[30] on Monday morning in the Queen's Bench Division, before the Lord Chief Justice and a special jury, to answer to a charge of having on the 24th of March published an obscene book. [...]

The Solicitor-General in opening the case, said the two defendants were indicted for having published an obscene book under statutes which prohibited the publication of matter calculated to corrupt and destroy the morals of the people. Those in authority in the City of London were placed in the dilemma of either allowing this work to be sown broadcast over the whole city or to institute this prosecution. The police purchased some of the pamphlets, and the question to be decided was whether the defendants were entitled to sell for the sum of 6*d.* the book referred to to every person to whom it might occur that it was interesting or exciting to a morbid appetite to purchase a book of this description, and the question was whether the book was an obscene publication.

The Lord Chief Justice asked if that were so. Suppose, for instance, the book was not obscene, that its effect were to vitiate the public morals, although it were free from any objection in point of language, still, he thought, in point of law, persons publishing it would be liable.

The Solicitor-General said he used the word obscene in the sense of corrupting the morals of the public. The learned gentleman then explained the nature of the book. The work was not couched in vulgar language, and the defendants did not affirm and vouch for all the statements made on medical authority contained within it. The author of the work was an American physician.

The Lord Chief Justice said the work appeared to have been first published in America, and first introduced into this country forty years ago.[31] [...]

The Solicitor-General, continuing, said it appeared to him important to bear in mind that a question of this sort did not simply depend upon the nature of the thing published, but in a great degree on the mode of publication. It was not a question whether a work of this kind might be submitted to a college of physicians, but whether it could be sold in the streets of London. [...]

William Simmons, of the City Detective Force, proved purchasing the book of Mrs. Besant, in the presence of Mr. Bradlaugh, on the 24th of March.—Edwin Williams gave similar evidence as to the purchase of a second copy of the work.—Robert Outram, detective-sergeant in the City Police Force, proved the execution of the warrant, in company with the two last-named witnesses. He read the warrant to the defendants and searched the premises, but did not find any books. Mr. Bradlaugh said they had no more copies of the book on the premises except a few they should require for the defence. [...]

The Lord Chief Justice said the proof of the sale of the two copies had been given, and to prove further sales would not add to the cogency of the case.

This concluded the case for the prosecution.

Mrs. Besant then rose to address the Court for the defence, and continued speaking until the Court rose.

The trial was resumed on Tuesday morning, when Mrs. Besant resumed her address, towards the close of which she said, however the trial might go, whether the defence succeeded or not, it would be the duty of the defendants, steadily and persistently, in no spirit of defiance, but simply in their duty as citizens, to press this subject on the attention of their fellow-countrymen, and to risk even fine and imprisonment in order to bring salvation and happiness to the poor in future. Having referred to other natural checks upon the population as she termed them, Mrs. Besant said there was only one argument against preventable checks that deserved consideration. She was referring to Mr. Darwin's argument as to the survival of the fittest and the struggle for existence, when[32]

The Lord Chief Justice said it was well worthy of Dr. Darwin's consideration whether the results were not twofold, and that while out of the struggle and competition for existence might come in a smaller number a still higher and gifted race, that upon the masses the effect might be deteriorating.

Mrs. Besant said that was just the point she desired to put. She denied that she had any idea of limiting marriage, or that she desired it should take place late in life. That was not the object of the book. She repudiated any idea of a bad intent in the publication of such a book as this. Its publication at the low price of 6*d*. was to promote its circulation among the poor. The prosecution, it was said, had been instituted to prevent the book from being scattered broadcast throughout the country. But if it was so, it would be a consequence of this ill-advised prosecution; for, previously, the whole sale was not above 700 in the course of a year. And why should the circulation of this book be prevented? There was no restriction on the sale of the works of Bull and Chavasse.[33] She had herself obtained the work of Dr. Bull from the respectable publishers, through the post, and so, too, the work of Dr. Chevasse. Before this prosecution the sale of these works was far larger than of the book now prosecuted—though, since this prosecution, no doubt the sale had become enormous, and it had risen from 700 a year to 120,000. Such was the result of trying to stop the circulation of a book which had been in circulation for forty years.[34] [...]

The further hearing was resumed on Wednesday morning by Mr. Bradlaugh continuing his address to the jury. He submitted, firstly, that the essay indicted was an essay on the population question. Secondly, that the subject was one lawfully to be discussed. Thirdly, that it could be heard over and over again that over-population was the fruitful source of poverty, ignorance, crime, vice, and misery; and that, therefore, the advocacy of prudential checks to population was not merely lawful, but highly moral. It was monstrous to charge him with having committed a criminal offence in publishing a book that was chaste in comparison with 'Carpenter's Physiology,' placed by the Government in the hands of boys and girls to study.[35] [...] Comparing some passages in the book to the work of Dr. Maryon Simms,[36] and which were accompanied with plates, he said it was too bad to ask the jury to send him to prison because he had given for 6*d.* prescriptions that had been publicly printed for the past fifty years. [...]

The Solicitor-General, in replying upon the whole case, said the defendants having challenged their prosecution, the authorities had no alternative but to accept it. He did not say all that the defendants said as to their motives, but he was willing to invite them to say that their motives were good.

The Lord Chief Justice: But they are distinctly charged with intending to deprave.

The Solicitor-General: Yes; because a man must be taken to intend that which is the natural consequence of his acts.

The Lord Chief Justice: No doubt.

The Solicitor-General: If the effect be to deprave, they must be taken to intend to deprave.

The Lord Chief Justice: But you acquit them of the intent. It was rather a startling thing to hear that the prosecution was willing to say that the defendants did not intend to corrupt morality, and ask the jury at the same time to say that they were guilty of doing so.

The Solicitor-General: There is a sect in India who advocate murder.

The Lord Chief Justice: Yes; but they intend murder.

The Solicitor-General said that his contention was that the effect of the whole work was to corrupt and deprave. He could not admit the motives which the defendants claimed on their own behalf, but he would ask the jury to accept them for the sake of argument. The defendants said it was desirable that certain courses should be adopted, and which he (the Solicitor-General) said were contrary to the laws of God and man. It was a filthy book, and one which no well-thinking husband would allow his wife to read. He called upon the jury to decide the issue by the aid of a little manly common sense.

The Lord Chief Justice, in summing up, said that they must all agree that this was a most ill-advised prosecution. The defendants had been indicted for having published the work with the intention of corrupting and vitiating public morals. The law declared every publication which outraged decency was illegal. If this was not a work of that character, the defendants were entitled to be acquitted. There was not a single word in the pamphlet which would have the effect of exciting the passions, but it dealt only with dry physiological technicalities. The question was whether the checks proposed for preventing over-population were such as were opposed to morality. It was for them to say if they adopted the Solicitor-General's views, that they were contrary to the laws of God and man. There could be no doubt of the *bonâ fides* of defendants, in publishing this book to relieve the misery of the poor and for the bettering the condition of humanity. It was a question whether the indications for the guidance of married people might not have an injurious effect on public morality by indicating to the unmarried how they might avert the consequences of immoral conduct.

THE VERDICT

The jury retired at a quarter to one o'clock, to consider the verdict. After an absence of one hour and thirty-five minutes they returned into court with a verdict that the work is calculated to debase public morals, but we entirely exonerate the defendants of any corrupt motive in publishing it. [...]

A verdict of Guilty was then entered.

Matthew Arnold, 'Copyright', *Fortnightly Review*, 159 (March 1880), 319-34 [321-9, 332-4]

Arnold (1822–88) is now mainly famous as a literary and social critic, but he was also concerned with the implications of the professionalization and regulation of writing (typically, Arnold retained copyright of this article, reprinting it in *Irish Essays and Others* (London: Smith, Elder and Co., 1882, 444–80)). His article is a useful collage of arguments and tropes derived from a variety of sources that date back to the five-year debate preceding the 1842 Copyright Act. In 1876, a Royal Commission was set up to examine British and international copyright law. The commission's report, published two years later, attempted to clarify the law and close loopholes. International copyright was eventually ratified by the 1885 Berne Convention (to which America was not a signatory).

A Royal Commission on Copyright has lately been sitting, and has made its report. 'We have arrived at a conclusion,' the report declares, 'that copyright should continue to be treated by law as a proprietary right, and that it is not expedient to substitute a right to a royalty, or any other of a similar kind.'

This opening sentence of the report refers to a great battle. The Commissioners have come, they say, to a conclusion, 'that copyright should continue to be treated as a *proprietary right*.' Here has been the point of conflict, as to the proprietary right of the author, as to his right of property in his production. Never perhaps do men shew themselves so earnest, so pertinacious, so untiringly ingenious, as when they have under discussion the right and idea of property. [...]

In England our laws give [the author] the property in his work for forty-two years, or for his own life and seven years afterwards, whichever period is longest. In France, the law gives him the property in his work for his own life, and his widow's life, and for twenty years afterwards if he leave children; for ten years, if he have other heirs. In Germany, the property in his work is for his life and thirty years afterwards. In Italy, for his life and forty years afterwards, with a further period during which a royalty has to be paid upon it to his heirs. In the United States, the author's property in his work is guaranteed for twenty-eight years from publication, with the right of renewal to himself, his wife, or his children, for fourteen years more.

[...] Property is the creation of law. It is an effect given by society and its laws to that natural instinct in man which makes him seek to enjoy ownership in what he produces, acquires, or has. The effect is given because the instinct is natural, and because society, which makes the laws, is itself composed of men who feel the instinct. The instinct is natural, and in general society will comply with it.[37] But there are certain cases in which society will not comply with it, or will comply with it in a very limited degree only; and what has determined society in these cases to refuse or greatly limit its compliance with the instinct of ownership, is the difficulty of giving effect to it, the disadvantage of trying to give effect to it in spite of such difficulty.

There is no property, people often say, in ideas, in spoken words; and it is inferred that there ought to be no property in ideas and words when they are embodied in a book. But why is there no property in ideas and in spoken words, while there is property in ideas and words when they come in a book? A brilliant talker may very well have the instinct of ownership in his good sayings, and all the more if he must and can only talk them and not write them. He might be glad of power to prevent the appropriation of them by other people, to fix the conditions on which alone the appropriation should be allowed, and to derive profit from allowing it. Society, again, may well feel sympathy with his instinct of ownership, and a disposition to assist and favour a production which gives it so much pleasure. But we are met by the difficulty, the insuperable difficulty, of giving effect to the producer's instinct of ownership in this case, of securing to him the disposal of his spoken ideas and words. Accordingly, effect is not given to it, and in such spoken ideas and words there is no property.

[...] And now to apply this to the question of copyright. The instinct of an author to desire ownership in his production, and profit from that ownership, is natural. The author is an interesting person, and society may, and probably will, be even more ready, rather than less ready, to aid in giving effect to the instinct in his case than in the case of others, if it can be done without grave inconvenience. But there is difficulty in securing his ownership. His production is a production particularly difficult to keep at his own disposal, particularly easy for others to appropriate. His claim to some benefit of ownership, however, is generally admitted, and he has ownership given to him for a limited term of years. He finds a publisher, and in concert with him he exercises his ownership; and the result in England of this concert between author and publisher is, that English books are exceedingly dear. A strong desire for cheaper books begins to be felt. Here is the real importance of Sir Louis Mallet's contention, and Mr. Farrer's.[38] 'To Englishmen,' says Sir Louis Mallet, 'easy access to the contemporary literature of their own language is only possible on the condition of exile; England is the only country in which English books are scarce or dear.' 'Nothing can be more intolerable,' says Mr. Farrer, 'than a system of copyright-law under which the inhabitants of the mother-country, in which the books are produced, are the only persons in the world who are prevented from obtaining cheap editions of them.' An impatience [...] at the dearness of English books, a desire to have them cheaper, has therefore to be added to the original difficulty of securing the author's ownership in a kind of production which is by nature hard to keep at his disposal, easy to appropriate. An increased difficulty of securing his ownership is the result. [...]

But yet to secure, so far as without intolerable inconvenience it can be done, the benefits of ownership in his production to the author, every one, or almost every one, professes to desire. And in general, those who profess to desire this do really mean, I think, what they say; and there is no disposition in their mind to put the author off with benefits which are illusory. But Mr. Farrer and others propose, no doubt without intending the poor author any harm, a mode of benefit to him from his productions which does seem quite illusory. The proposal is to set all the world free to print and sell his work as soon as it appears, on condition of paying him a royalty of ten per cent. But both authors and publishers, and all who have the most experience in the matter, and the nearest interest, unite in saying that the author's benefit under this plan would be precarious and illusory. The poor man pursuing his ten per cent. over Great Britain and Ireland would be pitiable enough. But what shall we say of him pursuing his ten per cent. over all the British Dominions; what shall we say of him pursuing it, under an international copyright on this plan between all English-speaking people, over the United States of America? [...]

The Royal Commission reported against this plan of a royalty, and in favour of continuing the present plan of securing by law to the author an ownership in his work for a limited term of years. The Commissioners have proposed what would, in my opinion, be a very great improvement upon the present arrangement: instead of a copyright for forty-two years, or for life and seven years after, whichever period is longest, they propose to give, as in Germany, a copyright for the author's life and for thirty years after. [...]

And yet the natural facts, in England as in France, are as Michel Lévy states them in his conversation with Madame Sand;[39] there is a need for cheaper books, the need will have to be satisfied, and it may be satisfied without loss to either author or publisher. The strength of the dissatisfaction of Sir Louis Mallet and Mr. Farrer with the actual course of the book-trade in England, is that the course of our book-trade goes counter to those natural facts. Sooner or later it will have to adjust itself to them, or there will be an explosion of discontent likely enough to sweep away copyright, and to destroy the author's benefit from his work by reducing it to some such illusory benefit as that offered by the royalty plan of Mr. Farrer. As our nation grows more civilised, as a real love of reading comes to prevail more widely, the system which keeps up the present exorbitant price of new books in England, the system of lending-libraries from which books are hired, will be seen to be, as it is, eccentric, artificial, and unsatisfactory in the highest degree. It is a machinery for the multiplication and protection of bad literature, and for keeping good books dear. In general, a book which is worth a man's reading is worth his possessing. The plan of having one's books from a lending-library leads to reading imperfectly and without discrimination, to glancing at books and not going through them, or rather to going through, for the most part, a quantity of the least profitable sort of books only—novels—and of but glancing at whatever is more serious. Every genuine reader will feel that the book he cares to possess, and the number of genuine readers amongst us, in spite of all our shortcomings, is on the increase [...]

The three shilling book is our great want, the book at three shillings or half-a-crown, like the books of the *format Lévy*, shapely and seemly, and as acceptable to the eye as the far dearer books which we have now. [...] A cheap literature hideous and ignoble of aspect, like the tawdry novels which flare in the bookshelves of our railway-stations, and which seem designed, as so much else that is produced for the use of our middle-class seems designed for people with a low standard of life, is not what is wanted. A sense of beauty and fitness ought to be satisfied in the form and aspect of the books we read, as well as by their contents. The contents offered us for next to nothing, but in hideous and ignoble form and aspect, is not what one desires. A man would willingly pay higher, but in the measure of his means, for what he values, in order to have it in worthy form. But our present prices are prohibitive. The taste for beautiful books is a charming and humane taste for the rich man, though really, as has been already said, our ordinary dear books gratify this taste not a bit better than the French cheaper ones. However, the taste for beautiful books requires expense, no doubt, to be fully gratified; and in larger paper copies and exquisite bindings the rich man may gratify it still, even when we have reformed our book-trade [...]

The Americans, as is well known, have at present, to quote the words of an American, Mr. George Putnam, who has published on this question of copyright a pamphlet very temperate and, in general, very judicious, 'no regulation to prevent the use, without remuneration, of the literary property of foreign authors.' Mr. Putnam adds: 'The United States is, therefore, at present the only country itself possessing a literature of importance, and making a large use of the literature of the world, which has done nothing to recognise and protect by law the rights of foreign authors of whose property it is enjoying the benefit, or to obtain a similar recognition and protection for its own authors abroad.'[40] [...]

Still, on the whole, the spirit of the American community and government is the spirit, I suppose, of a middle-class society of our race, and this is not a spirit of delicacy. One could not say that in their public acts they showed, in general, a spirit of delicacy. [...] [C]ertainly they have not shown that spirit in dealing with authors,— even with their own. They deal with authors, domestic and foreign, much as Manchester, perhaps, might be disposed, if left to itself, to deal with them; as if, provided a sharp bargain was made and *a good thing*, as the phrase is, was got out of it, that was all which could be desired, and the community might exult. [...]

The important question is whether American opinion, if we give it time, is likely to cease insisting on the condition that English books, in order to acquire copyright in America, must be manufactured and published there; is likely to recognise the English author and publisher as Siamese twins, one of whom is not to be imported without importing the other. Is there any chance, in short, of the Americans, accustomed to cheap English books, submitting to the dearness of English books which is brought about in England by what, in spite of all my attachment to certain English publishers, I must call our highly eccentric, artificial, and unsatisfactory system of book-trade? I confess I see no chance of it whatever. There is a mountain of natural difficulty in the way, there is the irresistible opposition of things.

Here [...] lies the real gist [...] The Americans ought not to submit to our absurd system of dear books; I am sure they will not, and, as a lover of civilisation, I should be sorry, though I am an author, if they did. I hope they will give us copyright; but I hope, also, they will stick to Michel Lévy's excellent doctrine: 'Cheap books are a necessity, and a necessity which need bring, moreover, no loss to either authors or publishers.'

NOTES TO SECTION III

1. Libel had been redefined in 1812 as 'words of another, calculated to bring him into *hatred, ridicule, or contempt*' (Mitchell, *Newspaper Press Directory*, 1847, 40). It was redefined again in 6 & 7 Vict., c. 96, 'Lord Campbell's Act' (not to be confused with the Obscene Publications Act of 1857, also called by that name). The latter added that libel 'must involve, *personal malice*, or *gross negligence*' (ibid. 56). Several detailed overviews of the legal position of print media were published in the nineteenth century, including James Patterson's *The Liberty of the Press, Speech and Public Worship, being Commentaries on the Liberty of the Subject and the Laws of England* (London: Macmillan, 1880).

2. Kathryn Temple's *Scandal Nation: Law and Authorship in Britain, 1750–1832* (London: Cornell University Press, 2003) is particularly illuminating on the interconnectedness of print media regulation and the concept of nationality.

3. See Ernest Alfred Vizetelly, *Émile Zola: Novelist and Reformer. An Account of his Life and Work*, i (London: John Lane, 1904), 274–93.

4. 'Information' is here used in a legal sense, meaning a formal written accusation presented to a magistrate to begin court proceedings.

5. The *True Sun* (1832–7) was edited by the radicals Samuel Laman Blanchard and William Johnson Fox.

6. A complex play on words: 'burking' meant murdering by suffocation, but it is also possibly a reference to Burke's *Peerage & Baronetage*, a genealogical tree of aristocrats, first published in 1826. A third layer of meaning is its possible reference to the image of Edmund Burke as a political reactionary, projected by his 1790 *Reflections on the Revolution in France*.

7. i.e. out of work.

8. John Walter II, the proprietor of *The Times*, had placed Thomas Barnes (1785–1841) in the editor's chair in 1817, where he was to remain until his death. In 1832 Walter purchased Bear Wood, an estate in Berkshire, in order to be elected to Parliament for that county.

9. Charles Rollin (1661–1741) published his *Histoire ancienne* between 1730 and 1738. It was soon translated into English.

10. See Charles Dickens, *Nicholas Nickleby* (1838–9), ch. 52, where the phrase refers to class distinctions. A coal-heaver demands a shave because the previous week the barber had shaved a baker. The barber refuses to shave the coal-heaver because 'It's necessary to draw the line somewheres ... if we was to get any lower than bakers, our customers would desert us.'

11. The prestige of this list should not be underestimated. Bulwer-Lytton (1803–73): one of the best-selling authors of the 1830s; Bohn (1796–1884): the major specialist publisher in cheap reprints who bought up vast numbers of copyrights; Cruikshank (1792–1878), famous cartoonist; Howitt (1792–1879), author, editor of periodicals, translator; Briton (1771–1852): writer on architecture, whose autobiography had recently appeared; Colburn (?– 1855), chief publisher of novels at mid-century; Richard Hengist Horne (1802–84), friend of Howitt, editor of periodicals, author. The identity of Macfarlane is less certain: the name may refer to the author of *Duty* (1856) and a few other religious works.

12. The case of *Boosey* v. *Purday* had taken place in 1849.

13. i.e. after the Napoleonic wars that ended in 1815.

14. France agreed the following year; America not until 1891.

15. Ernest Jones (1819–69), Chartist leader, author, and editor.

16. Wilkes and Foggle: minor booksellers. Note the low status of the support for Jones.

17. Novello, a major music publisher from 1830, was vigilant in protecting his copyrights (though himself guilty of infringement). Novello was also treasurer of the Association for the Repeal of Taxes on Knowledge.

18. Initial reports of the battle were indeed ambiguous: several papers report it as the 'Fall of Sebastopol'. Only during the week starting Monday 9 October was it reported as 'the Battle of the Alma': see *The Times*, 1–24 October.

19. The *Edinburgh Guardian* (1853–5), the *Spectator* (1828–) and the *Examiner* (1808–81): all weeklies, independent liberal/progressive in outlook.

20. i.e. *Holts'* was claiming to be a 'class' publication, one containing only a single kind of information aimed—in theory—at a very specific social group. Thus *The Builder* was aimed at architects, the *Athenaeum* at literary men, and so on.

21. Joseph Timm was solicitor to the Board of Trade.

22. For remarks on Holyoake, see the Introduction to this section.

23. Roebuck instituted an enquiry on the condition of the army, inspired largely by critical reports sent by William Howard Russell of *The Times*.

24. See next extract for informtation on Cockburn.

25. *The Confessional Unmasked* was originally published in 1852, a direct outcome of the famous case for libel brought against the Catholic convert Cardinal Newman by a defrocked Italian Catholic priest, Dr Achilli.

26. i.e. a barrister who serves as a part-time judge in a city.

27. *Original Note*: Probably Milton's pro se defensio contra Alexandrum Morum [1655—eds.].

28. Pierre Bayle, *An Historical and Critical Dictionary ... Translated into English with many additions and corrections made by the author* (London: C. Harper, 1710). There were several later editions.

30. i.e. came to court as they had promised.

31. The *Weekly Times* indicates the author and title of the pamphlet only very late in the article in a section not reproduced here. Charles Knowlton's *Fruits of Philosophy* had been initially published in New York in 1832. It was first published in Britain the following year by James Watson; Holyoake (described in the Introduction to this section) had distributed it from 1834.

32. This breaking off is a typical sign of the pressure under which newspaper compositors had to work at the cheap end of the market: cf. Knight in Section IV.

33. Thomas Bull, *Hints to Mothers, for the management of health during the period of pregnancy, and in the lying-in room ...* (London: Longman, 1837), with numerous later editions; Pye Henry Chevasse [*sic*], *Woman, as Wife and Mother* (Birmingham, 1871). Chevasse was

a well-respected figure, fellow of the Royal College of Surgeons of England and one-time president of Queen's College Medicochirurgical Society.

34. Sales rose to about 300,000 in the two and a half years following the prosecution: see Chandrasekhar (ed.), *Reproductive Physiology and Birth Control* (London: Transaction Publishers, 2002), 45.

35. William Benjamin Carpenter, *A Manual of Physiology, Including Physiological Anatomy, etc.* (London: John Churchill, 1846), and numerous later editions.

36. James Marion Sims [*sic*] (1813–83), celebrated as 'the father of American gynaecology', had published *Clinical Notes on Uterine Surgery* in 1866. Recent research has uncovered his countless experimental operations on slave women without anaesthetic.

37. In a section not reproduced here, Arnold writes of the 'natural right' to property. In English law personal property was not in fact a 'natural right' since 'nature has given the earth and all its products equally to all' (John Sangster, *The Rights and Duties of Property* (London: Whittaker and Co., 1851), 11).

38. Sir Louis Mallet (1823–90), Civil Servant and economist, 'the independent man of the Copyright Commission, questioning everything that others take for granted' (*The Times*, 1 June 1878, 11); Farrer was also on the Commission, a Civil Servant at the Board of Trade.

39. Arnold's article had opened with a lengthy account of the French novelist George Sand's relation with her publisher, Michel Lévy. Arnold had just published an essay on Sand in *Mixed Essays* (1879).

40. George Haven Putnam, activist American publisher (1844–1930), had printed *An Analysis of Mr. R. Pearsall Smith's Scheme for International Copyright* in 1880. Putnam led the battle for international copyright in America, which was finally won in 1891.

IV

PUBLISHING, PRINTING, COMMUNICATION

INTRODUCTION

Publishing and printing were major beneficiaries of the industrial revolution. Technological advances in the production and distribution of print media were crucial for constituting and supplying a mass reading public. New printing and communication technologies, however, can never be considered in isolation when discussing changes in the production of print media. As George Dodd neatly declared in 1843, the conundrum was 'Whether we say that cheap literature has given a spur to printing, or that printing has given a spur to cheap literature, or, which is perhaps the most correct of the three, that each has received advancement from the other.'[1] This section follows Dodd's approach in that while it offers contrasting interpretations of the forces driving the growth of publishing, it ultimately demonstrates the nexus of factors upon which the supply of print media depended.

One group of articles in this section exemplifies the narrative of technological progress characteristic of the Victorian period ('Friends, Brethren'; Knight; Wynter, 'Who is Mr Reuter?'). These articles describe key technological developments that altered the format and production methods of different print media, and which, in so doing, fed into the changing structure of the publishing industry as a whole. A second group of essays, while equally concerned with the supply and distribution of texts, focuses on the institutional practices of publishing and bookselling (Besant; Chapman; Heinemann; Wynter, 'Our Modern Mercury'). This latter group interrogates the tensions caused by the conflicting interests of the different stakeholders in the cycle of literary production. Thus, in this section, there is a balance between articles which detail the processes by which newspapers and books are made, and articles on the relationship between authors, printers, booksellers, and publishers.

Charles Knight's piece is from a well-known series of essays published by the *Penny Magazine* in 1833, which describe the stages involved in the journal's production. Knight's self-reflexive series emphasizes the link between the technology and the economics of publishing. He demonstrates the way that the industrialization of the printing process helped make cheap literature viable. Stereotyping, for example, encouraged the production of German and French versions of the *Penny Magazine*. Knight's ardent belief in progress nevertheless has to be set against the opening article from the *Poor Man's Guardian*, wherein, intriguingly, a group of its working readers asks the journal to justify its use of the steam press to disseminate its attacks upon industrialism. The two articles, which were published within months of each other, embody antithetical interpretations of the impact of printing technology.

Two essays by Andrew Wynter, both from the early 1860s, examine the development of communication and distribution networks. The spread of the railways, both as a form of communication and as a source of leisure, enjoyed an almost symbiotic relationship with the growth of print. In 1830 there were fewer than 100 miles of railway operating in Britain; by 1850 there were 6,600 miles of track.[2] The speed and spread of the railway network provided a significant opportunity for publishers and booksellers: metropolitan newspapers, for example, reached an increasingly national market and challenged the local dominance of provincial papers. W. H. Smith and Son was the principal firm to organize newspaper distribution via the railways; yet Wynter's article recounts how it also took advantage of the railway network for selling and circulating books. In November 1848 W. H. Smith and Son opened their first bookstall at Euston station. These soon became ubiquitous, the firm even running a successful circulating library enabling borrowers to pick up a book at one station and drop it off at another (see Section VII for a related article on the phenomenon of 'Railway Reading'). Like the railways, the national and international telegraph network was also extensively developed in the 1850s. Wynter's second essay traces the rise to prominence of Reuters telegraph agency, which became a habitual source of information for newspapers. Domestic and international news was communicated almost instantaneously by telegraph; newspaper readers were thus able to enjoy a greater imaginative connection not only with the rest of the nation but with far-off corners of the world.

Wynter's essay on the railways, revealing their role as both a distribution network and retailing space, is one example of the way changes in the publishing industry improved the supply of texts. The most crudely deterministic factor in the availability of reading matter, however, was price, and whether book prices were to be set by booksellers or publishers was a key battleground in the early 1850s. The Bookselling Question came to the fore in 1852, when the publisher John Chapman led a successful campaign against an early version of the net book agreement.[3] Chapman's report in this section demonstrates the way that the commercial interests of booksellers, authors, and publishers intersected with the desire for cheap literature.

The two final articles examine the role of publishers in terms of their relations with libraries, authors, printers, and booksellers. Walter Besant charts the rise and fall of a peculiar phenomenon of nineteenth-century publishing, the three-volume novel. A cartel-like relationship between publishers and circulating libraries ensured that the triple-decker survived as a staple media form. While authors and publishers intermittently chafed against its constraints, the economic power of the circulating libraries, particularly Mudie's and W. H. Smith, meant that the format survived from the late 1820s until the early 1890s. Its longevity illustrates the extent to which the economics of publishing could determine literary formats.

Walter Besant was one of the driving forces behind the foundation of the Society of Authors in 1884, which campaigned vigorously to improve the conditions of writers. Faced with the Society, with the organized purchasing power of the circulating libraries, and with the general strength of the union movement that represented the different groups working in the printing trade, William Heinemann's article argues that publishers too needed their own professional organization. Heinemann's unashamed desire to improve the lot of publishers stems from an industrial model that assumes publishers, authors, printers, libraries, and booksellers all have conflicting rather than complementary roles. He thereby raises the question of the structural relationship between those groups responsible for the printing, publishing, and retailing of print media.

FURTHER READING:

Barnes, *Free Trade*; Bennett; Coover; Dodd; Eliot; Feltes; Howe; Jordan and Patten; Keating; Knight, *Old Printer*, *Passages of a Working Life*; Moore; Reed; Sutherland, *Victorian Fiction*, *Victorian Novelists*; Twyman; Weedon.

'Friends, Brethren, and Fellow-Countrymen', *Poor Man's Guardian*, 13 April 1833, 113-15 [113-14]

The *Poor Man's Guardian* was associated with the National Union of the Working Classes, an organization set up by Henry Hetherington and William Lovett in 1831 to campaign for universal suffrage and trade union rights (see also p. 85 above). In this article, a group of Union members suggests a contradiction between the radicalism of the journal and the printing technology it used.

❧

Friends, Brethren, and Fellow-Countrymen,

It is with sorrow and indignation we call your attention to the subjoined communication, which we received last week, from a few individuals styling themselves 'Members of the National Union of the Working Classes.'

[*To the Editor of the Poor Man's Guardian*]

Sɪʀ,—We, the undersigned Members of the National Union of the Working Classes, having heard that the *Guardian* is worked by machinery, wish to know if it is the case, as we consider it inconsistent with what you advocate in the pages of the *Guardian*.

John Rogers	Thomas Perrott
James Milett	George Duffy
J. Davis	Francis Thomas
James Hand	William Plume
James Boston	E. Borton
John Summers	T. Maxwell

P.S.—The six and ninth classes request you will insert this in the *Guardian*.⁴

These persons may be members of the Union, for all we know to the contrary. They may also be very honest and well-disposed men. The circumstance of their giving their names, and the Numbers of their classes, would seem to argue this. At the same time, judging them by the tendency of their conduct, it is difficult not to suspect their motives—or giving them credit for sincerity, it is impossible to be indifferent to the consequences of their blindness. These consequences must inevitably be to weaken our influence—to injure *themselves*, and to play the game of our common enemy. At a moment when we have gathered up a revolutionary power, such as never before existed in England, they ask us whether the report is true that the *Guardian* is worked by machinery?—And then, assuming it to be true, they say '*it is inconsistent with what you advocate in the pages of the Guardian.*' Both the report and the inference are false. It is false that the *Guardian* is worked by machinery (in the sense imputed), and it is equally false that (were it even true) we should be acting inconsistently with our principles. The *Guardian* is worked by *manual labour*, not by *steam power*. It is certainly worked by a machine, and so do the twelve 'undersigned members' eat their dinners with a machine; a knife is a machine, and so is a fork or a spoon. To say that we ought not to use machinery at all, is to say we ought to renounce civilization altogether, and become a horde of destitute savages.—And to say that we ought not to work the *Guardian* with machinery, is to say we ought not to work it at all!—The *Guardian* could no more be printed without a machine than could the earth be cultivated without tools, or a man live without air. Different degrees of mechanical power may indeed belong to the machines employed. Some economise, or supersede the necessity of human labour more than others. But is this an argument against machines? Why, in God's name, what could be a better blessing to man than to have all his work done by machinery if possible? Is it not his primeval curse to be obliged to live by the sweat of his brow? And would *he* not be the greatest benefactor of man who would deliver him from this curse, and make his life one of comparative ease and abundance? [...]

But were it even the fact (which it is not) that Mr. H. caused a few individuals to lose their employment by sending his *Guardian* to a machine, we maintain he would have a perfect right to do so, and that those who would prevent him, or punish him for it, are in their hearts tyrants, who only want the opportunity to inflict on others what they now suffer themselves. Suppose Mr. H. could get his paper printed by a machine in half the time, and for half the price, that a common hand-press would cost—should he on the one hand deprive his family of the saving—a saving perhaps necessary to their existence—and, on the other, deny his subscribers the accommodations of *early time* and *latest news*, because forsooth, a few individuals *might* be inconvenienced by the change? [...]

[Charles Knight], 'The Commercial History of a Penny Magazine', *Penny Magazine*, 2 (1833) 377–84; 417–24; 465–72; 505–11 [377–9, 466–72, 508]

Knight (1791–1873) was the publisher for the Society for Diffusion of Useful Knowledge, which launched the *Penny Magazine* in 1832 (see the Brougham in Section I). His vast publishing output also included the *Penny Cyclopaedia*, *Pictorial Shakespeare*, and *Pictorial Bible*. He was regularly perceived as initiating the dissemination of cheap, improving literature in the 1830s and 1840s. Knight's article demonstrates the way technological advances in printing helped to facilitate the publication of cheap journals. It also exemplifies belief in the ability of industrial progress to further social and political enlightenment.

The process of printing, when compared with that of writing, is unquestionably a cheap process; provided a sufficient number of copies of any particular book are printed, so as to render the proportion of the first expense upon a single copy inconsiderable. If, for example, it were required, even at the present time, to print a single copy, or even three or four copies, only of any production, the cost of printing would be greater than the cost of transcribing. It is when hundreds, and especially thousands, of the same work are demanded that the great value of the printing press in making knowledge cheap, is particularly shown. [...] For some years after the invention of printing, many of the ingenious, learned, and enterprising men who devoted themselves to the new art which was to change the face of society, were ruined, because they could not sell cheaply unless they printed a considerable number of a book; and there were not readers enough to take off the stock which they thus accumulated. In time, however, as the facilities for acquiring knowledge which printing afforded created many readers, the trade of printing books became one of less general risk; and dealers in literature could afford more and more to dispense with individual patronage, and rely upon the public demand. After the experience of three centuries and a half, the power of reading has become so generally diffused, that a work like the

'Penny Magazine,' which requires a sale of 60,000 or 70,000 copies, before any profit can accrue, may be undertaken, with a reliance alone upon the general demand arising out of the extended desire of knowledge. The periodical sale of 160,000 copies of this work is the extreme point which literature has yet reached, in contrast with the promise of the Earl of Arundel to our first printer, to take of him a reasonable quantity of copies, and give him a buck and a doe yearly.[5]

It has been said, that 'the bent of civilization is to make good things cheap.' There can be no doubt whatever, that in all the processes in which science is applied the article produced is not only made better but cheaper; and the more 'the bent of civilization' leads to an extension of demand, the more will scientific knowledge, and the division of labour, be called into employment. But this is peculiarly the case in all *copying* processes, among which printing is the foremost. [...] The cost of authorship, of designs for wood-cuts, and of the wood-cuts themselves, of the 'Penny Magazine,' for example, required to produce a yearly volume, amounts, in round numbers, to 3,000*l.*, or 60,000 shillings. If 120,000 copies are sold, that expense is sixpence upon each volume; if 60,000, one shilling; if 10,000, six shillings; if 3,000, one pound. The purchasers, therefore, of a twelve-months' numbers of the 'Penny Magazine,' for which less than four shillings is paid to the publisher, buy not only sixty-four sheets of printed paper, but as much labour of literature and art as would cost a pound if only 3,000 copies were sold, and six shillings if only 10,000 were sold. Those, therefore, who attempt to persuade the public that cheap books must *essentially* be bad books, are very shallow, or very prejudiced reasoners. The complete reverse is the truth. The cheapness ensures a very large number of purchasers; and the larger the number the greater the power of commercially realizing the means for a liberal outlay upon those matters in which the excellence of a book chiefly consists,—its text, and its illustrations. It is no doubt true that some cheap books must incidentally be bad books. That will be the case, if the condition of great cheapness is attempted with the probability of a small demand. Under such circumstances, the book must either be worthless, or the publishers must sustain severe loss. In cheap publications, the great object to be aimed at, is *certainty* of sale; and that certainty can only be attained by carrying the principle of excellence as far as can be compatible with commercial advantage. The first element of this certainty is an adequate demand.

The almost universal circulation of our 'Penny Magazine' in the United Kingdom; its republication in the United States of America; the establishment of works of similar character, (in all respects imitations,) in France, Belgium, Germany, and Russia; and the plans already formed and announced for extending such publications to Italy, Holland, Poland, and the Brazils,—these circumstances have led us to think that a popular account of all the processes necessary for its production would be of very general interest. [...]

In the petition of Sweynheim and Pannartz to the Pope, which we have already quoted, one passage shows that the demand for paper which had been created by the new art of printing, was supplied with difficulty.[6] 'If you peruse the catalogue of the works printed by us, you will admire how and where we could procure a sufficient quantity of paper, or even rags, for such a number of volumes.' The total of their books amounted to 12,475 volumes. If we average each volume at 50 sheets, of the same size as the 'Penny Magazine,' (which is indeed the size of the early folios,) we find that the quantity of paper thus printed upon was about 1250 reams. Now, this is as near as may be the quantity required for three numbers only of the 'Penny Magazine;' or one twentieth of the quantity annually consumed in printing sixty-four numbers. In weight the quantity for our annual consumption amounts to 500,000 lbs. But then the total annual production of first class paper (that is, writing and printing paper), in the United Kingdom, is about 50,000,000 lbs., or about 100 times as much as that used for the 'Penny Magazine,' and more than 2000 times as much as the paper used in the 12,475 volumes of the poor German printers. It is not unlikely, therefore, that some of our readers may admire how and where *we* can now procure a sufficient quantity of rags for such an immense production of printing and writing paper. We will endeavour to explain how this is managed.

The material of which the sheet of paper which the reader now holds in his hand is formed, existed, a few months ago, perhaps in the shape of a tattered frock, whose shreds, exposed for years to the sun and wind, covered the sturdy loins of the shepherd watching his sheep on the plains of Hungary;—or it might have formed part of the coarse blue shirt of the Italian sailor, on board some little trading vessel of the Mediterranean [...]—or might have accompanied every revolution of a fashionable coat in the shape of lining—having travelled from St. James's to St. Giles's—from Bond Street to Monmouth Street—from Rag Fair to the Dublin Liberty—till man disowned the vesture, and the kennel-sweeper claimed its miserable remains. [...] In each or all of these forms, and in hundreds more which it would be useless to describe, this sheet of paper a short time since might have existed. The rags of our own country do not furnish a fifth part of what we consume in the manufacture of paper. France, Holland, and Belgium prohibit, under severe penalties, the exportation of rags, because they require them for their own long-established manufactories. Spain and Portugal also prohibit their exportation. Italy and Germany furnish the principal supplies of linen rags, both to Great Britain and the United States. [...]

The paper upon which the 'Penny Magazine' is printed is chiefly manufactured at Albury Mill, near Guildford, belonging to Mr. Magnay. Paper-mills in the south of England are set in motion by water-power—that is, they are placed upon some small stream, which, being dammed up, sets the wheels in motion, as in a flour-mill. In the north of England, where coal is abundant, paper-mills employ steam-power; and in the present mode of manufacturing paper, in which heat is essential, it is probable that the article can be produced at a lower rate by this process. A paper-mill moved by water-power, is generally a very agreeable object. It is in most instances situated in some pretty valley, through which the little river glides;—and as it is important that the water, (which is not only employed for turning the wheels, but for converting the rags into pulp) should be of the purest quality, the stream is generally one of those transparent ones which are so common in England—now bubbling over pebbly shallows, and now sleeping in quiet depths. The paper-mill at Albury is of this picturesque character. [...]

Let us now examine a printing office a little more in detail. In Mr. Clowes's establishment, which we noticed in our last Number, we enter a very long room, in which from fifty to sixty compositors are constantly employed.[7] Each man works at a sort of desk called a frame, and in most instances he has the desk or frame to himself. [...] They are cleanly, well-dressed, intelligent looking, active artisans; not much thinking about the matter of the work they have in hand, but properly intent upon picking up as many letters in the hour as may be compatible with following their copy correctly, and of producing what is called a clean *proof*,—that is, a proof, or first impression, with very few mistakes of words or letters.

[...] No one unacquainted with the details of a printing-office can conceive the great differences between the correctness of one compositor and of another. The differences in the talent, the acquired knowledge, and even the moral habits of different men, are the causes of these remarkable variations. A *proof* shall be brought to the reader produced by the joint labour of two or three compositors of different degrees of merit. In a particular part of it he will find one letter constantly substituted for another, although the sense is upon the whole given correctly: this is the work of the careless and slovenly compositor, who does not take the trouble to look over the types as he sets them up line by line. He is a bad economist of his own time; for he has to correct all these faults at last, without making any charge for his correction; and he corrects them with much less ease in the second stage than in the first. Again, in another part of the proof, although the merely literal faults may be very few, there is a perpetual substitution of one word for another. This is the work of the ignorant or conceited compositor, who jumps at the meaning of his author, and thus contrives to produce the most ludicrous errors in his original proofs, and to insinuate some error or other into the most carefully corrected book. We have seen proofs in which an ode to a Grecian *urn* was translated into an ode to a Grecian *nose*; in which Queen Mab was drawn by a team of little *attorneys*, instead of the little '*atomies*' of Shakespeare; and the *aromatic* principles of the English constitution, instead of the *democratic*, made us think of a Persian court, rich with all delicate odours, instead of the House of Commons and the hustings. [...]

When the ordinary reader of a newspaper, or of a book, meets with an occasional blunder either of a letter or a word, he is apt to cry out upon the carelessness with which the newspaper or book is printed. It is in the very nature of the process of producing words and sentences by the putting together of moveable types, that a great many blunders should be made by the compositor in the first stage, which nothing but the strictest vigilance can detect and get rid of. The ordinary process of correction is for the printer's reader to look upon the proof, while another person, generally a boy, reads the copy aloud. As he proceeds the reader marks [...] all the errors which present themselves upon a first perusal. The proof then goes back to the compositor; and here a business of great labour and difficulty ensues. The omitted words and letters have to be introduced, and the incorrect words and letters have to be replaced by the correct. The introduction of two or three words will sometimes derange the order of a dozen lines; and the omission of a sentence will involve the re-arrangement of many pages. In this tedious process new blunders are oftentimes created; and these again can only be remedied by after vigilance. The first corrections being perfected, the reader has what is called a *revise*. He compares this with his first proof, and ascertains that all his corrections have been properly made. In this stage of the business the proof generally goes to the author; and it is rarely that the most practised author does not feel it necessary to make considerable alterations. The complicated process of correction is again to be gone over. The printer's reader and the author have again revises; and what they again correct is again attended to. The proof being now tolerably perfect, the labour of another reader is in most large establishments called in. It is his business to *read for press*—that is, to search for the minutest errors with a spirit of the most industrious criticism. The author has often to be consulted upon the queries of this captious personage, who ought to be as acute in discovering a blunder, as a conveyancer in finding out a flaw in a title-deed. But in spite of all this activity, blunders *do* creep in; and the greatest mortification that an author can experience is the lot of almost every author,—namely, to take up his book, after the copies have gone out to the world, and find some absurdly obvious mistake, which glares upon him when he first opens the book, and which, in spite of his conviction that it was never there before, has most likely escaped his own eye, and that of every other hunter of errors that the best printing-office can produce.

[...] We subjoin a wood-cut which exhibits the compositor composing in his frame, and a second frame which more distinctly shows the shape of a pair of cases. Standing against the empty frame to the left is a form of four folio pages, supposed to represent the form of the 'Penny Magazine;' at the other end of the same frame is an empty chase similar to that in which the pages are wedged up.

FIG. 3. 'The Compositor', *Penny Magazine*, 2 (1833), 469.

It is in this stage, when the pages of the 'Penny Magazine' have been rendered as correct as the care of several readers can ensure, and when the original wood-cuts have been inserted in their proper places, that the process of *stereotyping* commences.[8] This process is by no means universally applied to all printed books. Its peculiar advantages are confined to works in very large demand, and of which the demand is continued long after the first publication. [...] [There follows a long description of the process of stereotyping, whereby a mould, taken from the arranged movable type, is then cast and finished in order to create a reproduction of the original page type— eds.]

[T]here is another advantage which stereotyping gives us, in allowing us to multiply casts to any extent. We can assist foreign nations in the production of 'Penny Magazines;' and we can thus not only obtain the high moral advantage of giving a tone to the popular literature of other nations, which shall be favourable to peace, and a right understanding of our common interests, but we can improve our own 'Penny Magazine' out of the profit which accrues from the sale of these casts. The American Government has a tariff, or duty, of 33 per cent. upon all foreign books imported into the United States. This tariff would prevent the 'Penny Magazine' being sold at two cents (nearly a penny), and would probably advance it to three cents. We send our pages stereotyped to a bookseller at New York, who employs American labour and American paper in working them off. By thus avoiding the tariff he can sell the 'Penny Magazine' at two cents. Further, the art of wood-cutting is imperfectly understood in France and Germany. We sell, therefore, to France and Germany casts of our wood-cuts, at a tenth of what it would cost them to have them re-engraved. These countries are thus enabled to produce their '*Magasin Pittoresque*,' and their '𝔓fenig-𝔐agazin.'[9] This literary intercourse may appear to some people to be of trifling importance; but that circumstance cannot be uninteresting which has a tendency to direct the popular reading of four great countries into the same channels; and which, by lessening the cost of producing cheap books in each of the countries, leaves some capital free in each to be devoted to other intellectual objects. [...]

And this brings us to the great and paramount advantage of the stereotype process, namely, the economy of capital. The inherent difficulty of the business of a publisher consists in the mistakes he may make in calculating the demand for a particular book. The demand for broad-cloth, or bacon, or any other article of physical necessity, does not greatly vary. The demand for books depends, in a certain degree, upon fashion, and the prevailing current of public opinion. In books of a merely temporary interest, or which are addressed only to particular classes, and deal with particular modes of thought, a publisher often loses very considerably by over-printing. In this case the copies which remain locked up in his warehouse for years, and are at last sold for waste-paper, absorb so much capital that might have been applied to other literary purposes if the demand for them had not ceased. But in books of universal interest, which address themselves to all classes, and which consequently may be sold cheap in the expectation of a large sale, the risk of over-production is very much diminished. But the publisher must still watch the demand. He must not run too much before it with his supply, for he may be ruined by his stock;—he must not lag too much behind it with his supply, for he may thus lose the market. Before the first Number of the 'Penny Magazine' was issued, it was impossible to say whether the periodical demand for the work would be 20,000 or 100,000 copies. Stereotyping came to the solution of the difficulty. It enabled the publisher then, and it enables him now, to adjust the supply exactly to the demand. One hundred and six Numbers have been published, and yet the supply of any one has not fallen behind the demand a single day. Twenty million 'Penny Magazines' have been issued from the commencement; and yet the publisher has rarely more than 2 or 300,000 in his warehouse. A small quantity of each number can be worked off from the stereotype plates at a day's notice; and a little foresight, therefore, can always ensure that the market shall be supplied, while the stock is kept low. This is the great secret of all commercial success. [...]

If the difficulties that existed in producing any considerable number of newspapers before the invention of the printing machine were almost insurmountable, equally striking will the advantages of that invention appear when we consider its application to such a work as the 'Penny Magazine.' Let us suppose that the instruction of the people had gone on uninterruptedly in the schools of mutual instruction, and that the mechanical means for supplying the demand for knowledge thus created had sustained no improvement. In this series of papers we have endeavoured constantly to show that the price at which a book can be sold depends in great part upon the number printed of that book. But at the same time it must be borne in mind, that the number of any particular work thus produced must be limited by the mechanical means of production. If the demand for knowledge had led to the establishment of the 'Penny Magazine' before the invention of the printing machine, it is probable that the sale of twenty thousand copies would have been considered the utmost that could have been calculated upon. This invention has forced on other departments of printing, and larger presses have therefore been constructed to compete in some degree with the capacity of the machine for printing a large *form* of types. Twenty years ago there probably was no press in England large enough to work off a double number of the 'Penny Magazine.' One thousand perfect copies, therefore, could only have been daily produced at one press by the labour of two men. The machine produces sixteen thousand copies. If the demand for the 'Penny Magazine,' printed thus slowly by the press, had reached twenty thousand, it would have required two presses to produce that twenty thousand in the same time, namely, ten days, in which we now produce one hundred and sixty thousand by the machine; and it would have required one press to be at work one hundred and sixty days, or sixteen presses for ten days, to effect the same results as the machine now effects in ten days. [...]

John Chapman, *A Report of the Proceedings of a Meeting (Consisting Chiefly of Authors), held 4 May, at the House of Mr. John Chapman, 142, Strand, for the Purpose of Hastening the Removal of the Trade Restrictions on the Commerce of Literature* (London, 1852), 17–21

Between December 1829 and 1852, the Booksellers' Association sought to uphold an agreement that prohibited booksellers retailing books at more than 10 per cent below their set price. The association argued that underselling harmed the trade by enforcing aggressive competition and reducing profits. In 1852 the publisher John Chapman, who had previously tried to sell imported American books at 30 per cent below their usual price, began a campaign against the association in the name of free trade. The extract below stems from a meeting Chapman organized to garner support from notable authors; attendees included Dickens, Wilkie Collins, Richard Hengist Horne, and George Eliot. On 19 May Lord Campbell ruled against the Booksellers' Association; it was not until 1 January 1900 that a Net Book Agreement was finally introduced.

A REPLY TO THE ARGUMENTS ADDUCED IN SUPPORT OF THE BOOKSELLERS' ASSOCIATION

The material producers of books, publishers, unlike most other manufacturers, fix and advertise the retail prices of their productions, and the distributing agents, or booksellers, are remunerated in the shape of a discount from the published prices. The discount ranges from 25 to about 42 per cent. According to Mr. Murray,[10] it has been the custom of the trade to allow 25 per cent discount for at least 100 years; the allowance has therefore been increasing instead of diminishing, as it ought to have done—rates of profit being generally graduated in an inverse proportion to the increase of business and facilities for its transaction. And, accordingly, a considerable number of booksellers have declared unnecessary the large discounts now allowed, by offering to divide them with their customers; but powerful monopolists and men lacking enterprise have combined to prevent the adoption of the system of small profits, in order that they may continue to enjoy the large ones, or reap other indirect, but apparently no less substantial, advantages of monopoly. Thus originated the Booksellers' Association, the object of which is, to keep the price of books artificially high. [...]

My endeavour to point out the injury which this Association inflicts on the public and on literary men, and to prove the applicability of free-trade principles to bookselling and publishing, has called forth several arguments from the literary protectionists in vindication of their restrictive system. Of these arguments the principal is, that free trade would do away with a large number of existing booksellers both in the metropolis and in the provinces. Mr. William Longman says, that the main question is, whether free trade would or would not injure the retail booksellers.[11] But the public, which preferred cheap bread to continuing the guarantee of protected profits to the farmers, will hardly consider the maintenance of any given number of book-sellers an object of even equal importance with that of getting cheap books. Unrestrained competition will accurately determine how many booksellers are needful for the efficient distribution of all the books which are published. Those who object to competition, when applied to the sale of books, are bound, in consistency, to oppose its adoption in all other departments of trade. [...]

Another argument in favour of the Association is the alleged unanimity of the booksellers in their desire for protection. But this apparent unanimity is not real. If the booksellers are actually such a happy family as they are asserted to be, whence the necessity for the oppressive coercion so constantly practised? How Mr. W. Longman could reconcile his attestation to Lord Campbell of the voluntary submission of the trade to the restrictions opposed, with his subsequent appeal to his Lordship in justification of processes which ruin the dissentients, it is difficult to understand.[12]

Mr. Simms of Manchester told Lord Campbell that he represented the whole trade of the town.[13] Now I possess evidence that, after considerable effort to convert the Manchester booksellers into members of the Association, there still remained six heretics. Whether sufficient force has since been applied to *dragoon* all these into orthodoxy, I am not aware. The following extract from a letter addressed to me by Messrs. Burge and Perrin of Manchester will show how *they* were reconciled, in the words of Lord Campbell, 'to the true faith.'[14]

'We received notice from the secretary of the London Association, that, unless, we previously signed the rules, our accounts in London would be closed after a certain day. We allowed the day to pass, and then wrote to our agents in London for a supply of books, and from them we received a letter by next post, stating that they were reluctantly compelled to decline our order in consequence of our not belonging to the Association, but that they trusted we should reconsider the matter. Having no option, we then consulted with two other firms in Manchester who were in the same position, and, together with them, waited upon the secretary of the Manchester Association and signed the rules.'

I have indubitable proofs that the same methods have been adopted at Birmingham, and am assured that persons have been employed in that town to purchase books from suspected booksellers in order to discover whether they disobeyed the rules of the combination. [...]

The motives of the literary-protectionists are various [...] But the following is, I believe, an adequate explanation [...] At their trade sales, Messrs. Longman and Co. allow about 30 per cent. discount to purchasers, and rarely give the extra advantage of charging 25 books as 24 or 13 as 12; whereas Mr. Murray, in common with two or three other publishers, allows at his trade sales $33\frac{1}{3}$ per cent. discount, and gives the extra advantage of charging 25 books as 24, and very often 13 as 12, which, considered as an additional discount, amounts to $7\frac{1}{3}$ in the one case, and $11\frac{1}{3}$ in the other, more than is usually allowed by Messrs. Longman and Co. It thus appears that, though competition is not permissible to the retail booksellers, it is perfectly legitimate for the publisher to practise it within the limits of the trade; in fact, a main reason why the bookseller is subjected to the system of protection, which he is assured is for his exclusive benefit, is, that the practice of competition is found to produce a rich return to the underselling publisher in proportion as the privilege is withheld from the retail bookseller. I feel sure Mr. Murray is unconscious of the inconsistency; but it certainly takes one rather by surprise to find that the very man who recently designated the few booksellers acting on the principles of free trade, as 'interested and ill-informed persons,' 'solitary upstarts,' and 'undersellers,' who 'endeavour to filch away the customers from old-established houses,' should himself prove to be *the great underseller* of his trade.

The refusal to sell off the 'remainders' of unsuccessful works is another part of the protectionist system. I have just shown how, by enforcing protection on the booksellers, the underselling publisher can secure to himself an undue share of their co-operation; but he may make assurance doubly sure by a practical pledge that he will never reduce the published prices of any of his publications, even though the public should have steadily refused to buy at the prices fixed upon them, and when, therefore, as speculations, they have proved total failures. This system is adopted by the most eminent of the publishers, and the booksellers are therefore tempted, within certain narrow limits, to purchase more largely from a house offering such a pledge, than they otherwise might do. I say within certain narrow limits, for an attempt to promote the sale of books by a manoeuvre, however skilful, which shall have reference to the booksellers only, cannot possibly result in a success equal to that which would be achieved by a direct appeal to the public. The system acted upon in Lackington's day was that of destroying a portion of the edition of any unsuccessful book, in order to make the remainder artificially dear;[15] the modern publisher who hoards his stock has not made much advance upon the commercial ideas of that time; he crowds one warehouse after another with books which, while they are valueless to himself, he refuses to give to the public at such prices as 'demand' would fix upon them. If the eminent publisher who is especially distinguished by this practice would sell at their ascertained market values such of his publications as are not in demand at their original prices, he would redeem thousands of pounds else irrevocably lost, and would render tens of thousands of handsome volumes available to the public. [...]

The members of the Booksellers' Association allege that, in fixing the retail prices and discounts of books, they are doing no more than the proprietors of patented articles do. In asserting this, they assert what is simply not true. Were all proprietors of patented articles and their agents to unite and fix certain rates of profit—were they to say to all patentees, 'Your commodities shall not be brought before the public unless you agree to our percentage;' and to all agents, 'We will ruin you if you take less than these percentages'—then, indeed, there would be an analogy. As it is, however, for the sale of every newly-invented article the patentee makes his own terms with his agents; and it is just this liberty possessed by the patentee, that is contended for by the advocates of literary free-trade; namely, that every author and every publisher shall be able to fix his own conditions of sale.

[Andrew Wynter], 'Our Modern Mercury', *Once a Week*, 4 (2 February 1861), 160-3.

Andrew Wynter (1819-76), physician and author, devoted much of his career to the study of the insane. He published articles in the *Edinburgh* and *Quarterly* reviews, as well as short entertaining sketches of contemporary life in *Once a Week* (1859-80), a successful 3*d*. miscellany. These were later collected and republished in volume form. Here, Wynter details the growth of W. H. Smith and its use of the railway network to both disseminate and retail newspapers, novels, and periodicals.

It is often the case that the history of a single firm, is the history of a great social revolution in a country of rapid development, such as Great Britain. What ages seem to separate us from the time, little more than a quarter of a century ago, when it took two days to convey any important item of intelligence between London and Liverpool. Then the *Times* in the north was fresh two days after date! In those days, say thirty-five years ago, all newspapers sent into the country passed through the Post-office. [...] It struck Mr. Smith, the father of the present head of the extensive firm near St. Clement's Danes Church, that instead of waiting for the night mail, the morning papers might be despatched by the quick morning coaches, thus enabling the community at Birmingham to read the London morning news, and the great cities of Liverpool, Manchester, and other neighbouring towns, to get the papers on the first instead of the second morning after publication. This was a simple idea, and destined to be of immense importance to the community, and one would have thought that its advantages would speedily have been taken advantage of. The experiment, however, was only another example of the length of time it takes to make the public leave their old ruts, but of the ultimate triumph of all good ideas if sufficiently persevered in. Mr. Smith laboured long and earnestly in this new direction before it began to tell. As the morning papers in those days made no editions expressly for early trains, it often happened that the coaches started before they were out—this was Mr Smith's first difficulty, which he overcame by establishing express carts to overtake them. On great occasions, these express carts went the whole journey at a very heavy expense; but the prize was commensurate—the conveyance of important news before any other medium of communication. Thus Smith's express carried the news to Dublin of the death of George IV., before the government messenger arrived.[16] Again, during the excitement of the Reform Bill, the craving for early intelligence made Smith's expresses famous throughout the north. Even at the latest period of the coaching time, however, one man, who is still in the establishment, was able to carry all the papers to the coaches under his arm, and now six tons of the *Times* newspaper alone, are despatched every day by the early trains; and the preparation of packing and folding, carried on in the great room in the Strand, is one of the most remarkable sights in London. [...]

The penny morning papers are beginning to monopolize the public market; and the thousands which daily leave Messrs. Smiths' for the country is a proof that hundreds of thousands in the provinces now see a daily paper who never enjoyed that luxury before. As the *Telegraph, Star*, and *Standard* have thus spread themselves over the country, all the high-priced daily papers, with the exception of the *Times* only, have lost a considerable part of their circulation, and must eventually come down to the standard penny, if they would avoid destruction. Whilst we note this revolution among the daily papers, it is equally clear that the old slovenly scissors and paste weekly journal is going to the wall. People, as soon as they grow accustomed to see a cheap morning paper, will not tolerate a mere stale jumble of the week's news patched together without method or originality. [...]

It is impossible to calculate the fruits which spring indirectly from any new discovery. Who would have imagined that the introduction of railways would be a powerful and direct means of increasing a thousand-fold the influence of Belles Lettres, and of scattering throughout the country the literary treasures that find their birth as a natural consequence in great capitals? The institution of railway libraries by Messrs. Smith is, we think, one of the most remarkable features of the present day. On the first establishment of railways, the porters were allowed to keep book-stalls for their own emolument. Low-class intellects, of course, could only appreciate low-class literature, consequently these stalls at last became mere disseminators of literary trash and rubbish, and were quite a nuisance. It was evident

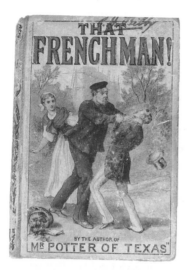

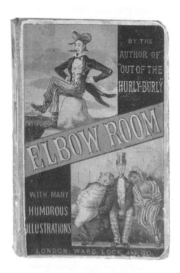
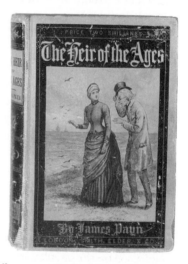

FIG. 4. A selection of 'Yellow-back' railway novels. Archibald Clavering Gunter, *That Frenchman!* (London: George Routledge and Sons, 1889); Mary Elizabeth Braddon, *One Life—One Love* (London: Simpkin, Marshall, Hamilton, Kent & Co., 1891); Max Adeler, *Elbow-Room: A Novel without a plot* (London: Ward, Lock and Co., 1876); James Payn, *The Heir of the Ages* (London: Smith, Elder & Co., 1887).

that the note of public taste had been struck a whole octave too low. At this juncture, the stalls of nearly all the railway stations fell into the hands of Mr. W. H. Smith; and a book for the journey speedily became as a great a necessity as a railway rug or cap. Our readers must have observed that a certain class of literature was called into existence to fill that new want. The shilling series of Routledge were the true offspring of the railway libraries.[17] Even their highly-embellished covers were of the rapid school of design, calculated to ensnare the eye of the passing traveller. It cannot be denied that this new style of literature had its evil as well as its good side, and had a tendency to deteriorate our current literature with a certain slang and fast element which boded anything but good for the future. It was speedily discovered that higher priced books, such as are published by Messrs. Murray and Longman, seldom found a sale at these stalls, and the circulating population would feed on no literary food but that which was of an exciting, stimulating character. In this country, however, things have a tendency to work straight, and it occurred to Mr. W. H. Smith that every book-stall could be turned into a circulating library, fed by the central depôt in London. Listen to this, young ladies in remote villages, eaten out by *ennui*, and pining to read the last new novel! Imagine one of the largest booksellers in the metropolis proposing to pour without stint all the resources of his establishment into your remote Stoke Pogis, and you will find this unheard-of proposition is now an actual and accomplished fact. At the present moment almost every railway in Great Britain and Ireland, with the exception of the Great Western, is in literary possession of Mr W. H. Smith. At two hundred stations, metropolitan, suburban, and provincial, a great circulating library is opened, which can command the whole resources of an unlimited supply of first-class books: and to appreciate this fact we must remember the state of things it displaces. In the country village the circulating library is generally an appendage to the general shop. A couple of hundred thumbed volumes, mostly of the Edgeworth, Hannah More, or Sir Charles Grandison class, form the chief stock-in-trade.[18] If by any chance a new novel loses its way down into one of these villages, in a couple of months' time a resident may have a chance of reading it. But all this is now changed. In Mr W. H. Smith's circulating library the reader may have any book he may choose to order down by the next morning train, regardless of its value. Imagine Southey living in this age, and whilst he enjoyed his lovely Cumberland Lake, having a stream of new books down from London fresh and fresh, at an annual cost a little more than one volume would have cost him in his day![19] The subscriber to the railway library has simply to present his ticket to the book-stall keeper, wherever he may be, to get the book he wants, if it be in stock; if not, a requisition is forwarded to the house in the Strand, and he gets it by the next day. He can get the book he wants with a great deal more certainty, and almost as quickly even in the North of England, than he could by sending to the next country town. If he is travelling he may exchange his books at any station where he may happen to be. [...]

Amid the hum of the mighty Babylon, we easily overlook the noiseless and unostentatious growth of such an establishment as that of Messrs. W. H. Smith & Co. Within thirty-five years, by the exercise of intelligence, perseverance, and industry, this house has grown from a mere stationer's shop and newspaper agency, employing half-a-dozen persons, to a mighty establishment, employing two hundred clerks and five hundred men and boys; and whilst Mr. Smith has thus toiled to place himself in the position of a greater employer of labour, his efforts tend most powerfully to civilize and elevate the intelligence of the nation.

Along every line of rail which traverses the country in every direction, these libraries are posted, and become wells of English undefiled. They have established a propaganda of culture in the remotest as well as in the most cultivated spots of the island; and their proprietor, in building up his own fortune, is doing no small service towards the educational movement in this country.

[Andrew Wynter], 'Who is Mr. Reuter?' *Once a Week*, 4 (23 February 1861), 243–6

In November 1851 the first cross-channel telegraph cable began operating between Britain and France. A month previously, Paul Julius Reuter (1816–99) had opened an office in London. This would become the home of Reuters, an international institution devoted to disseminating telegraphed news. Reuter had previously run a telegraph agency from Aachen, Germany, supplying German and Belgian newspapers. This essay was subsequently republished in *Our Social Bees* (1866).

All the world is asking this question. Is the mysterious individual who tells us through the public press what battles have been won or lost—what kings have decamped, or what words emperors have spoken an hour since in far-off countries, which will shake the political world to its foundation—is this Mr. Reuter an institution or a myth? Must we count his name like one of those which have an existence in the heathen mythology only, or is he a man like ourselves, having 'feelings, organs, dimensions,' &c.? If he be, by what extraordinary organization does he manage to gather up over night a summary of events over the entire continent, and to place it before us as a startling interlude between coffee and toast at the breakfast-table? Nay, how is it that through his mouth—if we may so term it—we hear for the first time of a successful battle in China, or of the madness of the Southern slave states in America? To answer all these questions is the purpose of the present paper, and we may claim the privilege of being the first to satisfy the public inquiries relative to this very interesting subject. Mr. Reuter's history is like that of all courageous and energetic men, who, seizing upon a new idea, work it persistently and silently, until one fine morning, from comparative obscurity they suddenly find their names famous.

The practical success of the first working telegraph on the continent—that between Berlin and Aix-la-Chapelle in 1849—convinced Mr. Reuter, in common with every thinking man on the continent, that a new era in correspondence had arisen, and he determined to avail himself of its facilities for the public advantage. The first office for the furtherance of telegraphic communication was opened at Aix-la-Chapelle, an admirable spot lying so conveniently between the east and west of Europe. This office formed the first centre of that organization which has since gathered up into the hands of one man for all general and public purposes the scattered electric wires of the world. In order to correct breaks in the most direct line of transmitting news, he had to supplement the wire with contrivances of his own, so as to insure priority of information. Thus, the better to gain time in the journey between Aix-le-Chapelle and Brussels, he employed a service of carrier-pigeons. By this means on this distance alone he was enabled to anticipate the mail train between the two places by six or eight hours. In order to ensure regularity and safeness in transmission, each message was despatched by three different pigeons, which made the passage from Brussels to Aix-la-Chapelle in an average period of one hour. When the telegraphic line was extended from Aix-la-Chapelle to Quiev-rain, on the Belgio-French frontier, and the French Government extended their line from Paris to Valenciennes, there remained a gap of only five miles in the line of telegraph between the French and Prussian capitals, but insignificant as this space was, the delay thereby occasioned was enormous. To obviate this, relays of saddled horses were always kept in readiness to forward despatches between the two points.

As line after line was opened in succession, each was made sub-servient to his system, and when the cable between Calais and Dover was successfully laid in 1851, Mr. Reuter, who had become a natur-alised subject of Her Majesty, transferred his office to London, which thenceforth was put in connection with the principal continental cities. Up to this time Mr. Reuter confined his attention to the conveyance of commercial despatches, but it now struck him that the time was arrived for making the telegraph the handmaid of the press. [...] [F]or a third time in 1858, Mr. Reuter made his offer to the press. This time, however, he sent his telegrams for one whole month to all the editors in London, leaving it to their option whether they used them or not. The quickness with which Mr. Reuter received his telegrams, and the accuracy of the information they contained, were soon appreciated, and one newspaper after another became subscribers. His telegrams did not attract particular notice, simply because no great public event gave him an opportunity of showing the value of his system. So matters went on until the 9th of February, 1859. On that day the Emperor made his famous speech, in which he threatened Austria through her ambassador.[20] His ominous words were uttered at 1 P.M. in the Tuileries, and at 2 P.M the speech was published in a third edition of the *Times*, and had shaken the Stock Exchange to its foundation. This was a dramatic hit, and thenceforward every one looked out for Mr Reuter's telegrams. [...]

The newspapers of the chief provincial towns were not long in availing themselves of his system, which ended in depriving the metropolis of the monopoly of early intelligence. The daily papers of the great towns of the north of England and of Ireland possess exactly the same early telegrams as the London daily papers, by means of Mr. Reuter's system, which posts England well up in the news of the world, at her furthest extremities, as she is in the metropolis itself.

News from England is in the like manner conveyed by Mr. Reuter to all the chief continental cities. Thus the people of St. Petersburg may read every morning abstracts of the previous night's debate in the British Houses of Parliament.

What Mr. Reuter has already done for Europe, he is about to do for the other quarters of the globe. It will have been observed that all our earliest information from America, India, and China, the Cape, and even Australia, is derived from this gentleman's telegrams. In all these countries he has located agents, who transmit him news in anticipation of the mails. There being no direct telegraphic communication between England and those countries, Mr. Reuter avails himself of every telegraphic line *en route*. Messages from America, for instance, are telegraphed up to the latest moment to the last port in the Atlantic where the steamer touches; they are then landed either at Queenstown, Londonderry, Galway, Liverpool, or Southampton, whence they are telegraphed to London. News from the East is received in an accelerated manner, by a similar method. All the telegrams first come into the hands of Mr. Reuter, whose day offices are near the Exchange, and whose night offices are in Finsbury Square—thus this gentleman is without doubt, as regards the affairs of the world, the best informed man in it. He gives his political telegrams to the press alone, and never allows them on any account to be communicated beforehand to merchants and bankers for the purpose of speculation.

In order to make the separation between the political and commercial departments of his establishment the more complete, he has removed the former to Waterloo Place at the West End, whilst the latter remains at the city offices. These offices are open day and night; the day staff of clerks working from 10 A.M. till 6 P.M., and the night staff, a far more numerous one, in consequence of the far longer hours of work, being engaged, in relays, from 6 P.M. one evening till 10 A.M. next day. All the offices are connected together by the electric wire, and to still further facilitate the transmission of telegrams to the different newspapers, the wires are being continued from the West End Office right into the editor's room of each journal, who, by means of Wheatstone's universal telegraphic apparatus, is enabled to read off his own messages instead of receiving them as heretofore, by messenger.[21] The pedestrian, as he walks along Fleet Street and the Strand, will perceive high over head what might be termed the political spinal cord of the metropolis; every here and there it gives off right and left fine filaments; these are going to the *Globe*, the *Sun*, the *Morning Post*, the *Herald*, the *Standard*, the *Telegraph*, and all the other daily papers which line this great thoroughfare. These are the lines by which Mr. Reuter puts the whole British public in possession of the thoughts, and records the actions of the rest of the world; and as we watch the wires ruling their sharp outlines against the sky, for all we know they are conveying words which may affect the destinies of millions yet unborn.

William Heinemann, 'The Hardships of Publishing', *Athenaeum*, 3 December 1892, 779–80

Heinemann (1863–1920) launched his publishing firm in 1890. Its fiction list included well-known figures such as Sarah Grand, Rudyard Kipling, and Robert Louis Stevenson. This article, which was later expanded into a pamphlet, provoked a fierce debate in a prestigious literary weekly, the *Athenaeum* (1828–1921), between authors and publishers. Walter Besant published several letters in response defending the rights of authors. Heinemann helped to set up the Publishers' Association of Great Britain and Ireland in 1896.

May I be allowed through your valuable columns to say a word with regard to the curious condition of the English publisher of to-day? I do so hesitatingly, and my remarks must be regarded as tentative rather than conclusive.

A year and a half has gone by since the introduction of the American Copyright Act, from which some of us hoped so much, and I do not see that we are in a better or in a worse position than we were before.[22] [...]

The colonial market (as every one knows who has had anything to do with publishing during the last few years) has, on account of heavy failures in the colonies and the general depression of trade, been steadily deteriorating, and few except cheap books find buyers in the colonies.

With our home market things are, perhaps, not quite so bad, but they are bad enough to force upon all of us engaged in the distribution of books a look round—a stock-taking of what is really going on. We are oscillating between the Scylla of those who provide us with raw material and the Charybdis of those for whom our ready-made wares are intended. Happy the 'doughty Ulysses' who, steering clear of these dangerous rocks, is enabled to cast his anchor in the safe harbour of success.

Let us consider these two dangers independently and see how we can save our fragile craft from shipwreck and utter destruction.

The providers of raw material can be divided roughly into two divisions, viz., the authors, editors, and compilers of our publications, and the printers, paper-makers, binders, &c., who put the produce of the former into a saleable form. For convenience's sake let us look at the latter first, and leave the proud knights of the pen to be last (they take care that they are not least) in our calculations.

Perhaps the three classes enumerated share in equal proportion the attention of the collective London publishing world, for while the printers are the more important to the publishers of high-price books, paper-makers and binders unquestionably run the cheap-book publishers to a 'nice figure' per annum. Printers' wages have increased steadily for years past until it has become imperative to employ non-union houses for work of an inferior order, such, for instance, as the setting of ordinary fiction. Higher-class printing is more expensive now than it ever was, and not only do the master printers make smaller profits, but the publishers have to pay higher prices for first-class work. The same increase in prices has taken place with very similar results among binders in London, and the only appreciable difference to the good is the fall in the prices of paper—a temporary fall, we are told, and due only to over-production and excessive competition. On the whole, it is certain that the price of book production is not less, perhaps it is higher, than it was a few years ago before the adoption of the Eight Hours Bill.[23] It certainly is higher with all the best work, and the enormous number of books (statistically about 75 per cent.) which are printed in only small editions.

To this must be added the fact that the public are more fastidious now with regard to print, paper, and general get-up, and that they make, if not a united, in places, at least a definite stand against the horrible stuff that they used to buy under the good-natured generalization of 'books.' These increased expenditures are brought about by the trades union of printers, the trades union of binders, and the unconscious union of the public.

And now come our authors, who have also put themselves together in a trades union—a trades union more complete, more dangerous to the employer, more definite in its object, and more determined in its demands than any of the other unions—conducted, besides, with intelligence, with foresight, with purity of purpose, but unquestionably and avowedly against the publisher. No one has had better opportunity than myself to test the courteous spirit and fair dealing of the Authors' Society, and I will be second to none in acknowledging the services rendered by Mr. Besant and his colleagues in certain directions.[24] But with all deference, I will say that they have done harm too—not voluntarily, but accidentally. I will not dwell on a number of very inaccurate and very unreliable handbooks which they have published, because I do not fancy that these have penetrated very far, so that the errors they contain can hardly have become very widespread. But I will at least mention the surprise felt by our American *confrères* at the lethargic attitude of the London publishers when the Authors' Society takes upon itself to judge as to the proper way a book should appear, the proper remuneration the author should receive ('if he respects himself, and if the publisher is honest!'), and best of all when it calculates the cost of publication, &c., with a disregard to that heavy item—our working expenses—which is delicious in its airiness. In the latter function the position of the Authors' Society is as naïve as if we publishers were to sit down and write fiction or poetry instead of publishing what others have written.

It would lead too far, perhaps, to enter into the surprising results that have already come of advice given indiscriminately to authors. I could adduce dozens of the most comical mistakes which aspiring or comparatively new authors (helped by just a little vanity) have thus been made to fall into. Irrespective of published price of the book he was offering, I was told by an author who had just issued one *un*successful book, that no honest publisher would dare to offer him less nowadays than twopence in the shilling royalty and something down. Another budding novelist, who had made two or three failures and had published one fairly successful bookstall book, declared that a member of the council of the Authors' Society had assured him that any publisher would jump at his next book if he were allowed to publish it on the basis of a royalty of 25 per cent. with a substantial sum down, &c. [...]

But I must not dwell longer on the subject of our authors, except to come to the point, and, that is, that their prices have gone up with leaps and bounds of late; that royalties are actually being paid which, with the increase in the cost of production, leave to the publisher barely his working expenses; and that they, as well as printers and binders, have a trades union which has formed a decided front, determined on concerted action, not perhaps *against us*, but *for* themselves.

And now come those to whom we sell our books—not the public, because we seldom reach them except through the middleman, the bookseller and the librarian. The former has, as we all know, by means of the abominable discount system, been reduced to all sorts of outside devices simply to keep body and soul together.[25] He sells throughout the country anything that may be in demand besides books—fancy goods, stationery, newspapers, pipes, and tobacco—in fact, anything which the public will buy. I know a country town with over 20,000 inhabitants, and one bookseller only, who combines with his calling of purveyor of literature the garrulous profession of Figaro.[26] That is more or less the condition of things throughout England and Ireland (Scotland occupying an entirely different position, and being, for the smallness of its population, a marvellously good book market). [...]

But the general rule remains that bookselling is about as profitable as the backing of horses, with less chances and similar risks. To reduce these risks to the narrowest limit is, of course, the steady aim of all engaged in the trade, and the result is that, with the exception of a small number of firms of high standing, and with a large turnover, they become daily less inclined to stock books. Our travellers visit them regularly, and, in order to get a 'line,' they have to offer books at reductions which amount in some instances to 50 per cent. off the published price. Those publishers who issue series at 6s., or 3s. 6d., or 2s. 6d., or 2s. find, with the increased number of these issues, a corresponding disinclination on the part of 'the trade' to take up new volumes. Better terms are, therefore, offered as an inducement, with the result that we are at the present moment cutting prices to an extent that will land us all in the workhouse if we do not make some timely and united stand against this increasing danger.

It is the same with the libraries, and in their instance we are far more to be blamed than with regard to the booksellers, because most of these establishments flourish. When, for example, certain big libraries began to take large numbers of three-volume novels, they only too naturally gave preference to those publishers who would sell these novels at the price fixed by themselves. At first these terms were looked upon as secret, but they soon leaked out, and we are now requested by every little library in the kingdom to supply it on the same terms as we supply the big libraries. I cannot say in how far publishers give way in this, and whether further inroads are likely to be made by the big libraries on the present prices. One thing is certain, viz., that if they do make further demands, they will act together, with strength and determination; while we cut one another's throat!

I have thus stated in general terms the outside dangers which threaten us. Without trespassing too much on your space, I should just like to add a word about our internal condition, and then—if I may—draw one or two conclusions. These internal conditions are simple indeed—in that they add to our growing danger. A statement of the facts will, I fancy, suffice. Clerks', book-keepers', &c., wages are higher than they were, and they are not likely to decrease—on account of the increased requirements of our middle-classes. We are besides, for various reasons, compelled to employ higher-class labour than we could when the business was less complex, before there were serial issues, colonial and continental libraries, when translations were *raræ aves*,[27] and when a casual ten-pound note was the Ultima Thule[28] of our ambitions from America, &c. We are further, on account of the rapid distribution, required to carry more stock than we used to do, so as to supply possible immediate demand—but with the risk of accumulating unsaleable stuff; and we have a press-list and gratis-list on our table which is growing with the rapidity of a sugar cane. Closely connected with this is the enormous increase in necessary advertising, and the appearance of that ubiquitous gentleman the literary agent, who has to be paid by some one, and to whose keep, I suspect, a not inconsiderable quota must be contributed, indirectly, if not directly, by the publisher. However, 'Genug des grausamen Spiels.'[29] Every publisher knows himself and feels daily the many extra and increasing demands that are sprung upon him from every quarter of his firmament. What, therefore, is his position? Can nothing be done to protect the interests at stake? Should we not at least grapple with the danger, before it is too late, being, as we are, in a position assailed on all hands by the most powerful of modern weapons in trade— trades unions? Let me enumerate them again. There is the printers' trades union, the binders' trades union, the authors' trades union, the librarians' union (in so far as they act together), and the miserable union of starving competition among our best friends the booksellers.

Let us therefore also form ourselves into a brotherly band, and stand together against the inroads that are being made on our common interests. Let it be the duty of such a body to arrange in all friendship and good feeling with the Authors' Society what percentages and profits are fair, and to see that the basis of their combined calculations represents both parties to this bargain. Let them confer with the printers about the proper rate they should be paid for such incomprehensible vagaries as 'corrections,' 'extras,' 'overtime,' &c. And with the binders they could easily come to an understanding. Let them further arrange with the libraries what prices are fair, when it is right that cheap editions should be issued, and what help and special advantages libraries should expect and give, with regard, for instance, to remainders, &c.

And lastly, let us not overlook a sacred duty, which is to do what we can to improve the condition of the bookseller, and to stem with sound regulations the flowing tide of discounts. I call upon the heads of my profession, of which I am only a humble minor, to look to this. Let those historic houses who are the pride of English literature take the matter in hand speedily and energetically, and I promise them that we younger ones will rally around them one and all. We want a publishers' union, a publishers' society, a publishers' club.

Walter Besant, 'The Rise and Fall of the "Three Decker" ', *The Dial*, 17 (1 October 1894), 185-6

The three-volume novel costing 31*s*. 6*d*. survived for over six decades thanks to the purchasing influence of the circulating libraries. In June 1894, following longstanding complaints, Mudie's and W. H. Smith finally withdrew their support by announcing that they would pay no more than 4*s*. per volume for fiction. The rejection of the 'triple-decker' by Walter Besant (1836–1901) is significant because, as well as being a novelist, he edited *The Author* (1890–   ), the journal of the Society of Authors (Besant had helped found the society in 1884). This article, written for a progressive American literary periodical, *The Dial* (1880–1929), explains why authors disliked the three-volume format.

There are three institutions in this country which pass the understanding of the American. Since we are able to understand them very well, some of our insular conceit is accounted for. If you think of it, indeed, that level of intelligence which enables us to understand anything which your people cannot understand is something to be proud of. These three institutions are the House of Lords, the Established Church, and the Three Volume Novel—the 'Three Decker.' The first two of these, in spite of long continued and determined attacks, are stronger than ever. The last of these, with which I have been intimately connected for five and twenty years, has just received a blow which threatens to be mortal. Often assailed, long derided, much abused, the Three Volume Novel has been stabbed at last in a vital part and by the hand of its oldest friend. It is not dead: it will, perhaps, partly recover; but it is doomed to carry on a languishing, lame, and limp existence for the future. The history of the Three Decker and the curiously artificial character of its publication and price forms a little chapter in our branch of English literature that may not be without interest to American readers. At least, one may explain the genesis and the meaning of an institution which is full of absurdity; which exists in no other country; which will shortly be numbered among the things of the past.

The English novel in its popular form, as an article of daily or constant consumption, was born and grew up in the last century. It appeared in one, two, or more volumes, as the author chose; there was no rule or practice as to length. 'The History of Tom Jones' took three or four times as much space in the telling as that of 'The Vicar of Wakefield.'[30] The woes of Clarissa could not be contracted in the narrow limits which contained the adventures of Rasselas.[31] But the volumes themselves were generally of equal length, forming a small octavo containing from twenty to thirty thousand words. And between the years 1750 and 1800 these volumes were priced at three shillings each, so that a novel in three volumes was sold for nine shillings and one in four volumes for twelve shillings. The reading (and purchasing) public of that time was mostly found in the towns: in every large town, and in many smaller towns, there were literary coteries, clubs, and societies, a few of which were important enough to occupy a place in the history of literature. [. . .] And the habit of reading, as the most delightful form of recreation, went on growing. People read faster as well as more; they devoured books. No purse was long enough to buy all the books that one could read; therefore they lent to each other; therefore they combined their resources and formed book clubs; therefore the circulating libraries came into existence. It was not that we ceased to buy books: it was that we could no longer afford to buy a tenth part of the books we wanted to read, and that we clubbed together and passed on the books from hand to hand.

All this took place in the latter half of the last century. Then followed a long war—a war of three and twenty years, nearly a quarter of a century—when Great Britain stood in arms for a time against the whole of Western Europe, the one undefeated enemy of military despotism. I fear we are forgetting, as a nation, that long conflict: what it meant for the liberties of the world; the sacrifices which we made to maintain it. These sacrifices fell with the greatest weight upon the professional classes, those in which were found the reading public. They could no longer afford to buy books at all; the book clubs increased in number: so did circulating libraries. The booksellers, finding that their buyers were growing fewer, had to raise the price of their books. And from 1790 to 1850 the price of novels (not to mention other branches) ran up from three shillings a volume to ten shillings and sixpence a volume. At the same time the number of

volumes gradually became limited to three at the most, and was
seldom under three. For forty years or so this arbitrary rule has
prevailed. The novel has had to be in three volumes; the price has
been, nominally, thirty-one shillings and sixpence; the only purchasers have been the circulating libraries.

Other changes have occurred: the book clubs, with very few
exceptions, have been dissolved; the circulating libraries, for practical
purposes, have been reduced to two—Mudie's and Smith's: these two
have long since refused to pay the nominal price of thirty-one shillings
and sixpence, and have obtained the novels at fifteen shillings a copy,
and in some cases at very much less.

Again, forty years ago the reprint of a novel in a cheap form was a
rare event; only the most popular novelists were so honored, and then
after a long interval. It is now the custom to bring out a new and cheap
edition of every novel the least above the average. This edition
appears about nine months after the first; the price varies from three
shillings and sixpence to six shillings.

We have, therefore, this remarkable custom in the publishing of
novels. We bring out the first edition exclusively for the readers of
Mudie's and Smith's libraries. These number about 250,000, reckoning about four to each subscribing family. That is to say, in a home
population of 37,000,000, and a colonial population of 15,000,000,
without counting India, whose educated natives read our literature
extensively, we keep everybody waiting for our best works of fiction
until this lucky quarter of a million has had a nine months' run among
them. Of late, there have been revolts here and there. Two or three of
our best and most popular novelists have refused to recognise the
Three Volume rule. Mr. Louis Stevenson is one; Mr. Rudyard
Kipling is another. And now the two libraries themselves—supposed
to be the props and pillars of the old system—have announced to the
trade that in future they will only give eleven shillings a copy instead
of fifteen shillings for the Three Volume novel, and they will make it a
condition that they shall have the exclusive use of it—*i.e.*, that there is
to be no cheap edition—for twelve months after the first publication.
I dare say American readers have heard of the storm which during the
whole summer has raged about this question. The Society of Authors,
taking counsel of its novelist members, have declared against
the Three Volume system altogether. Some of the publishers have

advertised that they will issue no more novels in that form. Those of our novelists who are already engaged ahead for the old form—I am myself one of these—will break away from it as soon as they can. And although the old form will linger on for some time, its tyranny is now past. Henceforth, in this country as in the States, we shall appeal to the whole reading public at the very outset; and we shall ask them, for the present, to buy our stories in one volume at the price of six shillings. And here again—because we really are a most illogical race—the six shillings means four shillings and sixpence, for the retail bookseller has to take off twenty-five per cent from the nominal price.

It is often advanced in newspapers that this revolt means a demand for shorter stories. The statement is made in ignorance. The Three Volume novel ranges from one hundred thousand words to three hundred thousand words in length. The one volume novel has exactly the same range. For instance, Mr. Louis Stevenson will be found, as a rule, somewhat under one hundred thousand words. 'Marcella,' on the other hand, now in one volume, is nearly three hundred thousand words.[32] The only demand, in fact, for a shorter story—I do not mean the 'short story,' which is another thing—is raised, so far as I can see, by those who write reviews for the London papers. Readers, when they get hold of a good novel, care not how long it is. Who would wish 'Vanity Fair' to be reduced by a single page? When we are in good company we are loth to leave them: there are even characters with whom one would like to live for years. A long novel which is also tedious is, indeed—but then I, for one, never allow myself to be bored by a tedious novel.

And this—if you have had patience to read so far—is the history of the rise, the growth, the greatness, and the fall, of that mysterious institution, the Three Volume Novel.

NOTES TO SECTION IV

1. George Dodd, *Days at the Factories* (London: Charles Knight and Co., 1843), 236.
2. Michael Freeman, *Railways and the Victorian Imagination* (New Haven: Yale University Press, 1999), 1.

3. The Net Book Agreement came into force in 1900 and lasted until 1995. It meant that publishers allowed a trade discount to booksellers on condition that books were sold to the public at not less than their net price fixed by the publisher. See Heinemann below.

4. The National Union of the Working Classes was divided into 'classes' for meeting purposes; thus, in London, there were over one hundred classes, each of twenty-five members.

5. The earl made the promise to William Caxton (c.1422–91).

6. Conrad Sweynheym (c.1430–76) and Arnold Pannartz (c.1430–76) began the first printing shop in Italy and published the first Bible in Italian.

7. Clowes was the printing firm responsible for the *Penny Magazine*; in the 1820s it was reputed to be the largest printing firm in the world. See Francis B. Head, 'The Printer's Devil', *Quarterly Review*, 65 (December 1839), 1–30.

8. Stereotyping was made commercially successful by Earl Stanhope (1753–1816), after he purchased the patent rights in 1803. The introduction of stereotyping into publishing was crucial in the mass production of books in the 1840s and 1850s.

9. *Le Magasin Pittoresque* (1833–1914) was launched by Martin Bossage and published in Paris; *Das Pfennig-Magazin der Gesellschaft zur Verbreitung gemeinnütziger Kentnisse* (1833–42) was published in Leipzig by the German office of Bossage.

10. John Murray (1808–92) took over the family publishing business on the death of his father in 1843; he was a strong supporter of the Booksellers' Association.

11. William Longman (1813–77) became a partner in the family publishing firm of Longman, Browne, Green, and Longmans, in 1839; he was Chairman of the Booksellers' Association in 1852.

12. See Section IX n. 14. Campbell adjudicated the dispute.

13. George Simms, a Manchester publisher, gave evidence to Lord Campbell for the Booksellers' Association on 14 April 1852.

14. Burge and Perrin was a Manchester publishing firm; William Perrin spoke for the undersellers at a meeting with Lord Campbell on 17 May 1852.

15. James Lackington (1746–1815), a bookseller who made his fortune by underselling; he bought up remaindered books and sold them at dramatically reduced prices.

16. George IV died in 1830.

17. George Routledge's shilling Railway Library was one of most prominent series of cheap reprints and was launched in 1848. See

F. A. Munby, *The House of Routledge 1834–1934. With a History of Kegan Paul, Trench, Trübner and Other Associated Firms* (London: Routledge, 1934), 29–32.

18. Maria Edgeworth (1767–1849); Hannah More (1745–1833); Samuel Richardson published *Sir Charles Grandison* in 1753–4. All three figures would have been very dated by the 1860s.

19. Robert Southey (1774–1843), Romantic poet who lived for most of his life at Greta Hall, Keswick, Cumberland.

20. Napoleon III obliquely threatened the Austrian ambassador on New Year's Day 1859 in the run-up to the Franco-Sardinian alliance against Austria. Wynter appears to have confused this with a speech given on 7 February, when Napoleon III opened the French legislature.

21. In 1840 Charles Wheatstone developed a Universal Dial Telegraph that did not require incoming messages to be read by a trained telegraphist. It was widely used in the 1850s and 1860s.

22. See Section III above, esp. Arnold.

23. During the early 1890s there was a vociferous campaign for the passing of an Eight Hours Bill, which would limit the working day of miners to eight hours. It was, however, a strike by bookbinders in November 1891 that forced the adoption of an eight-hour day.

24. On Besant, see subsequent headnote.

25. The 1890s saw the build-up of a campaign against the problem of underselling. Buyers could receive up to 3*d.* in the shilling discount.

26. Figaro was a barber in Pierre Beaumarchais's plays, *Le Barbier de Seville* (1775) and *Le Mariage de Figaro* (1778).

27. 'Rare birds.'

28. i.e. the limit.

29. 'Enough of this cruel play.'

30. Henry Fielding, *The History of Tom Jones* (1749); Oliver Goldsmith, *The Vicar of Wakefield* (1766).

31. Samuel Richardson's gargantuan *Clarissa* (1747–8) is many times longer than Samuel Johnson's slim *The History of Rasselas, Prince of Abissinia* (1759).

32. Mrs Humphrey Ward, *Marcella* (London: Smith, Elder & Co., 1894).

V

INVESTIGATING THE POPULAR,
1840s–1860s

INTRODUCTION

This section, the longest in the Reader and located at its core, is concerned with vital questions in media theory and media history: what does the term 'popular' mean and how is it to be investigated? Does 'popular' mean primarily 'produced by the people', 'produced for an idea of the people', or 'consumed by a large number of people'? Our section emphasizes the latter while acknowledging its links with the first two. Even Bennett Johns, who starts out with the notion that street ballads are 'popular' in the sense of an authentic expression of a folk spirit, goes on to show that all of the 'Poetry of Seven Dials' is in fact produced as a commodity for a metropolitan audience to consume.

In this section we not only investigate nineteenth-century theorizations of the 'popular' but also what kinds of text the term and its cognates were attached to. Just as 'the people' did not produce popular texts, neither did they determine what texts were labelled 'popular'. Popular texts were instead defined as such by those with greater social and cultural capital: indeed, the very usage of the term, whatever its definition, was implicated in status difference. But to call something 'popular' was not only to look down upon it. It does not only indicate a vertical relation to the object described but a horizontal one to the addressees of the description: it created group cohesion through the labelling of an inferior other outside that group. Thus Johns, quoting and referring to classical authors, not only ensures he displays cultural capital superior to that of the poetry of the street, but solidarity with the high-status readers of the *Quarterly Review*. Usage of the term 'popular' therefore emerges as always political and always ready for tactical redefinition.

The question of when popular print media began is inevitably caught up in the politics and ambiguity of the term. It has been claimed that the *Penny Magazine* initiated popular print media because its first issue sold 213,241.[1] Others place the beginnings a decade or two earlier with the sales in the tens of thousands of Byron and

Scott. Rymer below suggests even earlier origins. Here we wish to define the 'popular' not only in terms of very large numbers sold within a specified time, however, but also in terms of a sustained industrial mode of production. Like the commentators we cite, we have omitted newspapers (these have a section of their own below). We have instead concentrated on what Rymer called 'imaginative' verbal texts, and mainly penny weekly fiction magazines at that. We have also omitted texts concerned with overtly parliamentary-political messages, such as Chartist novels and poetry. These latter are also sometimes claimed for the 'popular', yet they tended to be produced not primarily for profit but for utopian ideals that existed beyond the cash register: they are texts produced for an idea of what the 'people' should be and should desire, rather than for what purchasers actually desired. Dalziel called the popular texts of our definition the 'Purified Penny Press' and its difference from Regency and earlier material is marked either implicitly or explicitly by Collins, Oliphant, and Johns. Indeed such morally pure texts lack the grotesque glamour of the earlier material or the subversive excitements of Chartist or pornographic works.[2] Rather, they recycle and vary the already-known in ways that uncannily prefigure Hollywood genre movies.[3]

Our definition causes the 1840s to emerge as the time when popular print media arose in a widespread form, Rymer's article appearing at its inception. In the 1840s numerous factors coincided to enable the rise of serial fiction that sold hundreds of thousands of parts per week. As Section IV shows, the technology was firmly in place: improved paper-making and speedier printing processes were prerequisites that had been exploited since the 1820s. But it was not until the 1840s that the second prerequisite occurred: the social conditions that enabled the technology to fulfil its potential. In that decade literacy amongst poorer social groups increased dramatically, especially amongst women. Later in the decade a drop in prices for staple foodstuffs simultaneous with rising wages liberated cash for inessentials such as reading matter. Later again, the removal of the window tax in 1851 meant that windows could be made larger and so made poor dwellings lighter (Dickens believed the window tax to be more of an obstacle to the spread of reading than the Taxes on Knowledge).[4]

The third prerequisite involved the establishment of the practices of popular reading, which for us is closely tied to seriality. Cheap serial fiction had appeared before Dickens (e.g. the *Penny Novelist*, 1832–3), but *Pickwick* in 1836–7 had shown that it could be highly lucrative: imitators at the cheap end included Edward Lloyd, who quickly brought out the *Penny Pickwick* by 'Bos' (1837–9, 112 numbers), *Oliver Twiss* (1838–9), and others. Lloyd is most famous, though, for publishing 'Penny Dreadfuls' or 'Penny Bloods', of which *Lives of the Most Notorious Highwaymen* is often considered the first: it came out in 60 parts the same year as *Pickwick*. But while successful, both *Pickwick* and the Bloods were fundamentally niche market. There was little for the vast middle that the popular is produced for. In 1842 the *Family Herald* (–1940) was launched by George Biggs. It was the first of the four highest-selling penny fiction magazines of the mid-nineteenth century. Unillustrated itself, its formula (which may be gleaned from the Collins below) was soon combined with illustrations by the *London Journal* (1845–1928), *Reynolds's Miscellany* (1847–69), and *Cassell's Illustrated Family Paper* (1853–67). It was the *London Journal* and *Cassell's* that fought over J. F. Smith's services in the mid-1850s, as noted by Oliphant: two industrial giants, each with sustained circulations of hundreds of thousands, tussling over what Rymer would call a 'star'. By the mid-1850s the 'popular' in our definition was fully established.

The case of Smith proves all too well Rymer's point about the ephemerality of the popular. Smith was one of the best-selling serial fiction writers of the entire nineteenth century but is now forgotten. He was rivalled only by a handful of other now obscure names such as Pierce Egan the Younger (1814–80) and Charlotte May Brame (1836–84; also known as 'Bertha M. Clay'), together with North American women writers such as E. D. E. N. Southworth (1819–99), Harriet Lewis (1841–78) and May Agnes Fleming (1840–80). All were published in huge quantities throughout the Anglophone world as well as in translation. They should not be confused with what are today often called Victorian 'popular' writers who published mainly in volumes at mid-century: Mary Braddon, for example, was not particularly successful in the market for penny fiction. It was not until the 1890s, when the price of volume-form fiction dropped dramatically, that the volume entered to any great extent the same market as penny serial fiction.[5] In light of the ephemerality of the popular, we include an example of the thing itself, a complete episode of a serial novel

by J. F. Smith from *The London Journal*, a magazine described by
Collins and Oliphant. While this episode was chosen for its typicality,
we also wanted to provoke reflection on whether the commentaries
were accurate in their assessments, and on what they omit that we
might consider important today.

The Collins article below, the central piece of this central section,
raises important questions about the methodology of this Reader. It is
perhaps the most widely read article today on nineteenth-century
mass-market writing and was well known in the nineteenth century
too.[6] It has usually been read as a generally accurate description, even
when, as today, its class attitudes have become obvious. In fact, the
article is almost entirely overdetermined by the specific context of its
writing; it comprises many falsifications mixed with a modicum of
truth to render the lies more convincing. Even its stylish consum-
ability stems partly from the deployment of a skills-base ('good
writing') in a local skirmish over loss of profits. Collins's account of
the 'Unknown Public' is the result of an attempt to maintain a very
limited private network of print culture producers through coded
public pronouncements comprehensible only to members of his
circle. For example, the article deploys a gentlemanly, comic-modest
style appropriate for a Dickens publication and attempts a 'research
method' already legitimated by another friend. Given its falsifications,
why has it been so cited? This again is overdetermined. Its continuing
fame rests partly on the status of its author, a friend of the canonical
Dickens, partly on its seductive readability—and, more recently, also
on the prominent place it is assigned in Altick's still standard account
of the Common Reader. The Collins then acts as another confirm-
ation of an *a priori* assumption of this Reader, that Victorian media
texts functioned not only to unite a wider public into an 'imagined
community' but were often just as concerned to create and maintain
smaller networks amongst media producers themselves.

Finally, it may be useful to point out a few of the recurrent tropes
connected to the idea of the 'popular'. Many can be observed else
where in this reader as well as in the pieces below. They include the
marked separation of the patriarchal from the popular in Rymer and
Oliphant, the idea of a heroic man of letters who will unite the
fractured market and thereby make the English nation strong (Collins,
Johns), the failure of 'improving literature' (Oliphant), the idea of

progress (Johns, Oliphant), a casual violence in the representation of the non-British, and an awareness of the popular's moral and political innocuousness that is linked nonetheless to an anxiety that it may not be as harmless as it seems.

FURTHER READING:

Altick, *Common Reader*; Anderson; Ashton; Bennett; Collison; Haywood; Hindley, *Curiosities*, *Life and Times*; Hughes and Lund; James, *Fiction Print*, Jordan and Patten; King, *London Journal*; Neuberg; Vincent, *Literacy*.

The Editor [J. Malcolm Rymer], 'Popular Writing', *Queen's Magazine: A Monthly Miscellany of Literature and Art*, 1 (1842), 99–103

Rymer is best known for his penny-part novels written for the publisher Edward Lloyd. While authorship of individual works often remains uncertain in this cultural zone, the famous *Ada the Betrayed* (original *c.*1844) and *Varney the Vampyre* (orig. *c.*1844) may well be Rymer's. In the extract below, Rymer is at the beginning of his career, editing a sixpenny monthly, yet both clearly aware of what was being produced elsewhere in the market and uncannily prescient of what he would produce himself in a year or two.

> Black spirits and white,
> Blue spirits and grey,
> Mingle, mingle, mingle,
> Mingle while you may.[7]

The following epistle to our Editorship has suggested to us some ideas on popular writing, which we hope will be extremely popular, if we rightly understand the term to mean that which everybody reads:—

To the Editor of the Queen's Magazine

SIR,—

Should your literary staff not be full, I think I could offer you such terms and arrangements, with a view of supplying a small article each month, which you would not object to. My style is strictly *popular*.

I am, Sir,
Your obedient servant
* * * *

Cerulean powers! what is a popular style? Shall we attempt to define popular writing? Shade of Horace Walpole! cease for a 'moment to shake thy grisly locks' at George Robins, and tell us what is popular writing?[8] Why, an old helmet as large as the diving-bell at the Polytechnic, and a defunct warrior, thirty feet high, to be sure.[9] The Castle of Otranto is exceedingly popular. What say you,

Mrs. Radcliffe?—I perfectly agree with Walpole. The Mysteries of Udolpho comprises every department of popular writing.[10] But, hark! the castle clock tolls the solemn hour of midnight! I must away. Smollett, what is popular writing? Life, my boy, life—real life. Ask Fielding.[11] Ha! Miss Porter, Burney, Edgeworth, Lewis,[12]—Pray what is popular writing? Envious shadows, and substances demure, you answer not. Why gaze you thus upon each other? What is popular writing? What constitutes its popularity? Let us be didactic. Imaginative literature is, after all, but of recent growth; it is a sort of parasitical plant, clinging around the huge oak of classicality. It is, comparatively, but recently that the masses of the community have become pleased with works of fiction. To cultivate the imagination was for many 'monkish years' a grievous sin; and the printing press was a familiar object long before a romance or novel issued from it. [. . .]

Suddenly, towards the middle of the eighteenth century, novels and romances assumed new characters. The disjointed witticisms and weak licentiousness of the early writers, gave place to delicate distresses and vapid sentimentality. [. . .]

Neck-and-neck, if we may be allowed the phrase, with the above-mentioned species of novel, ran the blood and murder romance, so that the lovers of fiction had their choice of a dish of highly seasoned horrors [. . .]

The historical novel was then unknown. The Newgate Calendar had not a name.[13] The libelous novel never appeared. The fashionable novel of the present day comes nearest to the old style of any, only the modern are more narcotic than the ancient, because we can read with greater complacency a flimsy record of vices and punctilios of another age than of our own.

Each of these was extremely popular in its day; and the principal singularity about the whole subject, consists in the rapidity with which the bulk of the nation has at different times altered its taste. The arbitrary changes of fashion in garments are mild and gradual in comparison with the sudden popular freaks with regard to popular writing. The real secret may be, that there is so little good writing now-a-days, that the highest reputations are in great measure artificial, consequently their rapid rise, and as rapid fall; but certain it is, that no popular author can reasonably count upon his popularity above eight or ten years. After that time, he has generally the mortification to find, that like an old almanac, he is out of date. This is a sad state of things; for time *was* when there was a certain standard of literary excellence, which not only carried an author, if he wished it, to a green old age, but preserved his reputation unscathed through succeeding generations. Which of our present 'popular writers' will be remembered in 1942? [...]

Popular writing, then, we conceive, is to be divided into two great portions. The most popular is that which common, everyday people understand; and the next is, that which the aforesaid people are ashamed to say they do not understand.

The former must just reach the vague comprehension of the mass of mankind, and the latter must be so good as to be backed by the opinions of those with whom the herd are afraid to differ. We do not pretend to say that there is nothing between these extremes worthy of consideration or remark; we only draw a broad line of distinction between the two extremes—as we should say the water of the sea is salt, and that of a river flowing into it fresh, although they might so mingle at their junction as to render it impossible to say where the one ceased or the other began.

If an author, then, wishes to become popular in the sense in which we use the term, that is, to be read by the majority, and praised and fêted, he should, ere he begins to write, study well the animals for whom he is about to cater. A popular speaker has said, that he commenced his career in oratory by 'getting up' the most supreme contempt for his audiences; but, without going so far as that contemptuous gentleman, it is absolutely necessary for a popular author of the first class, to take care that he writes to the capacities of his readers, or they will have their revenge by condemning all that they don't understand. Here, of course, we only allude to those writers who are themselves some degree removed above the multitude. Your really first-rate, high flying, popular writer, is he who will condemn this essay in toto, and say that the public is a most discerning, learned, and artful public, for that he writes his very best, and yet is a 'very popular writer.' To such a gentleman and his logic[14] we have nothing to say, except that he is just what he says he is, 'a very popular writer,' and a happy man. [...]

But it may be said, How are we to account for the taste which maintained so long for works of terror and blood—those romances which abounded with mysterious horrors, and revelled in the super-natural? Most easily. It is the privilege of the ignorant and the weak to love superstition. The only strong mental sensation they are capable of is *fear*. The dishes of horrors served up by a Radcliffe, a Walker, or a Lewis, served as the piquant sauces to the plain meat, nicely done, of a Richardson, a Mackenzie, or a Burney.[15] Is the superstitious terror of a nursery maid, who reads by her allowance of rushlight with indescribable dismay, 'The Blood Spangled Monk, or the Inhuman Shriek,' to be called a love of imaginative literature?[16] As well we might accuse her of a sublime notion of the supernatural, when she threatens one of her infant charges with the immediate appearance of a mysterious personage, known in many establishments as 'The Old Man,' 'Bogie,' &c. The taste for the horrible is by no means surprising. It has been, and ever will be. There are millions of minds that have no resource between vapid sentimentality, and the ridiculous spectra of the nursery.

We would, therefore, say to a young author who pants for 'popularity,' 'if you sicken at pointless dialogue and silly adventures, do a little of the haunted castle and midnight murder business, and you will attain your object. Never mind ridicule; the ridicule of a fastiduous minority. There are still thousands who are ready to echo the sentiment of the lady in the pit of Covent Garden Theatre, who, upon witnessing the pantomime of The Castle of Otranto, said, 'It would have been a very pretty piece, if they hadn't made such fun of it.'[17]

Imaginative literature, until very lately, did not present sufficient inducements to men of education and talent to throw themselves into its arena. Before Sir Walter Scott's time we had, comparatively, few writers of any eminence in the novel line. The enormous profits which that literary cormorant procured by his works, turned the attention of writers of all grades and conditions to the subject of novel and romance writing. That such a change was beneficial, there can be no doubt; but that it was pleasant to the majority of readers of such works, there is very great doubt. The disappointed governesses, cashiered ladies maids, and small literary men, who used to write the bulk of the volumes on the shelves of the circulating libraries, suited a large class of readers, who are now forced to eat dishes they neither comprehend nor like, or to seek their proper food in an under current of minor publications, they are ashamed to patronise. The extraordinary success of Sir Walter Scott in the line of historical romance, gave a mortal blow to the old novel and romance school, which it never can recover; that is to say, a blow to its popularity—viewing popularity as a fashion. Far be it from us to say, that there are not thousands of 'most respectable people,' who prefer in their hearts 'The Midnight Blast and the Moat of Blood,' or 'Sir Charles Grandison,' to the whole tribe of Waverly novels, and their imitators.[18] Scott, however, brought a new class of readers into the market; persons who, before his time, repudiated all novel reading as waste of time; and, as a matter of course, by thus extending the popularity of works of fiction, the remuneration of the authors of such works became proportionably greater.

From this circumstance, then, we may date the origin of the vast influx of novels and romances with which we are now deluged. They began to pay! Instead of thirty or forty pounds for a novel in seven volumes, the first publishers began to give from hundreds to thousands for three volumes of inanity.

The star system, borrowed from the theatrical world, prevailed in full force. Every needy gentleman and dowager in difficulties commenced novelist. Authors, who before would have shrunk from any literary labour of so trivial a character, were allured into the magic circle of romance. [...] All this was popular writing; but still the witless gentlemen, the sentimental young ladies with weak eyes, the aspiring people who stand at the corner of Bury Street, to see the carriages 'go to a Levee,'[19] were not quite pleased: they adored Scott, but in their hearts thought him 'rather dry.' They wanted back again the epistolary romances, nor were they allowed to linger long with hope deferred. The Minerva Press sprung, Phoenix-like, from the ashes of its former glory, and the 'Fashionable Novel' appeared, not as before, in five or seven small volumes, printed in soot and water, on thin cartridge paper, but looking as respectable as Waverley itself.[20] The success, as might have been anticipated, of 'The Fashionable Novel,' or Minerva Press Novel, in disguise, was immense. People were, as usual, taken in by appearances, and they re-read all their old friends in new dresses; the frivolity of the eighteenth century was only exchanged for the frivolity of the nineteenth. [...] There were the same small miseries and delicate distresses, the same pointless conversations and foolish misconstructions. [...]

The popular writing of the day, then, appears to us mainly to consist of two kinds: namely, the stirring and alarming adventurous novel, in which each page contains a striking incident; and the personal fashionable novel, which we have sufficiently described. These two classes of novels are the fair representatives of the old romance and the old epistolary fashionable novel. When we use the term popular, we mean it in the sense in which we have all along used it, namely, to mean the greatest number of readers. The transcendentalism of a Bulwer—the heaven knows what of an Ainsworth—the pathos of a Dickens—all find admirers;[21] but if the dear public would be candid, they would say that the first they did not at all understand—the second they were tired of—and the third fairly bothered them.

J. F. Smith, complete episode, *The Will and the Way*, from *The London Journal and Weekly Record of Literature, Science and Art*, 16 (15 January 1853), 289–92

J. F. Smith's serial novel *Minnigrey* (1851–2) had broken all sales records: the circulation of *The London Journal*, an illustrated penny fiction weekly, rose to over 500,000 a week while it ran there. *The Will and the Way* (1852–3) consolidated this success. It was reprinted numerous times both in serial and book forms, and given in at least seven theatrical versions in 1853 alone. The complete episode printed here is typical Smith, from the fake authority of the invented epigraphs and odd classical allusion, to the universal moralizings and exploitation of topical items in the news even while the tale is set thirty years in the past (relevant here is the 'modernization' of India under Governor Dalhousie). In this episode, Meeran is recovering from a duel with his rival in love, Henry Ashton.

THE WILL AND THE WAY.

by the author of
'The Jesuit,' 'The Prelate,' 'Minnigrey,' Etc.

CHAPTER XL.

> The strongest resolutions oft are wrung:
> From the heart's weakness; passion's voice
> Drowning weak conscience's whisperings.
> Old Play.

Although still weak, and suffering from his wound, Meeran Hafaz no longer kept his couch—despite the remonstrances of his medical attendants and the entreaties of the Khan, he persisted in leaving it: the physical pain he endured was nothing weighed in the scale against the mental torture to which his forced inactivity had condemned him. With the young Indian, life was action; he was a being of impulse—a creature to whom excitement and emotion were as necessary as the fulcrum to the lever, or the main-spring to the watch; his mental

THE

LONDON JOURNAL:

And Weekly Record of Literature, Science, and Art.

No. 412.—Vol. XVI.   FOR THE WEEK ENDING JANUARY 15, 1853.   [Price One Penny.

[ELLEN DE VERE AND THE AYAH IN THE PICTURE GALLERY.]

THE WILL AND THE WAY.

BY THE AUTHOR OF
THE JESUIT," "THE PRELATE," "MINNIGREY," ETC.

CHAPTER XL.

The strongest resolutions oft are wrong
From the heart's weakness; passion's voice
Drowning weak conscience's whisperings.
                                        OLD PLAY.

ALTHOUGH still weak, and suffering from his wound, Meeran Hafas no longer kept his couch—despite the remonstrances of his medical attendants and the entreaties of the Khan, he persisted in leaving it: the physical pain he endured was nothing weighed in the scale against the mental torture to which his forced inactivity had condemned him. With the young Indian, life was action; he was a being of impulse—a creature to whom excitement and emotion were as necessary as the fulcrum to the lever, or the main-spring to the watch; his mental enjoyments proceeded rather from that quick sensibility which admires the beautiful in art and nature, than the intellectual analysis and appreciation of it. Thus, without being a sensualist in taste, he was a materialist: fine as the line of demarcation is, it is perfectly possible to draw it.

The first feeling of consolation he experienced since the morning of the duel, was from the visit of the ayah, who came to inform him that his rival had actually departed on his journey to Italy. The intelligence appeared to afford him mingled satisfaction and regret: satisfaction, that he was no longer basking in the light of Ellen's beauty, breathing his heart's young hopes, impassioned vows, into her willing ear—risting yet closer the delicious bonds which knit their like one soul together; regret, that he had escaped him—for on his couch of agony—compared to which Ixion's wheel must have been a bed of roses—he had sworn a fearful oath to have the life of Henry Ashton.

"'Tis well!" he said, a faint smile illuminating his pale features, like a fading sunbeam resting on a corse. "I can breathe more freely now I know that seas divide them! Never, never, must they meet again!"

Zara—who, as usual, had seated herself upon the ground—gazed for an instant upon her foster-son with a cold, mocking expression of contempt.

"Seas divide them!" she repeated; "resolution, long ere this, would have placed a grave between your rival and yourself! This land of gloom and shadows has broken the temper of your soul, Meeran, or you would never prate of seas—they may be crossed! The grave," she continued, lowering her voice, "is narrower than the sea—its depths are less profound—*but they are impassable!* When before did one of your race receive an insult, and let the insulter live?"

The countenance of Meeran became darkly shadowed: the words of the temptress had roused all that was evil in his nature, and recalled the scene of his humiliation so vividly before him, that again he saw the flashing eye of his insulting rival, the curl of his scornful lip, as, in the presence of Ellen and her friends, he crushed his pride and trampled on his pretensions, by reminding him of the charity extended by the Ashtons to his father.

"He *shall* die!" he muttered between his clenched teeth; "but not yet—not yet! It would be envy, not revenge, to slay him in his dream of happiness, his trusting confidence in the bright future; for what is death?—a momentary pang—oblivion—rest! No," he added, "he must *madden*-first—when, one by one, I have stripped life of its illusions—when I have wrung his heart till the strained nerves are dead to every sense of agony—when hope and feeling are alike extinct —then, and not till then, will I place my heel upon his neck, and crush the reptile! I can no longer torture—I must humble ere I destroy!"

"Words!" replied the ayah, "words! Long ere this I had mixed for him the draught, which is our own land rids love and ambition of their foes—hate, of its victim—but for the fear that Ellen's lips might taste it!"

It had frequently been in the power of the speaker to perpetrate the crime she meditated; for since her arrival at the abbey she had daily made coffee for the drawing-room; her foster-child preferred it after the manner of the East, and Zara had prepared it for her from childhood.

"Thank heaven," exclaimed Meeran, whose very heart trembled at the thought of risk to Ellen, "you did not attempt it!"

Their further conversation was interrupted by the Khan, who came to announce the visit of the warrener to his young charge: there was a degree of sadness in the tone in which the old man spoke to him—for he felt that confidence no longer existed between them, and that the estrangement was becoming wider every hour.

"Admit him!" exclaimed Meeran, impatiently; and the next moment, Will Sidelor, who had followed closely on the steps of his conductor, entered the apartment, which the renegade quitted: he did not wish to be directed a second time to wait in the antechamber, under the insulting pretext of preventing intrusion.

"Well," demanded his employer, impatiently, "have you succeeded?"

"I had succeeded," replied the ruffian, "and the packet was made in my possession, when——"

"Pshaw!" interrupted Meeran—who, in his contempt for the sordidness of the instrument he descended to employ, imagined that the warrener was merely trying to extort more gold from him, by some well fabricated tale—"I am no niggard, to drive a huckster's bargain with a thing like thee! Name thy price, man, and give me the packet!"

FIG. 5. 'Ellen De Vere and the Ayah in the Picture Gallery', *The London Journal: A Weekly Record of Literature, Science and Art*, 16 (15 January 1853), 289.

enjoyments proceeded rather from that quick sensibility which admires the beautiful in art and nature, than the intellectual analysis and appreciation of it. Thus, without being a sensualist in taste, he was a materialist: fine as the line of demarcation is, it is perfectly possible to draw it.

The first feeling of consolation he experienced since the morning of the duel, was from the visit of the ayah, who came to inform him that his rival had actually departed on his journey to Italy. The intelligence appeared to afford him mingled satisfaction and regret: satisfaction, that he was no longer basking in the light of Ellen's beauty, breathing his heart's young hope, impassioned vows, into her willing ear—riveting yet closer the delicious bonds which knit them like one soul together; regret, that he had escaped him—for on his couch of agony—compared to which Ixion's wheel must have been a bed of roses—he had sworn a fearful oath to have the life of Henry Ashton.

"'Tis well!' he said, a faint smile illuminating his pale features, like a fading sunbeam resting on a corse. 'I can breathe more freely now I know that seas divide them! Never, never, must they meet again!'

Zara—who, as usual, had seated herself upon the ground—gazed for an instant upon her foster-son with a cold, mocking expression of contempt.

'Seas divide them!' she repeated; 'resolution, long ere this, would have placed a grave between your rival and yourself! This land of gloom and shadows has broken the temper of your soul, Meeran, or you would never prate of seas—they may be crossed! The grave,' she continued, lowering her voice, 'is narrower than the sea—its depths are less profound—*but they are impassable!* When before did one of your race receive an insult, and let the insulter live?'

The countenance of Meeran became darkly shadowed: the words of the temptress had roused all that was evil in his nature, and recalled the scene of his humiliation so vividly before him, that again he saw the flashing eye of his insulting rival, the curl of his scornful lip, as, in the presence of Ellen and her friends, he crushed his pride and trampled on his pretensions, by reminding him of the charity extended by the Ashtons to his father.

'He *shall* die!' he muttered between his clenched teeth; 'but not yet—not yet! It would be envy, not revenge, to slay him in his dream of happiness, his trusting confidence in the bright future; for what is death?—a momentary pang—oblivion—rest! No,' he added, 'he must *awaken* first—when, one by one, I have stripped life of its illusions—when I have wrung his heart till the strained nerves are dead to every sense of agony—when hope and feeling are alike extinct—then, and not till then, will I place my heel upon his neck, and crush the reptile! I can no longer torture—I must humble ere I destroy!'

'Words!' replied the ayah, 'words! Long ere this I had mixed for him the draught, which in our own land rids love and ambition of their rival—hate, of its victim—but for the fear that Ellen's lips might taste it!'

It had frequently been in the power of the speaker to perpetrate the crime she meditated; for since her arrival at the abbey she had daily made coffee for the drawing-room: her foster-child preferred it after the manner of the East, and Zara had prepared it for her from childhood.

'Thank heaven,' exclaimed Meeran, whose very heart trembled at the thought of risk to Ellen, 'you did not attempt it!'

Their further conversation was interrupted by the Khan, who came to announce the visit of the warrener to his young charge: there was a degree of sadness in the tone in which the old man spoke to him—for he felt that confidence no longer existed between them, and that the estrangement was becoming wider every hour.

'Admit him!' exclaimed Meeran, impatiently; and the next moment, Will Sideler, who had followed closely on the steps of his conductor, entered the apartment, which the renegade quitted: he did not wish to be directed a second time to wait in the antechamber, under the insulting pretext of preventing intrusion.

'Well,' demanded his employer, impatiently, 'have you succeeded?'

'I had succeeded,' replied the ruffian, 'and the packet was safe in my possession, when—'

'Pshaw!' interrupted Meeran—who, in his contempt for the sordidness of the instrument he descended to employ, imagined that the warrener was merely trying to extort more gold from him, by some well fabricated tale—'I am no niggard, to drive a huckster's bargain with a thing like thee! Name thy price, man, and give me the packet!'

Will Sideler felt nettled; the undisguised contempt of the young Indian piqued even him, to whom gold was an idol, and virtue and honesty marketable commodities—valued only for they would bring.

'I haven't got it,' he answered, sulkily.

'Liar!' exclaimed the disappointed Meeran.

'He speaks the truth!' said the ayah, who had been observing the fellow closely. 'You forget the proverb of the Indian sage, that a spoonful of honey catches more flies than a tun of vinegar: vile as this pariah is, the lust of gold is not his only motive in serving you— you may trust him!'

As Zara spoke in the language of the East, the warrener could not divine whether her speech applied to him or not; but, being naturally of a suspicious nature, he concluded that it did.

'The woman may say what she pleases, young sir,' he observed; 'but I have spoken the truth. I had the packet, but it has been taken from me.'

'By whom?'

'That is what I wish to know,' continued the ruffian, with a fierce look.

'By force?' demanded his employer.

'No; by cunning!'

In as few words as possible, he proceeded to inform Meeran of his double adventure with the lawyer and the pretended Bow Street officers— for reflection had convinced him that his escape must have been connived at, and, consequently, their characters assumed. How his intentions had been foreseen, it puzzled him to tell: his suspicions rested on the Khan, but he dared not utter them—he was too much in his power.

The fellow told his tale so clearly, and with so many expressions of anger at the clever way to which he had been outwitted, that Meeran Hafaz was convinced that he spoke the truth. Still he was at a loss to imagine how his scheme had transpired, or by whom it had been defeated. His suspicions, unlike those of the warrener, fell upon Colonel Mowbray, whom he knew to be capable of any act, however deceitful or treacherous: not that he imagined the colonel himself had undertaken the character of the Bow Street officer—his person was too well known to Will Sidler for him to have attempted that; besides, he had not been absent from the hall a single night. The more he reflected, the more he felt intrigued.

'Should you know the men again?' he asked.

'From a thousand!' replied the warrener. 'I may forget the features of friends—of those whom I have loved, or who have loved me—but never of those whom I hate! The principal was a tall, dark man, with something of the air of a gentleman—but it did not appear natural to him. The lower part of his face was muffled in a shawl; but once, when it fell, I discovered that he wore a moustache.'

The description tallied so well with Captain Elton, that Meeran was struck by it, and he determined to ascertain, before the speaker left the house, whether his suspicions were correct or not; but for the instant he had matter of deeper moment to reflect upon.

No sooner had the ayah quitted the apartment and left him alone with his agent, than the young Indian seated himself in an easy chair; a table with a lamp was placed between him and Will Sideler, upon whose features the light shed its full glare. Meeran sat for several minutes with his eyes fixed intently upon him: the glance seemed to penetrate to the very brain of the ruffian, searching its hidden thought. At first he appeared restless, like a bird when first fascinated by the gaze of the rattlesnake; gradually, however, his shifting orbs became fixed—he had no longer the power to remove them to any other object—he felt as if there was a spell upon them!

'You can be faithful?' inquired the young man.

'To those who trust me,' replied the warrener, breathing with difficulty.

'And love gold?'

'Show me the poor man who does not,' answered the fellow, quickly; 'without it, liberty becomes bondage; it is the rod which enables the few to govern the many. Earth groans beneath its fetters. It is a taskmaster, and mankind its slaves!'

'Right!' said Meeran, with a bitter smile. 'He who first dug the yellow devil from its mine, stamped it with an impress, and called it by the name of money, forged the first chain. The links were scattered, but civilisation gradually united them till they enchained the globe. You have no great love, I believe, for this Sir William Mowbray?'

'I hate him!' exclaimed Will Sideler, fiercely; the mad fool has been my persecutor through life! First, he dismissed me from my place of keeper; now, as warrener; but I shall not die till I have been revenged upon him! The dream, the hope of it, has haunted me too many years for that! The oppressor and the oppressed become equal,' he continued, 'when the one has no further tyranny to inflict—and the other no injustice to endure!'

'How so?' demanded his employer, curiously.

'There is no longer any fear between them!' was the reply.

'The death of your former master, then,' observed the young Indian, endeavouring to speak in a careless tone; would it not grieve you?'

'About as much as that of the serpent who had stung me!' replied Will Sideler; 'I have the same cause to hate them both!'

A long and whispered conversation followed, during which their chairs were gradually drawn closer; and their words came thick and slowly, as though the conscious lips reluctantly gave egress to the sounds, or their hearts paused to gather strength to frame them. Meeran appeared like some fallen angel, scorning and loathing the thing it tempted—and the warrener, like avarice grovelling at the feet of, and offering up its soul to, Mammon. To his bewildered mind, the sum proffered by the youth for the fearful service he required, sounded like a fable; yet, strange to say, dearly as he loved the yellow dross, alone it was not sufficient to decide him.

'Thine is a costly soul, Master Sidler!' observed the Indian, sinking back in his seat and regarding him with a look in which curiosity and disgust were curiously mingled. 'The sum I have named might have purchased the conscience of a priest—the honour of a noble! Name your price?'

'The gold is sufficient,' replied the old man; 'more than sufficient; but there is one more thing that I require.'

'Name it?'

'My old place as keeper on the lands of Carrow; friends grew cold, and my enemies scoffed and jeered at me when it was taken from me. I must have that back again; promise me, and our bargain is concluded. Colonel Mowbray, I am certain, will not refuse a request from you.'

The glance which accompanied the observation, even more than the tone in which it was made, conveyed to Meeran that the speaker was perfectly aware of the mutual understanding between the brother of his intended victim and himself.

'Be it so,' he said; 'the place you covet shall be yours!'

'And the gold?' eagerly added the warrener.

'Shall be counted down to the last piece *when you have earned it!*' replied Meeran, disdainfully; for he was one of those contradictory beings whom passion might drive to crime, yet could not descend to meanness. Like most natives of the East, he recked but little of the sacrifice of life, when it stood in the way of his purpose or his ambition.

'Have you still the means of obtaining admission to the old pavilion at the end of the park?' he inquired.

Sideler assured him that he had, not only to the summer-house where he had been in the habit of meeting the ayah, to receive her letters for Meeran—but to the abbey itself, if necessary.

'Leave it to me!' he added; I have so long contemplated the thing you wish, that I have calculated every chance!'

'And why did you not accomplish it?' demanded the tempter.

'I lacked two motives—the last outrage, and the reward! You have supplied the one—Sir William Mowbray, the other!'

Again Meeran Hafaz passed gold into the eager palm of the calculating ruffian, whose eyes sparkled with excitement as he grasped it.

'In a few days,' he muttered, as he thrust the coin into his gibern, 'you shall hear of me: there will be news to stir the country far and near!'

The rival of our hero in the love of Ellen, had not forgotten the warrener's description of the person who had so cleverly outwitted him in the affair of the will. Satisfied that his agent was not to blame, he paid him as lavishly, perhaps, as he would have done had he succeeded. He saw that the master-key to his soul was gold, and he dispensed it with no niggard hand.

Making the usual signal with his hands, the Hindoo boy entered the apartment. Knowing that he could rely upon his fidelity, his master had directed him to wait in the antechamber, and at once inform him if any one approached during his conference with the warrener: the precaution was chiefly levelled at his old confidant and tutor.

Had he been as well acquainted with the localities of Bungalore Hall as Lady Harebell, it was not against the Khan that his suspicions would have been directed.

The boy retired after having received his orders, and presently returned with the renegade, whom Meeran had sent him to seek. There was an expression of sadness upon the usually stern countenance of the old man, as he gazed upon the young Indian and his uncouth visitor; for he felt assured that the confidence between two beings of such opposite characters could only be the confidence of crime.

'Where is Captain Elton?' inquired his charge.

The Khan informed him that he was in the drawing-room.

'Send him to me directly!' continued Meeran; 'and fear not to disturb him. He will come joyfully,' he added, with a slight expression of scorn; 'for he is a borrower!'

The instant the speaker and Will Sideler were left alone, he directed the latter to conceal himself behind the curtains of the bed—but in such a position that he could observe the countenance of his intended visitor. He next locked the casket, which remained open upon the table, and placed the key in his bosom.

'Stir not! if possible, breathe not!' he said to his confederate. 'Probably you will see the man who thwarted you in your late attempt upon the lawyer.'

The ruffian grasped his heavy stick with a threatening air.

'Not for your life!' added the speaker. 'There must be no violence; at least not here. Cunning must be met with cunning. The fool has played his cards: it is yet to be seen who will win the game!'

When the scheming adventurer entered the room, he inquired, in the blandest tone possible, after the health of his young friend—who smiled as he heard the word, for he knew exactly the value of the captain's friendship.

'Weak—too weak to write!' he replied; 'or I should have answered your note before. I am not one of those who forget their obligations!'

His late second protested against the word, assuring him that he felt too happy in having had the occasion to serve him.

'Let me see,' continued Meeran, pretending to search for the key; 'five hundred pounds, I think, was the sum named in your note?'

'Exactly!' said the captain, who had written to borrow the sum of the young Indian, in order to enable him to execute his design of carrying off the daughter of Sir Jasper Pepper.

'Where can the key be?' exclaimed Meeran, with a well-affected air of vexation. Tut! Tut! I remember! Look in upon me in the morning, and it shall be at your disposal.'

A shade of disappointment overspread the countenance of his visitor, who hinted that he should be obliged to start for London at an early hour, where the death of a relative had unexpectedly rendered his presence necessary.

'In that case,' said his friend, 'visit me again before you retire to rest. You need not fear disturbing me—I seldom sleep. By-the-bye,' he added; 'do you think of depriving us of your presence for any lengthened period?'

'About three days,' was the reply.

Captain Elton felt anxious to return to the drawing-room. He feared to absent himself for an instant from the side of his intended victim, lest her resolution should waver, and the rich prize escape him. With many apologies for the briefness of his visit, he withdrew, promising to return as soon as the guests should leave the drawing-room.

"'Tis he!' said Will Sideler, stepping from his place of concealment, as soon as the speaker had left the apartment.

'I thought so!' observed Meeran, carelessly.

'But for your caution, I should have strangled him as he stood!'

'Leave him to me!' replied the youth, with a cold smile; 'you heard what he said? I shall see him again before he retires to rest.'

With these words he dismissed the warrener, who was conducted from the house by the Hindoo boy, who appeared to have suddenly grown in great favour with his master.

When Captain Elton renewed his visit to Meeran Hafaz, at a much later hour, he found him smoking his hookah, on a couch, with a cup of fragrant coffee before him. Its rich aroma filled the room.

'What a delicious perfume!' he exclaimed.

'It is made,' replied the youth, 'from the most precious berries of Arabia. What wine is to the European, coffee is to the Oriental. He is as difficult in its choice as a Frenchman of his claret or an Englishman of his port. After all,' he added, 'wine is a gross beverage; the enjoyment it procures is too material. The excitement procured by coffee is far more exhilarating—more ethereal. It has this advantage, too: it never leaves an aching head behind. You smile! I see I shall not make a convert of you!'

'On the contrary,' replied his visitor—who felt how important it was that he should not oversleep the hour appointed for the elopement with Miss Pepper, and recollected that coffee, at a late hour, invariably kept him awake—'I am more than half a convert already. With your permission, I will join you.'

Meeran clapped his hands, and directed the Hindoo boy to bring coffee for the captain. In a few minutes the attendant returned, bearing a small cup of porcelain upon a salver, filled with the exquisite beverage, prepared after the manner of the East: that is to say, as strong as if it had been distilled, and unpolluted by the presence of milk or saccharine matter. The exquisitely painted cup was contained in a larger one of filagree silver, to prevent the heat from incommoding the hand, the Orientals never using saucers A small crystal flask of rosoglio and a glass were upon the salver beside it.

Had not the attention of Captain Elton been absorbed by the delicious fragrance which the coffee exhaled, he must have noticed that the hand of the Hindoo boy trembled as he presented it to him.

'Exquisite!' exclaimed he, with an air of satisfaction, after repeatedly sipping the beverage. 'Ah, my dear fellow, you have done me an injury instead of kindness!'

'How so?' inquired Meeran, earnestly.

'You have given me a taste which I shall not have the means of gratifying; and heaven knows my sins were numerous and expensive enough already. Who, after tasting such nectar, can reconcile himself to the insipid, watery decoction, which passes under the name of coffee in England?'

By this time the speaker had drained the last drop, and began to assist himself to the rosoglio.

'I feel a lightness, a buoyancy of heart and spirit,' he continued. 'I wish, on my return, you would suffer your attendant to instruct my rascal of a valet how to prepare it?'

'Right willingly!' replied the Indian, with a smile. 'By-the-bye,' he added, pointing at the same time to a roll of notes upon the table, 'there is the sum you require. Will it be sufficient?'

For very shame, his visitor—who mentally cursed his stupidity for not having asked for more—was compelled to acknowledge that it would. He was profuse in his thanks and professions of friendship—all of which Meeran answered with a smile.

'Shall I give you an acknowledgment?' demanded the captain, after carefully counting the notes, and placing them in his pocket-book.

The offer was declined, as being unnecessary between such friends as they were.

The captain could not avoid thinking, as he retired to his room to prepare for his departure, what a *simple* person the young Indian was—so confident and childlike; and he mentally resolved that, if anything occurred to blight his matrimonial prospects with Miss Pepper, to cultivate his friendship to the last; for he felt convinced that, in judicious hands, Meeran Hafaz would prove as good as an annuity.

With all his shrewdness, the scheming Captain Elton was but a poor judge of character. Strong passions and designs lie deep, and seldom leave any trace by which they can be guessed at on the surface. The shallowest waters are the easiest ruffled.

Great was the consternation at Bungalore Hall, on the following morning, when it was discovered that the daughter of Sir Jasper and three of his guests had disappeared: Captain Elton, Isabel, and her cousin Herbert. General Bouchier was in a perfect fury. At the first reproach which he addressed to Lady Harebell, whom he most unjustly suspected of being a party to her daughter's elopement, her ladyship took refuge in hysterics.

Instant pursuit was resolved on. Sir Jasper and the general started as soon as the carriage could be got ready—not that there was much hope of overtaking them, for the fugitives had at least four hours start of them.

'My dear Lady Harebell,' observed a good-natured friend to the disconsolate widow, 'the general will relent!'

'Never!'

'Yes he will! Your daughter has made a brilliant match! you have managed it capitally!'

'I manage it!' repeated her ladyship, who had but small faith in any relenting on the part of General Bouchier. 'I would sooner have seen Isabel in her grave, than the wife of her cousin!'

'Why so?' demanded the lady.

'*He is a beggar!*'

In that word all her objections were comprised. Poverty was a crime which no virtue could atone for—no genius palliate! Had her daughter's husband been a bankrupt in honour, in the world's esteem, and all which constitutes the ornament of life, and yet been rich—she could have forgiven her; but to marry for love—preposterous! Lady

Harebell almost doubted if she really were the mother of a girl capable of such an absurdity.

It must be confessed that the disappointment was very provoking, just as her hope of securing a rich husband, both for herself and Isabel, were changing into certainties. Little did she dream that her daughter's disobedience had been, in all probability, the means of saving her own life, by preventing her entering into a contest with Meeran Hafaz, who would have crushed her with as little remorse as he felt in removing her accomplice, Captain Elton, from his path. Fortunately the man whom she designed to honour with her hand, was made of more pliable material than the young Indian.

During the day, most of the guests left the hall. Lady Harebell was too ill to be removed, and Colonel Mowbray remained to attend to his wounded friend. It did not suit either of their plans to quit the neighbourhood.

CHAPTER XLI.

Old visions haunt the creaking floors—
    Old sorrows sit and wail—
Whilst still the night-winds out of doors
    Like burly bailiffs rail!
Old visions haunt the floors above;
    The walls with wrinkles frown;
And people say who pass that way,
    'T were well the house were down.
                              CHARLES SWAIN[22]

FROM the day of the departure of the two travellers, a deep gloom seemed to have settled on the spirits of the inhabitants of Carrow Abbey; even the domestics felt its chilling influence. Like a sunbeam which had been admitted into the recesses of some long-closed vault and suddenly withdrawn, the old mansion appeared more lonely from the absence of our hero and his friend Walter Mowbray, whose brief visit had given something like life and animation to the place. It is the privilege of youth to impart the sunshine of its dreams and hopes to all around; for if age is forbidden to participate, it at least can sympathise with them—and in that sympathy sees its own pleasures and pursuits reflected in Time's inverted mirror. Poor Ellen! the separation from her lover was the first serious sorrow she had experienced since the death of her parents; her heart collapsed like a tender flower deprived of the dew which should refresh its leaves, and add to their perfume and beauty.

How often would she recall to mind each word the absent one had spoken—his thoughts and looks as they wandered together by the lake, or he sat on a pile of cushions at her feet, in the old drawing-room, reading some favourite poet's page—pausing at every verse to participate in the enjoyment his task afforded her—to gaze into her eyes, and receive his thanks in the eloquent tear which trembled on the silken fringes of their drooping lids!

Still her grief was not without hope. 'He will return!' she thought, and her heart bounded at the words: she found courage in them to struggle with the feelings which oppressed her.

If at times the fear that, in the sunny land he was about to visit, her lover would find one more fair, more gifted, and more worthy of him, presented itself, she instantly dismissed it from her mind as an act of treason to the absent, and atoned for the involuntary crime by mentally renewing her vows of constancy and fidelity, no matter what difficulties might arise, or influence be used, to shake them.

Wisely and beautifully has it been said by the poet of old, that ' God is love!' for it tempers the weakest soul, gives strength to the feeble, energy to the strong—arms us with patience and endurance—teaches the heart, like faith, to believe against reason, to trust despite of doubt—filling it with richest harmonies—it adds even to our appreciation of the beautiful in nature; never are our sensibilities so keenly excited as when under its delicious influence; it is the soul of the universe—without it the world would be a desert, and life endurance—not enjoyment.

Love has its sorrows, as spring-time has its showers: without them, the flowers and feelings would both wither, by basking in too much sunshine.

The effect produced upon the baronet was equally marked; he again became silent and gloomy, shutting himself within the library to commune with his thoughts, or find oblivion, if possible, in those of others. A smile was never seen upon his countenance, unless when Ellen visited him, when he exerted himself to appear cheerful for her sake.

More than once the generous-hearted man reproached himself with selfishness, in having permitted her lover to depart—so sensitive was he in analysing his own motives, so indulgent towards the feelings of others.

As for old Martin, the groom, Mrs. Jarmy and the butler both declared, that he had grown more morose and silent than ever—there was no getting a word from him. The instant he had taken his meals, he retreated to his usual place of refuge—the stable—and passed half the night in wandering about the house and grounds; his spirit appeared more restless than ever.

Kitty, the youngest of the housemaids, who was looked upon as a very giddy sort of person by the rest of the household—having only reached the age of forty-four—was sure that he had something upon his mind; and Nicholls, the grey-headed butler, although he did not care to confess it, was very much of the same opinion. The only person in the family to whom the absence of the young men appeared to be a relief, was the ayah. There was an air of satisfaction in her manner, and a mocking expression in her dark eye, as she listened to the regrets and suppositions of those around her, which deeply offended the worthy house-keeper, who more than once declared that she looked like an evil thing rejoicing in the desolation she had caused.

Martin was of the same way of thinking, but he was more cautious how he expressed his opinions; yet it was evident to those who understood the old man's ways, that he had taken a strong antipathy to Zara, of whose movements, for weeks past, he had been a close observer.

Ellen had remained later than usual in the library, conversing with her uncle, whose spirits appeared more and more depressed; and her feelings gradually assumed the tone of the speaker's, as she listened to his rich and mellow voice, descanting on the future when he spoke of Henry and herself, it was full of hope and promise—when he alluded to himself, it was despondency, but without fear.

'Dream on, dearest Ellen,' he said; 'for your life has many a bright and joyous hour in store: it were to accuse the goodness of Providence to doubt it—to break our trust in virtue! I shall not live to witness your happiness,' he added; but if the dead are permitted to revisit earth, my spirit shall watch over it and share it!'

'Speak not of dying!' exclaimed Ellen, casting her arms with filial affection round his neck, and gazing with innocent confidence upon his noble features, which sorrow, more than time, had invested with the character of age; 'why should you have these sad anticipations?'

'I cannot shake them off,' replied the baronet; 'they haunt me like my own shadow! I have striven against them, but in vain: there are sympathies and warnings we cannot account for. Have you not heard,' he added, 'how Umfriville de Mowbray, our ancestor, foretold his own death, on the eve of Bosworth field?'

'But you are not going to battle!' observed his niece, with a faint attempt to smile; 'he was on the point of a fierce encounter, where lives were to be risked, and men were to struggle on the red field for mastery.'

'I cannot reason, Ellen,' said Sir William, 'I can only feel; for several days the presentiment has oppressed me! If I have named it to you,' he added, think not that it proceeds from weakness: no; it is that I would prepare you for the loss of one who has loved you like a father!'

The head of the orphan, like some gentle flower which the heavy dews of night oppress, sank upon his breast.

'I have taken every human means,' he continued, 'to secure your happiness; 'no stern guardian, when I am gone, can interpose between you and your lover! In my will, I have given my consent, without condition or reservation, to your marriage with Henry Ashton. I need not say how deep a blessing followed it. The world, perhaps, may condemn me for weakness in so doing; but what care we for its opinions, its censure, or its praise? hearts are our world—we know no other!'

The feelings of the grateful and affectionate girl became too strong to be controlled, and she wept audibly upon his breast.

'Father!' she murmured; 'my kind, my second father!'

At this moment the turret clock struck the hour of midnight.

'So late!' exclaimed the baronet, with surprise, at the same time ringing the bell to summon one of the domestics to light his niece to her room. 'Good night, Ellen! time flies so swiftly when speaking with those we love, that I have failed to note his steps!'

He gently released himself from her embrace, and kissed her on the forehead.

Again he rang, and paused—but no one answered.

'The servants have all retired to rest,' he said; 'no matter! I will accompany you through the picture-gallery myself.'

Ellen would not hear of his quitting the library. She knew how much he disliked visiting the gallery, which contained the veiled portrait of his faithless wife. She had no childish, superstitious dread, and positively refused the offer.

'You mock me, uncle!' she said, at the same time taking up one of the candles from the table. What should I fear? I would as soon pass through the picture-gallery at midnight as at the hour of noon! I am not a child, to be startled at shadows!'

Sir William smiled sadly—for he guessed her motive—and once more bade her good night.

Ellen entered the great hall, where the lamp was still burning, and mounting the massive, carved oaken staircase, proceeded along the north corridor, which terminated in a door leading to the picture-gallery: as she opened it, a gust of wind extinguished the taper in her hand. She paused for an instant: suddenly recollecting that she had left one of the windows open, she felt ashamed at her momentary want of decision.

'I have but to cross it,' she thought; ' and I am in my own chamber, where Zara is doubtless tired of waiting for me!'

So well was she acquainted with the locality, that she could have traversed it blindfold. With a light step, she had passed more than half the length of the apartment, when her ear was startled by a faint, rustling sound: at first she thought that her imagination must have deceived her—it was repeated! Without slackening her speed, she turned her head towards the spot whence the sound proceeded—and saw, indistinctly, a shadowy, dark figure crouching down by the side of a large Indian cabinet, and a pair of dark eyes, which shone like a tiger's in the dark, fixed upon her.

How the heart of the orphan beat—she could almost hear its throbbings! and yet she neither screamed nor hesitated, although the sound of her own voice would have been a relief to her. She remembered the words, the anticipations of her uncle—and affection nerved her with desperate courage. Silently she pursued her way till she reached the door at the end of the gallery, and, placing her hand upon the lock, it trembled so, she could not open it; and, to add to her terror, she fancied she heard a light step behind her.

'What stupid person,' she exclaimed, half-aloud, 'has turned the key?'

The words saved her—the footstep was arrested.

Grasping the handle with a convulsive effort, it turned in her hand, and she entered a second corridor, at the end of which was her own apartment.

'Bring me a light, Zara!' she called, in as firm a tone as she could command; 'mine is extinguished!'

The next moment the door of her room opened, and the ayah appeared, with a lighted taper in her hand.

With all her treachery and waywardness of character, the Indian nurse loved her foster-child with an affection second only to her slavish devotion to Meeran Hafaz; and when she saw the quivering lip, the pale cheek, and glance of terror of the affrighted girl, she demanded what had happened.

Fortunately she spoke in Hindostanee.

'Hush!' said Ellen, in the same language. 'Not a word—a breath! There is some ruffian in the picture gallery: I saw the glare of his fierce eye fixed on me!'

The ayah drew a long, glittering blade from beneath the folds of her dress, and passed with the rapidity of thought between her young mistress and the door of the picture-gallery. At that moment she was really beautiful in her fidelity, as she stood, fierce as a lioness guarding her threatened young—her nostrils dilated with passion, her hand pressing the weapon, which she well knew how to use.

'Fear not!' she whispered; 'they must shed my heart's blood before they injure you!'

'It is not my life,' replied the orphan with sudden recollection, 'but one far more precious than mine, which is threatened!'

'Whose!' demanded Zara, in a tone of surprise.

'My uncle's! My dear, loved uncle's!'

The manner of the ayah suddenly changed: probably she more than guessed who the intruder was.

'Your imagination has deceived you!' she answered, coolly; 'what danger can threaten your gloomy kinsman, in his own mansion? Come to your chamber!'

'I must descend to the library!' frantically urged Ellen.

'Folly—dreams!'

It was in vain that she entreated Zara to accompany her: the woman either did not or would not believe that the danger to Sir William was real. Desperate at her refusal, Ellen suddenly snatched both the lamp and weapon from her hands: thus armed, the affectionate girl feared nothing.

'Remain!' she said, in a resolute tone. 'I can descend alone!' And, without waiting for a reply, she disappeared down a second staircase, which led to the servants' hall.

'I must follow her!' muttered the ayah. 'Should it be the man I think, and he encounter Ellen, she will need my presence to protect her!'

As she was about to descend, with this intention, the door of the picture-gallery partly opened, and a man peered cautiously into the corridor.

'Hist! Zara—Zara—is that you?' he said.

It was the warrener.

'You here!' impatiently exclaimed the Indian woman; 'escape instantly! Know you not that you are discovered?'

'No matter!'

'That an alarm is given?'

'I know where to hide myself; besides, I have locked the door at the other end of the gallery,' added the ruffian. 'I was a fool to be deceived by the artifice of a girl! Had I been certain that she had seen me, I would have strangled her!'

'Strangled her!' repeated the horror-stricken ayah.

'Yes—quietly.'

'Fool!' she whispered; 'it was my foster-child, who is dearer to him you serve than all his gold—and he is rich, even in the land of princes! Had you harmed a hair of her head,' she continued, with increased vehemence, 'Meeran would have invented torments to punish you!'

Will Sideler gave a low whistle, as if to congratulate himself upon having escaped so serious a blunder.

'Now, then, away!' she continued, 'and be more cautious for the future! Remember that Meeran Hafaz is as fearful as an enemy as he is generous as a friend!'

'I do not need your caution,' he replied. 'I could serve him in this for the mere pleasure of serving him!'

'How so?'

'I hate Sir William Mowbray!'

The ayah paused an instant, and smiled.

'You smile!' he added; 'do you doubt me?'

'No.'

'Why did you smile, then?'

'To find thou wert a thing less ignoble and mercenary than my imagination had painted thee!'

(To be continued in our next.)

[Margaret Oliphant], 'The Byways of Literature: Reading for the Million', *Blackwood's Edinburgh Magazine*, 84 (August 1858), 200–16 [200–9, 211, 214–15]

Oliphant (1828–97), like many women authors in the nineteenth century, wrote to support her extended family. Despite her radical politics, she was a long-serving contributor to the Tory *Blackwood's* and wrote many novels for its publishers. The extract negotiates her personal convictions with editorial requirements. Despite the acuteness of many remarks, Oliphant's selection has led her astray over several points (see the Notes for details).

Not very long ago we spent, perforce, an idle summer-day in one of the most important of our English cathedral towns [. . .] and had with us the restless company of a child. So sight-seeing was rather out of our *rôle* for the moment. We were too languid in interest to care even for the cathedral, the echoing solemn nave of which our small companion was more awed than pleased with. Our alternative was not a very dignified one; we invested a sixpence in a most miscellaneous and varied collection of literature, and retired with the small heroine who loved the living daisies outside better than the dead effigies within, to the verdant turf of the cathedral close. [. . .]

[W]e strewed upon the grass around us, while our little companion filled her basket with daisies, our sixpenny store of literature, strangely incongruous with the scene. Grave literature and learning, decorum and dignity, the authorities of society, stood represented in those grave old houses, from which no careless human eye looked out; and scattered over the daisies, with the wind among their leaves, lay the unauthoritative, undignified, unlearned broadsheets, which represent literature to a great portion of our country people, despite of all the better provision made for their pleasure. There could not possibly be a more marked or total contrast than between the object of our immediate attention and the scene.

Yet the contrast of itself was not without its suggestion. Progress is something more than the cant of the age [. . .] When all the world whirls and changes, one inconstant, inconsistent, unexplainable being remains always the same. There are no new capabilities to be found out in him, no undiscovered depths from which science can conjure up forces and powers unknown. Progress is but a word for this last and greatest of God's works, meaning what goes on outside of him— the story of the accessories by which he is surrounded. That nature which was only perfect in the earliest days of its earliest possessor, and which will be perfect again only when the world's full chronicle is completed, makes no progress. Comforts increase, power grows, science expands and widens, but the man who is in the midst of all does not change.

Progress rules over science, over manufactures, over all the inge-nuities and wisdoms of the race. There is not a workman in existence so perfect but he may learn something of which his work shall be the better. The only things which escape this wide rule of increase are the creative art and the individual man. Here [...] lie rustling upon the fresh grass these dreary sheets of printed paper, flimsy pages, made to kindle fires withal to-morrow; which prove to us, beyond the possi-bility of doubting, that good sense, good thought, truth, excellence, or refinement of any kind, are by no means included in what is called the spread of literature, and that the human mind has made no particular advance in any direction, to judge from the mental condition of those multitudes of people who find their weekly delectation in publications such as these.

No, the lesser arts progress, but the greater art does not share in the advancement. We print a great deal better than we used to do, but the matter to be printed shows by no means a corresponding improve-ment. It is three hundred years, or thereabout, since we had our Shakespeare, and such another has not come again. We can no more produce another *Hamlet*, than we can build another cathedral like that at Canterbury. [...] True, every kind of publication has in-creased tenfold; and there is scarcely a house or a room in the country, down to the very boundary-line where poverty subsides into want, or rather where want meets destitution, in which something readable is not to be found. [...] Let us give the masses all credit for their gift of reading; but before we glorify ourselves over the march of intelligence, let us pause first to look into their books.

These unfortunate masses! When first the schoolmaster began to be abroad, how tenderly we took care of the improvement of their minds, and how zealously exerted ourselves to make literature a universal dominie, graciously enlightening the neophyte on every subject under heaven! Does anybody remember now the Societies for the Diffusion of Knowledge—the Penny Magazines and Cyclopædias through which the streams of *useful* information fell benignly upon the lower orders?[23]—how we laboured to bring ourselves down to the capacity of that unknown intelligence, the working man!—how we benevolently volunteered to amuse him in a profitable and edifying way, by histories and descriptions of the ingenious crafts, and nice accounts of how they make pins, and laces, and china, or how a steam-engine is put together! What a delightful ideal dwelt then in our inexperienced thoughts! Would any one have supposed that this intellectual creation, austerely brought up upon facts and figures, could ever own a guilty longing for stories, or verses, or other such amusements of a frivolous race? The idea was insulting to all our hopes and exertions; and when, by-and-by, the horrid numerals of a statistical account disclosed to us the fatal certainty that the multitude, like ourselves, loved amusement better than instruction—that working men, too, preferred *Guy Mannering* to the *Novum Organum*, and that Byron was more to the purpose than Bacon even in the library of a mechanics' institute—the chill of disappointed expectation consequent upon the discovery is not to be described.[24] So the penny cyclopædias dropped one by one into oblivion, and nobody missed them; and lo, rushing into the empty space, the mushroom growth of a sudden impulse, rapid and multitudinous to meet the occasion, came springing up a host of penny magazines—spontaneous and natural publications, which professed no artificial mission, and aimed at no class-improvement, but were the simple supply of an existing demand—wares such as the customer wanted, and the market was suitable for. [...]

There are few words so difficult to define as that term literature, which is in everybody's mouth. To confine its meaning to that which we call literature, is about as exclusive and limited a notion as it is to confine that other term society to the fashionable world, which claims the name in sublime disdain of all competitors. Almost as numerous as the distinct 'circles' which, upward to the highest *haut monde*,[25] and downwards to the genteelest coterie of a village, each calls itself by the all-comprehending name, are the widespread oligarchies and democracies of that Republic of Letters, which, like most other republics, claims throughout its ranks a noisy equality, pleasantly varied by the arrogance of individual despotisms. Let us not delude ourselves with the idea that literature is fully represented by that small central body of its forces of whom everybody knows every individual name. Nay, not everybody—only everybody who is anybody—not the everybody who reads the *London Journal* and the *Family Herald*. That eminent group, with which we at least do ourselves the credit to claim acquaintance, are only the chance oligarchs who stand up head and shoulders above the mass of their co-aspirants—whom, by virtue of that accident of stature, other countries see over our cliffs and channels, whom above a certain level of society it is impossible to avoid seeing—nay, even necessary and inevitable to know something of— and whose works are forming the last ring in that big old tree called English literature. But it matters very little to the people in the valley whether a man stands on the top of the hill or only on the side of it— nay, for all their purposes, the lowest slope, being nearest, is the best; and so in the underground, quite out of sight and ken of the heroes, spreads thick and darkly an undiscriminated multitude—undiscriminated by the critics, by the authorities, by the general vision, but widely visible to individual eyes, to admiring coteries, and multitudinous lower classes, who buy, and read, and praise, and encourage, and, under the veil of their own obscurity, bestow a certain singular low-lying Jack-o'-lantern celebrity, which nobody out of these regions is aware of, and which is the oddest travestie and paraphrase of fame. [...]

[O]ne genuine natural appetite, at least, if nothing more, displays itself most prominently in this 'reading for the million.' It is that love of stories which distinguishes all primitive minds, and which has its strongest development in savages and children. No disparagement to our friends of the multitude. They, too, share with the children and the savages a certain absolute and first-hand contact with things and facts, which throws out philosophy. Events great and grievous come upon them as upon their social superiors; but necessity thrusts them on without the lingering which we have time to make over our graves and shipwrecks. They have to gulp down their sob in the midst of the common work, which, by the compensation of Providence, is the best practical consoler; and with always the first absolute need of nature before them—the necessity to earn their daily bread—live, and are constrained to live a life outside of themselves—not of contemplation, but of activity. So it comes about that these labouring multitudes stand somewhat in the same position as, perhaps, the very knights of romance held four or five hundred years ago. It is not that they differ in natural intelligence from the classes above them; it is not that the delf is duller than the porcelain; it is only that we have got so many centuries ahead by dint of our exemption from manual labours and necessities. They are still among the dragons and the giants, where hard hands and strength of arm are more in demand than thoughts and fancies. We have gained the thoughtful ways of civilisation, when we smile at Archimage, and find St George's hideous adversary a fabulous creation.[26] Our leisure accordingly plays with all fancies, all inventions—all matters of thought and reason; whereas their leisure, brief and rapid, and sharpened with the day's fatigue, loves, above all things, a story, and finds in that just the amount of mental excitation which makes it somehow a semi-intellectual pleasure. For it is a story, for the story's sake; not a story because it is a good story—a work of genius—a revelation of nature. The simple practical mind is a great deal more absolute than that. Merit is quite a secondary consideration; it is the narrative which is the thing. What does a child care for the probabilities of fiction, for the wit of dialogue, or the grace of style? It is likely they bore him, detaining as they do the current of events with which his interest is linked; and though we will not say quite so much as this for the liking of the multitude, yet the principle is the same. [. . .]

This principle of mind is just what the societies for the diffusion of knowledge did not find out, and which we fear even the philanthropist of the day, who does popular lectures, persists in ignoring. People working face to face with the primitive powers—people in whose understanding poverty does not mean a smaller house, or fewer servants, or a difficulty about one's butcher's bill, but means real hunger, cold, and nakedness, are not people to be amused with abstractions. And it has often occurred to ourselves, that were all these benevolent, noble, right honourable, and distinguished lecturers to be replaced by so many minstrels of the antique strain, yet of a modern fashion—men with stories on their lips, fresh, new, and living—not stories written in books which anybody can read who has a mind—that the effect would be something quite beyond our modern calm and even level of interest. It has pleased one of our great novelists in recent days to read certain stories of his own to an elegant and refined public, most of whom had read them before, and went to look at the author with purely unexcited and philosophical minds.[27] We presume the audience had what they wanted, and were satisfied; and so probably had the distinguished writer, reader, and actor, who made this entertainment for their benefit; yet after all, though it is becoming common, it is not the most dignified meeting this between the story-teller and his auditory. The relations between them are changed for the time, and not agreeably changed. Somehow it seems a sin against good taste and the reticence of genius, that the writer, with his own voice, should bring out and emphasize those 'points' already singled out by popular approbation, which are sure to 'bring down the house.' [...] But let the story-teller bring us a tale fresh from his own conception, and unfamiliar to the world, and the circumstances are changed. It is possible even that this might be the 'something new' after which this fatigued capital toils with persever-ance so praiseworthy. Suppose Mr Thackeray and Mr Dickens, instead of monthly numbers yellow and green, had a monthly assem-bly, and gave forth the story to a visible public, moved by all the visible emotions over which these magicians exercise their subtle power,—would not that be an experiment sufficient to reinvigorate with all its pristine force the flagging serial—possibly even by the prompt criticism of the audience to bestow a certain benefit upon the tale? [...]

Every single page of our sixpennyworth of periodicals proves more strongly this natural taste; and now it is about time that we should see what the manner of these stories is. In the first place, they have one particular and marked distinction—they are not of the class of those multitudinous tales which the art of criticism once patronised, and now extinguishes; the fiction feminine, which fills with mild domestic volumes the middle class of this species of literature. The lowest range, like the highest range, admits no women.[28] We cannot take it upon us to say what this fact teaches, or if it teaches anything; but it is curious enough as a distinction. And if any one supposes that here, in this special branch of literature provided for the multitude, anything about the said multitude is to be found, a more entire mistake could not be imagined. It is only the higher classes who can find a hero in a tailor, or amuse themselves with the details of a workman's household and economy. An Alton Locke may find a countess to fall in love with him, but is no hero for the sempstress, who makes her romance out of quite different materials; and whereas we can please ourselves with *Mary Barton*, our poor neighbours share no such humble taste, but luxuriate in ineffable splendours of architecture and upholstery, and love to concern themselves with the romantic fortunes of a Gertrude de Brent and a Gerald St Maur.[29] [...] When the future historian of this century seeks information about the life and manners of our poorer classes, he will find no kind of popular print so entirely destitute of the details he seeks as those penny miscellanies which are solely read by the poor, yet are full of tales about the rich. We suppose, though it is rather contrary to the theory which brings poetry—and fiction as a development of poetry—most close to the heart when it expounds what that heart itself feels without being able to express—that this too is a natural sentiment. In our nobler and loftier sorrows, it comforts us to hear of others who have borne the like affliction; but in our more sordid and petty pangs do we prefer to escape rather into regions where such things are impossible, to forget our mean surroundings in imaginary splendour, and ignore our miserable little cares in a fancied association with the magnificent and lavish? Is this the interpretation? We are unable to pronounce judgment on our own authority; but it would certainly seem so, looking at the proofs before us. [...] The multitude not only ignores itself in its reading, but suffers itself to be misrepresented, and takes its view of the humbler individuals in its fictions from its fine hero's superb point of vision, and not from its own actual knowledge; so that it is safer to be contemptuous of the masses when you address themselves directly, than it is to show the same disdain to those who have no personal concern with the matter [...] What has to be read in the workshop and kitchen must be enacted at club and boudoir; there must be lackeys at the door, splendid as any macaw of the Zoological Gardens, and stately gentlemen in white neckcloths to usher the visitor up-stairs. As for the ineffable creatures who are up-stairs, when one reaches that superlative region, what pen can do justice to them? Yet we presume the mere hearing of them—their silken couches, their 'dashing carriages,' their jewels, their dresses, and their lovers—must somehow please the poor maiden who has none of these fine things, and never will have, yet who cannot help associating them with grandeur and happiness, and a life like a fairy tale. And so the stories run: even poor superior high-minded governesses, and refined poverty in elegant distress, those staple commodities of fiction, do not flourish in the penny periodicals; *that* public does not care to know how careful gentility makes both ends meet, or how the gentlewoman who has seen better days suffers delicate martyrdom. Enough of the commonplace hardships of life are, we presume, in their own lot, and their choice is to hear of those to whom such hardships are impossible, and whose very troubles are fine and splendid, and out of the common way.

To illustrate this, we can hardly do better than give our readers a passing glimpse of one of those tales, of itself rather 'superior,' and aiming at something beyond the pretensions of most of the class; superior, that is to say, in intention, though not in carrying out. It is contained in one of the most exemplary and well-intentioned of penny serials—the *Cassell's Illustrated Paper*—which gives its readers sundry other things besides stories, and is a highly moral and edifying publication. This story is distinct from all the others, in being a story of benevolence and philanthropy, but is like the rest in choosing personages of fashion and rank for its agents.[30] The heroine, a young lady called Ada Pemberton, has been changed from a mere young lady of fashion into the highest model of human perfectibility by becoming a teacher in a ragged school. She 'tells her footman, who waited for her at some little distance, where to order the carriage to meet her,' before 'she takes her way to the blind alley,' where one of her protegées lives; and when she has reached home, and descended to the drawing-room, this is her description, as she appeared to her fashionable lover, whom the groom of the chambers has just announced as 'Mr Gerald St Maur!'

'Her long and abundant hair, with its golden ripples glittering in the morning sun, was not, as he had often seen it before, elaborately plaited and expanded by Pertinette, and its beauty hidden by ribbons and laces, but was simply braided round her oval face; one long thick tress, of what the initiated call "the back hair," was plaited, and brought like a coronet round the small Grecian head, while a rich coil of similar plaits formed a scroll behind, and fell in loops on the shoulders. A simple lilac bâtiste, very ample, and embroidered richly with white, fitted her fine form, while all her adornment consisted in a collar and sleeves of fine lace, a gold chain round her long white throat, merely to secure the watch hidden in her bosom, and which was now become no idle ornament or fine-lady appendage, but a faithful monitor, marking those hours every one of which had its appointed duty. A miniature, richly set, of her brother, formed her brooch, and those of her father and mother clasped two thick cables of gold round her wrists. She had a little black silk apron, with pockets full of ragged-school reports, lists of the wants of children in her own little class, practical directions from Ellen St Ange and Jem Goodman, a note-book, a pencil, her charity-purse, and several prospectuses connected with different temperance and ragged-school meetings. What a contrast to the pockets of her fine flounced silks before that memorable evening of her first visit to the Green Fields Ragged School!'

This angelical Ada has her hand kissed, and exclaims, as she 'snatches it away,' 'Come, none of your foreign gallantry here!' upon which the lover with the fine name announces that he is to kiss the Queen's hand the next day, and they fall into brisk conversation; which ends with a mental resolve on the part of the gentleman, when he leaves her, in spite of considerable annoyance at her ragged-school enthusiasm—'I shall formally propose;' and a meditation on the part of the lady—'I think he will propose; more than once he was on the point of doing so,' with which thrilling suggestion this number, and our acquaintance with the history of these very fine people, comes to an abrupt termination.

[...] Fame has fled out of those refined circles where everybody professes criticism—fled to take refuge underground, and to bestow itself upon heroes unknown to you; for alas! human nature is narrow-minded, and sees nothing which is not immediately under its own observation. We, for our own part, had supposed ourselves aware of the names at least of all the English lights of literature—but our recent investigations have undeceived us. Here is one personage, for instance, whom rival publications vie for the possession of, and whom the happy successful competitor advertises with all the glow and effusion of conscious triumph,—J. F.; nay, let us be particular,—

John Frederick Smith, Esq.[31] This gentleman is a great author, though nobody (who is anybody) ever was aware of it. We have no doubt that nothing but a conspiracy of spiteful critics could have kept his name so long veiled under this envious obscurity. He is 'the author of "Dick Tarleton," "Phases of Life," "The Soldier of Fortune," "The Young Pretender," ' &c.; yet we protest we never read a word of his writings, nor heard a whisper of his existence, until we spread out our sixpenny budget of light literature upon the June daisies. What matter? his portrait, from a photograph by Mayall, may be had in those regions where his sway is acknowledged; and the everybody, who is nobody, bestows upon him that deep-rolling subterraneous universal applause which is fame.[32] [...]

We have not touched upon a half, or indeed a tenth part, of that reading for the million which has become so multitudinous. We have not even attempted to notice the countless swarms of serial stories, separate publications issued like the magazines in weekly numbers, printed on the worst paper, with the worst type and poorest illustrations of which the arts are capable, which, we believe, are about as popular as the periodicals themselves;—these are bought by the very poorest classes, but they are by no means *cheap* literature, though the weekly pennyworth, we presume, persuades these humble readers into supposing so—nor the penny papers, which, though bought by everybody, undoubtedly address themselves to the multitude. [...] The apologists and the assailants of this large portion of the community have equally ignored the fact, that it is a varied and fluctuating mass, as uncertain and changeable as any other class of the community, acted upon by peculiar and not very favourable circumstances, but acting with the same fickleness, short-sightedness, and inconsistency which rule over everybody else, that forms the lower order and basis of our commonweal. They are not to be kept in perpetual lecturedom any more than we are; they are not inspired by a heroical antipathy to their betters, nor possessed with an incurable political fever like model Chartists in novels; neither do they surpass their neighbours in honesty, sincerity, and single-mindedness, as some of us would have the world to suppose. Circumstances alone distinguish them, as it is circumstances which distinguish the other extreme of society. [...] As a general principle, they have no leisure to concern themselves with those problems of common life which all the philosophers in the world cannot solve, nor to consider those hard conditions of existence under which they and we and all the race labour on towards the restoration of all things. It is much easier to conclude that something arbitrary can mend all, and to escape out of the real difficulties into those fictitious regions of delight, where every difficulty is made to be smoothed away—those superlative and dazzling regions of wealth and eminence, where, to the hard-labouring and poverty-pinched, it is hard to explain where the shadows lie.

Whether the existing literature of the multitude is improvable, we will not take upon us to say; but certainly no one ever will improve it efficiently without taking into full account all the class-characteristics which have helped it into being.

[Wilkie Collins], 'The Unknown Public', *Household Words*, 18 (21 August 1858), 217-22

Bradbury and Evans, the respectable publishers of Dickens's *Household Words* (1850–9), had secretly bought the *London Journal* in 1857. They had assigned its editorship to a friend of Dickens and Collins, Mark Lemon, who was currently also the editor of *Punch* (also owned by Bradbury and Evans). Lemon's attempts to rebrand the *Journal* as London-centred, English, and male-dominated, resulted in a huge loss of readership and a massive drop in profits. Bradley and Evans were furious. Collins's account codedly defends Lemon and other members of their circle involved in the débâcle, though it came out too late: Bradbury and Evans had sold the *London Journal* to its original owner, George Stiff, in June, and Lemon had retired to *Punch* in disgrace. Under Stiff the *Journal* immediately returned to its former practices. It was soon back to the high circulation Collins claims for it here.

Do the subscribers to this journal, the customers at the eminent publishing-houses, the members of book-clubs and circulating libraries, and the purchasers and borrowers of newspapers and reviews, compose altogether the great bulk of the reading public of England? There was a time when, if anybody had put this question to me, I, for one, should certainly have answered, Yes.

I know better now. I know that that the public just now mentioned, viewed as an audience for literature, is nothing more than a minority.

This discovery (which I venture to consider equally new and surprising) dawned upon me gradually. I made my first approaches towards it, in walking about London, more especially in the second and third rate neighborhoods. At such times, whenever I passed a small stationer's or small tobacconist's shop, I became conscious, mechanically as it were, of certain publications which invariably occupied the windows. These publications all appeared to be of the same small quarto size; they seemed to consist merely of a few unbound pages; each one of them had a picture on the upper half of the front leaf, and a quantity of small print on the under. I noticed just as much as this, for some time, and no more. None of the gentlemen who are so good as to guide my taste in literary matters, had ever directed my attention towards these mysterious publications. My favorite Review is, as I firmly believe, at this very day, unconscious of their existence. My enterprising librarian who forces all sorts of books on my attention that I don't want to read, because he has bought whole editions of them at a great bargain, has never yet tried me with the limp unbound picture quarto of the small shops. Day after day, and week after week, the mysterious publications haunted my walks, go where I might; and, still, I was too inconceivably careless to stop and notice them in detail. I left London and travelled about England. The neglected publications followed me. There they were in every town, large or small. I saw them in fruit-shops, in oyster-shops, in lollypop-shops. Villages even—picturesque, strong-smelling vil-lages—were not free from them. Wherever the speculative daring of one man could open a shop, and the human appetites and necessities of his fellow mortals could keep it from shutting up again, there, as it appeared to me, the unbound picture quarto instantly entered, set itself up obtrusively in the window, and insisted on being looked at by everybody. 'Buy me, borrow me, stare at me, steal me—do anything, O inattentive stranger, except contemptuously pass me by!'

Under this sort of compulsion, it was not long before I began to stop at shop-windows and look attentively at these all-pervading specimens of what was to me a new species of literary production. I made acquaintance with one of them among the deserts of West Cornwall, with another in a populous thoroughfare of Whitechapel, with a third in a dreary little lost town at the north of Scotland. I went into a lovely county of South Wales; the modest railway had not penetrated to it, but the audacious picture quarto had found it out. Who could resist this perpetual, this inevitable, this magnificently unlimited appeal to notice and patronage? From looking in at the windows of the shops, I got on to entering the shops themselves, to buying specimens of this locust-flight of small publications, to making strict examination of them from the first page to the last, and finally, to instituting inquiries about them in all sorts of well-informed quarters. The result—the astonishing result—has been the discovery of an Unknown Public; a public to be counted by millions; the mysterious, the unfathomable, the universal public of the penny-novel Journals.[33]

I have five of these journals now before me, represented by one sample copy, bought hap-hazard, of each. There are many more; but these five represent the successful and well-established members of the literary family. The eldest of them is a stout lad of fifteen years standing. The youngest is an infant of three months old.[34] All five are sold at the same price of one penny; all five are published regularly once a week; all five contain about the same quantity of matter. The weekly circulation of the most successful of the five is now publicly advertised (and, as I am informed, without exaggeration) at half a Million. Taking the other four as attaining altogether to a circulation of another half million (which is probably much under the right estimate) we have a sale of a Million weekly for five penny journals.[35] Reckoning only three readers to each copy sold, the result is *a public of three millions*—a public unknown to the literary world; unknown, as disciples, to the whole body of professed critics; unknown, as customers, at the great libraries and the great publishing houses; unknown, as an audience, to the distinguished English writers of our own time. A reading public of three millions which lies right out of the pale of literary civilisation is a phenomenon worth examining—a mystery which the sharpest man among us may not find it easy to solve.

In the first place, who are the three million—the Unknown Public— as I have ventured to call them? The known reading public—the minority already referred to—are easily discovered and classified. There is the religious public, with booksellers and literature of its own, which includes reviews and newspapers as well as books. There is the public which reads for information, and devotes itself to Histories, Biographies, Essays, Treatises, Voyages and Travels. There is the public which reads for amusement, and patronises the Circulating Libraries and the railway book-stalls. There is, lastly, the public which reads nothing but newspapers. We all know where to lay our hands on the people who represent these various classes. We see the books they like on their tables. We meet them out at dinner, and hear them talk of their favourite authors. We know, if we are at all conversant with literary matters, even the very districts of London in which certain classes of people live who are to be depended upon beforehand as the picked readers for certain kinds of books. But what do we know of the enormous outlawed majority—of the lost literary tribes—of the prodigious, the overwhelming three millions? Absolutely nothing.

I, myself—and I say it to my sorrow—have a very large circle of acquaintance. Ever since I undertook the interesting task of exploring the Unknown Public, I have been trying to discover among my dear friends and my bitter enemies, both alike on my visiting list, a subscriber to a penny novel-journal—and I have never yet succeeded in the attempt. [...]

In the absence, therefore, of any positive information on the subject, it is only possible to pursue the investigation which occupies these pages by accepting such negative evidence as may help us to guess with more or less accuracy, at the social position, the habits, the tastes, and the average intelligence of the Unknown Public. Arguing carefully by inference, we may hope, in this matter, to arrive, by a circuitous road, at something like a safe, if not a satisfactory, conclusion.

To begin with, it may be fairly assumed—seeing that the staple commodity of each one of the five journals before me, is composed of Stories—that the Unknown Public reads for its amusement more than for its information.

Judging by my own experience, I should be inclined to add, that the Unknown Public looks to quantity rather than quality in spending its penny a week on literature. In buying my five specimen copies, at five different shops, I purposely approached the individual behind the counter, on each occasion, in the character of a member of the Unknown Public—say, Number Three Million and One—who wished to be guided in laying out a penny entirely by the recommendation of the shopkeeper himself. I expected, by this course of proceeding, to hear a little popular criticism, and to get at what the conditions of success might be, in a branch of literature which was quite new to me. No such result, however, occurred in any case. The dialogue between buyer and seller always took some such practical turn as this:

Number Three Million and One.—'I want to take in one of the penny journals. Which do you recommend?'

Enterprising Publisher.—'Some likes one, and some likes another. They're all good pennorths. Seen this one?'

'Yes.'

'Seen that one?'

'No.'

'Look what a pennorth!'

'Yes—but about the stories in this one? Are they as good, now, as the stories in that one?'

'Well, you see, some likes one, and some likes another. Sometimes I sells more of one, and sometimes I sells more of another. Take 'em all the year round, and there ain't a pin, as I knows of, to choose between 'em. There's just about as much in one as there is in another. All good pennorths. Why, Lord bless your soul, just take 'em up and look for yourself, and say if they ain't good pennorths! Look what a lot of print in every one of 'em! My eye! What a lot of print for the money!'

I never got any farther than this, try as I might. And yet, I found the shopkeepers, both men and women, ready enough to talk on other topics. On each occasion, so far from receiving any practical hints that I was interrupting business, I found myself sociably delayed in the shop, after I had made my purchase, as if I had been an old acquaintance. I got all sorts of curious information on all sorts of subjects,— excepting the good pennorth of print in my pocket. [...]

Having, inferentially, arrived at the two conclusions that the Unknown Public reads for amusement, and that it looks to quantity in its reading, rather than to quality, I might have found it difficult to proceed further towards the making of new discoveries, but for the existence of a very remarkable aid to inquiry, which is common to all the penny novel-journals alike. The peculiar facilities to which I now refer, are presented in the Answers to Correspondents. The page containing these is, beyond all comparison, the most interesting page in the penny journals. There is no earthly subject that it is possible to discuss, no private affair that it is possible to conceive, which the amazing Unknown Public will not confide to the Editor in the form of a question, and which the still more amazing editor will not set himself seriously and resolutely to answer. Hidden under cover of initials, or Christian names, or conventional signatures, such as Subscriber, Constant Reader, and so forth, the editor's correspondents seem, many of them, to judge by the published answers to their questions, utterly impervious to the senses of ridicule or shame. Young girls beset by perplexities which are usually supposed to be reserved for a mother's or an elder sister's ear only, consult the editor. Married women, who have committed little frailties consult the editor. Male jilts in deadly fear of actions for breach of promise of marriage, consult the editor. Ladies whose complexions are on the wane, and who wish to know the best artificial means of restoring them, consult the editor. Gentlemen who want to dye their hair, and get rid of their corns, consult the editor. Inconceivably dense ignorance, inconceivably petty malice, and inconceivably complacent vanity, all consult the editor, and all, wonderful to relate, get serious answers from him. No mortal position is too difficult for this wonderful man; there is no change of character as general referee, which he is not prepared to assume on the instant. Now he is a father, now a mother, now a schoolmaster, now a confessor, now a doctor, now a lawyer, now a young lady's confidante, now a young gentleman's bosom friend, now a lecturer on morals, and now an authority in cookery.[36]

However, our present business is not with the editor, but with his readers. As a means of getting at the average intelligence of the Unknown Public,—as a means of testing the general amount of education which they have acquired, and of ascertaining what share of taste and delicacy they have inherited from Nature—these extraordinary Answers to Correspondents may fairly be produced in detail, to serve us for a guide. [...]

A reader of a penny novel-journal who wants a receipt[37] for gingerbread. A reader who complains of fullness in his throat. Several readers who want cures for grey hair, for warts, for sores on the head, for nervousness, and for worms. Two readers who have trifled with Woman's Affections, and who want to know if Woman can sue them for breach of promise of marriage. A reader who wants to know what the sacred initials I.H.S. mean, and how to get rid of small-pox marks. Another reader who desires to be informed what an esquire is. Another who cannot tell how to pronounce picturesque and acquiescence. Another who requires to be told that *chiar'oscuro* is a term used by painters. Three readers who want to know how to soften ivory, how to get a divorce, and how to make black varnish. A reader who is not certain what the word Poems means; not certain the Mazeppa was written by Lord Byron; not certain whether there are such things in the world as printed and published lives of Napoleon Bonaparte. [...]

I have already said that the staple commodity of the journals appears to be formed of stories. The five specimen copies of the five separate weekly publications now before me, contain, altogether, ten serial stories, one reprint of a famous novel (to be hereafter referred to), and seven short tales, each of which begins and ends in one number. The remaining pages are filled up with miscellaneous contributions, in literature and art, drawn from every conceivable source. Pickings from Punch and Plato; wood-engravings, representing notorious people and views of famous places, which strongly suggest that the original blocks have seen better days in other periodicals;[38] modern and ancient anecdotes; short memoirs; scraps of poetry; choice morsels of general information; household receipts, riddles, and extracts from moral writers; all appear in the most orderly manner, arranged under separate heads, and cut up neatly into short paragraphs. However, the prominent feature in each journal is the serial story, which is placed, in every case, as the first article, and which is illustrated by the only wood-engraving that appears to have been expressly cut for the purpose. To the serial story, therefore, we may fairly devote our chief attention, because it is clearly regarded as the chief attraction of these very singular publications.

Two of my specimen-copies contain, respectively, the first chapters of new stories. In the case of the other three, I found the stories in various stages of progress. The first thing that struck me, after reading the separate weekly portions of all five, was their extraordinary sameness. Each portion purported to be written (and no doubt was written) by a different author, and yet all five might have been produced by the same man. Each part of each successive story, settled down in turn, as I read it, to the same dead level of the smoothest and flattest conventionality. A combination of fierce melodrama and meek domestic sentiment; short dialogues and paragraphs on the French pattern, with moral English reflections of the sort that occur on the top lines of children's copy-books; incidents and characters taken from the old exhausted mines of the circulating library, and presented as complacently and confidently as if they were original ideas; descriptions and reflections for the beginning of the number, and a 'strong situation,' dragged in by the neck and shoulders, for the end— formed the common literary sources from which the five authors drew their weekly supply; all collecting it by the same means; all carrying it in the same quantities; all pouring it out before the attentive public in the same way. After reading my samples of these stories, I understood why it was that the fictions of the regularly-established writers for the penny journals are never republished.[39] There is, I honestly believe, no man, woman, or child in England, not a member of the Unknown Public, who could be got to read them. The one thing which it is possible to advance in their favour is, that there is apparently no wickedness in them. There seems to be an intense in-dwelling respectability in their dulness. If they lead to no intellectual result, even of the humblest kind, they may have, at least, this negative advantage, that they can do no moral harm. If it be objected that I am condemning these stories after having merely read one number of each of them, I have only to ask in return, whether anybody ever waits to go all through a novel before passing an opinion on the goodness or the badness of it? [...]

And this sort of writing appeals to a monster audience of at least three millions! The former proprietor of one of these penny journals commissioned a thoroughly competent person to translate The Count of Monte Christo, for his periodical.[40] He knew that there was hardly a language in the civilized world into which that consummate specimen of the rare and difficult art of story-telling had not been translated. In France, in England, in America, in Russia, in Germany, in Italy, in Spain, Alexandre Dumas had held hundreds of thousands of readers breathless. The proprietor of the penny journal naturally thought that he could do as much with the Unknown Public. Strange to say, the result of this apparently certain experiment was a failure. The circulation of the journal in question seriously decreased from the time when the first of living story-tellers became a contributor to it! The same experiment was tried with the Mysteries of Paris and The Wandering Jew, only to produce the same result.[41] Another penny journal gave Dumas a commission to write a new story, expressly for translation in its columns. The speculation was tried, and once again the inscrutable Unknown Public held back the hand of welcome from the spoilt child of a whole world of novel-readers.

How is this to be accounted for? Does a rigid moral sense permeate the Unknown Public from one end of it to the other, and did the productions of the French novelists shock that sense from the very outset? The page containing the Answers to Correspondents would be enough in itself to dispose of this theory. But there are other and better means of arriving at the truth, which render any further reference to the correspondents' page unnecessary. Some time since, an eminent novelist (the only living English author, with a literary position, who has, as yet, written for the Unknown Public) produced his new novel in a penny journal. No shadow of a moral objection has ever been urged by any readers against the works published by the author of It is Never Too Late to Mend; but even he, unless I have been greatly misinformed, failed to make the impression that had been anticipated on the impenetrable Three Millions. The great success of his novel was not obtained in its original serial form, but in its republished form, when it appealed from the Unknown to the Known Public. Clearly, the moral obstacle was not the obstacle which militated against the success of Alexandre Dumas and Eugène Sue.[42]

What was it, then? Plainly this, as I believe. The Unknown Public is, in a literary sense, hardly beginning, as yet, to learn to read. The members of it are evidently, in the mass, from no fault of theirs, still ignorant of almost everything which is generally known and understood among readers whom circumstances have placed, socially and intellectually, in the rank above them. The mere references in Monte Christo, The Mysteries of Paris, and White Lies (the scene of this last English fiction having been laid on French ground), to foreign names, titles, manners, and customs, puzzled the Unknown Public on the threshold. Look back at the answers to correspondents, and then say, out of fifty subscribers to a penny journal, how many are likely to know, for example, that Mademoiselle means Miss? Besides the difficulty in appealing to the penny audience caused at the beginning by such simple obstacles as this, there was the great additional difficulty, in the case of all three of the fictions just mentioned, of accustoming untried readers to the delicacies and subtleties of literary art. An immense public has been discovered: the next thing to be done is, in a literary sense, to teach that public how to read.

An attempt, to the credit of one of the penny journals, is already being made. I have mentioned, in one place, a reprint of a novel, and later, a remarkable exception to the drearily common-place character of the rest of the stories. In both these cases I refer to one and the same fiction—to the Kenilworth of Sir Walter Scott, which is now being reprinted as a serial attraction in a penny journal. Here is the great master of modern fiction appealing, at this time of day, to a new public, and (amazing anomaly!) marching in company with writers who have the rudiments of their craft still to learn! To my mind, one result seems certain. If Kenilworth be appreciated by the Unknown Public, then the very best men among living English writers will one of these days be called on, as a matter of necessity, to make their appearance in the pages of the penny journals.[43]

Meanwhile, it is perhaps hardly too much to say, that the future of English fiction may rest with this Unknown Public, which is now waiting to be taught the difference between a good book and a bad. It is probably a question of time only. The largest audience for periodical literature, in this age of periodicals, must obey the universal law of progress, and must, sooner or later, learn to discriminate. When that period comes, the readers who rank by millions, will be the readers who give the widest reputations, who return the richest rewards, and who will, therefore, command the service of the best writers of their time. A great, an unparalleled prospect awaits, perhaps, the coming generation of English novelists. To the penny journals of the present time belongs the credit of having discovered a new public. When that public shall discover its need of a great writer, the great writer will have such an audience as has never yet been known.

[Bennett G. Johns], 'The Poetry of Seven Dials', *Quarterly Review*, 122 (April 1867), 382-406

When this article came out, the *Quarterly* had just changed editor. Once a Tory organ, now it offered a more dialogic approach to politics—the Liberal Gladstone would soon publish a piece in it on the Reform Act, for instance. The immediate occasion of 'The Poetry of Seven Dials' was the extension of the franchise in 1867 which once again provoked anxiety about the politics of popular culture: Arnold's *Culture and Anarchy* (1869) is only the most famous of a large number of texts inspired by the reform and its attendant demonstrations. Johns (1820/1–1900), chaplain at the Blind School in London, was known for his publications on the education of the disadvantaged.

ANDREW FLETCHER of Saltoun once said 'he knew a wise friend who believed that if a man were permitted to make all the Ballads of a nation, he need not care who should make the laws.'[44] Ingenious M. Meusnier de Querlon, too, once seriously projected the writing of a history of his country by a chronological series of Songs and Ballads; and, beyond a doubt, honest Andrew's words contain a considerable amount of truth, however difficult his more airy Gallic neighbour might have found it to make his history a complete one.[45] [...]

There have been Ballads and Songs in every age of every civilized country, which gave utterance, not simply to the noble thoughts of some rapt minstrel or inspired bard, but to the deep and passionate longings, the undying patriotism, the heroic patience, the invincible courage, the sublime self-sacrifice, the rapture or the agony of a whole people; and it was this that lent immortal fire and music to the lips of the singer; though his verse may have lacked the martial splendour of a Macaulay, or the smooth and subtle strength of an Aytoun.[46] So far, therefore, we may well endorse the dictum of worthy Mr. Fletcher; and still be a long way from making Acts of Parliament out of Ballads. But there comes a time in the history of every highly-civilized people, amid all the golden fruits of Religion, Philosophy, Art, Poetry, Science, Discovery, and Wealth, with the baser results of

Luxury and Refinement, when the Nation no longer speaks as a whole. The classes that in a simpler age were more or less one, or bound together by the tie of common duties, needs, and pleasures, become selfish and distinct. Each begins to have its own heroes, poets, teachers, maxims and favourite rules; and then, amid the clash of conflicting creeds, the jargons of schools, the cries of hungry ambition, the lofty reasonings of the philosopher, the proud flights of science and of song, the insatiable cravings of increasing wealth, and the dreams of self-indulgence,—among the great, the mighty, the rich, and the prosperous,—the words of the lower and poorer classes pass unheeded and almost unknown beyond their own immediate circle.

And yet this very circle, narrow as it comparatively is, in the midst of a great country like England, and in the heart of the mightiest city in the world, has its own pet heroes, poets, and teachers, its own favourite maxims, sayings, and rules; and, above all, its own Literature; with which few but the multitude of ardent disciples have any real acquaintance. Of that Literature Mr. Catnach[47] and his successors, Disley and Fortey, are the High-priests; Seven Dials is the shrine;[48] while the question of authorship in the majority of cases is as great a mystery as that of the Homeric poems themselves. [...]

Catnach is still the presiding genius of all the neighbouring grimy streets, and the Literature, though somewhat fallen from its ancient glory, includes that wonderful domain of 'Halfpenny Ballads' to which we are now about to introduce our readers; forming, more or less, a separate class by themselves; distinct, as will be seen, in subject, style, and beauty. We have now before us a catalogue containing five or six hundred of these Ballads, and out of them, with considerable care—as choice flowers out of a dainty garden—about a hundred have been selected [...] No mere selection, indeed, can give a true idea of all their varied beauties, or even of the innumerable topics on which they touch; so lofty is the flight of genius, so various are the themes which poesy seizes on, ennobles, and makes her own for ever; but we have done what we could in the difficult task, and those ardent readers whose thirst shall still be unquenched must go themselves to the fountain head.

The Ballads may be roughly divided into about eight classes, 'Famous Men and Women', 'Historical', 'Modern Events', 'Religious', 'Miscellaneous', 'Murder', 'Political', 'The Royal Family'. The modes

THE
NAUGHTY LORD & THE GAY YOUNG LADY,
DAMAGES, £10,000.

There is a pretty piece of work,
　It is up in high life,
Upon my word an amorous lord,
　Seduced another man's wife;
She was a lady of title,
　She was charming, young, and fair,
With her daddy and her mammy once
　She lived in Belgrave Square.

The trial now is over,
　And his lordship, with a frown,
For kissing Lady Nelly
　Has to pay ten thousand pounds.

Lord G—— was a naughty lord,
　Oh! how could he engage,
To seduce young Lady Ellen,—
　He is sixty years of age.
The verdict of the jury
　Made his lordship quake and jump,
Ten thousand pounds he has to pay,
　For playing tiddly bump.

Lady Nelly left her husband,
　And would with his lordship be,
She would trim his lordship's whiskers
　As she sat upon his knee.

Some said oh, lack-a-daisy,
　She was in a comical way!
His lordship was bald-pated,
　And his hair and whiskers grey.

My lord was very fond of lamb,—
　The cook said so at least,—
And neighbours you must understand
　He liked the belly piece.
His lordship loved the lady,
　And the lady she loved he,
His lordship played by music,
　The tune called fiddle-de-dee.

His lordship when he heard the news,
　Caused his eyes to flash like fire then
He looked around, ten thousand pounds
　His lordship holloaed, "wire-em."
He sold his hat, he pawned his coat,
　To pay the browns, we find,
And then he run round Hyde Park sqre,
　With his shirt hanging out behind.

Sweet Ellen was a daughter
　Of my Lord and Lady C——
And once lived in a mansion,
　Yes she did in Belgrave Square,

Sweet Ellen had an husbund,
　An honest upright man,
And his lordship went a trespassing
　Upon her husband's land.

My lord was fond of sporting,
　And hunting of the hare,
He has to pay ten thousand pounds,
　The damage to repair;
His lordship played the fiddle,
　Down in Scotia's land, 'tis said,
And his lordship must have fiddled well
　Both in and out of bed.

Now all young lords take warning,
　When a hunting you do go,
In the evening or the morning
　Pray beware of "Tally-ho!"
If you are caught a trespassing
　On other people's ground,
Perhaps you'll be like old Lord G—
　Made to pay ten thousand pounds.

The lady's injured husband,
　Has nobly gained the day,
And beat old Mr December,
　Who seduced young Lady May.

H. Disley, Printer, 57, High Street, St. Giles, London.

FIG. 6. 'The Naughty Lord and The Gay Young Lady' (*c*.1840), *Curiosities of Street Literature* (London: Reeves and Turner, 1871), 134.

of treatments are so curious, the metres employed so lawless, the beauties and the blots so many and so unexpected, that the difficulty is where to begin and what to select. The critic is fairly distracted by the infinite variety that besets and captivates him. The only way, there-fore, in such a garden of roses, is to begin boldly, pluck the first flower that comes to hand, and arrange the bouquet as we best may. We turn, therefore, to 'Famous Men and Women,' and light at once on the fair name of Florence Nightingale, as 'The Nightingale in the East.' It's a far stretch from 'Seven Dials' to the Crimea, but the poet, nothing daunted by the greatness of his subject, thus plunges *in medias res*,-[49]

> 'On a dark and lonely night on the Crimea's dread shore
> There had been bloodshed and strife on the morning before,
> The dead and the dying lay bleeding around,
> Some crying for help—there's none to be found;
> Now God in his mercy he pitied their cries,
> And the soldier so cheerful in the morning do rise;
> So forward, my lads, may your hearts never fail,
> You're cheered by the presence of a sweet Nightingale.'[50]

There is a fine abruptness in the three opening lines, but in spite of the rough music of the second, the whole picture is at once before the reader's eye; and in the midst of dead and dying heroes, some silent for ever, and some crying madly for help in their last agony, is the poet's fit occasion for obeying the great canon of 'Nec deus intersit, &c.,'[51] and making a bold dash for the heroine in the closing line. [...] Yet, in utter defiance of this horrible scene of carnage and confusion, the grim woodcut at the head of the Ballad represents our fair countrywoman as seated cosily by the side of a downy four-post bed, and handing a basin of Hot Gruel (with Brandy in it beyond all doubt) to a stalwart but 'dismantled' Dragoon, propped up with pillows and looking the very picture of easy comfort. [...]

Under our second heading of 'Historical,' we have a dozen or two ballads, the titles of which sufficiently indicate their several subjects. [...] For example, 'The Battle of Boulogne' thus opens:

> 'On the second of August, eighteen hundred and one,
> We sailed with Lord Nelson the port of Boulogne,
> For to cut out their shipping which was all in vain,
> But to our misfortune they were all moored and chained,

and after crawling heavily through six or seven like stanzas, winds up with a single verse, which reveals in the most bare-faced way the drift of the whole poem, viz., to draw money from an admiring crowd for the benefit of the six 'dismantled' mariners who on a Saturday evening may be found in the New Cut or Leather Lane, each without arms or without legs [...]

But these impostors are well known in the profession as belonging to the thieves' kitchen; and we are bound to add that, throughout the whole range of ballads, there is scarcely another trace to be found of the Muse's degradation to the baser purposes of mendicity. [...]

Our next section of 'Modern Events' is characterised throughout by such a general sameness of treatment as to need few examples by way of illustration. They are clearly written, for the most part, hastily, on the spur of the moment; and though they may command a good sale at first, they do so not by the wit, beauty, or aptness of the verse, but by the absorbing interest of the calamity which it describes. Thus, say, an appalling accident happens in London; the news spreads like wildfire throughout the city, and gives rise to rumours, even more dreadful than the reality. Before night it is embalmed in verse by one out of five or six well-known bards who get their living by writing for Seven Dials, and then chanting their own strains to the people. The inspiration of the poet is swift, the execution of the work rapid,[52] but the pay is small. 'I gets a shilling a copy for my verses' (says one) 'besides what I can make by selling 'em.' But the verses are ready and go to press at once. A thousand or two copies are struck off instantly, and the 'Orfle Calamity' is soon flying all over London from the mouths of a dozen or twenty minstrels, in the New Cut, in Leather Lane, Houndsditch, Bermondsey, Whitechapel, High Street, Totten-ham-court-road—or wherever a crowd of listeners can be easily and safely called together. If the subject admits of it, two minstrels chant the same strain,

> 'In lofty verse
> Pathetic they alternately rehearse,'[53]

each taking a line in turn, and each vying with the other in doleful tragedy of look and voice. A moment suffices to give out in sepulchral accents, 'Dreadful Accident this day on the Ice in Regent's Park,' and then the dirge begins—

'You feeling Christians, both high and low
O listen to this sad tale of woe;
On that fatal Tuesday boys and men so brave
In the Regent's Park met a watery grave.
Their cries were dreadful—see the parent's wild,
O God of Heaven in mercy save my child!
For the ice gave way, the people lined the shore
Upwards of fifty sank to rise no more
   (*Then in full chorus from both voices*)
In Regent's Park, O hear those dreadful cries,
They sank that Tuesday never more to rise.'[54]

The dismal horror attending on a dozen such verses shouted out *con spirito* in the midst of a busy thoroughfare, spreads rapidly, and the crowd thickens as they stand aghast, all intently listening, and all eager to buy [...]

Such a ballad is sure to be popular, and unless the weather is unusually cold or wet, a couple of active singers will dispose of twenty or thirty dozen copies in a single day. And in this way an edition of 5000 or 10,000 soon runs off, to the extreme advantage of Mr. Catnach, if not to the immortality of the poet. [...]

We pass on, therefore, to the next division of our subject, the 'Religious Ballads;' and here we come upon an entirely new stratum, and with one step dash headlong into the raging waters of religious controversy between the Protestant and Romish Churches. With the exception of a single sheet, which contains 'Patient Job,' and 'The Hymn of May,' all the Ballads are clearly the work of a red-hot Irish Papist, armed with all the resources of an unscrupulous tongue [...] for the express edification of the lower orders of Irish Papists, who yet haunt the grimiest dens and courts of Whitechapel, St. Giles's, and the New Cut. [...]

[W]e must be content to pass on to our next section of 'Miscellaneous' Ballads, of which, however, we almost despair of giving our readers any adequate notion by mere extracts. We wander from grave to gay, from lively to severe, from boisterous fun to faint satire, to touches of mild sentiment and mysterious bathos, until we fancy that all the blazing metaphors and fiery denunciations of the 'Protestant Drum' school must be an entire myth. Yet they issue from the same press, and find a sale among the same appreciating admirers. [...]

It is fairly entrancing to hear of a maiden whose cheeks were roses, eyes serene, distilling balmy dew, 'fairer than Pandora, or Venus, Juno, Dido, or Diaphy,'[55] the centre of graces, 'the godess [sic] of harmony;' [...]

From the domain of sentiment, beauty, and romance, we now pass to the ghastly regions of crime, especially that of 'Murder,' which no less a critic and philosopher than Thomas De Quincey has treated as 'one of the Fine Arts,' and made the subject of one of his most brilliant Essays, but which here comes before us in all its naked deformity; in spite of some considerable variety in the mode of treatment.[56] Of these 'Dying Speeches and Confessions' we have thirteen before us, stretching from the famous murder of Maria Martin by W. Corder in the Red Barn (1825) down to J. R. Jeffery's murder of his little boy in October, 1866.[57] Many of these are clearly by the same hand, probably one of the five or six well-known authors, who also chant their own verses in the streets. 'I gets', says one of the fraternity, 'I gets a shilling a copy for the verses *written by the wretched culprit* the night previous to the execution.'[58] 'And I,' says another, 'did the helegy on Rush. I didn't write it to horder; I knew that they would want a copy of verses from the wretched culprit.[59] And when the publisher (Mr. Catnach) read it; 'that's the thing for the streets,' he says. But I only got a shilling for it.' 'It's the same poet that does 'em all,' says a third authority, 'and the same tip; *no more nor a bob for nothing.*' This was paltry pay under any circumstances, but still more so when we find from Mr. Mayhew that in the case of the chief modern murders these 'Execution Ballads' commanded a most enormous sale; thus,

Of Rush's murder.. .. .. 2,500,000 copies.
Of the Mannings .. .. 2,500,000 ,,
Of Courvoisier .. .. 1,666,000 ,,
Of Greenacre .. .. 1,666,000 ,,
Of Corder (Maria Martin) 166,000   ,,[60]

So that Catnach must have reaped a golden harvest for many a long day, even if sold to the street patterers or singers at the low rate of 3*d.* a dozen.

The 'Dying Speech and Confession Ballad,' strictly so called, is said to have been unknown in the trade until the year 1820,[61] when a change in the law prolonged the term of existence between the trial and death of the criminal. 'Before that,' says a street patterer,[62] 'there wasn't no time for lamentation; sentence to-day, scragging to-morrow, or, leastways, Friday to Monday.' And with regard to this matter of *time*, it must also be noted that many of the most popular Ballads being composed on the spur of the moment for the purpose of being sung while all London is ringing with the event, all niceties of rhyme, metre, and orthography have to be utterly disregarded.

As far as can be ascertained, the sale of Ballads in Rush's case far exceeded that of any now before us. Even that of Müller did not amount to more than forty or fifty thousand copies—though no modern murder ever surpassed it in atrocity, or in the profound interest which it excited throughout England.[63] And this difference is no doubt to be explained by the fact that since Rush's day the daily penny newspapers have almost forestalled the Halfpenny Ballads by giving a full account of the different enormities in all their minute and hideous details. The force of public opinion, too, thus exerted through the Press, has been brought to bear on the question of crime, and much of the morbid sympathy which found expression in the case of such a monster as Rush, had died away in 1864, when detectives tracked Müller across the Atlantic, and brought him back to be hanged by an English hangman, in the presence of an English mob. To every one of the murderers [...] stern justice is meted out with inflexible severity. [...]

'The Political Ballads' are ten in number, of which seven are devoted to the special subject of Reform, the ridicule of 'Johnny Russell,' and the express glorification of 'Gladstone, Beales, Bright, and Co.'[64] The remaining three are 'John Bull and the Taxes,' 'Stop the Beer on Sunday,' and a 'Political Litany on the present Session of Parliament,' amusing enough in their way, but of which a verse or two will amply suffice as specimens. [...]

The 'Political Litany' differs from all our other ballads in being entirely in prose, and for the most part is rather a bitter satire on the noble Earl Russell (then Prime Minister, February, 1866), whom the poet irreverently addresses as 'O dearly bought and never to be forgotten, Johnny,' while he is equally severe on Johnny's coadjutors in office, as a single sentence will prove:—

When the *Whigs*[65] shall cease to be a milk and water set, and prove to the people of England that like good and trusty servants, they will stick up for their rights, and pass such measures as will be for the benefit of the nation at large; then and not till then shall we consider them as trumps, and look upon them with confidence.' [...]

As for the question of Reform itself, it's a mere *cry* and nothing more. His interrogators insult the little statesman by hoping that 'Reform will so apply to railways that they shall supply a sufficient number of surgeons with splints and bandages to each train, with a good supply of coffins for those who are headstrong enough to travel by rail.' As to the processions, and grand 'Agricultural Hall meetings,' they are '*vox et præterea nihil*,'[66]—

> 'Many they aloud will shout,
> For Reform, Reform,
> *Scarcely knowing what about*
> Bawl Reform, Reform.'

Such was the state of things only a few months ago; but alas for the fickleness of the crowd, the intelligent artisan, and the 'working man,' by the time we get to the date of 'The Reform Battle in Hyde Park' all is changed.[67] The noble Earl and all his Whiggish allies are for a time clean wiped out and forgotten, and the poet now reserves all his vials of wrath for

> 'The titled tories who keep you down
> Which you cannot endure,
> And the reason I to tell am bound
> You're but working men—and poor.'

There are some ten other stanzas of a like calibre, but though Mr. Catnach has enriched them with a most graphic woodcut (*date* 1832) representing one Bishop, the Duke of Wellington, and Sir Robert Peel, headed by 'little Johnny' carrying a banner of 'Victoria and Reform,' all issuing in triumph from 'St. Stephen's School', the whole thing is a mere piece of idle banter, which never rises above the level of a noisy chorus between people and bobbies, roughs and iron railings. [...]

The Royal Ballads are but three in number,—on the death of the Prince Consort, the marriage of the Prince of Wales, and the birth of his eldest son,—and of these we may take, as a sample, the 'Elegy on the Death of H.R.H. Prince Albert,' surmounted by a portrait of the 'Prince as he appeared on the morning of his Marriage,' and edged with a broad margin of black. The poet is lost in grief, and his mournful numbers flow heavily as he tells of 'Britannia lamenting and calling on the daughters of Britain to join in sorrowful condolence with their beloved Queen:

> 'We grieve for thy loss, Queen Victoria
> And all over Britain deplore
> Thy Consort, thy own dearest Consort
> Is gone, and thy Albert's no more.' [...]

This may be very homely sympathy, but it is respectful and hearty. The poet hardly dares to intrude on the privacy of the Royal mourners, but with kindly hand touches on the many virtues of the departed Prince [...]

These Halfpenny Sheets form almost the entire poetry of Seven Dials, and though they teach little or no history, they show, at least, what kind of Poetry finds the most favourable reception and the readiest sale among our lowest classes. As far as we can ascertain, there are in London eight or ten publishers of the Fortey and Disley stamp—though not on so large a scale. Of Ballad-singers and patterers of prose recitations (such as the 'Political Catechism') there may be about a hundred scattered over the metropolis, who haunt such localities as the New Cut, Tottenham Court Road, Whitechapel, and Clerkenwell Green; and according to the weather, the state of trade, and the character of their wares, earn a scanty or a jovial living by chanting such strains as we have now laid before our readers. 'Songs if they're over-religious,' says one minstrel, 'don't sell at all; though a tidy moral does werry well. But a good, awful murder's the thing. I've knowed,' says our authority, 'a man sell a ream a day of *them*,[68]—that's twenty dozen you know;' and this sale may go on for days, so that, with forty or fifty men at work as minstrels, a popular Ballad will soon attain a circulation of thirty or forty or fifty thousand. Now and then 'Catnach' himself composes a Song, and in this case is saved the cost of copyright, though his expenses are very trifling, even when he has to purchase it. If one of the patterers writes a ballad on a taking subject, he hastens at once to Seven Dials, where, if accepted,

his reward is 'a glass of rum, a slice of cake, and five dozen copies,'—
which, if the accident or murder be a very awful one, are struck off for
him while he waits. A murder always sells well, so does a fire, or a
fearful railway accident. A good love story embracing

'infidi perjuria nautae
Deceptamque dolo nympham'[69]

often does fairly; but Politics among the lowest class are a drug. Even
the famous *'Ballad on Pam's death didn't do much* except among the
better sort of people;' and though the roughs are fond enough of
shouting *Reform*, they don't care, it would seem, to spend money on
it.[70]

We have submitted this wretched doggrel to our readers, that they
may form some idea of the kind of Street Literature which is still
popular with so many of the lower classes. It is humiliating, in the
midst of all the schools and teaching of the present day, to find such
rubbish continually poured forth, and eagerly read. Still there are
some redeeming features in this weary waste. *Taken as a whole*, the
moral tone of the ballads, if not lofty, is certainly not bad; and the
number of single stanzas that could not be quoted in these pages on
account of their gross or indecent language is very small; while that of
entire Ballads, to be excluded on the same ground, is still smaller.

Compared with a volume of the famous 'Roxburghe Ballads,'
which range between the years 1560 and 1700, our present five
hundred from Seven Dials are models of purity and cleanliness.
[...] For open indecency and grosser pruriency we must go to a
class of songs and song-books, authors and customers, of a higher
class; to penny and twopenny and sixpenny packets of uncleaness, to
some of the minor Music Halls, where delicacies are to be had at a
price beyond the reach of the New Cut. The men who wrote the filthy
Ballads in the Roxburghe Collection were of a far higher class then
those who write for Seven Dials; and they found higher readers amid
the wide-spread deep depravity of their day. [...] But there are yet in
the minds and hearts of the poorest class, who can read and enjoy a
Halfpenny Ballad on the 'Awful Accident in Hyde Park,' deeper
feelings, and purer tastes ready to spring up under the least culture,
and, if fairly appealed to, to be brought out into full life and bear
abundant and goodly fruit. They have no particular relish for bad

spelling, or for faulty rhyme. Feeling and intelligence, a sense of such inborn goodness as Miss Nightingale's; a love of fair play, and an old-fashioned liking for what is true and brave; a keen sense of the ludicrous, and a deep current of loyalty to the throne and to their native land, yet linger in the thousands who look to Seven Dials for inspiration. If any real poet should arise who would be content to sing in good, plain, honest Saxon, such topics as they love to hear; of men and women great in goodness or in vice, of life and death in their widest sense, of crime and disaster, of human sorrows and joys whether in Chick Lane or in Windsor Castle; he would achieve an immortality not far below that of the 'silver clarion' of Tennyson himself. We do not despair of his advent, and the sooner he comes the better for Seven Dials; and for us all.

NOTES TO SECTION V

1. Scott Bennett, 'Revolutions in Thought: Serial Publication and the Mass Market for Reading', in Joanne Shattock and Michael Woolf (eds.), *The Victorian Periodical Press: Samplings and Soundings* (Leicester: Leicester University Press, 1982), 225-57.

2. See Margaret Dalziel, *Popular Fiction 100 Years Ago: An Unexplored Tract of Literary History* (London : Cohen & West, 1957).

3. There is a vast amount of work on Hollywood genre: see, for instance, Steve Neale, *Genre and Hollywood* (London: Routledge, 2000).

4. Richard Altick, *The English Common Reader: A Social History of the Mass Reading Public, 1800–1900* (1957; Columbus, Oh.: Ohio University Press, 1998), 92.

5. Simon Eliot, *Some Patterns and Trends in British Publishing* 41. See also Besant in Section IV.

6. See e.g. Thomas Wright, 'Concerning the Unknown Public', *Nineteenth Century*, 13 (February 1883), 279-96.

7. Cf. *Macbeth*, IV. I.

8. Horace Walpole (1717-97), author of what is generally considered the first Gothic romance, *The Castle of Otranto* (1765). George Robins was the auctioneer at the sale of Walpole's collection in 1842.

9. The Polytechnic Institution at 39 Regent's Street, London, opened in 1838. One of its main attractions was a diving bell in which visitors could descend to the bottom of a glass tank.

10. Radcliffe had received the unheard of sum of £500 from her publishers G. & J. Robinson for her Gothic novel *The Mysteries of Udolpho* (1794), a sum well justified in view of its phenomenal sales.

11. Tobias Smollett (1721–71), novelist, poet, historian, editor, here mentioned for his picaresque novels such as *The Adventures of Roderick Random* (1747); Henry Fielding (1707–54), most famous for the picaresque novels *Joseph Andrews* (1842) and *Tom Jones* (1849).

12. Jane Porter (1776–1850), prolific writer of novels in various genres; Fanny Burney (1752–1840) and Maria Edgeworth (1767–1849) were novelists much admired by Jane Austen; Matthew Lewis (1775–1818) was notorious for his scandalous Gothic novel *The Monk* (1796).

13. Newgate was a prison in London: Newgate Calendars were records of crimes, published irregularly 1773–1826.

14. *Original note*: Logic:—John James is dead. A donkey is dead. Ergo, John James is a donkey. We offer this, with humility, to the Private Teacher's Asylum in Gower Street [i.e. University College London. Professors derived their income from fees paid by students—Eds.].

15. George Walker, author of Gothic novels such as *The Haunted Castle: A Norman Romance* (1794), *Theodore Cyphon, or, The Benevolent Jew* (1796), *Don Raphael: A Romance* (1803). Samuel Richardson (1689–1761) printer and author of *Pamela* (1740–41), *Clarissa* (1747–48); Henry Mackenzie (1745–1831), author of *The Man of Feeling* (1771). Our thanks to Eileen Curran for explaining the identity of Walker.

16. Rymer was soon to publish *The Black Monk; or, the Secret of the Grey Turret. A Romance* (Lloyd, 1844), followed by *Varney the Vampyre; or, the Feast of Blood. A Romance* (Lloyd, 1845–7) and many other serials of similar title.

17. *Harlequin and the Giant Helmet; or, The Castle of Otranto* was the recent Christmas pantomime at Covent Garden, opening on 26 December 1840.

18. *The Midnight Blast* is unidentified (probably an invented title); *Sir Charles Grandison* (1753–4) by Samuel Richardson attempts to delineate the perfect man of honour in its eponymous hero.

19. Bury Street is near the aristocratic St James's Square and Pall Mall.

20. *Original note*: A lady of our acquaintance unhesitatingly purchases a book, if it possesses what she calls 'respectable and interesting covers'. The covers, paper, and printing, she calls 'the amenities of literature'. [The Minerva Press, founded by William Lane in 1790, was both printer and circulating library, specializing in material aimed at young ladies.—Eds.]

21. The German philosopher Immanuel Kant (1724–1804) is generally considered the initiator of transcendentalism, which is concerned with discovering the conditions that make possible our perceptions of the world. Rymer is here linking the novelist Edward Bulwer (-Lytton) (1803–73) to writers such as Coleridge and Carlyle who were influenced by Kant. Harrison Ainsworth (1805–82) was best known for his Newgate novels (see above, pp. 38–9).

22. Swain (1801–74) was the *London Journal*'s most commonly printed poet at this period.

23. See Sections I and IV above, especially Brougham and Knight.

24. *Guy Mannering* (1815), historical novel by Walter Scott; *Novum Organum* (1620), philosophical treatise in Latin by Francis Bacon.

25. High society.

26. Archimago is an evil enchanter who battles St. George in Spenser's *Faerie Queene* (1552–99).

27. Dickens had started giving his public readings only a few months previously, in April 1858.

28. Untrue. American women novelists had sold very well in Britain since at least 1851 and Harriet Beecher Stowe's *Uncle Tom's Cabin*, though these were not entirely 'mild' or 'domestic'.

29. *Alton Locke* (1850), novel by Charles Kingsley about an artisan hero who becomes a Chartist (see Cooper in Section II); *Mary Barton* (1848), novel by Elizabeth Gaskell about working-class life in Manchester. On the other characters, see later in this extract.

30. The anonymous serial is called *Hope Evermore; or, Something to Do. A Tale of the Ragged Schools*, serialized in *Cassell's Illustrated Family Paper* (1858). Despite Oliphant's claims to the contrary, most of this novel is devoted to scenes amongst the poor and includes sordid, moralistic portraits of alcoholics (Cassell promoted teetotalism). Oliphant quotes from the episode of 26 June 1858 (NS 2: 59).

31. For more on Smith, see Andrew King, *The London Journal 1845–83: Periodicals, Production and Gender* (Aldershot: Ashgate, 2004).

32. John Edwin Mayall (1810–1901) was a photographer of royalty and celebrities. Smith's portrait, taken from a photograph of Mayall, appeared on the front page of *Cassell's Illustrated Family Paper*, dated 22 May 1858.

33. *Original note*: It may be as well to explain that I use this awkward compound word in order to mark the distinction between a penny journal and a penny newspaper. The 'journal' is what I am now writing about. The 'newspaper' is an entirely different subject, with which this article has no connection.

34. The first must refer to the *Family Herald* although it was not illus-
    trated: an early indication of Collins's lack of accuracy. The 'infant'
    almost certainly refers to *The Guide to Literature, Science, Art and
    General Information* (1858–9, NS 1861–7), founded by Stiff as a rival to
    Lemon's *London Journal*. It was based on the same formula as the
    London Journal under Stiff and was accordingly successful. Stiff
    combined it with the *Journal* when he bought the latter.

35. Lemon's *Journal* claimed a circulation of half a million in adverts, but
    the figure is inaccurate: the other four had higher circulations.

36. Lemon severely curtailed such correspondence and was much
    sterner and contemptuous in his replies than had been usual in the
    Journal. Collins's ridicule is another justification of Lemon's
    practices.

37. i.e. recipe.

38. All of the leading illustrated journals made use of specially commis-
    sioned wood-blocks and only occasionally recycled prints.

39. Untrue. The best-selling serials were also made available in volume
    form, some still being reprinted as late as the 1930s.

40. Alexandre Dumas, *The Count of Monte Christo* [*sic*] (1844–5), trans-
    lated by John Taylor Sinnett in the *Journal* (1846–7), when it was
    owned by Stiff. Collins's account of a supposed decrease is false,
    designed to justify Lemon's decision to turn the *Journal* into a purely
    'English' periodical.

41. Eugène Sue's *The Mysteries of Paris* (1842–3) and *The Wandering Jew*
    (1844–5). Sue (1804–57) was probably the best-selling author of the
    1840s, famous for his newspaper novels that came out in daily instal-
    ments (*feuilletons*). There were numerous translations in many lan-
    guages. The *Journal* had very successfully serialized his *Martin the
    Foundling* (1846–7) and *The Seven Cardinal Sins* (1847–8).

42. Charles Reade's *It is Never too Late to Mend* (1857) was the cause of his
    employment as a serialist for the *London Journal*. After *Cassell's* had
    poached J. F. Smith, Stiff commissioned Reade, another of the Dick-
    ens–Collins–Lemon circle, to write a serial, *White Lies*. *White Lies*
    proved such a disaster that it provoked Stiff's sale of the *Journal* to
    Bradbury and Evans.

43. Lemon extensively advertised his serialization of Walter Scott novels,
    including *Kenilworth*. They proved a flop.

44. *Original note*: These well-known words have been variously attrib-
    uted to men as different and as wide apart in every respect as Robert
    Burns and William Cobbett. But there is no doubt they belong to
    Honest Andrew. Vide 'Political Works,' 266; and Whately's 'Bacon',

p. 175. Fletcher died in 1716. [Fletcher was a Scottish landowner, politician and writer.—Eds.]

45. Anne-Gabriel Meusnier de Querlon (1702–80), usually noted for his libertine writings.

46. William Aytoun (1813–65), poet and critic, best known for his *Book of Ballads* (1855) under the pseudonym Bon Gaultier, for an edition of *Ballads of Scotland* (1858), and for his parody of spasmodic poetry which gave it its name (*Firmilian, or the Student of Badajoz; a Spasmodic Tragedy by T. Percy Jones*, 1854).

47. *Original note*: The most elaborate production of '*Jemmy Catnatch*', as he was popularly called, was 'An Attempt to Exhibit the Leading Events in the Queen's Life, in Cuts and Verse,' price 2d; printed on a folio sheet adorned with 12 cuts, interspersed with verses of descriptive poetry, and bearing date Dec. 10, 1821. Catnatch was then at the height of his fame as a printer of ballads in Monmouth-court, Seven Dials, where he spent a hardworking, busy life, and died in 1840, ætat. 49, having amassed a fortune of 10,000*l*. [...]

48. Henry Disley operated *c*.1835–55 and was based at 16 Arthur Street, London; William Fortey took over the stock and premises of Catnach and operated *c*.1840–80. Seven Dials is so named because seven roads meet there and because originally there was a sundial with seven faces in the centre. By the late eighteenth century it was already notorious as a meeting place for ne'er-do-wells.

49. Horace, *Ars Poetica*, 148, referring to how Homer begins his epics in the middle of the action.

50. *Original note*: In every extract from these ballads care has been taken to quote most exactly, *verbatim, literatim*—and if it were lawful to say so—*punctuatim*.

51. Horace, *Ars Poetica*, 191. The quotation refers to Horace's discouragement of divine intervention in tragedy unless the subject matter is worthy of it.

52. *Original note*: How rapid may be judged from the following fact. On Thursday, Feb. 21, a woman named Walker was brought before the magistrate and charged with robbing Mr. F. Brown, her master, a publican, to whom she had offered her services as a *man*. She was sent to prison, and there her sex was discovered. The next morning, at 10 a.m., two men and two women were singing her personal history and adventures in the New Cut, to a large but not select audience, under the title of 'The She Barman of Southwark.' It was great trash, but sold well.

53. *Original note*: C. Lamb's translation of V. Bourne. [Charles Lamb was a great admirer of the Latin and Greek poetry of Vincent Bourne

(1695–1747), a schoolmaster at Westminster. Bourne's *Poemata* (1734) was several times reprinted. Lamb made translations of nine of Bourne's poems. – Eds.]

54. The accidents occurred on 14 January 1867. There were actually no fatalities, as a section of the poem not here quoted eventually reveals.

55. *Original note*: Daphne?

56. [Thomas De Quincey], 'Murder Considered as One of the Fine Arts', *Blackwood's Edinburgh Magazine*, 26 (1826), 199–213.

57. William Corder murdered his pregnant love Maria Martin in 1827. John Jeffery was publicly hanged in October 1866 for the brutal murder of his son whom he believed not to be his. Both cases were famous for their confessions.

58. *Original note*: Mayhew's 'London Poor,' vol. iii.

59. In 1848 James Bloomfield Rush murdered Isaac Jermy and his son at Stanfield Hall, Norfolk.

60. *Original note*: See Mayhew, vol. i. 284.

61. *Original note*: The street singers say so, but in the 'Roxburghe Ballads' there are many professing to be written by criminals. [*A Book of Roxburghe Ballads*, edited by J. P. Collier, had been published by Longmans in 1847. They date from the sixteenth century and are actually much tamer than Johns later makes out. – Eds.]

62. *Original note*: Mayhew's 'London Poor.'

63. Franz Müller, found guilty of having robbed and beaten to death a banker, was executed in November 1864.

64. Earl John Russell (1792–1878), Whig politician whose efforts helped pass the 1832 Reform Bill. Prime Minister for a second time from October 1865, he resigned office in June 1866 after failing to get parliament further to extend the franchise; Edmond Beales [*sic*] (1803–81) was President of the Reform League and a key figure in the vast demonstration in Hyde Park on 23 July 1866 calling for male suffrage; John Bright (1811–88), MP for Birmingham 1857–85 and one of the leading political representatives of manufacturing classes, supported Gladstone's attempted Reform Bill in 1866.

65. *Original note*: In a very recent edition of this ballad, the word *Whigs* is amusingly converted into Tories, so as to apply to the present Government.

66. 'A voice and nothing more', i.e. all talk and no action.

67. In July 1866 the Reform League organized a meeting in Hyde Park which was banned by the Metropolitan police. Large crowds gathered outside the park nevertheless and, after scuffles with police, they broke some railings and masonry in their attempt to enter.

68. *Original note*: A ream costs him 3*s*. in Seven Dials, and these he retails at a halfpenny each, or even a penny, if the murder is a very fearful one, as in Müller's case, thus reaping a harvest of 250 or 300 per cent.

69. *Original note*: V. Bourne. 'Poemata'. [The translation reads 'the perjury of an unfaithful sailor and a nymph deceived by a trick'.— Eds.]

70. Lord Palmerston ('Pam'), prominent Tory and twice Prime Minister, died in October 1865.

VI

READING SPACES

INTRODUCTION

Victorian reading spaces suggest a variety of reading practices while simultaneously regulating access to different print media. As Roger Chartier has argued, 'reading is not already inscribed into a text'; rather, modes of reading are constituted by the spaces, gestures, and habits that govern the way communities of readers interact with texts.[1] The articles in this section correspondingly suggest that where and how reading was undertaken affected the meanings generated. Previous sections have shown that many arguments concerning print media had their roots in the belief that the reading of texts influenced subjectivity, especially an individual's class and/or gender identity. Such articles on the influence of print media are often premised on a model of reading where the text is transmitted directly from page to mind: the act of reading itself is dematerialized. In contrast, this section covers a variety of actual reading situations, from coffee-houses to mechanics' institutes.

The increase in the variety of reading spaces obviously played an important role in the growth of the reading public. Reading spaces that allowed for the sharing of texts were a principal means of gaining access to a wide range of books and periodicals the combined cost of which would have been too expensive for an individual. Texts were most evidently shared through the development of libraries, schools, and coffee-houses. Until at least mid-century, the rental of newspapers was also a common phenomenon in public houses. Several articles in this section demonstrate that texts were also shared through acts of collective reading, whether in school or around the family hearth.

Although public libraries and mechanics' institutes sought to encourage reading, much of the motivation for their development stemmed from the utilitarian belief in the improving value of literature. Mechanics' institutes were first set up to provide technical education to artisans in the 1820s; however, as William Newmarch's article describes, they soon metamorphosed into more genteel, all-purpose cultural institutions. Newmarch's article and the extract from the 1849 parliamentary select committee report on public libraries together exemplify the tension caused by the various top–down efforts to encourage reading. Attempts to attract working-class readers frequently conflicted with the desire to control the reading matter available. The admission of newspapers into the libraries of some mechanics' institutes was frowned on because of their political matter, while fiction was felt to be too diverting and not improving enough.

Before the establishment of large numbers of public libraries in the late 1880s and 1890s, circulating libraries constituted one of the principal spaces where readers could gain access to new publications. Circulating libraries became large, commercial operations in the 1840s and 1850s, and at the forefront of their development was Mudie's Select Library. Andrew Wynter's article focuses upon the way that Mudie's improved both the volume and the range of texts available to metropolitan and provincial readers. The power of circulating libraries was double-edged, though, for their large purchases of new novels meant that they could also regulate what was published and, ultimately, what was then read. Mudie's in particular was attacked for the way it restricted the price and morality of novels. In an 1885 pamphlet, *Literature at Nurse, or Circulating Morals*, George Moore famously labelled Mudie's as the 'British Matron' after it had refused to stock his novel *A Modern Lover*. Mudie reputedly wrote to Moore and told him that 'two ladies in the country had written to him to say that they disapproved of the book, and on that account he would not circulate it.'[2] Wynter's article should thus be read in conjunction with Walter Besant's attack on Mudie's role in sustaining the three-volume novel (see Section IV).

Reading was influenced by the physical nature of the reading space as much as by any regulation of the texts available. The article from *All the Year Round* notes that some working-class readers were discomforted by the enforced silence of the new public libraries. The articles by John Naule Allen, Henry Mayhew, and Sarah Stickney Ellis similarly stress the phenomenology of the reading process. Mayhew and Stickney Ellis typify the prevalence of aural and oral reading, albeit within very different contexts. In both, reading involves the physicality of a speaker reading a text aloud and, correspondingly, the process of interpreting texts through hearing them aloud. Oral reading offered a way of transmitting texts to those unable to read, and a different mode of reception. The London costermongers' boisterous, debated interpretations are the antithesis of the silent reading of the public library.

Stickney Ellis presents a very different model of oral reading. Her promotion of the practice of reading aloud within the home is one example of the ideological value placed on the figure of the woman reader. As Kate Flint has argued, domestic collective reading was believed to 'necessarily check the dangerous delights of *solitary* reading; was believed to aid family unity, and—as many autobiographies testified was indeed the case—served to initiate children to valued works of literature.'[3] One of the touchstones used to judge the morality of a text was whether it was suitable to be read together by a family, and this guideline is reflected in periodical titles such as *Household Words*, *Cassell's Illustrated Family Journal*, the *Family Herald*, *Sunday at Home* (1854–1940), and many others.

The different attempts to promote the habit of reading emphasize the way reading spaces were set up to wean the poor away from traditional forms of recreation, especially the public house. Conversely, the articles by Angus Reach and John Naule Allen, on coffee-houses and railway reading respectively, demonstrate that the reading habit spread through being integrated into the development of new forms of leisure and amusement. Reach, for example, argues that the number of coffee-houses expanded rapidly in the 1830s and 1840s because of their provision of cheap reading matter and cheap coffee in equal measure.

FURTHER READING:

Altick, *English Common Reader*; Brantlinger; Finkelstein and McCleery; Flint; Griest; Jordan and Patten; Keating; Kelly; King, 'Paradigm', King and Plunkett; Rose; St. Clair; Vincent, *Literacy*.

[William Newmarch], 'Mechanics Institutions', *Westminster Review*, 41 (June 1844), 416–45 [417–19, 433–6]

Under the editorship of William Edward Hickson between 1840 and 1851, the *Westminster* became notable for its commitment to legislative reform and popular education. Newmarch (1820–82), who would subsequently become a prominent economist and statistician, wrote this essay while working as a banker in Wakefield. His article is an intervention in a debate between Utilitarians over whether mechanics' institutes should provide instruction or amusement, and hence over what reading matter they should contain.

Our design in this paper is not to write a formal essay on the desirableness and necessity of popular education, and on the adaptation of societies formed on the principle of mechanics institutions materially to promote it. Into such general arguments it is not our intention at present to enter. Our object is altogether *practical*. We desire to assist mechanics institutions by bringing together such facts, and offering such suggestions, as are likely to be of service in the ordinary course of their management. We also desire to present a clear and correct outline of their progress to the present time, and of their actual condition, for the information of those persons who have paid little or no attention to the subject. We are the more inclined to this plain course, because we fear that there is too great a disposition in public writers to discharge their duty to the great question of the education of the people by the repetition of trite and commonplace reasons in its favour, to the neglect of more substantial and immediate kinds of assistance; and because we feel that not the least impediment to the advancement of the excellent institutions in question has been the neglect they have experienced from the more influential public journals.

We shall first define what is meant by a 'Mechanics Institution,' and then divide what we have to say into three divisions: namely,—

I. The origin and history of Mechanics Institutions.

II. Their condition at the present time. And,

III. Practical suggestions for their improvement, and assistance.

A 'Mechanics Institution,' then, is a voluntary association of a portion of the humbler classes of a town or locality, assisted by a few of the leading and wealthy inhabitants, to raise, by means of small periodical contributions, a fund to be expended in the instruction of its members in science, literature, and the arts, to the exclusion of controversial divinity, party politics, and subjects of local dispute, by means of a library of circulation, lectures, evening or day classes, and a reading room. The government of the society is commonly vested in a committee, chosen annually by the adult members, and composed of persons selected from the ordinary, and patron classes of subscribers, in the proportion sometimes of one-half, sometimes one-third, of the latter. Mechanics Institutions are not under the protection and regulation of any particular act, as are Friendly Societies, but stand in the same relation to the law as any other voluntary and unchartered associations of individuals.

I. *Origin and History of Mechanics Institutions.*—Although the late excellent Dr Birkbeck was not perhaps the individual inventor, he was, without dispute, the original founder of mechanics institutions.[4] The primitive 'mechanics institution' was a class of journeymen mechanics, formed by Dr Birkbeck at Glasgow, about February 1800, during the time that he was the Andersonian Lecturer in that city. The object of this class was the instruction of its members (who were expected to be labouring mechanics) in the 'scientific principles of their respective trades,' to the neglect, if not the exclusion, of other kinds of knowledge; and it is important to observe that, until the last few years, this limitation of instruction was considered to be the only legitimate basis on which to found the operations of these institutions. We shall see, before we conclude, how experience and circumstances have gradually extended this original idea.

We believe that the class formed by Dr Birkbeck at Glasgow continued to flourish for several years, under the care of the Professors who succeeded him in the Andersonian Institution.

In 1821, the 'School of Arts,' an institution analogous in plan and object to the Glasgow Society, was formed at Edinburgh, principally by the exertions of Mr Leonard Horner.[5] The real era of mechanics' institutions, however, was not until two or three years later. We believe the subject was first brought prominently before the public by Lord Brougham, in an article on the 'Scientific Education of the People' inserted in the 'Edinburgh Review' for October, 1824, and afterwards published as a pamphlet.[6]

In the course of 1825, mechanics institutions were formed in London and in several of the principal towns. Other institutions continued to be formed during the three or four succeeding years; and the period from 1825 to 1830 (both inclusive) may be considered, perhaps, as the first term in their history; that is, as the portion of time during which the ideas and principles which prompted and governed their formation in the first instance were most vigorous and active.

About 1831, we have reason to believe that both the establishment of new institutions began to slacken, and that the prosperity of those already in existence was, in general, materially on the decline. This state of things continued to about the end of 1835: the political excitement of those years was, probably, one chief cause of this declension; but the insufficiency of the means and scope of the institutions themselves, as we shall subsequently have to explain, was, no doubt, the principal reason.

Subsequent to 1835—in the course, perhaps, of 1836[7]—a revival took place in the condition of several institutions. This arose chiefly, from the lessons taught by past experience and failures, beginning to have their due influence in minor points of management, as well as in the greater matter of discovering the unsound parts of the original plan. The most important circumstances which have arisen out of this revival are, perhaps: (1) The virtual abandonment of the original idea that the operations of mechanics institutes should be confined to the instruction of 'working mechanics in the scientific principles of their respective trades,' as their *sole*, or at least their *greatly predominating* object; and the adoption of the more comprehensive purpose (still, however, not omitting or undervaluing the former) of providing for the humbler classes generally 'the largest amount of sound instruction combined with the largest amount of cheap and innocent amusement.' This change may be described in other words as the elevation of mechanics institutions from mere technical schools of arts for the use of operative artisans, into societies designed to meet, as far as their means will permit, all the intellectual wants of the poorer part of the population. This change is undoubtedly the most important event in their history. (2) The formation of LYCEUMS, a species of institutions which the deficiencies of the mechanics institutions appear to have called forth. (3) The successful adoption of the plan of 'Public Exhibitions of works of Nature and Art;' and (4) the establishment of 'Unions' among the institutions of particular districts with a view to the interchange of assistance and advice. On these three last particulars it will be needful to enter into some explanation.

First, as to LYCEUMS. We believe that, hitherto, these institutions have not extended beyond Manchester and its neighbourhood, where three of them were formed in 1838. The *principle* of their objects, government, and machinery appears to be identical with that of mechanics institutions. The differences between the two classes of institutions are, that the Lyceums are (1) cheaper in point of expense; (2) that they make more provision for the amusement of their members by means of concerts, tea parties, and *soirées*; (3) that they admit, with less restraint, works of light literature into their libraries of circulation, and newspapers into their reading rooms; (4) that their lectures are more frequent, treat of more popular and attractive subjects, and are delivered in a style more generally intelligible; and (5) that they provide for the instruction of females as well as males. [...]

We only have to say, in conclusion of this part of the subject, that we are most anxious to see adopted, in all cases, the rule of management already recognised in many mechanics institutes—namely— That the proper business of such institutions is to provide for the poorer classes, the largest possible amount of sound instruction, combined with the largest possible amount of cheap, innocent, and daily amusement.

We will now state, as fully as our small remaining space will permit, the means whereby this principle may be carried into practice.

(2) *Library.*—The library of a mechanics institution is its standing and staple source of support—the constant and abiding fund of interest and attraction when other means are suspended or impracticable. Let the library, then, contain books such as are likely to create a desire for reading—books which amuse without depraving the mind. Let there be a due proportion of books of science and useful

knowledge, but let there be also an extensive and judiciously chosen series of works of Fiction. [...] The Waverley Novels ought to be first and foremost in the catalogue of every mechanics institution library. We know personally, a man of some eminence at the present moment, who ascribes his acquisition of a desire for knowledge to the perusal of these novels, obtained by him when a lad from the library of a mechanics institution. To the fictions of Scott should be added the works of Edgeworth, Cooper, Dickens, and of many other authors whose names will occur to every one acquainted with the ordinary history of letters.[8] Let no one take fright at the idea of novel reading at a time when the strength with which the best and purest current of thought amongst us runs in the channel of fiction, is one of the most remarkable features in the intellectual condition of the age. There should also be a plentiful sprinkling of voyages and travels, and biography. [...]

(3) *Reading Room.*—This room should be (if possible) one of the most handsome, spacious, and attractive places of resort in the neighbourhood, because it should be designed to act as the antagonist of the beer-shop, the tavern, and the smoking-room. It should be filled with elegant, even luxurious furniture—adorned with pictures and sculptures—supplied with a profusion of periodical publications, and made the repository of a series of books of reference, and of works remarkable for the excellence of their pictorial embellishments. Wherever it is practicable, cheap and temperate refreshments, such as coffee, should be provided in connexion with this room. We shall rejoice to see the day when it is a chief point of rivalry among mechanics institutions to embellish and improve their reading rooms—in other words, their hotels, for the gratification of the intellect and the taste. The keepers of gaming tables and smoking rooms are well aware of the influence of handsome and commodious apartments in attracting customers, and it behoves the friends of a better system to press into their service every shaft from the quiver of the enemy which can be used with honour and advantage. [...]

(4) *Admission or Exclusion of Politics.*—The large and important question, 'How far and in what way, under present circumstances, instruction in political science can with success be made a branch of mechanics institution education,' cannot be discussed on the present occasion. The question is well worth an article devoted expressly to

its sole consideration, and probably at some future time we may be able to discuss it at adequate length; at present we have only a word or two to say concerning a subject which, although connected with the general question of the admission or exclusion of politics, is of itself, in our opinion, of very minor moment as regards present consequences, and has but a very slender bearing on the practical settlement of that question—we allude to the introduction of Local and London newspapers into reading rooms, to be there read in silence, like any of the literary periodicals. We are decidedly in favour of the admission of newspapers into mechanics institutions in this way, and we think that by the circumstance of such admission the present neutral character of these institutions would be in no way violated or impaired. Our main motive for holding this opinion is the consideration that every working man, and, in truth, every person who can spell, has a strong desire to have access to the current newspapers of the day, and in the country, especially to the local newspapers. We all know that this desire is gratified by going to the beer-house. The man has no taste probably for the beer, but he has an unconquerable, and let us say, a very natural taste for the newspaper. Now why should the poor man be exposed to the danger of intemperance and bad company, when his curiosity might be fully appeased without incurring any evil consequences at the mechanics institution? Why should the beer-house be permitted to possess exclusively a means of attraction so notoriously powerful and universal? If we want to attract the working man to the mechanics institution we must provide there those things in which he takes an interest—and mightiest among these, we contend, is the newspaper. [...]

Angus B. Reach, 'The Coffee Houses of London', *New Parley Library*, 1 (13 July 1844), 293–4

Coffee-houses proliferated during the 1820s and 1830s. Angus Reach's article explores their new-found position as one of the principal reading spaces for working-class male readers. Reach, a reporter for the *Morning Chronicle* and contributor to *Punch*, emphasizes that the coffee-house benefited from having neither the drunkenness of the public house nor the 'improving' atmosphere of mechanics' institutes. The *New Parley Library* was a 1d. illustrated miscellany—exactly the kind of journal that might be read over a leisurely cup of coffee.

Here and there in our more crowded thoroughfares—wherever pours, the live long day, the vast traffic of a principal London street—putting forth modest claims to notice for themselves and their wares, amid the glare and flaunting pretensions of their rivals and enemies, the GIN palaces, you may see the London *Coffee-houses*. They are in general quiet, almost sombre-looking places: they do not ape the gaudy brass work, gingerbread gilding, and coloured glass of the gin shops [. . .] The coffee-houses have no flash inscriptions to catch the eye; but they have books, magazines, newspapers, strewed thickly around. They are schools where instruction is meted out, as well as coffee sold. They are the public-houses of temperance. They are reading rooms as well as drinking rooms; and what you do in one way happily does not interfere with the other.

The London coffee-houses are a class quite *sui generis*.[9] You may easily distinguish them in the streets: they generally boast of an enormously broad window—as big as half-a-dozen common windows rolled into one; upon the sill are arranged some dozen tea-cups, presided over at each end by a tea and coffee-pot; while a plate or two of raw chops or steaks delicately intimate that something more substantial than coffee and bread-and-butter is to be had within. Backing the symbols of eatables and drinkables, there is usually arranged a perfect curtain of play-bills—for coffee-house windows and tobacconists' shops are favourite places for theatrical announce-

ments. There you have them all—comedy, tragedy, opera, and farce—
from the bill of fare at Drury Lane to the crowded *affiche*[10] of the
suburban saloon, in which, besides the cast of the play, you are
generally treated to a history of the plot, and picturesque description
of the scenery. Take them all in all, and you will have a very good
afternoon's play-bill reading; and poring over the announcements of
all the theatres in London is surely almost as good as going to one! But
let us enter. We are in a large, not very high, but generally very long
room, partitioned off into little boxes with a table in each. Upon the
walls—stuck upon hat-pins—you have more play-bills, and the eye is
caught by a long list of the good things ready almost at a moment's
notice, with the price of each attached. The whole place has an air of
stillness and repose, yet perhaps a hundred people are seated in the
different boxes, conning over books and newspapers, and sipping
their coffee at the same time. Orders are given in as different a tone,
from the loud bullying demand you hear in the public-house, as is the
quiet modest appearance of the damsel who executes them from the
flaunting air of the ringleted, flashy young lady who stands behind the
bar in a gin-palace. There is no quarrelling, no scuffling, no demands
for the police. There is indeed little conversation further than an
occasional—'The *Times* after you, if you please, Sir,' 'When you've
done with that magazine, I'll trouble you,' passing from one box to
another. Everybody is civil to his neighbour, and yet the company is
made up of a class who, were they at a public-house instead of a
coffee-house, in all probability, would be brawling and bullying, or
deeply immersed in such edifying discussions as to what four-legged
brute is to win the next Derby, or what two-legged bruie[11] is to win the
next prize-fight.

You see at a glance that the majority of the guests are working men;
fustian jackets are plentiful; and here and there you see laid on the
bench the straw basket containing the tools of their avocations. There
are no 'sporting characters' evidently; no 'gents', with cut-away New-
market coats,[12] and slang conversation [...] But there are respectable
men; hard-working and long-headed fellows, who think while they
hammer, and read when the hammering is over; who have an opinion
of their own, and can express it; who can feel deeply, as well as think
clearly, and who bring a homely philosophy to the forge and the loom.
We love to see hard horny hands—not very white perchance, or

Byronic in their formation—turn over the leaves of books and newspapers; and eyes, although heavy with the labours of the day, light up
as they pore over their contents. The working man, at least in towns,
is becoming more and more a reading man. He has his political faith,
and he can give a reason for the faith that is in him. The times are
passing away when senators said, 'What have low fellows, vulgar
mechanics, to do with the laws, but to obey them?' Cheap schools,
cheap publications, cheap lectures, and last, but not least, cheap
coffee and reading rooms, have worked wonders, and will work still
more.

Look at the number of publications spread about in lavish confusion in our ideal coffee-house. There are imaginative works, critical
work, political and philosophical works; newspapers fly about like
autumn leaves, and like them they enrich the soil on which they are
cast. Here we have them of all shades of politics indeed, urging all
manner of social theories, differing from each other in almost every
respect but in the most important respect—that of conveying knowledge: under different shapes they all do that. The reviews and
magazines are now a formidable host; embracing matter to suit
every taste; enriched, as I have seen them, with the most brilliant
essays, and the most rare fictions in the language. Here you have them
all. Almost every sheet which issues from the metropolitan periodical
press you find in the coffee-house; and for reading them (and you may
read from morning until night if you please) you pay—nothing.

In many coffee-houses, besides periodicals, a small library is kept,
consisting principally of works of fiction, and of entertaining and
useful information. The books may sometimes be a little greasy, to
be sure, the paper stained and thumbed, and the leaves dog-eared. But
what of that? We respect a stained dog-eared book. It is a veteran who
has seen service—not a mere gilt ornament to an unread library [...]

Well, you have your coffee; you are in a warm, comfortable, well-
lighted room; a library is at your beck and bidding: newspapers and
periodicals, native and foreign, are contesting each other's claims to
your notice. You may sit as long as you like, and read as much as you
like, and one or two pence is all the recompense demanded! Why at
home you would pay double the amount for one night's reading, of
one book or periodicals, from the circulating library. Here is knowledge, literary instruction, refined intellectualising pleasure, brought

within the reach of all who love its teaching. For what a man pays for a glass of gin, or a pint of porter at the public-house, he can have a more wholesome draught, a more comfortable place to enjoy it in, and a mental banquet, if he chooses, into the bargain. [...]

These establishments, too, are of quite modern growth, and they have opened up a new and extensive trade. Twenty-five years ago there were not above ten or twelve coffee-houses in London [...] Now, there are upwards of two thousand [...] Twenty-five years ago, you could not get a cup of coffee [...] for under the charge of a sixpence. Now, coffee—not of course very exquisitely flavoured, but still very drinkable—can be had from three-halfpence to three-pence per cup! [...] [I]n the vicinity of the Haymarket, there is an establishment of the kind which entertains from 1500 to 1600 people daily; the charge there is three-halfpence per cup for coffee; tea is somewhat dearer; forty-three papers are taken in daily, seven country papers, six foreign papers, twenty-four magazines per month, four quarterly reviews, and eleven weekly periodicals. Altogether about £400 a-year is expended on periodicals [...]

How different all this is from the tavern life of old [...] Knowledge is abroad over the world. It no longer sits enthroned in gilded saloons, apart from vulgar gaze. It is in the cottage, in the manufactory, shedding bright moral gleams over the dwellers in the crowded smoky streets and alleys. It is brought within the reach of all; and, although dandies may turn up their noses at the vulgarity of the cheap coffee-house, or philosophic pedants sneer at what they consider the quackery of the cheap scientific gallery, both the one and the other are doing their good work—fostering taste—encouraging and directing energy—sowing seeds which will one day spring up in rich harvests.

Mrs [Sarah Stickney] Ellis, 'The Art of Reading Well, as Connected with Social Improvement', in *The Young Ladies' Reader; or, Extracts from Modern Authors, adapted for Educational or Family Use* (London: Grant & Griffith, 1845), 1, 2–3, 7–8, 9–10, 12–13, 15, 16, 18

The Young Ladies' Reader was an offshoot of a series of conduct books published by Stickney Ellis (1812–72) in the late 1830s and 1840s, including *The Women of England* (1838) and *The Daughters of England* (1842). These books promoted women's importance through their moral and domestic influence. Ellis also ran a school for young women, Rawdon House, which educated its pupils according to her desired model of femininity. She flouted the idea that young ladies at home should read only 'Pope, Addison, Goldsmith, Johnson, and writers of this sterling class' (p. 19) and instead provided examples of more recent writing.

IF in our ideas of the *fine arts*, we include all those embellishments of civilized life which combine in a high degree the gratification of a refined taste, with the exercise of an enlightened intellect; then must reading aloud hold a prominent place amongst those arts which impart a charm to social intercourse, at the same time that they elevate and purify the associations of ordinary life.

The art of reading aloud, and reading *well*, is thus entitled to our serious consideration, inasmuch as it may be made a highly influential means of imparting a zest, and an interest, to domestic associations; and of investing with the charm of perpetual freshness the conversation of the family circle, the intercourse of friendship, and the communion of 'mutual minds'. [...]

The hurried manner in which most persons are now spending their lives, tends, perhaps more than any other cause, to destroy the interest and the advantage which might be derived from reading aloud. Mere snatches of time are all which the generality of people believe they can afford to give to a book; and thus, each volume of the vast number circulated by our libraries and book-societies, is snatched at by each separate member of a family, and supposed to be read as far as time will allow.

[...] Suppose a family to consist of ten members, each of whom indulges at intervals in an hour's silent and exclusive reading of any given book, and it must be a small book indeed which can be thoroughly read in an hour. According to this plan, ten separate hours must be consumed in order to enable each individual to say they have read the book at all, and that without the benefit of each other's impressions or remarks, and without those lively outbursts of thought and feeling which tend so much to render all such impressions forcible and lasting,—as regards the young, too, without the great advantage of the observations of age, and experience, to correct their sentiments and opinions.

Ten uninterrupted hours of social and family reading! What a sum of intellectual enjoyment might be gathered into that space of time! But then it must be *good* reading, or the enjoyment is exchanged for unspeakable annoyance. [...]

The art of reading, as now generally treated, would seem to consist in the mere recognition and utterance of certain signs of ideas, as they appear to us in their printed form. But it should never be forgotten that unless a *right* utterance is given to these signs, they fail to represent ideas; they are mere words, and nothing more; and such, in fact, are half the books now read aloud to us, according to the usual method. A perfect mastery over mere words should then be obtained, before much can be attempted in the way of adaptation of the voice; more especially as it cannot be expected that young children should enter either fully or clearly into the meaning of any writer. Set tunes, however, should be carefully avoided, because, when the habit of reading to a tune is once adopted, it is not easily laid aside; and as the mind matures, the eye having become so familiar with all common words that they can be uttered with facility by the organs of speech, there will come a time in the experience of all young persons, when they may with propriety be introduced to that higher branch of the study of reading, which requires a totally different exercise of mind from that of uttering mere words. It is now that they may safely enter upon a sphere of understanding and of thought, of which, at an earlier period, they could have formed none but very inadequate conceptions; and which, presented to them as it too frequently is, by faint and false glimpses, tends only to increase the labour and confusion in which they are necessarily involved, when attempting to carry on two distinct processes of thought at once. It is impossible to specify any particular age at which this study should commence, because the fitness for it must depend upon observation, experience, previous habits of thought, and individual capability of feeling and perception. Quick powers of sympathy have also much to do with reading well, because a correct tone and manner can only be attained by a just appreciation of the writer's meaning, entered into on the instant that his expressions have to be uttered.

As the most perfect music is that in which the air is exactly adapted to the words, so the most perfect reading is that in which the voice is so managed as to give to the sense its fullest and most entire expression. [...]

As music is to the ear, and to the passions, so is reading aloud to the ear, and to the mind. Yet, how amazing is the difference in the amount of time bestowed upon the one, and upon the other! It is no mean recommendation to the accomplishment of reading well, that it tends to promote family union and concord. A good book is like the conversation of an intelligent friend, and ought to be treated with the same respect. It forms, in fact, a safe rallying point, around which different tempers, feelings, and constitutions, can meet without jarring or discord; and in a far higher degree than music, it tends to draw each mind out of its petty cares and perplexities, to meet with other minds on common ground, where a wider extent of interest, and often a nobler range of thought, have the effect of shewing, by contrast, how trivial and unimportant are the little things of self in the great aggregate of human happiness and misery.

[...] On the other hand, the habit of silent and solitary reading has the inevitable effect, in a family, of opening different trains of thought and feelings, which tend rather to separate than unite, and which naturally induce habits of exclusive, selfish, and unprofitable musing. [...]

The habit of reading aloud, and reading well, is most especially important to women, because of the amount of time usually occupied by them in quiet and sedentary employments. Mind has so very little to do with a vast proportion of these employments, that for idle and unprofitable thoughts, for vague and endless musing, they are almost worse than nothing. [...]

The two principal errors into which young readers are apt to fall,—that of attaching too much importance to whatever affects the feelings and the passions, and too little to what belongs to the reasoning faculties, are equally likely to be corrected by the habit of reading aloud in families, and especially in the presence of intelligent and right-judging parents. [. . .] It is the free access to circulating libraries, the solitary and indiscriminate devouring of novels merely as such, and because they beguile the restless craving of a diseased imagination, which combine to constitute one of the greatest evils to which youth is liable. [. . .]

For the moral causes which operate on the well-being of nations, I am convinced we look too much to legislature, and too little to individual duty. We seek a panacea for the evils around us in the opinions of a new party, or the doctrines of some new sect; and persuading ourselves that some one great thing demands our exclusive attention, we overlook the many small things that make up the sum of life. But as a simultaneous effort throughout our land to render homes in general more attractive would do more towards keeping families united than the establishment of a new police for forcing fathers, husbands, and brothers to remain within their own doors; so any single object of attainment which has this tendency is richly worth our best endeavours; and to a highly improved method of reading aloud, I am sanguine enough to look for one amongst the many means of promoting social feeling, which ought not on any consideration to be neglected.

Report from the Select Committee on Public Libraries, Together with the Proceedings of the Committee, Minutes of Evidence, and Appendix (London: House of Commons, 1849), pp. vii–ix, 77–83, 124–5

In 1849 a parliamentary select committee examined the state of library provision. The committee was headed by William Ewart (1798–1869), the reforming Liberal MP for Dumfries, and included Joseph Brotherton (1783–1857), the first MP for Salford, Manchester, and Disraeli (1804–81), then head of the 'Young England' group of Tories. The committee's unflattering findings led to the passing of a bill in 1850 that allowed town councils to levy taxes for the creation of public libraries. The evidence given to the inquiry exposed the lack of accessible reading spaces for working-class readers and the failure of existing initiatives like mechanics' institutes.

Whatever may be our disappointment at the rarity of Public Libraries in the United Kingdom, we feel satisfaction in stating that the uniform current of the evidence tends to prove the increased qualifications of the people to appreciate and enjoy such institutions. Testimony, showing a great improvement in national habits and manners, is abundantly given in the evidence taken by the Committee. That they would be still further improved by the establishment of Public Libraries, it needs not even the high authority and ample evidence of the witnesses who appeared before the Committee to demonstrate.

There can be no greater proof of the fitness of the people for these institutions than their own independent efforts to create them. Evidence will be found in the subjoined Minutes of the extent of the Libraries connected with Mechanics' Institutes. Even in those useful places of resort of the temperate working classes, the Coffee-Houses of London (of which there are now nearly 2,000), it has been found necessary to supply the frequenters of them with a collection of books. The recent successful literary efforts of several of our working men is another reason for encouraging them by the formation of Public Libraries. The great practical education of an Englishman is derived from the incessant intercourse between man and man in trade, and from the interchange and collision of opinion elicited by our system of local self-government; both teaching him the most important of all lessons, the habit of self-control. But it would be wise to superadd to these rugged lessons of practical life some of the more softening and expanding influences which reading and which thought supply. It has been remarked by an American witness, that 'nothing strikes an American more forcibly than to see how little reading there is in England.'[13] This contrast (which we at once acknowledge and lament) arises partly from the wise application of the system of local self-government and local rating to the diffusion of universal education in America, and partly from the cheapness of books there; the great demand for which—in consequence of that very diffusion of education—springs from a class which cannot afford to pay for *dear* books. But these disadvantages on our part are additional reasons for giving, from other sources, greater facilities of reading to our fellow-countrymen. It would be a libel on their character, and an error in fact, to deny that they are sensible to the value and the blessings of reading. Scarcely any class appear to be so backward and benighted as to be impenetrable to such influences. We find that the efforts of a zealous parochial clergyman, the Rev. Mr. Brereton, to establish a self-supporting Library among the poorest part of our population in the parish of St. Martin's were successful. An increasing desire for such means of self-instruction exists in Spitalfields. Of our Village Libraries, for the rural population, an earnest promoter of them, the Rev. W. R. Fremantle, states that they are 'extending very much,' and that 'there is a very great and increasing inclination to make use of them on the part of the agricultural people of the country.'[14] But perhaps the most encouraging symptoms of a capability to appreciate books are traceable in the evidence of Mr. Imray, relating to the Libraries of the Ragged Schools of the Metropolis.[15] One of these he describes as frequented by about 100 constantly-varying readers, of a class approaching to mendicancy, who, though violent and ill-conducted at first, soon acquire perfect habits of order, and learn to take pleasure in reading. [...]

Amid the reasons in favour of the establishment of Public Libraries, we must not omit to consider the great extension which has been given, of late years, to the system of 'Lecturing' throughout the country. Half a century ago this system was comparatively unknown. The demand for 'Lectures,' especially in our trading and manufacturing districts, has called into existence a new class of men, and created, as it were, a new profession. The profits, as well as the influence, derivable from this pursuit, have attracted to it persons of superior education; who make a kind of periodical circuit in different districts of the country. It is almost a necessary consequence, that lectures should lead to reading. The lecturer himself frequently needs the assistance of books. His hearers naturally wish to pursue, by means of books, the subject on which his lectures have interested or instructed them. The power of access to standard works in a Public Library would tend to render the lecturer less superficial, and to promote investigation among his hearers. It would even be serviceable to our provincial press. It may often happen (as is shown in the evidence of Mr. Dawson[16]) that a journalist finds the necessity of consulting political, historical, and literary works. Students in the provinces (*see* the evidence of the same witness) are now constrained to collect together the scattered questions on which they wish to satisfy their minds, and make an occasional pilgrimage to London, to seek for a solution of their difficulties from the shelves of the British Museum. There can scarcely be a stronger proof than this of the necessity for creating Provincial Public Libraries. But the tendency of modern publication and of modern literature sets in this direction. A vast and increasing number of new popular works, cheap in price, condensed in form, and valuable in substance, is continually issuing from the British press. M. Guizot truly states that there is no such supply in France.[17] Even such useful popular publications as our best almanacs do not find their equals there. The supply of popular publications in parts of Germany and Italy is not greater, perhaps less, than that in France. This tendency towards popular publications in Great Britain—the result in a great degree of our superior capital and enterprise—would seem not only to facilitate, but to invite, the formation of Public Libraries. It is also truly observed that the establishment of such depositories of standard literature would lessen, or perhaps entirely destroy, the influence of frivolous, unsound, and dangerous works. Your Committee are glad to take this opportunity of echoing an opinion expressed by M. Van de Weyer:[18] 'I should positively say, (says M. Van de Weyer), that first-rate books ought to be put into the hands of the people instead of inferior publications. They enjoy and feel the beauties of the higher class of literature as deeply as any literary man; as in our theatres they applaud the very passages which a literary man would most admire.' This opinion is strongly confirmed by Mr. Imray, even as regards the readers in the Libraries of our Ragged Schools. Mr. Imray is asked, 'When they (the frequenters of such Libraries) read the better class of books, do they prefer them to the books you have spoken of' (the inferior books)?—*Answer.* 'So much so, that I do not think they would ever return to the lower class of books, after having read the other (the better) books.' Shall we therefore abandon the people to the influence of a low, enfeebling, and often pestilential literature, instead of enabling them to breathe a more pure, elevated, and congenial atmosphere?

But, it may be reasonably asked, in what mode can such institutions as Public Libraries be established and maintained? To this question Your Committee are bound, so far as they are able, to supply a practical answer.

The general want, in all such cases, is not so much the want of objects to be deposited, as of a depository for the reception of them. It is probable that, if buildings devoted to the purposes of a library or museum existed, and if the institutions for which they were erected were firmly and inalienably secured in some fixed and lasting society or corporation, and exempted from the burthen of local and general taxation, the materials to fill those buildings would easily, and in many cases voluntarily, be supplied. [...]

George Dawson, Esq., M.A, called in; and Examined.

1207. *Chairman.*] I BELIEVE you are very well acquainted with the manufacturing districts of this country?—I am.

1208. And the course of your pursuits as a lecturer has led you very much to understand the wants and feelings of the working class of this country?—Yes.

1209. You are familiar with all our manufacturing towns, are you not?—All of them.

1210. Both in England and Scotland?—Yes, in England and in Scotland.

1211. Has your attention been directed at all to the want of libraries in those towns accessible to the public?—Yes; I have gathered together the catalogues of all the libraries in the midland counties, with which I am well acquainted, for the purpose of preparing a report for the Association of Mechanics' Institutions.

1212. What has been the result of your observation ?—There are no free libraries, excepting about three or four. The chief libraries for operatives are those of the mechanics' institutions, and they are small. Many of the books are gift books, turned out of people's shelves, and are never used, and old magazines of different kinds, so that, out of 1,000 volumes, perhaps there may be only 400 or 500 useful ones. The rest are, many of them, only annual registers and old religious magazines that are never taken down from the shelves.

1213. Of course, the only persons admitted to use those books are the members of those mechanics' institutions themselves?—They are generally subscribers to the whole of the privileges of the institution. Some of those institutions let parties subscribe to the libraries alone; but, generally speaking, they must subscribe to the whole of the privileges of the institution before they can get at the library.

1214. There is a free library at Manchester, is there not?—Yes, an old one; Chetham's Library.

1215. You know of no other but Chetham's among the provincial libraries, which is quite accessible to the public?—There is the old town library of Leicester, which an order from a member of the town council admits you to. But that consists almost wholly of controversial divinity; and unless it may be that some clergyman comes and looks in occasionally, the greater part of the books are scarcely ever touched. The Old Town Library, it is called.

1216. Do you think there is any willingness on the part of the working classes to avail themselves of libraries, if they had free access to them?—Yes; in Nottingham they have an operative and artisans' library. The artisans' library is held in a room in one of the public buildings, and the subscription is small; but they refused to admit theological or political works, and many working men have withdrawn from it, and formed a new library, and the books are kept in public-houses, and there they go, and pay a small subscription, and perhaps take a glass of ale, and read.

1217. Can you give the Committee an idea of the character of those books?—They are mostly novels, or at least a large portion of them are novels; still there are a great many political works.

1218. Is there a willingness on the part of the working classes to study works that are rather of a deeper character than those, if they had the power of doing so?—Yes; we find that in regard to novels, which form the majority of books taken out, the proportion is diminishing, and the proportion of historical and philosophical works is increasing. The novels, in some libraries, are in the minority.

1219. Are you aware whether the publications of the different publishers who have issued a large amount of superior works for the reading of the people, has tended of late years to a deeper style of reading than formerly?—Much more so.

1220. Could you mention any of the works of that character which are most in request?—All Bohn's series are very much read.[19] They are historical works mostly; but the great defect in some of the mechanics' institutions is, that by their rules many of them do not admit political works or theological works into their libraries; some make no exception, and admit every kind of work, but many are fettered by those rules which admit of neither political nor theological works; consequently the working men do not trouble them much.

1221. How are those libraries managed?—By a committee of the institution.

1222. Mr. *Hamilton.*[20]] Do you suppose that the working classes prefer political and theological works?—The working classes prefer historical and political works; they do not trouble theological works much.

1223. Mr. *Thicknesse.*[21]] Are historical works much read by that class of the people?—Not unless they are political.

1224. Mr. *Hamilton.*] With regard to works on the arts and sciences, do you suppose the operatives would prefer reading them?— There is not so great a demand for those books as for historical books.

1225. Mr. *Charteris.*[22]] There is not so great a demand for scientific works in connexion with the various professions and trades?—The demand for books in relation to the different trades is limited, as compared with that for historical books and political books.

1226. Mr. *Wyld.*[23]] You are speaking of places where the operations carried on are mechanical?—Yes, of such places as Birmingham and Manchester.

1227. Where mostly there are many trades connected with the arts of design?—Yes.

1228. Mr. *Thicknesse.*] Do they not admit newspapers in the institution at Manchester?—Yes, and so they do almost in every institution; but that is done by admitting them to the news-room, as it is called, and that is regarded as a separate department.

1229. Do they not admit works of party politics?—In Manchester they do; they admit everything to the mechanics' institutions, but in Nottingham the operative library was founded because of the exclusion. I have a note of what a working man said about that; he said that he and nine other subscribers to the artisan's library seceded from it because they could not get such books on political and religious subjects as they wished to read. They 'clubbed' together and bought Howitt's History of Priestcraft,[24] and that was the beginning of operative libraries in Nottingham.

1230. Mr. *Hamilton.*] Can you state whether in Manchester the same preference exists for theological and political works, as distinguished from scientific or mechanical works?—Not in an equal degree; but still the greater demand is for historical and political works. There is one curious point I might notice, which is as to the proportion of issues to the number of volumes. It was found in the midland counties generally that there were six issues to one volume.

1231. Mr. *Wyld.*] As to the libraries in Birmingham, what are they?—They are all subscription libraries; there are Instruction Society Libraries, which are small, and the Polytechnic Institution Library is small, and the issues are about in the same proportion, six times the number of volumes; then if you subtract the number of volumes which never leave the shelves, you will find from that, each volume goes out nine or ten times in the course of the year. At the Leicester Library there are about 3,000 volumes and 13,000 issues; then if you subtract from that the books that never go out, some 2,500 books have 13,000 or 14,000 times to go out.

1232. Viscount *Ebrington.*[25]] In speaking of the absence of historical and political books from those libraries, you would hardly apply that to standard histories of the country, but to more recent works?—Yes.

1233. Are you aware whether the older historical writings are becoming more known, that is, the standard historical works as distinguished from more recent works, bearing more upon present politics; do you know whether those are circulated much?—Very much; for instance, Froissart's Chronicles is a work of great demand and very popular; and latterly the republication of the old Saxon Chronicles.[26]

1234. *Chairman.*] Have such books as Coxe's Revolutions of Europe an extensive circulation?[27]—Yes, and the translations from the French political histories have been much read.

1235. Do you think it would be desirable to have libraries containing books of every kind, so that people could take their choice?—Yes; there should be no restriction except a moral one, that is, excluding books of an immoral character.

1236. So that you would neither have political history excluded, nor have libraries restricted as to the subject of politics, but you would have a general library, where the reader might choose what suited his literary appetite?—Yes; in the best libraries there is no restriction.

1237. Do you feel convinced that if there were such libraries on an extensive scale they would be properly availed of by the people?— Yes, I am sure of that, because wherever they can get the means of having a library they take advantage of it; for instance, the Odd Fellows[28] have founded libraries in many towns, and some of the benefit societies have a library; at Birmingham the present cheap subscription-room is so full at night that it is quite inconvenient, and they will have to increase their accommodation; that is the case only where the subscription is reduced to the minimum; in Liverpool there is a mechanics' institution where they pay a penny a week to the library and lectures; they have never taken any subscription above a penny; they take none in advance, and they have a great number of working men.

1238. Mr. *Hamilton.*] Does the observation you have made with regard to the class of books extend to those other libraries also?—Yes.

1239. Are you acquainted with the public libraries in Scotland?— Not so well as with those in England. I have looked at the catalogues.

1240. Viscount *Ebrington.*] Are there books of travels and accounts of foreign countries in those libraries you have spoken of?—Yes, I have also observed among the working men a great spread of knowledge of French and German. And almost all English libraries are very deficient in modern foreign books. In the great library at Birmingham there are not a score of modern German books, and not more than 100 modern French books in French.

1241. Mr. *Hamilton*. Do you know anything of the London mechanics' libraries?—The literary institutions of London are little frequented by mechanics; they belong to the middle class almost exclusively.

1242. Are you able to state how the lower classes in London are supplied with literature?—By accident altogether. It is a scramble in London; whoever can get a penny buys a book. There is no provision in London in that respect for any poor person. The libraries in London, and throughout the country indeed, are closed at the only hours the working men can use them. The British Museum Library shuts at four, the Chetham Library shuts at four; they are closed at that hour because there shall not be fire or light in them. They are utterly useless to the working classes, who cannot take the books home. For them, in fact, libraries are not extant.

1243. *Chairman.*] If I understand you rightly, they do use the books which they buy themselves in the evenings?—Yes.

1244. Therefore in that case they run the risk of fire?—Yes; and in every case where the working men can form a society, they go and read there for hours of an evening.

1245. You think it desirable, and indeed almost indispensable, that libraries should be opened in the evening in order to be made available to the working classes?—Yes; it is the only hope for them, the libraries being open at night.

1246. And you think that, so opened, those libraries would be of great utility?—They would be very much used.

1247. As you have pursued your literary career in a number of the principal towns in this country, can you state whether or not it would be a great advantage to a literary man, even where connected with mere ephemeral literature, like that of a newspaper, to be able to avail himself of a library for the purpose of consultation?—Yes. In country towns he is obliged to make a list of points he wishes to elucidate, and if he is poor he waits till he comes to town, and then he goes to the Museum; and if he is better off, he comes up on purpose to settle those questions. I know a case of a person who came up in that way.

1248. Sir *H. Verney.*[29]] Where from?—From Leicester; but from not having made proper inquiry, when he got to London he found the Museum shut. That necessarily creates very great delay. There are many books which it is very necessary to refer to, which you cannot get in the country at all.

1249. *Chairman.*] You are speaking now of such books as ought to be attainable in all large towns?—Yes; and without some of them a man could not carry on a newspaper for six months. Supposing, for instance, he wanted to write an article on the Hungarian struggle, the chances are he could not get any thoroughly good work on Hungarian history or public documents connected with that country in Birmingham. Then he must come to London and run the chance of getting them even there.

1250. Therefore those public libraries are not only desirable to the working classes, but to the instructors of those working classes, as the men who contribute to the periodical literature and the newspapers of the country?—Yes.

1251. You are aware the schools of design have been much multiplied in this country?—Yes.

1252. Would not it be desirable that manufacturers, whose business is connected with design, should have ready access to such books as are connected with that design which belongs to their particular department?—Yes. In Birmingham everything depends upon design now, and the manufacturers purchase works and lend them to students in the painting rooms. I know the shifts the students are put to, because they come and borrow works of any man who has them; they will come to my house and get leave to sit an hour and copy them; therefore I know the great suffering the students go through to get them.

1253. Have you known instances of self-denial on the part of pupils to get books?—Yes. I have known men rise at five and work till eight for book-money, and then go to their day's work.

1254. In what towns have you known that?—In Birmingham. [. . .]

Samuel Smiles, Esq., called in; and Examined.[30]

1949. *Chairman.*] You reside at Leeds?—I do.

1950. Your habits have brought you a good deal into contact with the working classes of society?—A good deal; I was for eight years editor of a newspaper at Leeds, and brought very extensively into connexion with the working and the middle classes throughout the West Riding of Yorkshire.

1951. Has any attempt been made to form public libraries in that part of the country?—Yes, numerous attempts recently.

1952. Have they succeeded, or have they failed?— The popular libraries which have been formed up to a comparatively recent period, have generally been failures. They originated in this way: there was a desire felt to have a library, and so long as new books were bought, and an interest was felt in the scheme—so long as the books in the libraries were attractive, the people generally resorted to them; but so soon as the books became old and had been read out, they ceased to attract the readers, and in the end they were failures. I have a letter from Mr. Milburn, of Thirsk, the secretary of the Agricultural Society of Yorkshire, who says, 'There have been three public popular libraries formed here in my recollection; two are since dead.'

1953. Were those in an agricultural district?—Yes. 'They were formed by gifts; but when the books were all read over, there were no means provided or available to get new ones, the only means of keeping the thing up; I fear the same thing may await our mechanics' library,' just founded. I have no doubt that the same causes have operated very extensively to interfere with the success of the libraries formed up to a comparatively recent period.

1954. Mechanics' libraries have been formed in connexion with the mechanics' institutes?—Very extensively.

1955. But those were, of course, only accessible to the members of those institutes?—Yes.

1956. Have those libraries succeeded or failed?—I think they have been remarkably successful in the large towns, where the number of subscribers is so large as to enable them to purchase new books as they come out. The mechanics' institutes in the large towns, generally speaking, are not Institutes of mechanics; they are for the most part Institutes of the middle and respectable classes, and a small proportion, in some cases not so much as a half, of working men; a class superior to working men, and a small proportion of working men receiving comparatively high wages, support those institutions; generally speaking, they are not Mechanics' Institutes, and it is a misnomer to designate them as such.

1957. You have a sort of union of mechanics' institutes called the Yorkshire Union?—We have. I have before me the last report of the Yorkshire Union of mechanics' institutes, which gives a very large amount of information in a tabular view, of the institutes comprised in the Yorkshire Union. I find that all those institutions have attached to them libraries; some of them have lectures, and a large number of the institutions have recently formed classes; they find the classes to be exceedingly valuable portions of the institutions, necessary, in many cases, to keep them alive. Some have mutual improvement classes, but all, without exception, have libraries. They find in the libraries a bond of union, as it were, for the institution; that it is necessary to have a library to keep the institution together.

1958. Do you know the number of books in the libraries?—I do.

1959. What is the number of books in the institutes connected with the Yorkshire Union?—There are about 60,000 volumes; on the average, about 900 volumes to each library. The Yorkshire Union consists at present of 79 institutes, and there are at present seeking admission to the union 10 or 12 additional institutes. The total number of members in those institutes is about 16,000.

1960. What is the character of the books in the libraries?—There are all kinds, on history, political economy, statistics to a small extent, and a large proportion of works of fiction.

1961. What are the books principally read?—Works of fiction; but a taste for a better description of literature is evidently increasing. The numbers of issues of works on mechanics, philosophy, chemistry, and science, is on the increase, and historical works have been very much read of late years.

1962. Do you consider the taste of the people in that part of the country to have improved of late years?—I think their taste is decidedly improving.

1963. With that improvement in taste, has there been any improvement in their habits of order, temperance and character generally?—Amongst those who read, unquestionably there has.

1964. You think that reading produces a good effect upon them?—There is no doubt of it. But the misfortune is, that but a small proportion of the population in our large towns, and probably also in the agricultural districts, read. The general deficiency that we have to encounter in our neighbourhood is the want of elementary instruction to begin with. Even after the working people have learned to read, there is a want of opportunities of keeping up their reading. In the parish church at Leeds nearly one-half of the women who are married cannot sign their own names. But it is exceedingly probable that a large proportion of those women had learned to write when they were young, but had forgotten it for want of means and opportunities of practising it as they grew up.

1965. Do you think it of great importance not only that the means of early education should be given, but that means of using the information they have acquired should be supplied by means of public libraries?—It is most important.

1966. Have many of the mechanics' institutes libraries been augmented by donations?—Some of them have been entirely formed by donations; there is one little institution at Woodhouse, near Leeds, of which I officiate as president, which has been got together by a few young men, most of them members of a teetotal or temperance society,—a movement which has effected a great deal of good by withdrawing the working people from debasing pleasures, and leaving a good deal of time at liberty, which they find it necessary to occupy in more improving pleasures and pursuits than before; a man who keeps out of the beer-house finds it necessary to occupy his time with something; some of those young men, after they had joined those teetotal societies, felt it necessary to meet together in the evening for some purpose, and they resolved to join in a small literary institution. One or two active young men connected with it went about amongst the principal people of the neighbourhood, and solicited donations of books. They have also formed classes for young men, which are at present in operation, and very efficient. Not more than 5*l*., as the secretary informs me, has been spent in books, the whole library now consisting of about 500 volumes, which have been obtained by presents from those able and willing to give them.

1967. You think that, as the habit of temperance extends, not only the inclination but the necessity for reading extends with it, as a means of filling up the intervals of leisure which the working people have?—Yes; there is much valuable time thus liberated; and a taste for reading has sprung up, and is rapidly extending, encouraged by the numerous cheap publications now issuing from the press; and that taste must be satisfied.

1968. From the evidence given by you to-day, and the evidence given by Mr. Dawson a few days ago, it appears that it is a mistake to suppose that the mechanics' institutes are practically institutes for mechanics, and that in point of fact they comprehend only the higher class of mechanics, and the lower order of the middle classes?—I certainly think so.

1969. The persons upon whom it is now particularly desirable to act are persons in the lower classes of society, to whom these institutes do not extend?—Yes; there is a very large proportion of the working classes who are neither connected with any literary body nor any religious body, whom society does not look after in the slightest degree, who have no literary nor mental provision, and for whom libraries, or literary food of some description, is very desirable.

1970. Do not you think that it is desirable, considering the employment by day of the working classes, that the libraries should be open in the evening?—Very important; all those mechanics' institutes in Yorkshire are now open in the evening; this little institution, of which I spoke, is open only in the evening; the working men who formed it are so occupied during the day that they cannot use it, except during the evening.

John Naule Allen, 'Railway Reading. With a Few Hints to Travellers', *Ainsworth's Magazine*, 24 (1853), 483-7 [483-5]

When railway trips became a popular form of recreation in the 1850s, reading seemed the ideal way of passing the time *en route*. W. H. Smith's book stalls became common sights at railway stations (see Section IV, 'Our Modern Mercury'), and numerous publishers introduced their own cheap 'Railway Libraries'. *Ainsworth's Magazine* (1842–54) was filled with fiction, essays, and short comic sketches. Its desire to provide amusement is reflected in John Naule Allen's humorous article, which pokes fun at the new craze for railway reading.

NEXT to 'Our Lady of La Salette,' spirit-rapping, and the Chelsea ghost, I take Railway Reading to be beyond all disputation the greatest joke of the day.[31] I am quite aware that the funniest part of the book often happens to be its title-page; for instance, I have many a time seen 'Poems and Tales for the Woods, the Fields, and the Stream Sides,' and could never for the life of me conceive how it was possible for an author to be conceited enough to imagine that he could ever find a reader so silly as to peruse his book in preference to giving his eyes and thoughts to the woods, fields, and stream sides themselves, whilst he was amongst them. But never did I suppose it possible for I don't know how many intelligent publishers to commence I can't say how many libraries, for persons to read whilst travelling by railway! Why, did I not know them to be a very sensible body of men, I should have strange thoughts about these same publishers, which thoughts would have direct reference to Hanwell.[32] If I were a Frenchman, say, visiting England for a week or two, and possessed of that French aptitude to seize upon the appearance of appearances and state it as grave fact, I should certainly go home and write a large book on the manners and customs of the people of this nation, in which book I should not forget to declare that the publishers here were going mad, their complaint being a kind of railway mania.

Railway Reading!

Now I do not mean to say one word against the character of the books that rank under that head. Very many of them are excellent. But I do say, that if those works were read on railroads only, you might as well take and light the engine fire with them for the good they would do: and I wish to point out a great mistake—good-humouredly.

There are book-stalls at the principal stations all along the different lines. I am very glad of it. Many books are sold at those stalls, I believe. I am very glad of that. But did I for a moment think that these same books were perused whilst the train was on its way, and then 'laid on one side'—by which process many copies of Chaucer, Shakespeare, Milton, &c., are daily consigned to oblivion—I should be very sorry; for what writer would not rather that his book went unread than read badly? And I defy—and this, I beg to say, forms the principal argument of my paper—I defy the most constant of all 'constant readers' to make either head or tail of even a child's primer while in a travelling railway carriage.

Then what is the reason why persons, who never think of looking at a volume of any kind at other times, are found making shilling and half-crown literary investments at the railway stations? It is because such persons do so invest that I rejoice in the establishment of such stalls. Whilst walking about the platform they imagine it to be the easiest thing in the world to devour their mental food when the train is on its road—strange to say, inveterate travellers are apt to be thus deluded—but they soon find out their mistake, and put their intellectual banquet in their pocket, to be enjoyed, let us hope, by their home fireside.

Read in a railway carriage indeed! There is only one kind of man in the least competent to do so; and he is the very personage not to attempt it. I allude to the gentleman who could go to sleep in one—the dormouse biped who resembles a fat baby so much: only wrap him up well outside and stuff him well inside, and he would slumber soundly on a slack rope. But as he in all cases prefers sleeping to reading, he fails to affect our argument in the least.

Quite a different man to this was Mr James Johnson, shopkeeper, Tottenham-court-road, London. Buoyant yet grave, lively yet thoughtful, he was neither the butterfly nor the grub; yet each at times, and at other times a something between the two. I merely wish to give a short specimen of Mr Johnson's Railway Reading, and to briefly describe the delectable manner in which he conducted himself on a journey. [...]

Our book-buyer saw that his fellow passengers consisted of two ladies and two gentlemen. He also perceived that the work he had purchased was entitled 'Tristram Shandy,' or some such thing; also that its author was the Reverend Lawrence Sterne, or some such name. [...] [H]e took a piece of paper from his pocket which he folded straight; and then recommenced, holding his paper-assistant parallel with, and just below, the line he was reading. By this means he got on more steadily, and the passage assumed to Mr Johnson's senses the following form, with this difference: I make a distinction as to source and person, while to Mr. J. all appeared to emanate from the author of 'Tristram Shandy:'

Sterne—Nay, if you come to that, sir, have not the wisest of men in all ages, not excepting—

1st. Gentleman—Lord Palmerston and—

1st. Lady—Such a duck of a shawl that —

Sterne—Solomon himself—

2nd. Gentleman—Speaking of our foreign policy made this re-mark—

2nd. Lady—I always thought a Cashmere shawl, real Cashmere, mind you, looked better than anything. But, I forgot to tell you, you have not seen my little dogs, Fido and Dido?

Sterne—Have they not had their HOBBY-HORSES—

2nd. Lady—Positively the most sagacious animals—

1st. Lady—Indeed! You ought to give them every morning—

Sterne—Their running-horses—their coins and their cockle-shells, their drums and their trumpets, their fiddles, their pallets,—their maggots and their butterflies—

1st. Gentleman—And the balance of power becomes disarranged—

2nd. Gentleman—But so long as the Sultan—

Sterne—Rides his HOBBY-HORSE—

Here Mr Johnson felt himself becoming distracted very fast. He thought Sterne must be some madman whom he was not sane enough to fathom; so he took one of the wisest steps he had taken since he left home, and put the book in the inside pocket of his over-coat, promising himself to look into it again when he had arrived at his journey's end.

Henry Mayhew, 'The Literature of Costermongers', in *London Labour and the London Poor*, vol. i (London: Griffin, Bohn & Co., 1861), 25–6

Between 19 October 1849 and 12 December 1850 Henry Mayhew (1812–87) published a series of letters investigating the state of the urban poor in the failing newspaper, the *Morning Chronicle*. These he subsequently expanded into the four-volume *London Labour and the London Poor*. Written in the aftermath of a cholera epidemic in London that was aggravated by slum deprivation, the series saved the *Chronicle*. Mayhew's success owed much to his willingness to let his working-class subjects recount their own life-stories, including their reading habits.

It may appear anomalous to speak of the literature of an uneducated body, but even the costermongers have their tastes for books.[33] They are very fond of hearing any one read aloud to them, and listen very attentively. One man often reads the Sunday paper of the beer-shop to them, and on a fine summer's evening a costermonger, or any neighbour who has the advantage of being 'a schollard,' reads aloud to them in the courts they inhabit. What they love best to listen to—and, indeed, what they are most eager for—are Reynolds's periodicals, especially the 'Mysteries of the Court.'[34] 'They've got tired of Lloyd's blood-stained stories,'[35] said one man, who was in the habit of reading to them, 'and I'm satisfied that, of all London, Reynolds is the most popular man among them. They stuck to him in Trafalgar-square, and would again. They all say he's "a trump," and Feargus O'Connor's another trump with them.'[36]

One intelligent man considered that the spirit of curiosity manifested by costermongers, as regards the information or excitement derived from hearing stories read, augured well for the improvability of the class.

Another intelligent costermonger, who had recently read some of the cheap periodicals to ten or twelve men, women, and boys, all costermongers, gave me an account of the comments made by his auditors. They had assembled, after their day's work or their rounds, for the purpose of hearing my informant read the last number of some of the penny publications.

'The costermongers,' said my informant, 'are very fond of illustrations. I have known a man, what couldn't read, buy a periodical what had an illustration, a little out of the common way perhaps, just that he might learn from someone, who *could* read, what it was all about. They have all heard of Cruikshank, and they think everything funny is by him—funny scenes in a play and all. His "Bottle" was very much admired.[37] I heard one man say it was very prime, and showed what "lush" did; but I saw the same man,' added my informant, 'drunk three hours afterwards. Look you here, sir,' he continued, turning over a periodical, for he had the number with him, 'here's a portrait of "Catherine of Russia." "Tell us all about her," said one man to me last night; read it; what was she?" When I had read it,' my informant continued, 'another man, to whom I showed it, said, "Don't the cove as did that know a deal?" for they fancy—at least, a many do—that one man writes a whole periodical, or a whole newspaper. Now here,' proceeded my friend, 'you see's an engraving of a man hung up, burning over a fire, and some costers would go mad if they couldn't learn what he'd been doing, who he was, and all about him. "But about the picture?" they would say, and this is a very common question put by them whenever they see an engraving.

'Here's one of the passages that took their fancy wonderfully,' my informant observed.

"With glowing cheeks, flashing eyes, and palpitating bosom, Venetia Trelawney rushed back into the refreshment-room, where she threw herself into one of the arm-chairs already noticed. But scarcely had she thus sunk down upon the flocculent cushion, when a sharp click, as of some mechanism giving way, met her ears; and at the same instant her wrists were caught in manacles which sprang out of the arms of the treacherous chair, while two steel bands started from the richly carved back and grasped her shoulders. A shriek burst from her lips—she struggled violently, but all to no purpose: for she was a captive—and powerless!

"We should observe that the manacles and the steel bands which had thus fastened upon her, were covered with velvet, so that they inflicted no positive injury upon her, nor even produced the slightest abrasion of her fair and polished skin."

Here all my audience,' said the man to me, 'broke out with—"Aye! that's the way the harristocrats hooks it. There's nothing o' that sort among us; the rich has all the barrikin to themselves." "Yes, that's the b—[space] way the taxes goes in," shouted a woman.

'Anything about the police sets them a talking at once. This did when I read it:

"The Ebenezers still continued their fierce struggle, and, from the noise they made, seemed as if they were tearing each other to pieces, to the wild roar of a chorus of profane swearing. The alarm, as Bloomfield had predicted, was soon raised, and some two or three policemen, with their bull's-eyes, and still more effective truncheons, speedily restored order."

"The blessed crushers is everywhere," shouted one. "I wish I'd been there to have had a shy at the eslops,"[38] said another. And then a man sung out: "O, don't I like the Bobbys?"

'If there's any foreign language which can't be explained, I've seen the costers,' my informant went on, 'annoyed at it—quite annoyed. Another time I read part of one of Lloyd's numbers to them—but they like something spicier. One article in them—here it is—finishes in this way:

'The social habits and costumes of the Magyar *noblesse* have almost all the characteristics of the corresponding class in Ireland. This word *noblesse* is one of wide signification in Hungary; and one may with great truth say of this strange nation, that *"qui n'est point noble n'est rien."* '[39]

"I can't tumble to that barrikin," said a young fellow; "it's a jaw-breaker. But if this here—what d'ye call it, you talk about—was like the Irish, why they was a rum lot." "Noblesse," said a man that's considered a clever fellow, from having once learned his letters, though he can't read or write. "Noblesse! Blessed if I know what he's up to." Here there was a regular laugh.'

From other quarters I learned that some of the costermongers who were able to read, or loved to listen to reading, purchased their literature in a very commercial spirit, frequently buying the periodical which is the largest in size, because when 'they've got the reading out of it,' as they say, 'it's worth a halfpenny for the barrow.'

Tracts they will rarely listen to, but if any persevering man *will* read tracts, and state that he does it for their benefit and improvement, they listen without rudeness, though often with evident unwillingness. 'Sermons or tracts,' said one of their body to me, 'gives them the 'orrors.' Costermongers purchase, and not unfrequently, the first number of a penny periodical, 'to see what it's like.'

The tales of robbery and bloodshed, of heroic, eloquent, and gentlemanly highwaymen, or of gipsies turning out to be nobles, now interest the costermongers but little, although they found great delight in such stories a few years back. Works relating to Courts, potentates, or 'harristocrats,' are the most relished by these rude people.

Andrew Wynter, 'Mudie's Circulating Library', in *Subtle Brains and Lissom Fingers* (London: Robert Hardwicke, 1863), 165-72

Mudie's Select Library was the foremost circulating library and an iconic institution even in its own time. Charles Edward Mudie started to lend books from his Bloomsbury shop in 1843; a decade later he moved to the expanded premises in New Oxford Street that this article describes. Wynter's essay, first published in *Once a Week* (21 December 1861), examines the way Mudie's growth meant that subscribers had a volume of reading they could not otherwise afford (see p. 141 for a biographical note on Wynter).

TWENTY years is sufficient in these days entirely to revolutionize any speciality, trade, or profession, or indeed, for the matter of that, any mundane thing. If in our youth we had been asked to point out a particularly sleepy occupation on a level with the exertions of a genteel and advanced spinsterhood, we should have reverted instinctively to the circulating library, whose spiriting was generally performed by some meagre and somewhat sharp-visaged virgin in spectacles. The flow of well-thumbed fiction which she mildly regulated never gave signs of an uncontrollable exuberance of life, and the books of travel or adventure she dispensed speedily, became fossilized on her shelves. The circulating library of those days was a thing outside the bustling, active sphere of trade—a quiet eddy, as it were, in which placid minds took refuge. In these days, however, when the demands of society create such numberless new schemes, and erect into first-class occupations what were before insignificant handicrafts; when match-making has arrived at the dignity of a great manufacture, a single employer often consuming annually a dozen shiploads of timber, and great fortunes are made out of steel pens, is it to be wondered at that the spirit of enterprise has penetrated even into the sleepy old circulating library, and transformed it at once into a very mill-race of literary life?

Standing the other day at the counter at Mudie's, where the Subscribers exchange their books, we were a witness of the transformation one enterprizing and intelligent man has wrought in this branch of trade. The constant flood of people that are discharged from broughams and chariots into this emporium of books reminds one more of the Pantheon than of a mere circulating library. Doyle, in his 'Sketches of Society,'[40] has surely overlooked this famous sketching ground. If an artist could photograph the eager faces that throng the long counters of this establishment, he would be enabled to give us a rare picture-gallery of intelligence.

But in order to obtain a true idea of the importance this great circulating library has obtained as an educational element in society, we had better get an insight into the machinery by which the reading world is now so plentifully supplied with knowledge. Let us begin by saying that Mudie's Library, since its commencement, has issued to its subscribers not less than 1,263,000 volumes—it is true, a vast number of these in duplicates; nevertheless, they represent the amount of reading issued to the public by one establishment alone.

At the present moment the establishment owns no less than 800,000 volumes. If all these were to come home to roost at one

FIG. 7. 'Exchanging Books at Mudie's Library', *Living London*, ed. George R. Sims, iii (London: Cassell and Co., 1902), 96.

time, it would require a library almost as big as the British Museum to hold them. As it is, the house is one mass of books. Upstairs are contained the main reserves from which supplies are drafted for the grand saloon downstairs. This room is itself a sight. It is not a mere store-room, but a hall, decorated with Ionic columns, and such as would be considered a handsome assembly-room in any provincial town. The walls require no ceramic decorations, for they are lined with books, which themselves glow with colour. Here, perchance, a couple of thousand volumes of 'Livingstone's Travels' glow with green;[41] there stands a wall of light blue, representing the supply of some favourite novel; then, again, a bright red hue running half across the room testifies to the enormous demand for some work of adven-ture. Light iron galleries give access to the upper shelves, and an iron staircase leads to other books deposited in the well-lit, well-warmed vaults below. Light trucks are perpetually circulating about from room to room laden with books. Then, again, the spectator sees solid stacks of books piled about in odd places, just as he sees bricks stored near some rising building.

Descending into the vaults, he finds the shelves laden with parcels of books in their cerements of brown paper: these are the books that have already been read. They are not, however, as yet considered dead, as upon the issue of new works by their authors (supposing they be popular ones), they rise again, and live for a time a renewed life. Some, however, are utterly past and gone: there, in a huge pile, for instance, lies a large remnant of the 2,000 copies of 'Essays and Reviews,' originally issued to subscribers, the demand for which has almost entirely ceased; not far off are the exhausted 1,000 copies of the famous *Quarterly* number in which the 'Essays' were answered.[42]

But there are still rooms in which books out of demand are being made up for sale, to go the round of country circulating libraries, ere they are finally at peace. We were curious to inquire if volumes ever became exhausted in Mr. Mudie's hard service. Broken backs and torn leaves are treated in an infirmary, and volumes of standard value come out afresh in stouter and more brilliant binding than ever.

There is, however, such a thing as a charnel-house in this estab-lishment, where literature is, as it were, reduced to its old bones. Thousands of volumes thus read to death are pitched together in one heap. But would they not do for the butterman? was our natural query. Too dirty for that. Nor for old trunks? Much too greasy for that. What were they good for, then? For manure! Thus, when worn out as food for the mind, they are put to the service of producing food for our bodies!

The machinery by which all these books are distributed over the length and breadth of the three kingdoms—and even to France and Germany—equally partakes of the wholesale style in which everything is done in this establishment. Of old, it was thought a great thing to be able to get a supply of a dozen books at a time from a library, but Mr. Mudie sends whole libraries at once to some subscribers. Thus for the highest class subscription a hundred new books are despatched, and changed as often as required. This liberal arrangement has entirely superseded half the labour of country book-clubs, athenaeums, and literary societies. Instead of buying their books, they get them in the gross from Mr. Mudie, and of course can afford to supply their readers with a much larger number than they did of old for the same money.

It must not be supposed that this great lending library is constituted on the principle of the inferior ones we been so long accustomed to, where the bulk of the volumes consists of novels. This class of literature scarcely amounts to a third of the volumes circulated by Mr. Mudie. The great majority are composed of books of travel, adventure, biography, history, scientific works, and all the books of *genre*—as they say in painting—which are sought for by the public.

We can perhaps give a better idea of the nature of the most popular works by mentioning the circulation obtained by some of them. Macaulay had the honour of first bringing before the public the system of Mr. Mudie. In December, 1855, when vols. iii. and iv. of his 'History of England' were published, it was announced that 2,500 copies were at once supplied to this library.[43] The public looked on in astonishment: it was the number contained in many a respectable library. This number has, however, been far surpassed since. Of Livingstone's 'Travels in Africa' 3,250 copies were in circulation at one time. Here there was a union of religious readers and those fond of scientific travel and adventure, and at the lowest calculation not less than 30,000 readers must have been introduced to the work of the great South African traveller through the medium of this establishment. This alone is fame to a moderate man.

People are very fond of saying that nobody reads poetry now-a-days; yet 1,000 copies of 'Idylls of the King' were necessary to supply the demand for Tennyson's last new book. M'Clintock's 'Voyage in Search of Franklin' was another great success: 3,000 volumes were at one time 'reading.'[44] A very singular illustration of the effect of theological controversy upon a book was made evident when 'Essays and Reviews' were first published, inasmuch as fifty copies remained for some little time unread upon the shelves. As the idea arose that they were a little naughty, the demand began to increase, until ultimately Mr. Mudie had to place 2,000 copies in his library.

As a rule, novels have a short life, and not a merry one. We must except, however, some of the very first class, such as those of Miss Evans; 3,000 copies of 'Silas Marner,' for instance, were necessary to supply the demand.[45] Thackeray, Dickens, and Trollope are of course always asked for, and Carlyle and Kingsley, again, seem never out of fashion.

The peculiarities of readers are evinced by the style of their reading: thus one well-known and celebrated man confines himself to the Waverley Novels,—when 'Count Robert of Paris' is done, beginning again at 'Waverley.' Then there are the sluggish and the omnivorous readers. Many persons will read only one book during their subscription, whilst one lady, for her guinea subscription, read a number of volumes which, if purchased, would have cost her £200.

Town subscribers generally change their own books over the counter, and the bustle of the scene may be imagined when we say that, on the average, 1,000 exchanges are effected in the day, representing not less than 3,000 volumes. Suburban subscribers are supplied with their exchanges by cart, and those living in the country have their own boxes; these are of all sizes, from those holding four volumes to the monster packages holding one hundred. Upwards of a hundred of these boxes are received and sent out each day. Taken altogether, no less than 10,000 volumes are circulating diurnally through this establishment.

The amount of reading this represents is enormous, and it cannot be denied that, as an educating power, this great Circulating Library holds no mean position among the better classes of society. Its value to authors, moreover, cannot be lightly estimated, inasmuch as its machinery enables a bountiful supply of their works to be distributed to the remotest parts of the island, thereby increasing their reputation in an ever-widening circle. What a gulf of time seems to separate us from that age when the only means the great master-minds of our noble craft possessed of making themselves known to the world was that of cringing to some noble debauchee, or of beslavering a gouty earl in a sycophantish dedication!

'A Day at the London Free Libraries', *All the Year Round*, 35 (1892), 305-9 [305-8]

Relatively few public libraries were established following the parliamentary bill of 1850; it was not until the end of the century, especially in London, that they began to proliferate. *All the Year Round* details the organization and attraction of several of the new London free libraries. It sketches the different types of reader, and evokes working-class readers' discomfort at the libraries' regulation of their space.

'WELL, ta-ta, I am going to the club,' said he. 'And I to the free library,' said she. And they parted. But the words, overheard in the street, and from people who were quite up to date in the way of looks and equipment, suggested the coming to the front of the free library as a useful and pleasant social institution. A very just and general objection is indeed made to the title Free Library, and it is suggested that 'Public Library' is the proper description of what is in fact the common property of the public, and paid for out of the public funds. But anyhow the library, public and free, is becoming one of the features of the period, and is made use of by all classes of the community.

The growth of the free library was not very rapid from the date of the Act of Parliament authorizing its establishment, A.D. 1850, till within the last five years, when the number previously existing has been nearly doubled. In London especially the spread of public libraries has been rapid, and is going on at a rate that promises to leave no very extensive district unsupplied. [...]

Hearing first of one and then another of these public libraries opened here and there, the desire arises to see how they are moving along, and what use is made of them. There is our own suburban free library, which is only in a chrysalis state as yet, occupying three or four rooms in an ordinary house, and affording an adequate supply of newspapers and periodicals, but with only a limited store of books. Yet it is still already a great public convenience. From the moment the doors open there is a constant stream of people passing through the rooms. First of all, there are the youths and men of all ages, who are looking for means of earning a living, and who are searching the advertisement columns of situations vacant. Rather later we have a sprinkling of young women, who also want places, but who seem brighter and less dejected than the men. There are curates, too, who meet and converse, and write letters and postcards after consulting the clerical journals. Then we have ladies who have come to consult the oracles of fashion, and who muse and meditate over drawings of skirts and trains, and who wonder if the new style of hair will become them. Then there are the usual gentle old trots, who make out an hour or two over the newspaper or in quiet reverie over the fire. So the day goes on, till evening brings a fuller gathering of those who have been at work all day, who wade patiently through the monthly magazines and illustrated papers.

But twenty minutes on a tramcar brings us to a more important institution. Here is a pleasant, old-fashioned mansion in the midst of a well-wooded park, and among pleasant gardens, which is the home of the Free Library of Hammersmith. A handsome room, pleasantly overlooking lawns and flower-beds, is devoted to newspapers, and is well filled with readers at whatever hour it may be visited. But the adjoining lending library is the sight of the morning. There the space in front of the desks and counters of the librarians is filled with a cheerful, well-dressed crowd, the most part of whom are ladies— young ones predominating. Here are married ones giving an anxious glance every now and then to the outside, to make sure that Mabel is not playing tricks with baby and the perambulator. Here is Clara with the golden curls and her favourite novel under her arm, who is anxious, too, about the little terrier she left tied up to the railings outside. Mary, too, is among the crowd with the volumes of her five elder sisters as well as her own to change, and who has got a little mixed with it all. Yet, by means of the indicators, which madden only the candidate for books, and leave the librarian calm and unruffled— and the really good system, common now to public libraries in general—the work is got through with very little friction, and the throng about the counters, constantly renewed, is also constantly streaming away, volume under arm. [...]

But it may be as well to sample a district of an entirely different character. Bermondsey strikes one as being in most respects the opposite of Kensington—it is a district which does not attract genteel residents; its married ladies do not employ their afternoons in shopping, visiting, and gossiping; its young ladies are rarely artistic, literary, or critical, and being employed in jam factories, soap works, or other industries, have no great leisure for social amenities. [. . .]

[In Bermondsey] there rises before us a building high and handsome, in light brickwork, its broad windows all lighted up, and diffusing a cheering glow all round. It is the new public library, a building designed and built for a public library, and a very good model of what such a building should be. There is a handsome

FIG. 8. 'Ladies' Reading Room at a Free Library (Shepherd's Bush)',
Living London, ed. George R. Sims, iii
(London: Cassell and Co., 1902), 99.

entrance hall with tessellated floor, a fine news room, abundantly supplied with journals. On the same floor is the lending library, with abundant space for all requirements. On the floor above is a group of handsome rooms, well warmed and lighted, a magazine room, a reference library, not much used, and a 'ladies' room.' A ladies' room, says an authority on free libraries, means simply gossip. In this case, however, there is no gossip, for the sufficient reason that the room is empty. But even a little gossip is not a bad thing, and would be a relief from the somewhat oppressive silence that pervades the free library in general. Everywhere you see posted up, 'Silence!' 'Silence is requested,' and so faithfully is the injunction carried out by the public, that after a round of free libraries one has an impression of belonging to a race that has lost its power of speech. The silence really becomes oppressive, and one longs to hear a laugh or a whistle, or even a catcall, to break the solemn stillness of the scene.

Apart from this, which has nothing to do with Bermondsey in particular, what a noble foundation is this among the tanners and leather-dressers of Bermondsey, bringing cheerfulness and light into a neighbourhood somewhat gloomy and congested! Yet the people of Bermondsey do not crowd in as you might expect. A sprinkling of people are here—thirty or forty, perhaps, in the whole building. No doubt as the institution becomes better known, and as the young people grow up who have acquired a taste for reading, the use of this fine building will extend. But at the present time the working classes of the population are not much attracted by the library. The silence and good order are a little too much for them; they miss the freedom, the chaff, the jokes of out-of-doors and the full-flavoured hilarity of the public house. But while we are in South London there are many public libraries which will well repay a visit. Camberwell has a noble public library—the Livesy—owing much to the munificence of a wealthy founder; Clapham has recently built a fine library at a cost of four thousand pounds; Battersea has handsome new buildings devoted to public library and reading rooms; and Lambeth has taken the lead in establishing branch libraries in almost every quarter of its enormous circuit.

NOTES TO SECTION VI

1. Roger Chartier, 'Labourers and Voyagers: from the Text to the Reader', in David Finkelstein and Alistair McCleery (eds.), *The Book History Reader* (London: Routledge, 2002), 46.
2. George Moore, *Literature at Nurse, or Circulating Morals* (London: Vizetelly, 1885), 4.
3. Kate Flint, *The Woman Reader 1837–1914* (Oxford: Clarendon Press, 1993), 100.
4. George Birkbeck (1776–1841), Professor of Natural Philosophy at the Andersonian Institute, Glasgow; he later moved to London and, in 1824, helped found the London Mechanics' Institute.
5. Leonard Horner (1785–1864), Scottish geologist and reformer.
6. On Brougham, see Section I above.
7. *Original note*: We do not like to adopt a more *positive* manner of statement, because there is yet no collection of data on the subject (that we know of) sufficiently extensive and accurate to justify any one in treating the matter as settled and placed beyond dispute.
8. The Waverley novels are the influential series of Scottish historical novels published by Walter Scott, which began with *Waverley* (1814).
9. i.e. unique.
10. Notice.
11. i.e. brute
12. Newmarkets were long and close-fitting, often a sign of the sporting 'swell'.
13. Henry Stevens (1819–86), American librarian employed by the British Museum.
14. Rev. William Robert Fremantle, clergyman at Claydon (Buckinghamshire), gave evidence to the committee.
15. John Imray (1812–80), Scottish civil engineer, botanist, and medical researcher.
16. George Dawson (1821–76), Nonconformist minister and lecturer, prominent in Birmingham civic life.
17. François Guizot (1787–1872), statesmen and scholar, became French prime minister in 1847 but was overthrown in the 1848 revolution.
18. Jean Sylvain Van de Weyer (1802–74), Belgian Ambassador.
19. See Section III n. 11.
20. George Alexander Hamilton (1802–71), Tory politician, Financial Secretary to Treasury 1852, 1858–9.
21. Ralph Thicknesse, MP for Wigan.
22. Francis Richard Charteris (1818–1914), Peelite/liberal MP (1841–84), then 8th Earl of Wemyss.

23. James Wyld (1812–87), publisher; he held the title of Geographer to the Queen, and was MP for Bodmin 1847–52, 1857–68.

24. William Howitt (1792–1879), writer, journalist, and Quaker. His *Popular History of Priestcraft of All Ages and Nations* (1833) was strongly anti-clerical.

25. Hugh Fortescue Ebrington (1818–1905), Whig MP, Viscount Ebrington 1841–61, then succeeded as 3rd Earl of Fortescue.

26. The *Chronicles* by Jean Froissart (*c*.1337–*c*.1404) were written between 1369 and 1400. They concentrate on pageantry and the decadence of chivalry. The Anglo-Saxon Chronicles are a collection of manuscript histories written by monks from the ninth to the twelfth centuries: several cover the Norman Conquest. Both these texts were several times translated in the nineteenth century; the most likely reference here is to the version translated by John Allen Giles in 1847 for Bohn.

27. This refers almost certainly to the *History of the Revolutions in Europe* by Christophe-Guillaume Koch, translated from the French and reprinted numerous times in the 1830s and 1840s.

28. The Order of Odd Fellows is a benevolent society formed from the break-up of the medieval guild system. The name derives from how single members of different guilds (i.e. 'odd fellows') banded together.

29. Sir Harry Verney (1801–94), reforming Liberal MP, 2nd Baronet, of Claydon House, Buckinghamshire.

30. Samuel Smiles (1812–1904), journalist, writer, and businessman; best known for *Self-Help* (1859), which promoted working-class self-improvement.

31. Two shepherd girls saw an image of the Virgin Mary at La Salette, near Grenoble, in 1846; the cult of Our Lady of La Salette was authorized by the Catholic Church in 1850. The Chelsea Ghost appeared inside a house in September 1853; hundreds of people gathered outside waiting for its appearance.

32. Hanwell County Asylum opened in 1831.

33. Costermongers sold goods from barrows on the street.

34. G. W. M. Reynolds's best-selling serial fiction *The Mysteries of the Court of London* ran from 1850 to 1855, and described the intrigues and debauchery of the court of George IV.

35. See p. 167.

36. Fergus O'Connor (1796–1855), Chartist leader, journalist, and MP. Reynolds appeared on a Chartist platform in Trafalgar Square in 1848.

37. Cruikshank's 'Bottle' (1847) was a narrative series of prints showing the dangers of alcoholism. See also Section IX n. 18.

38. 'Eslops' was Cockney back-slang for 'police'.
39. 'Whoever is not at all noble is nothing'.
40. Richard Doyle (1824–83), cartoonist and illustrator, published *A Bird's Eye View of Society* in the *Cornhill Magazine* between 1861 and 1863.
41. David Livingstone (1813–73), Scottish explorer and missionary. The guinea edition of his *Missionary Travels and Researches in South Africa* (1857) had sold 30,000 by 1863 (Altick, *English Common Reader*, 388).
42. *Essays and Reviews* (John Parker and Son, 1860) was a collection of seven controversial theological essays (by Frederick Temple, chaplain to the Queen, and Benjamin Jowett, Regius Professor of Greek at Oxford, amongst others) that took account of recent researches into biblical history, as well as scientific discoveries in geology and biology. It caused an enormous media response, not just in the *Quarterly Review* (January 1861, vol. 109, 248–305).
43. See Section VIII n. 15.
44. Francis Leopold McClintock, *The Voyage of 'The Fox' in the Arctic Seas: a Narrative of the Discovery of the Fate of Sir John Franklin and his Companions* (London: John Murray, 1859).
45. Marian Evans (1819–80); real name of George Eliot.

VII

AUTHORS, JOURNALISTS,
REVIEWERS

INTRODUCTION

The business and practice of writing in the nineteenth century almost always involved moving between different modes of authorship. Categorizing writers simply as novelists, journalists, or critics invariably downplays the range of literary activities they were engaged in. It is more helpful to conceptualize nineteenth-century authorship in terms of the existence of a range of what Foucault called author-functions. Different author-functions were the product of the contrary publishing practices employed by distinct sectors of the literary marketplace; they also entailed different psychological relations between text and reader.

One major pressure upon authorship, in all its different forms, was the impetus towards professionalism, itself caused by the growth of the periodical press during the first half of the century. The commencement of a triumvirate of heavyweight Reviews in the first quarter of the nineteenth-century (see Section I), coupled with the advent of lighter periodicals like *Blackwood's* and *Fraser's Magazine* (1830–82), provided a new forum for critical discussion. In 1855 Walter Bagehot declared that, 'In this transition from ancient writing to modern, the review-like essay and the essay-like review fill a large space.'[1] Reviews and magazines, in part simply through their advent, but also through the multitudinous subjects they covered, provided significant new opportunities for writers to publish remunerative work. The article by George Henry Lewes, a stalwart of the *Westminster Review*, helps to explain why so many nineteenth-century writers published their work in the periodical press.

Fiction writers also benefited from the growth of the periodical press because, while Reviews did not include fiction, many miscellanies, journals, and magazines did. In particular, there was the growth of what Wilkie Collins called 'penny-novel journals' (see Section V). New novels were also published serially in separate monthly parts, each part normally costing a shilling. Dickens, famously, demonstrated the economic rewards this practice could generate with the *Posthumous Papers of the Pickwick Club*, the first number of which was issued in April 1836. Yet there were several other types of serial publication: Shand's article describes the different outlets available to novelists in the latter part of the century, particularly focusing on the importance of serial publication in newspapers in Britain and the colonies. As Graham Law has argued, from around the mid-1870s, the dominant mode of periodical publication 'moved from serialisation in single metropolitan magazines, whether monthlies like *Cornhill* or weeklies like *All the Year Round*, to syndication in groups of provincial weekly newspapers with complementary circulations.'[2]

The extracts from Lewes, Shand, and Braddon, emphasize that authors had to conform to the demands of different modes of publication. This might involve writing according to the political ethos of a specific journal. Alternatively, for a serial novelist, it meant keeping up with the industrial rhythm of weekly or monthly publication. In a letter to Bulwer-Lytton in 1862, Braddon declared that 'I have never written a line that has not been written against time—sometimes with a printer waiting outside the door.'[3] It also meant writing chapters that matched the space constraints of each instalment.

The contrast between the extracts by Braddon and Morley marks an important faultline in the character and status of nineteenth-century authorship. When in 1847 Lewes published his article in *Fraser's Magazine*, it was not signed. This was usual, for anonymity was a dominant convention in the monthly and quarterly periodical press until at least the 1860s. Anonymity allowed writers to undertake work for different periodicals, ventriloquizing the required viewpoints without literally subscribing to them.[4] In contrast, as the Braddon demonstrates, mass-market authors were usually named and could enjoy tremendous literary celebrity (see also Rymer in Section V). The convention of anonymous authorship in the higher-status periodical started to break down in the early 1860s, giving more prominence to individual writers over corporate voices. *Macmillan's Magazine* and the *Fortnightly Review*, launched in 1859 and 1865, were the first really respectable magazines to discard the convention, and Morley's article from the *Fortnightly* sketches the principal arguments in favour of signed authorship.

The development of journalism was determined by the same impetus towards professionalism that affected all forms of nineteenth-century writing. As a neologism for newspaper reportage, the word 'journalism' was itself coined only in the early 1830s. In a review of a French work, *Du Journalisme*, in 1833, a grateful Gibbons Merle declared that ' "Journalism" is a good name for the thing meant; at any rate it is compact, and when once in circulation is incapable of equivocal meanings. A word was sadly wanted.'[5] Until at least mid-century, most journalists were gentleman-amateurs. The low status attendant upon full-time newspaper reportage is exemplified by the disrepute endured by penny-a-liners, whose function is described in the article from *Chambers's Edinburgh Journal*.

The increased scale of the newspaper press, particularly after 1855, was instrumental in expanding the number of full-time journalists. The establishment of journalism as a profession, which encouraged an increase in the number of university-educated men becoming re-porters, also produced a long-desired rise in the status of journalists. This improvement in journalistic status was also aided by the fact that the decline in authorial anonymity also fed into newspaper practices. Individual journalists became more prominent; a trend that began with the work of special correspondents like William Howard Russell and his reporting of the Crimean War for *The Times*. W. T. Stead, through both his critical essays and his highly publicized trial and imprisonment following his exposé of child prostitution in 1885, is another key figure in promoting the power of the journalist. The outcry provoked by his report in the *Pall Mall Gazette*, the 'Maiden Tribute of Modern Babylon', directly led to a change of law in August 1885, which saw the age of consent raised for girls to 16. Stead's essay in this section, 'The Future of Journalism', is a crusading attempt to place journalists at the centre of the democratic political process.

In the final extract Charlotte O'Conor Eccles describes the trials of a provincial female journalist attempting to establish herself in Lon-don. The work offered to O'Conor Eccles, including the anonymous working-up of articles for better-known authors, highlights the less salubrious hack-work that women writers in particular could be forced into. Even when successful, the multiple literary activities O'Conor Eccles undertakes suggest the continuing overlap between journalists, reviewers, and novelists.

FURTHER READING:

Brake, Madden, and Jones, *Investigating Victorian Journalism*; Brake, *Print in Transition*; Cross; Edwards; Foucault; Gissing; King, *London Journal*; Law; McCalman; Onslow; Shattock, *Politics*; Sutherland, *Victorian Novelists*; Trollope; Wiener, *Innovators*; Woodmansee and Jaszi.

'Penny-a-Liners', *Chambers's Edinburgh Journal*, NS 3 (1 February 1845), 65–9 [65–66, 68–9]

Penny-a-liners were one of the few types of full-time journalist up to at least the 1850s. Freelance column-fillers, their income wholly depended on the volume of words they published. *Chambers's* article reflects their importance in the light of the press expansion of the 1840s. *Chambers's* (see below, p. 398) was an improving miscellany that sold at 1½ *d.* and did not employ penny-a-liners. This article's approach exemplifies its desire to combine popular education with recreation.

PENNY-A-LINERS are the stragglers of the London press—the foragers for stray news—the narrators of fires, street accidents, suicides, murders, police cases, and all the odds and ends that fill up the columns of newspapers in default of political opinions, debates, and foreign intelligence. They have no engagement with the press. They are often wholly unknown, except by name, to its conductors. Their plan of life is simply to contribute, to all journals alike, whatever scraps of news they may be able to collect. For this purpose they hang about hospitals, fire-offices, and coroners' courts; besiege police-officers, churchwardens, overseers, and magistrates; and are perpetually going about in watch for what the chapter of accidents may throw in their way. They are paid by the line for their contributions, and hence their designation; although, of late years, they have so far advanced in the world as to receive three-halfpence per line, instead of one penny, as formerly. They have of course an inducement to tell their stories at as great length as possible; and one of the chief miseries of London editors and sub-editors is to prune their exuberance—'cut them down,' as it is technically termed—by weeding their phraseology of all their super-abundant epithets and needless circumlocutions. There may be about sixty men known as having this off-and-on connexion with the press, besides perhaps as many more who pretend to the same connexion, and live by the frauds they commit under that assumption.

The penny-a-liner, humble and unknown as he is—gaining a precarious and generally miserable existence; having £10 in his pocket one week, the proceeds of some interesting murder, and starving the next because people are too moral or too fortunate to afford him, for the time, anything to write about—passes a life, we seriously believe, by no means deficient of enjoyment. Amidst all the occasional distresses of his situation, he must have some satisfaction in seeing the extensive circulation given, by the press at home and abroad, to his homely lucubrations. And his very duty or business involves a variety of scene and pursuit that cannot be otherwise than agreeable. [. . .]

Some penny-a-liners have circuits as extensive as the judges, and traverse periodically a certain district, narrating, in default of crimes and misfortunes, the details of parish squabbles, local elections, the appearance of the crops—anything that appears to them of sufficient public interest to warrant a paragraph. In some districts, the travelling penny-a-liner passes for a very great man, and receives no small attention, with good fare and free quarters, from inn and hotel keepers, from the hope that some day, in the Times or the Morning Chronicle, he will say a good word for the excellence of his accommodation, and the urbanity and good wines of the host—an expectation which the obscure penny-a-liner but rarely has an opportunity of fulfilling. He is also a person of some consequence with police-inspectors, whom he may have occasion in some future paragraph to designate as 'zealous and active officers.' Nor is his consideration less with parish orators; for if he cannot repeat their eloquence in full, he can manage to say in print that they delivered 'able speeches,' and that they were 'loudly and repeatedly cheered.' If the penny-a-liner of this kind have any faults besides his verbosity, it is his impudence. He has no scruples. A private house is not private to him; he lives by narrating incidents, and incidents he will have, at whatever sacrifice. It has happened ere this that the penny-a-liner has been ducked under a pump for his impertinent prying; that he has been left on a mud-bank by the indignant boatmen, for obtruding himself on the privacy of distinguished or royal personages in their own barge; and suffered various other like mishaps and indignities in the 'pursuit of knowledge under difficulties.'[6] Nay, the penny-a-liner has been known to suffer indignity with a willing mind, and even with delight, if it would aid him to write a report for the morning journals which no rival penny-a-liner could have the opportunity of supplying. He has been known to put on the livery of a great family, and wait upon the guests at table, napkin in hand, like any other footman, that he might gather the names of the distinguished guests, and describe their rich banquet next morning in the columns of all the journals. And when he could not do this by the connivance of the great man himself, he has bribed the butler, and been admitted as an extra hand for the extraordinary occasion. It is not often, however, that he is reduced to shifts like these; for the great man who gives a feast, or his great lady, is generally but too happy to have his or her magnificence duly emblazoned in the newspapers; and the confidential butler is instructed to treat the penny-a-liner well, give him all the particulars he desires, with meat and drink, and a fee into the bargain. [...]

There is, however, a far larger class of penny-a-liners, who never move for business out of the limits of the metropolis, and who, enjoying there a beat of their own, might chance to meet with unpleasant resistance if they were to set a foot professionally in any suburban or provincial walk which a brother of the trade had, from use and wont, appropriated to himself. It is curious to note how, without authority, and solely by the prescriptive right of prior occupation and long usage, men of this kind have contrived to parcel out the metropolis amongst them, each man reigning supreme penny-a-liner and representative of the press in his own district, and taking charge of its news to the exclusion of every competitor. Some of these districts are very large, and some comparatively small. A few of them, in the neighbourhood of the Strand and Westminster more especially, are quite overrun with these literary prowlers. [...] Generally speaking, the penny-a-liners of London may be divided into the following varieties:—the police-reporter, the fashionable reporter, the fireman, the accident and murder man, the inquest man, and the vestry man; with now and then a mingling of these various functions in the person of some more active and intelligent member of the fraternity. [...]

It may be stated, in conclusion, that the five morning journals of London pay on the average about L.1000 a-year each for penny-a-line reports; and that, with the smaller payments made by the evening and Sunday journals, the penny-a-liners share among them about L.7000 per annum. What the dishonest members of the fraternity draw from the public by their extortions and frauds, cannot be so easily calculated; but from the repeated instances that occur in which large sums are paid for suppressions, the whole amount must be very considerable.

In this slight description, it is trusted that, although many things have been omitted, enough has been said to throw light upon the means of livelihood of a singular and important class of the community, whose numbers are few, but whose influence is great. The talent of some of them, and the usefulness of most, have been freely acknowledged; and if the veil has been lifted to expose the roguery of others, it has not been done for the satisfaction of mere curiosity, but to clear the high-minded and independent press of London from the aspersions that the malpractices of these false pretenders to a connexion with it have too often brought upon its character.

[George Henry Lewes], 'The Condition of Authors in England, Germany, and France', *Fraser's Magazine for Town and Country*, 35 (1847), 285–95 [285–9, 292–5]

George Henry Lewes (1817–78), distinguished journalist, critic, and intellectual, supported himself through a wide range of literary activity. As well as articles on philosophy, science, drama, and literature, in 1847 his already published work included a novel, *Ranthorpe* (1847), and *A Biographical Dictionary of Philosophy* (1845–6). Lewes's article argues that the expansion of the periodical press was vital for the professionalization of authorship. *Fraser's Magazine* was a monthly miscellany whose own diversity demonstrates why the periodical press encouraged such polymathic authors.

Literature has become a profession. It is a means of subsistence, almost as certain as the bar or the church. The number of aspirants increases daily, and daily the circle of readers grows wider. That there are some evils inherent in such a state of things it would be folly to deny; but still greater folly would it be to see nothing beyond these evils. Bad or good, there is no evading the 'great fact,' now that it is so firmly established. We may deplore, but we cannot alter it. Declamation in such a cause is, therefore, worse than idle.

Some inquiry into the respective conditions of literature in England, Germany, and France, may not be without interest; and in the course of that inquiry we shall, perhaps, meet with some suggestions towards bettering the condition of English writers, which may be worth considering.

If we reflect upon the great aims of literature, we shall easily perceive how important it is that the lay teachers of the people should be men of an unmistakeable vocation. Literature should be a profession, not a trade. It should be a profession, just lucrative enough to furnish a decent subsistence to its members, but in no way lucrative enough to tempt speculators. As soon as its rewards are high enough and secure enough to tempt men to enter the lists for the sake of the reward, and parents think of it as an opening for their sons, from that moment it becomes vitiated. Then will the ranks, already so numerous, be swelled by an innumerable host of hungry pretenders. It will be—and, indeed, is, now fast approaching that state—like the army of Xerxes, swelled and encumbered by women, children, and ill-trained troops. It should be like a Macedonian phalanx, chosen, compact, and irresistible.[7]

Let not this be thought chimerical. By a calculation made some years ago, the authors of England amounted to many thousands. These, of course, included barristers with scarce briefs, physicians with few patients, clergymen on small livings, idle women, rich men, and a large crop of aspiring noodles; the professional authors formed but a small item in the sum total. Yet we have only to suppose the rewards of literature secure, and the pursuit lucrative, and we have then the far greater proportion of this number quitting their own professions, and taking seriously to that of literature.

It may, perhaps, be objected to our argument respecting literature as a profession for which parents should train their sons, that without great talent there could be no success, consequently, the undeserving would pay the penalty of misplaced ambition. To which we answer, that in literature, as in every thing else, personal interest will always precede anything short of splendid talents in obtaining the quiet lucrative positions, especially when government rewards are numerous. We have only to cast our eyes around us to see, even in the present small amount of patronage, how little falls to the share of real merit. [...]

In money payments to literary men England far surpasses either France or Germany. The booksellers are more generous in England; abroad, the governments. In making this assumption, we purposely exclude such exceptional cases as those of Dickens, Eugène Sue, and Thiers;[8] the extraordinary success of their works warrants extraordinary payments. Yet even here the advantage is greatly on the side of England; Dickens received 3000*l.* for one of his tiny Christmas stories, whereas Eugène Sue only received 4000*l.* for the ten volumes of his *Juif Errant*.[9]

But to descend into the ordinary current, we find able literary men in England making incomes *averaging* 300*l.* a-year, some less, of course, and some more; the same men would scarcely be able to keep body and soul together in France or Germany. A few curious facts will illustrate this. While Bulwer receives his 1000*l.*, and, in one or two instances, even 1500*l.* for a novel, and James probably little less, Balzac (and we have it on his own authority), with all his popularity, with all his fecundity, has a hard task to make 300*l.* a-year.[10] While our Quarterlies were paying often 50*l.* and, in some cases, even 100*l.* for one article, and to their ordinary contributors, sixteen and twenty guineas a sheet, the French Quarterlies were paying ordinary contributors at the following rate:—100 francs (4*l.*) a sheet; if the article, however, exceeded a sheet, no more than 100 francs was due; and an author's *article de début* was not paid for at all. Other contributors, whose names were an attraction, received of course higher prices; but the highest price ever paid by the *Revue des Deux Mondes* [. . .] was that paid to George Sand; and how much, think you, was that maximum?— 250 francs (10*l.*) a sheet![11] So that while a solid, plodding, well-informed Edinburgh Reviewer, was receiving twenty guineas a sheet, one of the greatest of French contemporaries was receiving half that sum, as the highest *honorarium* the review could bestow.

It is indeed to be deducted from the above statement, that the author of an article in a French review does not part with the copyright, as in the English reviews. He can reprint it elsewhere, and, in the case of a novel, obtain for it a price equal, if not exceeding, that which the review paid. But this, although it makes novel-writing considerably more lucrative, does not affect our position, because the authors of critical or philosophical articles have slender chance of being called upon to reprint their essays.

One great reason of this low payment for contributions is, of course, the limited sale of the *Revue*. At the time when the *Revue des Deux Mondes* had only one rival in France, its circulation, we believe, never exceeded 3000 copies, in spite of its having all France, Germany, England, and Italy, for a public. In England at the same time there were five Quarterlies, with REGINA, *Blackwood, Tait,* &c., most of them counting their subscribers by thousands, in spite of a public limited to our island. [. . .]

It may reasonably excite some surprise, how two such very literary countries as France and Germany should suffer literature to remain in so miserable a condition; whilst in England affairs look far more encouraging. It cannot be our greater wealth which makes the difference, because if our wealth be greater, our expenses are also heavier; because, moreover, our wealth, only a few years ago, did not operate at all in that way; our authors were as beggarly as those of our neighbours. The real cause we take to be the excellence and abundance of periodical literature. It is by our reviews, magazines, and journals, that the vast majority of professional authors earn their bread; and the astonishing mass of talent and energy which is thus thrown into periodical literature is not only quite unexampled abroad, but is, of course, owing to the certainty of moderate yet, on the whole, sufficient remuneration.

We are not deaf to the loud wailings set up (by periodical writers, too!) against periodical literature. We have heard—not patiently, indeed, but silently—the declamations uttered against this so-called disease of the age; how it fosters superficiality—how it ruins all earnestness—how it substitutes brilliancy for solidity, and wantonly sacrifices truth to effect; we have listened to so much eloquence, and read so much disquisition on the subject, that, were we only half as anxious to sacrifice truth to effect as are the eloquent declaimers whom we here oppose, we might round a period, or produce an essay on the evils of periodical literature, which (to speak it with the downcast eyes of modesty) should call forth the approbation of all those serious men who view with sorrow the squandered ability of our age. Why should we not? It would be far easier than to look calmly, closely into the matter. It is always a cheap thing this declamation. It covers a multitude of deficiencies. It is paid for as highly as honest labour in inquiry, and saves so much time! In the present instance, it could be done with so little fatigue, and would fall in so softly with the commonplaces of every reader, and would flatter the 'seriousness' of magazine readers, to whom great works are 'sacred,'—men who scorn 'cheap literature,' and read none other. Why should the present writer quit so easy a path for the rugged path of investigation? Simply, because he is a periodical writer; and though, perhaps, as ready to sacrifice truth, occasionally, to what he may foolishly deem more effective (always a questionable process), as any foolish writer of books, yet in the present instance, at any rate, it is clear to him that truth is worth all the rhetoric that could be brought to bear on the subject.

The truth then is, that, in these much-decried days of ours, there is no lack of laborious, thoughtful writers, devoting the fairest years of their lives to the production of works, which may stand beside those composed in any time,—so far, at least, as mere labour, honest inquiry, and weighty consideration of the matter can be reckoned; ability, for obvious reasons, we put out of the question. [...]

Periodical literature is a great thing. It is a potent instrument for the education of a people. It is the only decisive means of rescuing authorship from the badge of servility. Those who talk so magniloquently about serious works, who despise the essay-like and fragmentary nature of periodical literature, forget that while there are many men who can produce a good essay, there has at all times been a scarcity of those who can produce good works. A brilliant essay, or a thoughtful fragment, is not the less brilliant, is not the less thoughtful, because it is brief, because it does not exhaust the subject. And yet the author, in all probability, could neither continue his brilliancy through the 'vast expanse' of a work, nor could he, in attempting to exhaust his subject, continue in the same thoughtful strain, but would inevitably fall into the commonplaces which bolster up the heads of all but *very* remarkable men. [...]

In England the popular authors in all departments gain prizes; but there are few blanks to men of talent: for a great mass of journalists, critics, essayists, tale writers, jesters, there are means of decent subsistence. Talent commands a price; industry is not unrewarded.

As a specimen of what industry will do, even when backed by very little ability and limited acquirement, we may mention the case of a German, who, after a residence of a few years in England, learned the language sufficiently to write it well enough for biographical dictionaries, cyclopædias, and the like, and then earned something like 600*l.* a-year, as a hack-writer on Greek and Roman history and archaeology, aided by translations from the German, by editing Latin grammars, and contributing to various works of compilation. In this labour he displayed no talent of any sort, no original thinking, not even remarkable erudition; all he displayed was a ready knowledge of a few textbooks, and an untiring perseverance.

Now let us turn the tables. Having witnessed the superiority of England, let us gaze awhile at its inferiority. In money payments we surpass all nations; our publishers are the most liberal of

Mæcenases.[12] But in respect for the profession of literature, and in solicitude for the waning days of its members, we are on a level with the Esquimaux. John Bull is at all times ready to pay. Guineas are tangible, definite, of exchangeable value. But respect, solicitude, anticipative charity, are vague, impalpable motives, which move not his stolid soul. He will pay for a book; he will subscribe for the widow and children of a heart-broken, misery-broken author; but to anticipate that misery by prospective benevolence, is not an idea that would occur to him, or occurring, that would long torment him. [...]

To rescue men of letters from the sad necessity of living 'from hand to mouth,' and to enable them to labour seriously at serious works, without being haunted by the fear of poverty, without being forced to write down to the popular taste, government's best, and indeed only means is, to institute professorships, and open public offices to authors. It has been said, and with some show of justice, that government has no more to do with the remuneration of authorship than it has with the remuneration of other professions; literature being for the public, the public will pay for its wants. But in this argument one very important point is overlooked. Literature is a profession in which the author has not only to struggle against his brother authors, but also against a host of interlopers. Authors without engagements cannot step in and eke out their income with a little chancery practice, or a bit of common law; but lawyers without clients can and do step into the field of literature. Thus the professional author is surrounded with rivals, not only as hungry as himself, but willing and able to work for lower wages, because they are not, as he is, solely dependent upon literature. As this state of things is inevitable, it must be evident that some protection would be more justly bestowed upon authors than upon other professions. That protection should not be pensions, but employment.

Pensions there should be, but only for those who are old, or disabled by ill-health. It is ridiculous to name the present amount of the pensions; and somewhat disgraceful has been the bestowment of many of them.[13] Strange that no legislator has the courage to take some step in this direction! No man will deny the claim of a decayed author. The veteran writer, battered in long and hard-fought service— in that service grown old and almost useless, is surely as much entitled to a pension from the government as the veteran soldier. The man who has devoted his talents and energies to the laborious task of improving and amusing mankind, has done the State as much service as the man who marched at the head of a regiment, even if every march had been followed by a victory.

Mary Elizabeth Braddon, *The Doctor's Wife*, from *Temple Bar*, 10 (1864), 160-2, 309-12

In *The Doctor's Wife*, Braddon (1835–1915) adapted the plot of Flaubert's as-yet untranslated *Madame Bovary*. She included a fictional portrait of a sensation author, Sigismund Smith, probably based on J. F. Smith (see Section V). While Braddon sympathetically depicts the demands placed upon authors by publishers and readers, and the conventions of popular genres, her account is also implicitly patronizing in that, particularly after the publication of *Lady Audley's Secret* in three volumes (1862), she enjoyed much greater literary status than her fictional author. Smith exemplifies the stereotype of the popular author from which Braddon was determined to distance herself.

Mr. Sigismund Smith was a sensation author. That bitter term of reproach, 'sensation,' had not been invented for the terror of romancers in the fifty-second year of this present century; but the thing existed nevertheless in divers forms, and people wrote sensation novels as unconsciously as Monsieur Jourdain talked prose.[14] Sigismund Smith was the author of about half-a-dozen highly-spiced fictions, which enjoyed an immense popularity amongst the classes who like their literature as they like their tobacco—very strong. Sigismund had never in his life presented himself before the public in a complete form; he appeared in weekly numbers at a penny, and was always so appearing; and except on one occasion when he found himself, very greasy and dog's-eared at the edges, and not exactly pleasant to the sense of smell,—on the shelf of a humble librarian and newsvendor, who dealt in tobacco and sweetstuff as well as literature,—Sigismund had never known what it was to be bound. He was well paid for his work, and he was contented. He had his ambition, which was to write a great novel; and the archetype of this *magnum opus* was the dream which he carried about with him wherever he went, and fondly nursed by night and day. In the mean time he wrote for his public, which was a public that bought its literature in the same manner as its pudding—in penny slices.

There was very little to look at in the court below the window, so George Gilbert fell to watching his friend, whose rapid pen scratched along the paper in a breathless way, which indicated a dashing and Dumas-like style of literature, rather than the polished composition of a Johnson or an Addison. Sigismund only drew breath once, and then he paused to make frantic gashes at his shirt-collar with an inky bone paper-knife that lay upon the table.

'I'm only trying whether a man would cut his throat from right to left, or left to right,' Mr. Smith said, in answer to his friend's look of terror; 'it's as well to be true to nature; or as true as one can be, for a pound a page;—double-column pages, and eighty-one lines in a column. A man would cut his throat from left to right: he couldn't do it the other way, without making perfect slices of himself.'

'There's a suicide, then, in your story?' George said, with a look of awe.

'*A* suicide!' exclaimed Sigismund Smith; '*a* suicide in the *Smuggler's Bride*! why, it teems with suicides. There's the Duke of Port St. Martin's, who walls himself up alive in his own cellar; and there's Leonie de Pasdebasque, the ballet-dancer, who throws herself out of Count Caesar Maraschetti's private balloon; and there's Lilia, the dumb girl,—the penny public like dumb girls,—who sets fire to herself to escape from the—in fact, there's lots of them,' said Mr. Smith, dipping his pen in his ink, and hurrying wildly along the paper.

The boy came back before the last page was finished, and Mr. Smith detained him for five or ten minutes; at the end of which time he rolled up the manuscript, still damp, and dismissed the printer's emissary.

'Now, George,' he said, 'I can talk to you.'

Sigismund was the son of a Wareham attorney, and the two young men had been schoolfellows at the Classical and Commercial Academy in the Wareham Road. They had been schoolfellows, and were very sincerely attached to each other. Sigismund was supposed to be reading for the Bar; and for the first twelve months of his sojourn in the Temple the young man had worked honestly and conscientiously; but finding that his legal studies resulted in nothing but mental perplexity and confusion, Sigismund grew weary of waiting for the briefs that never came, and beguiled his leisure by the pursuit of literature.

He found literature a great deal more profitable and a great deal easier than the law; and he abandoned himself entirely to the composition of such works as are to be seen, garnished with striking illustrations, in the windows of humble newsvendors in the smaller and dingier thoroughfares of every large town. Sigismund gave himself wholly to this fascinating pursuit, and perhaps produced more sheets of that mysterious stuff which literary people call 'copy' than any other author of his age.

It would be almost impossible for me adequately to describe the difference between Sigismund Smith as he was known to the very few friends who knew anything at all about him, and Sigismund Smith as he appeared on paper.

In the narrow circle of his home Mr. Smith was a very mild young man, with the most placid blue eyes that ever looked out of a human head, and a good deal of light curling hair. He was a very mild young man. He could not have hit any one if he had tried ever so; and if you had hit him, I don't think he would have minded—much. It was not in him to be very angry; or to fall in love, to any serious extent; or to be desperate about anything. Perhaps it was that he exhausted all that was passionate in his nature in penny numbers, and had nothing left for the affairs of real life. People who were impressed by his fictions, and were curious to see him, generally left him with a strong sense of disappointment, if not indignation. They had their own idea of what the author of the *Smuggler's Bride* and *Lilia the Deserted* ought to be, and Mr. Smith did not at all come up to the popular standard; so the enthusiastic admirers of his romances were apt to complain of him as an impostor when they beheld him in private life.

Was this meek young man the Byronic hero they had pictured? Was this the author of *Colonel Montefiasco, or the Brand upon the Shoulder-blade?* They had imagined a splendid creature, half magician, half brigand, with a pale face and fierce black eyes, a tumbled mass of raven hair, a bare white throat, a long black-velvet dressing gown, and thin tapering hands with queer agate and onyx rings coiling up the flexible fingers.

And then the surroundings. An oak panelled-chamber, of course— black oak, with grotesque and diabolical carvings jutting out at the angles of the room; a crystal globe upon a porphyry pedestal; a mysterious picture, with a curtain drawn before it—certain death being the fate of him who dared to raise that curtain by so much as a corner. A mantel-piece of black marble, and a collection of pistols and scymetars, swords and yataghans,—especially yataghans,—glimmering and flashing in the firelight. A little show of eccentricity in the way of household pets: a bear under the sofa, and a tame cobra di capella coiled upon the hearth-rug. This was the sort of thing the penny public expected of Sigismund Smith; and, lo, here was a young man with perennial ink-smudges upon his face, and an untidy chamber in the Temple, with nothing more romantic than a waste-paper basket, a litter of old letters and tumbled proofs, and a cracked teapot simmering upon the hob. [...]

For very lack of employment, George grew to take an interest in his friend's labour, and asked him questions about the story that poured so rapidly from his hurrying pen.

'What's it all about, Sigismund?' he demanded. 'Is it funny?'

'Funny!' cried Mr. Smith, with a look of horror; 'I should think not, indeed. Who ever heard of penny numbers being funny? What the penny public want, is plot, and plenty of it; surprises, and plenty of 'em; mystery, as thick as a November fog. Don't you know the sort of thing? "The clock of St Paul's had just sounded eleven hours;"—it's generally a translation, you know, and St Paul's stands for Notre Dame;—"a man came to appear upon the quay which extends all itself the length between the bridges of Waterloo and London." There isn't any quay, you know; but you're obliged to have it so on account of the plot. "This man—who had a true head of vulture, the nose pointed, sharp, terrible; all that there is of most ferocious; the eyes cavernous, and full of a sombre fire—carried a bag upon his back. Presently, he stops himself. He regards with all his eyes the quay, nearly desert; the water, black and slimy, which stretches itself at his feet. He listens, but there is nothing. He bends himself upon the border of the quay. He puts aside the bag from his shoulders, and something of dull, heavy, slides slowly downwards and falls into the water. At the instant that the heavy burden sinks with a dull noise to the bottom of the river, there is a voice, loud and piercing, which seems to elevate itself out of the darkness: 'Philip Launay, what dost thou do there with the corpse of thy victim?' "

'That's the sort of thing for the penny public,' said Mr. Smith; 'or else a good strong combination story.'

'What do you call a combination story?' Mr. Gilbert asked inno-
cently.

'Why, you see, when you're doing four great stories a week for a
public that must have a continuous flow of incident, you can't be quite
as original as a strict sense of honour might prompt you to be; and the
next best thing you can do if you haven't got ideas of your own, is to
steal other people's ideas in an impartial manner. Don't empty one
man's pocket, but take a little bit all round. The combination novel
enables a young author to present his public with all the brightest
flowers of fiction neatly arranged into every variety of garland. I'm
doing a combination novel now—the *Heart of Midlothian* and the
Wandering Jew.[15] You've no idea how admirably the two stories
blend. In the first place, I throw my period back into the Middle
Ages—there's nothing like the Middle Ages for getting over the
difficulties of a story. Good gracious me! why, what is there that
isn't possible if you go back to the time of the Plantagenets? I make
Jeannie Deans a dumb girl,—there's twice the interest in her if you
make her dumb,—and I give her a goat and a tambourine, because,
you see, the artist likes that sort of thing for his illustrations. I think
you'd admit that I've very much improved upon Sir Walter Scott—a
delightful writer, I allow, but decidedly a failure in penny numbers—if
you were to run your eye over the story, George; there's only seventy-
eight numbers out yet, but you'll be able to judge of the plot. Of
course, I don't make Aureola,—I call my Jeannie "Aureola;" rather a
fine name, isn't it? and entirely my own invention,—of course I don't
make Aureola walk from Edinburgh to London.[16] What would be the
good of that? why, any body *could* walk it if they only took long
enough about it. I make her walk from London to ROME, to get a
Papal Bull for the release of her sister from the Tower of London.
That's something of a walk, I flatter myself; over the Alps—which
admits of Aureola's getting buried in the snow, and dug out again by a
Mount St. Bernard's dog; and then walled up alive by the monks
because they suspect her of being friendly to the Lollards, and dug out
again by Caesar Borgia, who happens to be travelling that way, and
asks a night's lodging, and hears Aureola's tambourine behind the
stone wall in his bedroom, and digs her out and falls in love with her;
and she escapes from his persecution out of a window, and lets herself
down the side of the mountain by means of her gauze scarf, and

dances her way to Rome, and obtains an audience of the Pope, and gets mixed up with the Jesuits;—and that's where I work into the *Wandering Jew*,' concluded Mr. Smith.

George Gilbert ventured to suggest that in the days when the Plantagenet ruled our happy isle, Ignatius Loyola had not yet founded his wonderful brotherhood; but Mr. Smith acknowledged this prosaic suggestion with a smile of supreme contempt.

'Oh, if you tie me down to facts,' he said, 'I can't write at all.'[17]

'But you like writing?'

'For the penny public? Oh, yes; I like writing for them. There's only one objection to the style—it's apt to give an author a tendency towards bodies.'

Mr. Gilbert was compelled to confess that this last remark was incomprehensible to him.

'Why, you see, the penny public require excitement,' said Mr. Smith; 'and in order to get the excitement up to a strong point, you're obliged to have recourse to bodies. Say your hero murders his father, and buries him in the coal-cellar in No. 1. What's the consequence? There's an undercurrent of the body in the coal-cellar running through every chapter, like the subject in a fugue or a symphony. You drop it in the treble, you catch it up in the bass; and then it goes sliding up into the treble again, and then drops down with a melodious groan into the bass; and so on to the end of the story. And when you've once had recourse to the stimulant of bodies, you're like a man who's accustomed to strong liquors, and to whose vitiated palate simple drinks seem flat and wishy-washy. I think there ought to be a literary temperance-pledge, by which the votaries of the ghastly and melodramatic school might bind themselves to the renunciation of the bowl and dagger, the midnight rendezvous, the secret grave dug by the lantern-light under a black grove of cypress, the white-robed figure gliding in the gray gloaming athwart a lonely churchyard, and all the alcoholic elements of fiction. But you see, George, it isn't so easy to turn teetotaller,' added Mr. Smith, doubtfully; 'and I scarcely know that it is so very wise to make the experiment. Are not reformed drunkards the dullest and most miserable of mankind? Isn't it better for a man to do his best in the style that is natural to him than to do badly in another man's line of business? *Box and Cox* is not a great work when criticised upon sternly aesthetic principles; but I would rather be the author of *Box and Cox*,[18] and hear my audience screaming with laughter from the rise of the curtain to the fall thereof, than write a dull five-act tragedy, in the unities of which Aristotle himself could find no flaw, but from whose performance panic-stricken spectators should slink away or ere the second act came to its dreary close. I think I should like to have been Guilbert de Pixérécourt, the father and prince of melodrama, the man whose dramas were acted thirty thousand times in France before he died (and how many times in England?); the man who reigned supreme over the playgoers of his time, and has not yet ceased to reign.[19] Who ever quotes any passage from the works of Guilbert de Pixérécourt, or remembers his name? But to this day his dramas are acted in every country theatre; his persecuted heroines weep and tremble; his murderous scoundrels run their two hours' career of villainy, to be dragged off scowling to subterranean dungeons, or to die impenitent and groaning at the feet of triumphant virtue. Before nine o'clock tonight there will be honest country folks trembling for the fate of Theresa, the Orphan of Geneva, and simple matrons weeping over the peril of the Wandering Boys.[20] But Guilbert de Pixérécourt was never a great man; he was only popular. If a man can't have a niche in the Walhalla, isn't it something to have his name in big letters in the play-bills on the boulevard?

John Morley, 'Anonymous Journalism,' *Fortnightly Review*, OS 8 NS 2 (1867), 287-92

The convention of anonymous authorship, which was used by most high-status reviews and magazines, began to break down in the 1860s, led by the launch of *Macmillan's Magazine* and the *Fortnightly Review* in 1859 and 1865 respectively. The discarding of anonymity by the *Fortnightly* was keyed into its rejection of any univocal editorial voice and/or political affiliation. John Morley (1838–1923), a future Liberal MP, who took over the editorship of the *Fortnightly Review* in January 1867, here outlines the arguments in favour of signed authorship.

ONE of the most striking characteristics of English society for a long time has been its artificial and unnatural silence. On every kind of subject men shrink from speaking the things which are clearest and most constant in their own minds. At no time has a cautious reserve sealed men's lips so fast. So far, this reserve may possibly have been a useful condition of the transformation of opinion which has been in progress beneath it. A half-hypocritical silence is no worse than hasty, half-sincere effusive speech. But silence cannot be an eternal condition of things. Men will not always continue to revere hollow and eviscerated conventions. Signs are not wanting that we are on the eve of an era of free speech. The dullest man as he walks serenely over the ashes of burnt-out ideas must now and again hear sounds as of the rush and crackle of flame beneath the thin stratum which he confounds with the solid everlasting earth. [...]

This change of temper presses more strongly than ever upon us the desirableness of making journalists responsible for what they write. If controversy is to become more sincere, more earnest, more direct, and if, therefore, there is to be more hard hitting, it is indispensable that those who take a part in it should give the strongest possible guarantee that they mean exactly what they profess to mean, neither more nor less, and that they are ready to stand by it. [...]

Still, everybody will agree that no journalist ought deliberately to write a word which he would feel disgraced by owning, however unwilling he might be actually to avow it on special grounds. Granting this much, in what way would signing his name affect what he wrote? In what way would it contribute to the improvement of journalism and the diffusion of sound views? Surely in the same way in which the exaction of personal responsibility operates in other fields of activity. First, the knowledge that his reputation was involved would stimulate him to take as much pains as he possibly could to write with cogency and effect. Then, apart from popularity and reputation, the consciousness of individual responsibility adds dignity and strength to a writer as it does to anybody else. A man may write anonymously with as much brilliance and mere cleverness, as if he were to sign his name, but the chances are very much against his writing with as much fervour and force in grave subjects. The sense that he personally, and not with an editor or an impersonal journal for buffer, is in contact with his readers, steadies a man wonderfully. Among other things, it makes him—odd as this may seem—far less ready to stoop to irrelevant personalities in discussion, because he is conscious that personalities may be in this case retorted, or their unbecomingness detected, whereas retort is impossible or futile against a journal. The knowledge that he has no mystic editorial aegis impresses him with the necessity of self-control. Again, the growth of free outspokenness would be promoted, inasmuch as a man with the fear of his friends and acquaintances before his eyes would barely like to perpetrate those small compliances with conventions, those too sage economies of truth, into which in weaker hours he may be seduced when he knows that their discrepancy with his avowed opinions is not likely to be discovered. The disuse of anonymity would protect the journalist against his own incidental weakness and complaisance, and that he should need this protection is not any more disgraceful to him than it is to the barrister that he should need an unwritten but a stringent law against the sordid practice of hugging.[21] As we are approaching a time when a good many questions which have hitherto been allowed to slumber will assuredly be opened, it is in the highest degree desirable that everybody with any influence—and even the most insignificant of journalists is not without it—should have every possible difficulty thrown in the way of this weak pliancy. The more obscure the journalist the more reason why he should be known. In the case of the chief writers on the *Saturday Review*, for example, or the *Pall*

Mall Gazette, or the *Spectator*, or the *Economist*, there is practically no anonymity. The general public may not know who are their instructors, but each of these writers has a circle of friends who know perfectly well what he writes, and to whose opinion therefore he is virtually responsible. It is, for one thing, because they are thus in fact not anonymous that their general tone is so respectable. But there is a mass of journalism written by one knows not whom, men who are only amenable to a very low public opinion in the people who know what they write, and yet who speak to, and from their position are able in some manner to lead, a public opinion of a far greater moment than that of their own circle. These are the truly mischievous persons, whom the compulsory disuse of anonymity would reduce to a more just level, or else by stimulating them to more conscientious effort would make more fit for the level which they already occupy.

One writer, in criticising Mr. Congreve's pamphlet, has taken up the ground that it is our business to answer a journalist's arguments, and not to insist on knowing who he is, or on pointing him out to other people as the scurrilous author of an article, from which we differ.[22] If all journalism consisted of controversies, in which A might have his say one day, and the editorial B might answer the next, this position might be satisfactory. It only requires a moment's thought to see that this is not an adequate account of journalism. Among other things, not every journal—certainly not the most important of all—will admit a single word on behalf of the other side. But controversy is the exception. As a rule, the writer of leading articles is in the position of an oracle, or a parson in the pulpit. People do not sit down to read what he has written in a critical attitude. They will quite willingly take all he says for gospel. Let us never forget that the exertion of mental activity upon public transactions, still more upon questions involving some powers of abstract thought, is thoroughly exceptional. A fallacy must be very staring indeed to strike the mind of the average reader of newspapers, if we consider the hasty way in which newspapers are read. Therefore, what we have to contend with in a journalist is not merely his arguments which we might answer, but his arguments and his position as oracle is well. One might easily deal with the orator in private controversy, but the orator and his tub together are impregnable. The assailants of anonymity want the teacher to leave his tub, to come down to the ordinary level of mortals, and to teach and fight on fair ground. They say, 'Your arguments we can reply to, but after the arguments are disposed of, the majority will still believe that your leading article was not without a certain divinity; we want the public to know your names and address, in order to dispel this worship, and to persuade them that you are a mere mortal, with no more title to have everything your own way than other mortals.' One journalist, indeed, has said that there is some kind of divinity, or I know not what, developed in you if you belong to the staff of a paper. The paper generates a spirit of its own, which enters into you when you take up your pen to write for it. If you are writing for one journal you will find yourself brilliant and bitter; if for another, your soul will be seized with pomposity and dulness; if for a third, over your spirit there steals either a fine fanciful subtlety, or else a pert and delicious self-confidence. This is partially true. The consciousness of association has a very strong and perceptible influence upon the mind of the writer. But then, this has nothing to do with the question of anonymity. It has a great deal to do with the purely professional question of the desirableness of having journals written by small bands of men. [...]

That there is this or that drawback to the disuse of anonymity, from a professional point of view, we cannot fairly deny. But they all sink into insignificance compared with the gigantic objection against the present system, that it entrusts the most important of social influences at this moment to what is, as far as the public is concerned, a secret society. The immeasurably momentous task of forming national opinion is entrusted to men who are, as a body, wholly irresponsible. Secrecy, whether partial or entire, demoralises. People assail the project of the ballot by insisting that if a citizen is performing a public function, he ought to perform it publicly, without any screen from the eyes of neighbours who are interested in knowing how he performs it. Yet the same people vow that a journalist—and a strong journalist wields a thousand times as much social power, for good or evil, as the most conscientious voter in any borough or county in Great Britain— cannot and ought not to perform *his* function except in as much secrecy as he can secure. For him it is an imperative necessity that he should work behind a screen. Theoretically, such a position is absolutely untenable, and the present anonymous system is far from working so well practically as to justify the continued neglect of a sound and unmistakable principle.

[Alexander Innes Shand], 'Contemporary Literature (No. IV). Novelists', *Blackwood's Edinburgh Magazine*, 125 (March 1879), 322-44 [322-3, 340-4]

Shand (1832–1907) was an assiduous contributor to *Blackwood's*, the *Saturday Review*, and *The Times*. This essay, in which Shand examines the publishing options open to fiction writers, is one of an eight-part series on the state of contemporary literature. As Shand describes, successful novelists rarely prospered through the sales of their novels alone; rather, they relied on the growing number of outlets for serial fiction. In addition to the well-established opportunities offered by British and American magazines, the 1870s saw the emergence of serial fiction being bought by syndicates of provincial and colonial newspapers.

As knowledge is increased, books are multiplied, but nothing in the way of books has been multiplied so fast as the Novel. In most branches of literature, the author is presumed to have had certain advantages of literary training. [. . .] But the novel-writer seems to be on a different footing altogether, and to belong by right of his vocation to an exceptional order of genius. Like the poet, he is born, not made. And when we say 'he,' of course we merely make conventional use of the masculine pronoun; for in reality, in the miscellaneous hosts of the novel-writers, the fair sex very largely predominates. There are many reasons why ladies should be more addicted to novel-writing than men. In the first place, they have far more leisure and fewer ways of disposing of it to their satisfaction. When the husband is hard at work, the wife may be occupied with those cares of the household which engross her thoughts, to the exclusion of lighter subjects, even when she is not actually bustling about her business. But then, on the other hand, she may have an easy income, plenty of servants, and no children, and be sorely put to it to kill the time. Or she may have a praiseworthy wish to take her share of the family labour, and turn to some profitable account such talents as Providence has bestowed on her. [. . .]

That notion [of being a novelist] does not so readily occur to a man. [...] In fact, the youth who betakes himself to poetry or novel-writing is likely to have a strong dash of the feminine in him. He wears his hair long, taking exquisite care of it in its studied disorder; he is in the habit of eschewing the shooting-coat for the frock-coat: and in that it must be confessed that he shows his appreciation of the suitable and of the essential elements of the art of dress. For he shrinks with womanly sensitiveness from the rougher masculine nature; he is scared by the stories which enliven the smoking-room, and which bring a blush to the sallow pallor of his cheek though there may really be no great harm in them. [...]

The profession of the novel-writer is said to be not what it once was. The trade, like most others, has been overstocked; and the profits have been declining accordingly, so far as the publication in book-form is concerned. As to the overstocking, there can be no question; and we do not see that time is likely to bring a remedy to that. The frenzy for scribbling shows every sign of spreading; and so long as the profit is not merely a secondary consideration, but authors are actually willing to pay for the honours of print, so long will they find publishers, and probably readers. But we believe that brighter days are in store for the craftsmen who unite skill to talent; and indeed the revolution in that direction is already in progress. We have adverted to the strange changes that have come about since the mere fact of putting his name to a novel was decidedly a feather in a man's cap, and the novelists of any note might be almost reckoned upon the fingers. Then a clever book was sure of an extensive sale: the last work of a man of mark and ability served as an advertisement of the next; and as reviews were comparatively few and far between, a laudatory article in the leading journal was in itself an encouragement to a second edition. Now praise has become cheap as novels have become common. Hardly anybody dreams of buying the three vol-umes; the circulating libraries are chary of their orders, passing a single copy through any number of hands; and the tardy approbation of the critics gives but slight impulse to the sale. So far as the best men are concerned, the misfortune is that they are habitually undersold. If no novels were brought out but those that were likely to pay their way handsomely, their writers might command the markets and make their terms for reasonable remuneration. Were only some score or so of books published in the season, librarians who had boxes to fill would be found to give their orders accordingly. As it is, they have any number of books, in every gradation of quality, to choose from; and 'lots' may always be picked up on exceedingly easy terms. There are publishers who do a regular trade in what may be fairly called rubbish, and it is there that the multiplication of inferior writers becomes most noxious to the profession as an art. [...]

If the professional novelist lived by the actual sale of his books, he would speedily cut the profession in disgust; and it is a curious speculation whether the strike of the skilled might starve the public and the librarians into more discriminating patronage. But luckily, both for the novelist and his readers, there are other channels open to him—and channels that are multiplying and widening. If he pass his story through a leading magazine, its fortune is half made in advance; and in respect to its future he is comparatively on velvet. He gets a handsome price for each instalment; nor does the circulation in serial form injure its subsequent publication: indeed we have been informed by experts who ought to know, that, according to their experience, it rather improves it. And the magazines that rely chiefly on their fiction are multiplying likewise, although scarcely in proportion to the increase of novel-writing; while there are illustrated papers that publish serials, and weekly literary and social papers which are borrowing leaves from the books of the French *feuilletons*.[23] Some of these pay well; others very indifferently; but, at all events, the man who has been aiming high has the certainty of hedging against an absolute miscarriage.

The medium of magazine-publication is an unspeakable boon to authors, for genius must live somehow, and is dependent on its comforts if not on luxury. [...] Yet unquestionably the very general practice of serial-writing is in some ways unfavourable to the better style of art. When Dickens was at the height of his fame, and his green covers in the flush of their popularity; when he used to ride out to Hampstead or Richmond, with his confidant Mr Forster, that he might lighten suspense as much as possible till he had heard the results of the sales, readers of the Life will remember with what thought he prepared each separate instalment for isolated effect. The temptation to do so is exceedingly strong, for the public is short-sighted and peremptory in its judgement; tameness is the one unpardonable sin; and it will seldom possess its soul in patience, because it may hope for brighter things in our next. There are magazines and magazines, as we have reason to know. There are editors who rest on their reputation, and can afford to stand on it; who prefer a consecutive and finished piece of work to the garish patchwork of forced sensation. But there are editors, again, who will have a succession of striking effects, like the *tableaux* that succeed each other on the stage, or the shifting scenes of a panorama. How is it possible to be fairly true to nature? how, indeed, can one avoid the wildest incongruities, if you have to scatter your murders and suicides at short intervals of a chapter or two? Even in the purely sensational point of view, you discount the possibilities of an effective climax. Yet, on the other hand, what in most cases becomes an abuse may possibly prove serviceable to certain authors. For the sense that each separate instalment is so far complete in itself may act as an antidote to listlessness and dulness. And should the story be dragging, the monthly *critiques* bring the vanity of authorship up to the mark again.

Then the author may arrange for simultaneous publication in some of the foreign magazines. The pirates of the United States are anticipated by the forwarding of early proof-sheets, which is altogether without prejudice to the popular writer reaping the barren glories of a cheap notoriety by being set in circulation through the cars and at the bookstalls in stitched covers, priced at a few cents. He makes his bargain in the meantime for some solid pudding. There is, of course, a very probable hitch; and the chances are that neither 'Harper's' nor 'The Atlantic' manage to make an opening for the English celebrity at the moment that suits his English publishers.[24] But failing that, or failing a well-paying magazine anywhere, there are other resources that begin to open to him. There is an immense demand for fiction in the flourishing Australasian colonies; and they are scarcely so successful in raising native novelists as in other classes of valuable stock. Besides, the range of colonial observation is circumscribed, and squatters and merchants there know enough of the gold-diggings, the export trade, the bushrangers, and the cattle-runs. They have cravings for the romance of the Old World, and enlightenment as to fashionable and political society. So it is no wonder that their enterprising newspaper proprietors have been tightening up their loosely printed columns of advertisements, and making room for novels 'by eminent hands.' In place of relying on the bursts of criminal and political sensation that come to them spasmodically by the European mails, they find it pays them to supply it daily or weekly, and they pay in return exceedingly well. So very general has this duplex system become, that a certain prolific novelist assures us, not only that he has never published a story except as a serial in the first instance, but that he has never published one which has not appeared simultaneously at least in one colony or foreign settlement, while the majority have done so in three or four, including, in one very recent case, even Yokohama: while another popular writer is accustomed to gauge civilization in foreign parts by the test, 'Do they or do they not take my serial novels?' and we are sorry to say that that flourishing colony, New Zealand, stands lowest in the scale when judged by this standard. Partly for similar reasons, this example is being followed by the periodical press in England. A group of country papers clubbed together, transact their business in the novel-market through a central agency that places itself directly in communication with the author. They can afford to offer him liberal terms, and weekly proofs are circulated among the subscribers. The people who buy are, for the most part, of the class who have few dealings with the circulating libraries, and rarely, indeed, read anything in the shape of a printed book. But, on the other hand, they are precisely the class who like to have good value for their pennies, and who conscientiously spell through each line in a page from the first column to the last. We can conceive what a refreshment to them an exciting story is, as a change from the advertisements of the antibilious pills and Mr Thorley's food for fattening cattle.[25] No doubt that taste will spread, while editors can afford to become proportionately enterprising in gratifying it. In the meantime, as we happen to know, one of those popular novelists we have just been mentioning, had the offer of selling his last book to the Association for an exceedingly handsome sum. Nay, to prove how far the system is capable of being worked, we may mention that the 'Pickwick Papers' have recently been republished in a cheap Sheffield journal. Thrown in for a penny with the miscellaneous matter, and read aloud in the family circle, they anticipate the schoolmaster in the lowest depths of the humblest social strata; and immigrants from the wilds of Kerry and Connemara are making the acquaintance of Mr Winkle and Mr Samuel Weller. We question whether these uneducated intelligences may not be as capable critics as many of their betters: they are at least as likely to prefer the freshness of nature to the artificial essences of the boudoirs and of the perfumers. And writers of merit may avail themselves of opening fields which are practically closed to the sentimentalists and false sensationalists. But though Baron Tauchnitz pays English authors liberally, the income derived from absolutely foreign sources—that is, in the way of translation—is but small.[26] The French praise and higgle, and do not generally avail themselves of British talent till the term of international copyright has expired, when they can translate the work for nothing; and the same, though perhaps in a less degree, may be said of the Germans.

W. T. Stead, 'The Future of Journalism', *Contemporary Review*, 50 (1886), 663–79 [663–6, 668–72, 675–6, 678]

William Thomas Stead (1849–1912) was a key figure in advancing the role of the professional journalist during the late nineteenth century. Stead became editor of the *Northern Echo* in 1871, aged only 22, and subsequently edited the *Pall Mall Gazette* between 1883 and 1890. The *Pall Mall Gazette*, an early proponent of the New Journalism, was where Stead published the 'Maiden Tribute of Modern Babylon' (1885). The article below is one of two significant essays on journalistic reform Stead published in the *Contemporary Review*, a monthly journal which promoted Liberalism and social reform.

A man without a newspaper is half-clad, and imperfectly furnished for the battle of life. From being persecuted and then contemptuously tolerated, it has become the rival of organized governments. Will it become their superior?

The future of journalism depends entirely upon the journalist. All that can be said is, that it offers opportunities and possibilities, of which a capable man can take advantage, superior to that of any other institution or profession known among men.

But everything depends upon the individual—the person. Impersonal journalism is effete. To influence men you must be a man, not a mock-uttering oracle. The democracy is under no awe of the mystic 'We.' Who is 'We'? they ask; and they are right. For all power should be associated with responsibility, and a leader of the people, if a journalist, needs a neck capable of being stretched quite as much as if he is a Prime Minister. For the proper development of a newspaper the personal element is indispensable. There must be loyalty to the chief far beyond the precincts of the editorial sanctum. Besides, as I shall presently explain, the personality of the editor is the essential centre-point of my whole idea of the true journalism of the governing and guiding order, as distinguished from journalism of the mere critical or paragraph-quilting species. Where there is the combination of the two elements, the distinct personality of a competent editor and the varied interests and influences of an ably conducted paper, it is not difficult to see that such an editor might, if he wished it, become far the most permanently influential Englishman in the Empire.

He would not govern the Empire, but his voice would be the most potent among all those whose counsels guide the holders of our Imperial sceptre; he might not 'wield at will the fierce democratie,'[27] but he would be the most authoritative interpreter of its wishes, and his influence, both upon the governed and the governors, would be incomparably greater than that of any other living man.

And how would he attain this dizzy pre-eminence? He would be more powerful than any, simply because, better than any other, he would know his facts. Even now, with his imperfect knowledge of facts, the journalist wields enormous influence. What would he be if he had so perfected the mechanism of his craft as to be master of the facts—especially of the dominant fact of all, the state of public opinion?

At present the journalistic assumption of uttering the opinion of the public is in most cases a hollow fraud. In the case of most London editors absolutely no attempt is made to ascertain what Demos really thinks. Opinions are exchanged in the office, in the club, or in the drawing-room; but any systematic attempt to gauge the opinion even of those whom he meets there is none. As for the opinion of Londoners, outside the limited range of their personal acquaintance, that remains to them, as to every one else, an inscrutable mystery. Outside London, everything of course is shrouded in even denser darkness. How many London editors, I wonder, ever look half-a-dozen times in the year into the sheets of their provincial contemporaries? Yet not one of them will not undertake to pronounce off-hand that public opinion will not tolerate this, or that public opinion insists on that. And all the while they know as much about public opinion as of the private opinion of the Grand Lama. It is about time that imposture should cease.

I am not for a moment advocating the more accurate and scientific gauging of public opinion in order that blind obedience should be paid to its decision, when ascertained. Far from it. The first duty of every true man, if he believes that public opinion is mistaken, is to set himself to change it. But whether we regard public opinion as the supreme authority in faith, morals and politics, or whether we merely regard it as so much force to be directed or absolutely checked, it is obviously of the first importance to know what it is that we have either to obey or to transform. But at present who is there who studies public opinion—I do not say scientifically, but even intelligently? [...]

What, then, should be the organization of a newspaper office from this point of view? [...]

First, then, the editor of a newspaper should either be personally acquainted with, or should be surrounded by trustworthy assistants who are personally acquainted with, every one whose opinion has any weight on any subject with which he has to deal. Nor should it be mere acquaintance. There should exist such relations of confidence as to render it possible for the editor to be put in possession of the views of any personage whose opinion he desires to know. [...]

The ideal of the journalist should be to be universally accessible— to know everyone and to hear everything. The old idea of a jealously shrouded impersonality has given way to its exact antithesis. Of course, if the personality of the editor is such as to detract from the usefulness of his writings, he had better stick to the old plan. But if the editor is a real man, who has convictions, and capacity to give them utterance in conversation as well as in print, the more people he sees at first hand the better—always provided that he leaves his mind room enough in the crowd to turn round on its own ground. All that I have said concerning the London editor applies *mutatis mutandis*[28] to his provincial brother. The provincial editor has one enormous advantage over the Londoner—one among many. He can cover the whole of his field. He can make the personal acquaintance of every leading public man and of all the local leaders in every department of human activity. From the mayor to the bellman, they are all within his compass, and as a rule, if he makes it his business, they are approachable enough. It is difficult, of course, when there is keen sensitiveness on the part of a functionary whom it has been necessary to scourge in your paper, and also in places where the party line is broad and deep. I never found any difficulty, however, in being on excellent terms with my Tory contemporaries in the North, although neither side was accustomed to give or seek quarter in print. [...]

This, however, is the mere *A B C* of the subject: it is so obvious that whoever aspires to lead and guide must take counsel with those who have the daily drudgery of administration to do, that there is no need to labour the point. What is much less generally recognized is that the newspaper ought to be in close and direct touch with either extremity of the social system, and with all intermediate grades. There is something inexpressibly pathetic in the dumbness of the masses of the people. Touch but a hair on the head of the well-to-do, and forthwith you hear his indignant protest in the columns of the *Times*. But the million, who have to suffer the rudest buffets of ill-fortune, the victims of official insolence and the brutality of the better-off, they are as dumb as the horse, which you may scourge to death without its uttering a sound. Newspapers will never really justify their claims to be the tribunes of the people until every victim of injustice—whether it be a harlot run in by a policeman greedy for blackmail, or a ticket-of-leave man hunted down by shadowy detectives,[29] or paupers baulked of their legal allowance of skilly[30]—sends in to the editorial sanctum their complaint of the injustice which they suffer. When men cease to complain of injustice, it is as if they sullenly confessed that God was dead. When they neglect to lay their wrongs before their fellows, it is as if they had lost all faith in the reality of that collective conscience of society which Milton finely calls 'God's secretary.' For every appeal to the public is a practical confession of a faith that shuts out despair. When there is prayer there is hope. To give utterance to the inarticulate moan of the voiceless is to let light into a dark place; it is almost equivalent to the enfranchisement of a class. A newspaper in this sense is a daily apostle of fraternity, a messenger who bringeth glad tidings of joy, of a great light that has risen upon those who sit in darkness and the shadow of death. I do not say that the editors of the *Times* and the *Daily News* should be on visiting terms with the thieves of the Seven Dials and the Harlots of the New Cut, but they should know those who call tell them what the Dialonians feel and what the outcasts in the New Cut suffer. [...]

How to attain this end is the great problem. It is an end that cannot be reached at a bound, but by steady, patient, constant growth. There are, however, two methods by which a newspaper can work towards that end: the first is by a system of major-generals, and the second by a system of journalistic travellers.

First, the system of major generals. When Cromwell was driven to undertake the governing of England he mapped out the towns into districts, and over each district he placed a man after his own heart, responsible to him for the peace and good government of the district under his care. That system *mutatis mutandis* might be adopted with advantage by a newspaper that wished to keep in hand the affairs of the whole country. A competent, intelligent, sympathetic man or woman, as nearly as possible the *alter ego* of the editor, should be planted in each district, and held responsible for keeping the editor informed of all that is going on within that area that needs attending to, either for encouragement, or for repression, or merely for observation and report.

That, it will be said, is but a development under a new name of the existing system of resident reporters and local correspondents. That is a great recommendation. But the development is immense—so immense, in fact, that there would be the greatest difficulty in securing persons competent for the discharge of the duties of the post. But by themselves they would be helpless. They need to be supplemented by two agencies—one local, the other central.

There is probably in every constituency in the land some one man or woman keenly in sympathy with the governing ideas of the newspaper in question. That may be said concerning any newspaper which has a soul and a creed, and a man at the head of it who is not afraid to say, in clear accents of unmistakable sincerity, 'This is the way; walk ye in it.' In the newspaper whose organization I am sketching there would be so many points of contact with the average Briton that there would be no doubt at all that there would be many persons sufficiently in sympathy with the direction to feel honoured by being asked to co-operate as voluntary unpaid associates with the editor. It would be the duty of the major-general to select with the utmost care, in each important centre in his district, one such associate, who would undertake to co-operate with the central office in ascertaining facts, in focusing opinion, and generally in assisting the editor to ascertain the direct views of his countrymen. There would be endless varieties among those who would act as associates. It might be a squire, or it might be a cobbler; it might be the clergyman's daughter, or a secularist newsagent, or a Methodist reporter. The one thing indispensable is that they are intelligent, keenly interested in the general policy of the paper, and willing to take some trouble to contribute to its efficiency and to extend its power. To each of these associates there will be posted copies of the paper, in recognition of their position and services, and in order to keep them in touch with the editorial mind. That is to say, from 600 to 1,000 persons scattered all over the United Kingdom would be placed on the free list, on condition they were willing to perform certain simple but very important duties.

The first of these is to reply at once, when inquiry is made from the head office, first as to their own opinion upon any disputed point, and secondly, what they believed to be the general opinion of their neighbours. [...]

That, however, is by no means the only duty that would be required from the hands of the volunteer deputy major-generals. Once or twice a year—sometimes oftener, sometimes not so often—a crisis may arise in which it is urgently necessary that the Cabinet and the House of Commons should be presented with an unmistakeable demonstration of what the opinion of the people really is. Such an occasion arose during the Bulgarian crisis in 1876, and when the Criminal Law Amendment Bill was in danger July before last.[31] Whenever such a time arrived it would be the duty of a deputy major-general to take steps to secure public expression of the popular feeling. He, or it might be she, might not be able to attend a public meeting, much less speak at one. But they could nevertheless set one going by setting the right people in motion. A requisition to the mayor in all cases where opinion is tolerably unanimous—the best method of procedure—could secure a free and open expression of the general feeling. Information explaining the issues before the country could be obtained from the central office, and the question could be freely and fully put before the democracy, and an opportunity afforded it of expressing its convictions on the question of the hour. The weakness of government by public meetings is, that there is so often no one to give the thing a start in the first place, and to keep interest up until the meeting is held, in the second. There is also the difficulty about the expenses, which in all cases should be met by a public collection. The meetings of the democracy should surely be self-supporting. Under the proposed scheme the local deputy would be the live coal which sets the place ablaze, and he would be able to have at command exactly the kind of information needed for the locality.

Just imagine the consequences, under our present system of government, of an arrangement by which a leading newspaper, convinced that the Government was pursuing a policy contrary to the general wishes of the community, was able to issue a three-line whip to its representatives which would secure the holding of a public meeting in every town-hall in the country, in order to express the popular view. [...]

I believe that, just as Cromwell found the secret of his new model in enlisting in the Parliamentary men who put a conscience to their work, so it is possible for the editor to enlist in the service of the State a picked body of volunteers, who will work as hard for England in the field of public and corrective action as others do in the service of their sects. It is a new field that is opened up—a new field, and a most tempting one, for it offers to the capable man or woman opportunities of public usefulness at present beyond his utmost dreams, and while apparently making them the humble interrogators of democracy, in reality enrols them as indispensable members of the greatest spiritual and educational and governing agency which England has yet seen. Such a newspaper would indeed be a great secular or civic church and democratic university, and if wisely directed and energetically worked, would come to be the very soul of our national unity; and its great central idea would be that of the self-sacrifice of the individual for the salvation of the community, the practical realization of the religious idea in national politics and social reform.

[Charlotte O'Conor Eccles], 'The Experiences of a Woman Journalist', *Blackwood's Edinburgh Magazine,* 153 (June 1893), 830-8

O'Conor Eccles (1863–1911) here provides an autobiographical account of her difficulties as a female journalist seeking work in Fleet Street. Beginning on a provincial newspaper, she subsequently worked for the short-lived London edition of the *New York Herald* (1835–1924), and contributed to many journals, including *Sketch* and *Windsor Magazine.* This article, published in the same year that the Society of Women Journalists was launched, shows the increasing number of women working as professional journalists and the effect of the figure of the educated and liberated New Woman, itself largely a media creation.

When I came to London to look for work on a newspaper, I had had a little experience on the provincial press—not very much indeed, but still sufficient to justify me in claiming to know something of my profession. I took to journalism, in the first instance, because magazine work was irregular and precarious, and I could not afford to waste time in trying if it was in me to write a good novel. [. . .] My aspirations were modest. I wanted to make £100 or £150 a-year, and was prepared to take anything that was offered me. What higher ambitions I may have had are beside the question. Looking back on that time, I am filled with a curious impersonal self-pity; it seems to me to have been very hard indeed. No doubt I was very soft. Nature and training were against me. I had not been brought up amongst women who worked for their living; was diffident, unwilling to ask favours, and full of that impulse that leads one to say, 'Pray don't mention, it will do at any time,' when money due to one is in question. To crown all, in the days when no one contemplated a journalistic career for me, I had been educated at convents in England and abroad, which is not the type of training that makes one enjoy facing the world.

Like all novices, I bore a letter of introduction to a great—a journalistically great—man. It was difficult to find him at home; but, after two or three failures, he received me politely, asked me what my capabilities were, glanced at the reviews of my book, and said he had, unfortunately, no work for me himself, but that he would give me some letters of introduction to other people. I was very happy. This was as good as an appointment. The penetrating reader will at once see what a very inexperienced young person I was. It took me quite three weeks to learn that such letters are not worth the paper they are written on [...] One is horribly handicapped in being a woman. A man meets other men at his club; he can be out and about at all hours; he can insist without being thought bold and forward; he is not presumed to be capable of undertaking only a limited class of subjects, but is set to anything. Mr. T. P. O'Connor, in one of his clever articles, tells a would-be journalist that the first essential is to get taken on in an office in any capacity. 'Go as an office-boy, if need be,' he says—I quote from memory—'but get into an office anyhow.'³² The immense difficulty a woman finds in getting into an office in any recognised capacity makes a journalistic beginning far harder for her than for a man. Where a man finds one obstacle, we find a dozen. Once a woman gets work, she is largely privileged as to times and places; but the aspirant has no privileges: she is a nuisance, an untried unfledged being, very much in the way, and to be got rid of at all hazards. [...]

I now scanned the advertisement columns daily, and answered everything likely to suit, with but little result. My replies were generally disregarded, else I got letters requesting me to take a share in a paper, or enclosing the prospectus of some literary and artistic venture, that for an annual guinea, &c. One day, however, to my great delight, the editor of a 'Society' journal asked me to call. He was a little man, and very civil—surely my chance had come. 'Could I write articles, "spicy" articles—the naughtier the better.' He showed me some specimens of what he wanted. I couldn't—and wouldn't—so that fell through. My next application was to one of the many Ladies' Employment Bureaux under distinguished patronage, no very likely quarter to be sure, but I really did not know what else to do. It was presided over by an elderly person of highly respectable and severe aspect. She did not unduly raise my expectation of obtaining literary work through her but said something might turn up, anyhow she would put down my name and requirements. My references were examined, she asked me all sorts of questions as to my parentage, position, &c., and finally the name of my book. When I answered that it was called 'Modern Men, by a Modern Maid,' there was an awful silence. 'Well,' said my interlocutor solemnly, 'I would sooner have my right hand cut off than publish a book with such a title.' In vain I falteringly protested there was not a line from cover to cover that she might not read with perfect safety. I did not think much of it; I acknowledged its faults in all humility, but innocuous I maintained it to be. She looked at me incredulously, and advised me to peruse the works of Miss Anne Beale, as well as certain publications of the Religious Tract Society.[33] Strange to be considered in one week neither bad enough nor good enough to secure a post. I left the Ladies' Employment Office with a sinking heart; not much chance for me there evidently, and for a long time I heard no more of it. Indeed months passed before I received a note from my disapproving acquaintance, asking me to call without delay, as she had heard of something likely to suit me. I came. She had had an application for a female detective, and at once pitched on me as a probable candidate. The connection between what I asked and what she offered was not clear; no doubt she thought a woman journalist, like the father of a family in the French play, was *capable de tout*.[34] [...]

However, about this time I saw that a literary man required a young lady as amanuensis, and I offered my services. [...] [N]ext day I knocked at the door and asked for Mr Dash. I was shown into a comfortable study, and a young man about nine-and-twenty or thirty entered the room—son or nephew, perhaps assistant. 'I have called to see Mr Dash,' I said; 'I come from Messrs Black & White.' 'I am Mr Dash,' was the reply. There was nothing of the benevolent spectacled Santa Claus in the man before me; but I concealed my surprise as well as I could, and began to talk business. I would not do as secretary, he thought—and I was inwardly thankful—but he might be able to utilise me otherwise. 'In point of fact,' he said, with engaging frankness, 'I am what you may call a literary sweater. I act as London correspondent to a number of papers, colonial and others, and make a good income by it.' (He insisted frequently on his income.) 'Now most of this work I get done for me by young ladies. I like them, whenever they can, to mention the names of shops where different fashionable dresses and so forth may be purchased, then I write afterwards to these shop-people, and say, "See here, I have given you a valuable advertisement in such-and-such papers. If you like to acknowledge it, I shall be very glad;" and,' he added, 'they nearly always *do* send a cheque by return.' This sounded queer to me. Till then I had never even heard of the journalist who accepts presents from tradespeople, and though told in such a matter-of-course fashion, it did not strike me as being what a gentleman would do. However, I remembered it was he, not I, who would write for those cheques, and made no comment. He went on to speak about magazine articles. 'I often,' he said, 'get a few notes on a subject from some well-known writer, headings, you know, a mere outline: these I have amplified by some of the ladies who write for me, and it is published under the better known name.' He showed me a rather long essay, as he spoke, purporting to be by a popular woman traveller, and told me that all she had written would just fill a half-sheet of note-paper. 'I will give you a guinea a column,' he said, 'for any journalistic work you do for me.' [...] I wrote three or four articles, and with the first and last sent a little note asking if they were suitable. A line reached me in reply saying Mr Dash was out of town, but would communicate with me on his return. I went on like this for three weeks or more, then hearing nothing further, and getting no payment, sent no more articles. [...]

My patience was exhausted. I had arrived at that stage when one ceases to struggle. Nothing I undertook seemed to prosper. Was there any use in trying farther? In this frame of mind I turned one day into the office of the 'New York Herald,' then but lately established in London, and having finished my business, something prompted me to ask the manager if a lady was wanted on the paper.[35] He did not know—indeed it was not to be expected that he should, seeing that he had nothing to do with the literary department; but he asked me a few questions, and advised me to send in anything that seemed likely to suit. [...] I was put on the staff at a salary of three guineas a-week. What happy months were those that followed! Each morning instructions were telegraphed to me; each evening I handed in my copy. Mr Stanhope was always pleasant to deal with, but the 'Herald' had a short lease of life.[36] After I left it I had another six months of enforced idleness; meantime, however, I had gained courage and experience, had learned my way about, had become acquainted with other women journalists, and obtained a certain footing. A beginning once made,

I got new work with the New Year—very hard work too. A weekly newspaper offered me 30s. a-week for all my time from nine in the morning till six in the evening. I did a column of 'mems.' on current events; two columns of educational news; a number of sub-leaders; two Ladies' Letters; Answers to Correspondents; a 'Children's Corner,' most troublesome of all, as it involved competitions and prizes; corrected all the proofs; and had in my hands the selection of matter for the weekly, and for an educational paper. Quite enough to do I found it. The weather was bitterly cold, and the piles of work through which I plodded seemed daily to increase. This went on for nearly a year, when I gave up coming everyday, and did six columns at home for £1 a-week instead. Out of evil came good. My editor, though exacting, was kindly; we became friends, and he has ever since been very helpful to me. I was offered the sub-editorship of a woman's paper, and on it learned all the mysteries of 'make up,' as once a-week I had to go down to the works and see it through the press. The head printer helped me over many a difficulty. By degrees things grew better. I made a connection with country papers; contributed a regular weekly letter to a journal of good standing; sold a serial story; and began to write, at first casually, then regularly, for more than one London paper. As here ended the worst of my struggle, I shall here end my narrative.

NOTES TO SECTION VII

1. [Walter Bagehot], 'The First Edinburgh Reviewers', *National Review*, 1 (1855), 256.
2. Graham Law, *Serializing Fiction in the Victorian Press* (Basingstoke: Palgrave, 2000), 33.
3. Quoted in Robert Lee Wolff, *Sensational Victorian: The Life and Fiction of Mary Elizabeth Braddon* (New York: Garland, 1979), 134.
4. See Laurel Brake, *Subjugated Knowledges: Journalism, Gender, and Literature in the Nineteenth Century* (Basingstoke: Macmillan, 1994), 10–11.
5. [Gibbons Merle], 'Journalism', *Westminster Review*, 18 (January 1833), 195.

6. The phrase derives from the title of a book by George Lillie Craik that was published by the Society for the Diffusion of Useful Knowledge in 1830.

7. Xerxes I (486–465 BC), Persian king, used a massive army in an attempt to invade Greece in 480 BC. The Macedonian phalanx, much used by Alexander the Great (356–323 BC) in his conquests of many lands (including Persia), was a lightly armed and mobile military unit.

8. On Sue, see Section V n. 38. Adolphe Thiers (1797–1877), French statesman, historian and journalist, founded the newspaper *Le National*.

9. Sue was actually given 100,000 francs for his daily serial *Le Juif errant* (*The Wandering Jew*, 1844–5) by the newspaper *Le Constitutionnel*—an unprecedented sum. To make his point, Lewes is not allowing for either the different purchasing power of different currencies nor using entirely appropriate exchange rates.

10. Edward Bulwer-Lytton (1803–83), novelist and playwright; G. P. R. James (1799–1860), historical novelist.

11. *Revue des Deux Mondes*, high-status French periodical (1829–) founded with a view to creating dialogue between France and America. George Sand, pen name of Amandine Aurore-Lucille Dupin (1804–76), French novelist and playwright, published a great deal in the *Revue* from the 1850s to the 1870s.

12. Maecenas (d. 8 BC), a Roman senator renowned as a patron of literature.

13. Writers were sometimes granted pensions from the Civil List, although this was at the discretion of the government then in office and sometimes owed much to personal and political connections.

14. The upstart central character in Molière's *Le Bourgeois gentilhomme* (1670) who is surprised to learn from his grammar teacher that he has been speaking prose all his life.

15. Walter Scott, *The Heart of Midlothian* (1818).

16. Jeannie Deans, the heroine of *Heart of Midlothian*, walked to London to see Queen Caroline to get a pardon for her sister, Effie.

17. Smith is unconcerned by chronology. The Lollards were heretics, following the religious ideas of John Wycliff (*c*.1330–84). Cesarè Borgia (1476–1507), Duke of Valentinois and Romagna, was notorious for murdering his political opponents. Ignatius Loyola (1499–1556) founded the Society of Jesus (Jesuits) in 1540.

18. John Maddison Morton's *Box and Cox* was a popular farce first performed at the Royal Lyceum, London, in 1847.

19. Charles Guilbert de Pixérécourt (1773–1844), French dramatist credited with inventing melodrama in its modern acceptation.

20. Starting in 1821 *Theresa, the Orphan of Geneva* was several times adapted from the original French of Brahain Ducange. There were also several adaptations of Pixérécourt's *Le Pélerin blanc* (1802) known as *The Wandering Boys.*

21. The practice of courting an attorney with the hope of gaining employment.

22. Richard Congreve, *Mr Broadhead and the Anonymous Press* (London: E. Truelove, 1867).

23. See Section V n. 38.

24. The *Atlantic Monthly*, a prominent American periodical, founded in Boston in 1857 by Oliver Wendell Holmes and James Russell Lowell; *Harper's Monthly Magazine*, founded in New York by the publishers Harper and Brothers in 1850, initially focused on publishing well-known British authors.

25. Thorley's was much advertised 'as used by her Majesty's stables', and even mentioned in Thackeray's *Adventures of Philip* (1862).

26. Christian Bernhard Tauchnitz, a German publisher well known for his reprints of British novels.

27. John Milton, *Paradise Regained* (bk. IV, l. 267).

28. 'With the necessary changes.'

29. A 'ticket-of-leave man' was a convict on parole.

30. 'Skilly' was a thin broth, usually of oatmeal or of water flavoured with meat.

31. A Bulgarian uprising in 1876 against Turkey, the governing power, provoked fierce debate in Britain because of the perceived brutality of Turkish troops' reprisals. The Criminal Law Amendment Bill refers to 'The Maiden Tribute' scandal.

32. See p. 361.

33. On Anne Beale, see Section II n. 28; on the Religious Tract Society, see Section II n. 4.

34. 'Capable of everything.'

35. The *New York Herald* (1835–1924) was founded by James Gordon Bennett. It became one the best-selling American papers, employing a variety of what would be seen in Britain as New Journalistic techniques (it was the very first paper to use the telegraph). It produced a London edition between 1889 and 1891, after opening an international office in Paris in 1887. Initially extremely hostile to women's rights, by the late 1880s it had come to realize the economic value of independent women.

36. Aubrey Stanhope, one of the editors of the *New York Herald*.

VIII

NEWSPAPERS

INTRODUCTION

In 1829 Gibbons Merle described the Press as 'one of those extraordinary combinations by which capital activity, and intellect, have produced wonderful results.'[1] This oft-repeated sentiment was one of many laudations of its political and commercial achievements. However, the mythology of 'the Press'—its overweening presence as a monolithic discursive and institutional entity—contrasts with the fragmented and fast-changing structure of the nineteenth-century newspaper industry. The opening article in this section, for example, is an overview of the press by Merle, written just prior to Victoria's accession. He describes a very different industry to the later articles by Wright, March-Phillips, and T. P. O'Connor. In 1832 *The Times* led the market with a daily sale of around 10,000 copies. Fifty years later the highest circulation was enjoyed by *Lloyd's Weekly Newspaper*, a Sunday publication with a broadly working-class readership and a weekly sale of around 750,000 copies.[2] Crucially, therefore, an ongoing rise in potential readers, combined with less restrictive regulation of the newspaper industry, led not only to a predictable growth in circulation, but to the development of new forms of newspaper.

Section III examined some of the legislative restrictions upon newspapers, while Section IV demonstrated the impact of communication networks such as the railways and the telegraph system. The present section builds on previous ones by focusing on the way legislative, political, and technological influences fed into the emergence of different types of newspaper, each with their distinctive style and content. One enormously successful new format, described below by Thomas Wright, was the development of mass-market weekly newspapers such as the *News of the World* (1843–), *Lloyd's Weekly Newspaper* (1842–1918), and *Reynolds's Weekly Newspaper* (1850–1967). These Sunday newspapers were aimed at the large number of readers who were either unable to afford a metropolitan daily or who did not have the leisure time to read one. Following the removal of the paper duty in 1861, *Reynolds's Weekly Newspaper* and *Lloyd's Weekly*

Newspaper reduced their prices from 2*d.* to 1*d.*, well below *The Times* (which had also reduced its price from 4*d.* to 3*d.*).

The eponymous newspapers of Edward Lloyd and G. W. M Reynolds demonstrate that publishers moved between different media forms in the same cultural zone, and the link between cheap fiction, periodicals, and newspapers is also evident in the similar anxieties each provoked. For example, the 1849 cartoon from *Punch* below, which attacks the prevalence of crime reportage in Sunday papers, replicates any number of responses to criminal narratives in cheap serial fiction. Similarly, Wright's article on the Sunday press, which parodies a barely disguised Reynolds as the editor of *Crusher's Newspaper*, exemplifies the fear caused by its supposedly demagogic political agitation.

The effective removal of the Stamp Duty in June 1855 was a key moment in the creation of a cheap national press. The articles from *Chambers's Journal* and the *Westminster Review* demonstrate the way these regulatory changes affected not only the economics of the newspaper industry but its function in everyday life. Price reductions, rises in circulation, and an increase in the frequency of publication were the most obvious changes. A penny daily press was made possible for the first time. The most successful of the new penny papers, the *Daily Telegraph*, went on sale in September 1855; by 1861 its circulation was approximately 141,000, well above the 65,000 copies sold by *The Times*.[3]

Provincial newspapers were similarly affected. Before 1855 most had been bi-weekly or thrice-weekly publications; following the legislative changes, many became dailies. In 1855, the *Manchester Guardian* (1821–) thus changed from bi-weekly to daily publication; and most major provincial cities soon had their own daily newspaper. As *Chambers's Journal* demonstrates, these structural changes meant that many families were now able to afford their own daily newspaper, which would be read in the home rather than in a public house or mechanics' institute. News being received with greater regularity and simultaneity, *Chambers's Journal* suggests that the daily thereby accentuated local communities' engagement with national events.

The optionality of the Stamp Duty was usually seen as the culminating triumph of the Whig belief in the benefits of a free market for print media. John Chapman's article, published in October 1855 in the immediate aftermath of the bill, is a good example of this myth-ology. Examining the symbiosis between the commercialization of the press and its political function, Chapman lauds *The Times* for its long-standing refusal of party-political patronage, which it was able to do because of its large advertising revenue.

The changing structure of the mid-century press laid the founda-tions for the New Journalism of the 1880s and 1890s. 'New Journal-ism' was a label coined by Matthew Arnold in 1887, and represented significant changes in the content and appearance of newspapers.[4] Arnold saw the character of New Journalism as an uncomplimentary reflection of the democracy introduced following the 1884 Reform Bill. It was also accused of importing the worst practices of American popular journalism. In Britain, its principal exponents included T. P. O'Connor, Frederick Greenwood, and W. T. Stead. New Journalism, as O'Connor's piece in this section argues, stood for a more human-interest style of reportage. It was associated with the introduction of bold headlines, interviews, illustrations, more sports reportage, and a lessening of parliamentary coverage.

One particular feature of New Journalism was the sustained use of dedicated women's columns. Most newspapers were implicitly gen-dered in their appeal in that 'news' usually meant information regard-ing the masculine political sphere (although the *Illustrated London News*, for example, had included regular fashion columns since the 1840s). This was challenged, however, by the advent of women's newspapers in the early 1860s, the development of which is discussed by Evelyn March-Phillips. Such publications shifted the very defin-ition of a newspaper by combining the illustrated paper with conven-tional features of the women's journal. They were also heavily reliant on advertising, particularly from the new department stores of the 1880s and 1890s. Whereas, famously, *The Times* used advertising revenue to consolidate its supposed political independence, March-Phillips highlights the questionable intimacy of women's newspapers with consumer culture.

FURTHER READING:

Andrewes; Beetham; Black; Brown; Collett; Grant; Hollis; Hunt; Jackson, Kate; Jones; Law; Lee; Wiener, *Papers for the Millions, Innovators*.

[Gibbons Merle], 'Newspaper Press', *Westminster Review*, 10 (1829), 216-37 [216-18, 222-3]

Merle's essay comes from a series of three published by the *Westminster Review*, which form one of the earliest systematic attempts to survey the British press. Merle was a London editor of many years' standing who began his editing career with the short-lived Tory *White Dwarf* in 1817. His article examines the state of the London newspaper press as an industry in the period prior to Victoria's accession; he details government regulation, circulation figures, and salary levels.

ON a former occasion [No. III] a somewhat general view was given of the state of the Newspaper Press in this country, one of those extraordinary combinations by which capital activity, and intellect, have produced wonderful results.[5] The daily press is undoubtedly one of the great powers of society, a power constantly interfering with, and controlling every other. It has an omnipresent vision—there is nothing too high for its grasp—nothing too minute for its attention. It occupies itself with all public affairs—and with all private concerns as soon as they come within the circle of public interest; and perhaps of all the grand machinery of social existence, it is that which is most constantly improving—and presenting from year to year new evidence of what wealth and industry and mind can do when coalescing for any important object. The purport of this article, however, is not to discuss the benefits, or to enlarge on the wonders wrought by the newspapers of England, but to give information as to the manner in which this important engine is made to move, and to communicate in an unadorned shape, those details which cannot but be interesting even if regarded as the mere statistics of the subject.

   The number of newspapers now published in the United Kingdom is three hundred and eight, of which eighty-nine appear in Scotland and Ireland. In London alone there are fifty-five, of which thirteen issue daily; viz. The Times, Morning Herald, Morning Chronicle, Morning Advertiser, Morning Journal, Morning Post and Public Ledger, all Morning papers; and the Globe, Courier, Sun, British

Traveller, Standard, and Star, Evening papers. The quantity of copies daily put into circulation by these establishments is, including their occasional supplements, about forty thousand, and the amount of profit derived by the revenue from their diurnal publication is 722*l.* 16*s.* 8*d.*; of this sum, 533*l.* 6*s.* 8*d.* is paid for stamps, being at the rate of 13*l.* 6*s.* 8*d.* per thousand stamps at 4*d.* each, with a discount of twenty per cent, allowed by the government in lieu of the former deductions, made upon unsold papers, &c., a penalty of 100*l.* being now incurred by the printing of even a single copy upon unstamped paper; 32*l.* is paid by the manufacturer for the Excise duty, the sum being calculated at about 8*s.* per ream upon the large and small paper, used by the different offices; and 157*l.* 10*s.* for advertisements, taking the number which appear in the thirteen daily papers, together at nine hundred.

Each of these advertisements pays a duty of 3*s.* 6*d.* to the government; and, as the present estimate total is calculated from the advertising contents of the several papers, in one day of the present month, which is not the advertising season, it would be fair perhaps, to take the average at one-fifth more, thus making the total amount paid to the revenue daily by the London morning and evening papers, about 750*l.*

Besides the London daily newspapers, there are several which are published twice and thrice a week; these are the London Gazette, the Record, the St. James's Chronicle (a paper connected with the establishment of the Standard), the Evening Mail, which is published at the office of the Times; the London Packet, and the English Chronicle, which is printed by the proprietors of the Morning Herald.

As to the respective numbers issued by each of the daily papers, it is not easy to be precise. The Times, according to a paragraph which lately appeared in that paper, distributes nearly ten thousand copies daily, and the Herald has probably a daily circulation of not less than eight thousand, whilst the Morning Chronicle, according to the statement which has been made by its proprietor, may be supposed to issue something more than four thousand daily, a small circulation certainly as to mere number when compared with the Times or the Herald, but yet sufficiently large to enable the Chronicle to stand its ground well. [...]

The weekly papers now published, are, the County Chronicle, Farmer's Journal, World, Atlas, Baldwin's County Herald, Dispatch, Examiner, Trades' Free Press, Life in London, Sunday Times, New Sunday Times, Weekly Times, Age, Englishman, Sunday Monitor, Sunday Advertiser, Bell's Messenger, Farmer's Chronicle, Sphynx, Spectator, John Bull, News, Observer, Old Soldier, and Weekly Courier; besides the three Literary Papers, The Atheneum, the Literary Gazette, and the Weekly Review; one or two Law Papers; and Cobbett's Register. Three of these, the New Sunday Times, the Old Soldier, and the Weekly Courier, are of no older date than the current year. The number of persons employed upon the daily newspapers, taking the average of the morning and evening papers, is upwards of six hundred; and that of the weekly papers, including those which appear two and three times per week, more than five hundred; making a total of more than eleven hundred; and if to this we add the number employed upon the provincial English papers, and upon those which appear in Ireland and Scotland, we shall have a grand total, of two thousand seven hundred. Employed upon each morning paper, there are an editor, a sub-editor, from ten to fourteen regular reporters, at salaries of four to six guineas per week, each; from thirty to thirty-five compositors in the printing office, some of whom being what is called full hands, that is, men who work the whole of their day, receive $2l.$ $8s.$ each, as wages, with some additions for over hours; whilst others, who are called supernumeraries, and who compose only a limited portion of matter called a galley, receive $1l.$ $3s.$ $6d.$ each; one or two readers, who correct the proofs as they come from the compositors, and who receive each, from two and a half, to three and a half guineas per week; a reading-boy, whose duty it is to read the copy aloud, whilst the reader makes his corrections upon the proof; a printer, who receives from four to six, or even eight guineas per week; and a certain number of men and boys to attend to the printing machine, and to take off the papers as they fall from the cylinders; a publisher and sub-publisher; two or more clerks in the office, to receive advertisements and keep the accounts; a porter, a number of errand boys, &c.

The salary of an editor, upon a respectable morning paper, is from $600l.$ to $1000l.$ per annum; and a subeditor receives from $400l.$ to $600l.$ per annum. We have heard that the editor of one of the leading morning papers, has $1000l.$ per annum; and that at least another $1000l.$ per annum, is paid to gentlemen not regularly on the establishment, for political articles; thus providing a variety of matter. Besides the regular reporters of a newspaper, there are several occasional, or as they are called, 'penny a line' reporters; from the circumstance of their furnishing articles of intelligence, at a fixed price per line; viz., $1\frac{1}{4}d$. or $1\frac{1}{2}d$. They are not attached to any particular newspaper. The aggregate charge for copy furnished by these persons, forms a considerable item in the weekly expenditure of a newspaper. The salaries paid by a first rate morning paper weekly, to its editors, reporters, and others on the establishment, do not amount to less than 180*l.* per week; and if to this be added the expenditure for occasional reporting—for assistance to the compositors—for foreign newspapers, and private correspondence, and various items which it is unnecessary to enumerate, we have a weekly expense of nearly 250*l.*

'Useful Sunday Literature for the Masses', *Punch*, 17 (1849), 116

The 1840s saw the advent of cheap weekly newspapers that were aimed at an artisan readership. They dominated the reading of working-class men in particular (see piece by Wright in this section). Their detailed criminal reportage was often perceived as a significant element of their appeal. *Punch* (1841–), already well established as the leading satirical journal, here attacks the sensational reportage of Sunday newspapers. It also implicitly satirizes those Utilitarians who believed in disseminating 'useful knowledge' to willing working-class readers.

USEFUL SUNDAY LITERATIRE FOR THE MEASSES; OR, MURDER MADE FAMILIAR.

Father of a Family (*reads*): "THE WRETCHED MURDERER IS SUPPOSED TO HAVE CUT THE THROATS OF THE THREE ELDEST CHILDREN, AND THEM TO HAVE KILLED THE BABY BY BEATING IT REPEATEDLY WITH A POKER.* * * * * IN PERSON HE IS OF A RATHER BLOATED APPEARANCE, WITH A BULL NECK, SMALL EYES, BROAD LARGE NOSE AND COARSE VULGAR MOUTH. HIS DRESS WAS A LIGHT BLUE COAT, WITH BRASS BUTTONS, ELEGANT YELLOW SUMMER VEST, AND SALT AND PEPPER TROUSERS. WHEN AT THE STATION HOUSE, HE EXPRESSED HIMSELF AS BEING RATHER 'PECKISH,' AND SAID HE SHOULD LIKE A BLACK PUDDING, WHICH, WITH A CUP OF COFFEE, WAS IMMEDIATELY PROCURED FOR HIM."

USEFUL SUNDAY LITERATURE FOR THE MASSES;
OR, MURDER MADE FAMILIAR.

Father of a Family (reads). "THE WRETCHED MURDERER IS SUPPOSED TO HAVE CUT THE THROATS OF HIS THREE ELDEST CHILDREN, AND THEN TO HAVE KILLED THE BABY BY BEATING IT REPEATEDLY WITH A POKER. * * * * * IN PERSON HE IS OF A RATHER BLOATED APPEARANCE, WITH A BULL NECK, SMALL EYES, BROAD LARGE NOSE, AND COARSE VULGAR MOUTH. HIS DRESS WAS A LIGHT BLUE COAT, WITH BRASS BUTTONS, ELEGANT YELLOW SUMMER VEST, AND PEPPER-AND-SALT TROWSERS. WHEN AT THE STATION HOUSE HE EXPRESSED HIMSELF AS BEING RATHER 'PECKISH,' AND SAID HE SHOULD LIKE A BLACK PUDDING, WHICH, WITH A CUP OF COFFEE, WAS IMMEDIATELY PROCURED FOR HIM."

FIG. 9. 'Useful Sunday Literature for the Masses', *Punch*, 17 (1849), 116.

'The Penny Daily Paper', *Chambers's Journal of Popular Literature, Science, and the Arts*, 4 (6 October 1855), 223–4

The abolition of Stamp Duty in 1855 meant that, for the first time, many people became regular purchasers of a daily newspaper. *Chambers's Journal* (1832–1956, with changes of title) was a weekly miscellany run by William and Robert Chambers, long-standing Edinburgh-based proponents of low-cost print media, and this article promotes the benefits of a cheap press. It particularly celebrates the way that the penny daily press increased the extent and speed of the flow of news around the country to forward the 'national mind'.

This is a novelty in our domestic experiences, and really it is a very pleasant one. There, each morning as we enter our parlour to breakfast, we find the little inexpensive sheet ready for us, with all the news of the preceding day, and the latest intelligence transmitted by telegraph. Four hundred miles as we are from London, matters that have transpired there at six in the morning, are presented in this modest intelligencer by breakfast-time. We never could afford such a luxury or convenience before; and in the city of our residence, though as populous as Rome, there actually never was till now a local daily paper to be purchased. This new enjoyment in life we owe to the late law, making the stamp optional. Thousands must feel the blessing as we do, and thousands must be thankful for it, as we are. Let the old weekly and twice a week papers rail or grumble about the change as they may, the public grasps at the penny daily paper as something it needs, and will, if possible, have. It sees no necessity for taking three days' news in one sheet twice a week, instead of daily, in order to make as much as possible go under one penny-stamp, and that stamp, after all, perhaps not needed for any purpose the reader has to do with. It wishes to know *each morning* what is going on. If the stamp prevented it from obtaining this knowledge each morning, then it will think the stamp well away, how well assured soever the old large papers may have been of the virtues of that red mark.

Such of the penny daily papers as we have seen are respectably conducted. The trash which was uttered in anticipation of their necessarily proving low in tone, like many similarly priced papers in America, is in the course of being triumphantly falsified. The almost equal nonsense of the attempts to prove that a power of posting and re-posting was necessary to every particular news-sheet, and that the stamp was only the fair compensation for the postage (anything to keep on the stamp!), is undergoing similar exposure, in the fact, that the unstamped papers find their way all over the country by cheaper means than the post. But, then, it is said, the penny papers cannot live. Not a week passes but the old papers have the pleasure of recording the death and burial of a few of them. That would be very serious, if true. But the failure of a number of rash speculations, out of the multitude, is not quite a proof that all the penny papers are to fail. What a powerful fact it is on the other side, that the *Manchester Examiner*[6] (a paper which had the manliness to favour the abolition of the stamp) has attained for its daily form a circulation of 14,000, which would be considerably larger if the mechanical means existed for printing the sheet in proper time! It is possible, however, that the unstamped daily sheet will not succeed in many towns at a penny, for want of a sufficiently large population. If so, let them be tried at a somewhat higher rate. It was not implied in the demand for an unstamped press, that all the press should thenceforth be published at a penny.

The public may felicitate itself on attaining anyhow an unstamped press. Public intelligence and opinion will now have unrestricted flow through the land, and the advance of the national mind will henceforth be at an accelerated rate. It is perhaps more wonderful that the blessing has been attained even now, than that it was withheld so long, considering that so many of the natural advocates of an unrestrained press were bound over by erroneous views of their own interests to oppose the measure. Every such acquisition by the public is indeed a wonder, for even liberals and political economists, as we see, cannot, in their own case, get over the idea, that the public, somehow, is made for the individual trader, not the individual trader for the public.

[John Chapman], 'The London Daily Press', *Westminster Review*, OS 64 NS 8 (October 1855), 492–521 [516–19]

The removal of Stamp Duty produced several articles on the history of the press, partly inspired by Frederick Knight Hunt's *The Fourth Estate* (1850). The moment was celebrated by the reformist *Westminster* and others as the historical culmination of the establishment of an independent press. In keeping with this confident atmosphere, the article below by Chapman, owner and editor of the *Westminster*, narrates a history of *The Times* that attributes its market domination to its early refusal of party-political patronage. Ironically, *The Times*'s prominence, so celebrated by Chapman, would soon disappear because of the penny newspapers encouraged by the removal of Stamp Duty.

RETURN OF THE NUMBER OF NEWSPAPER STAMPS ISSUED TO EACH OF THE FOLLOWING LONDON NEWSPAPER FOR THE FIRST SIX MONTHS OF 1855:—

Times	9,175,788
Morning Advertiser	1,034,618
Daily News	825,000
Morning Herald	554,000
Morning Post	465,000
Morning Chronicle	401,500
Globe	540,000
Sun	378,000
Standard	202,000

Instead of forming little more than one-fourth of the total circulation of the London Daily Press, as was the case a few years after the passing of the Reform Bill, *The Times* now monopolizes nearly three-fourths of it. From 2,744,000 in 1835, it has mounted to 18,350,000 in 1855, supposing the latter half of the year to equal the first half—an increase of nearly six hundred per cent. A large portion of this increase has been at the expense of the other daily newspapers, as the aggregate circulation of the London Daily Press has not kept pace with the increase which has taken place in the consumption of newspapers throughout the country generally. During the last thirty years, the total circulation of the London Daily Press has not increased much more than sixty per cent., while the total consumption of newspapers in Great Britain for the same period is not less than three hundred per cent. above what it was at the former period. When Lord John Russell brought forward his motion in favour of Parliamentary Reform, in 1822, he referred to the increased circulation of newspapers as an argument for the extension of the suffrage.[7] There were at that time, he said, no less than 23,600,000 newspapers circulated annually in the United Kingdom, which was more than double what the consumption had been thirty years previously. Of these 23,600,000, the London daily journals sold not less than 14,000,000, or about sixty per cent. of the whole. At present, in spite of the enormous sale of *The Times*, the aggregate circulation of the London Daily Press does not form more than twenty-five per cent. of the whole of the newspapers consumed annually in the United Kingdom. This difference in the relative proportion of the London Daily Press to the aggregate circulation, is chiefly owing to the more rapid increase of London and provincial weekly newspapers, especially the latter class. The fact is interesting to the politician and the statesman, in so far as it serves to show the strong Anglo-Saxon tendency to individualization, as opposed to the Gallic love of centralisation. We have no means of comparing the Paris and provincial circulation of newspapers; but it would surprise us very much to find the French provincial newspapers forming anything like the same proportion of the aggregate circulation as they constitute in Great Britain. [...]

But the main cause of the wonderful success of *The Times*, during the last sixteen years—for it is only since 1839 that it has risen so far beyond all competition—has been its faithful adherence to the rule laid down by the late Mr. Walter, of keeping itself clear of all party connexions.[8] By taking that course, it not only cut away all chance of rising into favour on a sudden popularity through the success of this or that class of politicians, but exposed itself to much obloquy and misrepresentation for its alleged want of principle, seeing that it advocated neither the one side nor the other of any great question, on mere party grounds, but dared to 'condemn any act detrimental to the public welfare,' irrespective of the men who formed the Ministry of the day. This was the cause of its being exposed to so much persecution from the underlings of Government in the early part of its career, and of its receiving so little credit or sympathy for those sufferings from either the Whig or the Tory party. Had the 'Gentleman of the Press' at that period been able to rise above trade considerations, or party feeling, they would have admired the downright honesty of Mr. Walter in refusing even the semblance of Government patronage in any shape; and the indomitable courage with which he struggled against the disgraceful attempts of Ministers to destroy the property he had created by his enterprize, because he refused to make his paper a party organ. Had *The Times* attached itself to either side, it would have been safe from persecution, as the understanding which then existed between the leaders of the two aristocratic parties would have prevented the infliction of such injustice as it was made to suffer. It was only in the case of a Pariah journal, which refused to swear allegiance to Pitt or Fox, or any of their successors, that the Government could thus venture to act with impunity.[9] [...]

We make no apology for having devoted so much space to the history of a newspaper which is now universally recognised as the leading organ of the public in this country. Some of the causes which have contributed to raise it to that proud eminence we have endeavoured to trace.

A Journeyman Engineer [Thomas Wright], *Some Habits and Customs of the Working Classes* (London: Tinsley Brothers, 1867), 31-6

This extract typifies an oft-expressed concern over the influence of the radical, platform-style oratory of the Sunday newspaper. Wright, a working-class autodidact with a strong belief in self-improvement, attacks the class-consciousness encouraged by its mode of address. Wright published three personal surveys of working-class life, *Some Habits and Customs*, *The Great Unwashed* (1868), and *Our New Masters* (1873), as well as articles in the *Contemporary Review* and *Nineteenth Century*.

There is, however one class of self-constituted friend to whom the working man should ever say, 'avoid thee;' a class whose chief object it is to 'put money in their purse,' and who adopt the character of the working man's friend as the readiest means of accomplishing that object. It is this class of friend who tells the working man that he is an outraged and oppressed individual, against whom all classes of society are leagued; and that it is to them—the said friends—and to no one else, that he must trust for guidance and protection. At the head of this peculiar class of friends stands the great C. G. B., or 'Alphabet' Crusher, proprietor of Crusher's newspaper.[10] Crusher's newspaper is the oldest of its class; but age has only increased its influence as the leading and most pronounced organ of the labouring classes, the most energetic discoverer and denouncer of the abuses to which those classes are subject at the hands of every other. Since the abolition of the paper duty, Crusher has had many rivals for the proud and profitable position of journalistic agitator and toady-in-chief to 'the working man;' but he has always acquitted himself in a manner that proves him paramount, and his paper can still boast of having the largest circulation in the small but not altogether unimportant world in which papers of its class are read. And the continuous success of the veteran Crusher in his own line of business is by no means surprising to those having a knowledge of the subject. [...]

A working man may be in constant employment, earning good wages, and enjoying good health; he may have a comfortable home, and be a depositor in the savings bank, and with all these advantages he may consider that he is a comparatively happy man. But let him become a reader of Crusher's newspaper, and he will soon find that, so far from having any claim to consider himself in any sense happy, he is one of the most oppressed and miserable of human beings. He will learn that he is the prey and victim of a 'bloated, vicious, blood-sucking aristocracy,' unjust taxation, unfair and unequal laws, and a host of other national and personal wrongs. He will be persuaded that the chief aim of capitalists and the employers of labour is to crush and 'grind him down,' and to annihilate 'the rights of labour.' In this conscientious and comforting publication he will find the government of his country described as an organized swindle, the principal design of which is to oppress and rob him, and to prevent him from ever attaining any elevation in the social scale. To corroborate this description the actions and conduct of the Government are distorted and commented upon in a style of unquestionable vigour, but of very questionable fairness. The members of the legislative and executive bodies, and all who are in any way actively concerned in carrying on the work of government, he will find described either as arrant fools or self-interested knaves, who, however they may differ about other matters, are unanimous upon the two points of enriching themselves, and of deliberately oppressing the working-classes. And, finally, he will be led to infer that all the friendship for, and interest in, the welfare of the working man, and all the administrative talent in the country, is centred in the We's of Crusher's newspaper.

'We are a nation that must be cracked up,' observed one of our most remarkable men to Mark Tapley, during the period of that jolly gentleman's residence in the American 'Eden;'[11] and though there are few persons who would like to speak as plainly as the Yankee Colonel, there are, I fancy, still fewer who object to being cracked up occasionally. And so it is with the working classes. They do not say that they *must* be cracked up, and they would scorn the idea of asking any one to crack them up; but still when they *are* cracked up they are pleased, and are disposed to view the motives of the flatterer in a favourable light. It is to this feeling that Crusher's newspaper, and others of the same class, are indebted for the influence they undoubtedly exert over a considerable portion of the working classes. In these journals the working man finds himself cracked up to an almost unlimited extent. He is described in their pages as an injured innocent, against whom every man's hand is raised; he is told that it is he who is the only real producer of the national wealth, and that it is he who, as the chief producer, should have the lion's share of the produce, out of which he is unjustly kept by a 'bloated aristocracy,' and a 'servile middle class.' In these papers he finds himself habitually alluded to in favourable terms as 'a bold bread winner,' or a 'brawny son of toil,' is applauded to the very echo for his 'sturdy independence,' 'rough common sense,' and a host of other good and great attributes of which he may or may not be possessed. And in addition to reading all these fine things about himself, the working man, in this kind of papers, has the satisfaction of seeing his enemies (that is, according to these said journals, all who are in a higher rank of society than himself) denounced in the most emphatic language.

The working man who reads and believes in newspapers of the 'Crusher' class soon becomes a discontented and unhappy person, and learns to regard himself as an oppressed member of society, on whom all other ranks of society constantly wage warfare. He becomes a person of intensely class feeling, and believes in the sentiment that whatever is beneficial to or approved by people above him, must necessarily be antagonistic to his interest, as in a foregone conclusion; and, while he constantly rails against the aristocracy, thus speaking of them as the natural and avowed enemies of the working classes, he is himself generally the most aristocratic—in his own offensive sense of the word—of working men. Whenever a man of this kind is by any chance 'clothed in a little brief authority' he exerts that authority to its utmost limits and exacts the honour due to it with the greatest rigour. [. . .] And men of this kind, narrow-minded, ignorant, ill-informed men, whose ideas upon the constitution of society and the relative position and value of its various sections have been derived from the toadying of papers whose circulation depends on their persistent writing up of 'The working man' are among the greatest obstacles to the social progress of the working classes. They are men of little strength of mind, and, being fooled to the top of their bent, are firmly impressed with the belief that themselves, and their class, *are* perfect; and that consequently there remains nothing more for them to do in the way of self-improvement, with any view to aiding in the work of their own advancement. All such disadvantages as they labour under, they assume are entirely attributable to the general wrong-doings and special machinations against them of the rich and powerful, and they lay the flattering unction to their souls that their friends of the agitator persuasion will yet find them a royal road to wealth and social elevation. Hugging themselves in this belief, they remain stationary, grumbling at their position, but refusing to 'move on,' and are as a mill-stone about the neck of the more liberal, intelligent, and energetic section of the working classes, who have learned and are striving to carry out the principle that working men themselves must be the chief workers in achieving their own elevation, and that denial and self-improvement are primary means to the desired end.

'A Conservative Journalist', 'Why is the Provincial Press Radical?' *National Review*, 7 (July 1886), 678-82

Provincial newspapers enjoyed several decades of prosperity after 1855. The largest became daily publications printing news telegraphed from London; within their localities they consequently provided strong competition to their metropolitan rivals. The *National Review*, launched in 1883, was a monthly closely connected to the Conservative party. This pseudonymous article, which appeared in a publication in which most articles were clearly signed, seeks to explain why so many provincial newspapers supported the Liberal party. Its publication follows the Liberal Gladstone's re-election as Prime Minister in 1886, after he had been in power since 1880.

THE reason the Provincial Press is chiefly Radical is to be found in an examination of the genesis of newspapers. The opinionated newspaper is a creation of quite recent times. In the beginning of this century the pamphlet was still supreme as the medium of political discussion, and scarcely any journal had then emerged from the character of a news letter. During the last fifty years, however, the opinionated journal has become the rule, the pamphlet has become almost extinct, and although there are still a few newspapers that do not profess to have any political creed, their pretended neutrality is really a cloak for mild Radicalism. Their neutrality consists in avoiding subjects upon which there is any very decided difference of opinion, and such views as they happen to express consist of accepted platitudes. These independent journals are chiefly owned by Conservatives, who take great pains to impress you with the rigour of their personal creed, and their attitude illustrates, in a striking manner, the answer I am about to give to the question, Why the Provincial Press has, in the main, been Radical.

The newspaper owes its origin to the business instinct of the printer. A country stationer would, in the first instance, be merely an agent for a city printer, who would do for the town in question all the printing it needed. When the printing of the town had risen to a certain regular demand, the stationer would start a press of his own, and, in course of time, would employ a man to assist him. As soon as this stage was reached, the stationer would find his man at one time overwhelmed with work and at another quite idle. He would then resolve to get an apprentice or two, and, that there should be no idle time, he issues a small weekly sheet that would serve the treble purpose of keeping his hands employed, of advertising his name, and creating a new branch of business. The sheet at first would contain only local gossip, brief reports of meetings, and police cases, local advertisements, and no opinions. It would shortly become advisable, from a business point of view, to have opinions, and the printer calculates that in a population of, say 5,000, one thousand of the houses are inhabited by possible buyers of small means, and, perhaps, fifty houses by those who buy London newspapers and reviews. He, therefore, considers the disposition of the thousand householders, and he finds that the majority of these are of the class that would like to be better off than they are, and to this extent are dissatisfied with institutions that Radical politicians tell them are prejudicial to their prosperity. He thereupon concludes that it will be more remunerative to him to express opinions calculated to foster this dissatisfaction, and thus please the thousand possible buyers; if he can throw in a little abuse of the odd fifty, so much the better. The only thing that will restrain him will be a reflection that his stationery business was more dependent on the fifty than the thousand, so that, in the nett result, we may conclude the politics of his journal will be Radical, tempered by profits on stationery.

This represents the origin of most if not all the newspapers that came into being in the provinces up to fifty years ago, even in the large towns, and the same thing is going on now. The necessities of the printer was the origin, in this manner, even of the large daily papers in the provinces whose earnings now show a total of many thousands per year. They developed from the meagre weekly sheet into the well-filled, solid pages published on market day, and then twice a week and thrice a week, and finally some thirty or forty years ago they became daily papers, larger in size on some days than others, but still daily, and in all cases more or less antagonistic to capital, to land, and to possession, and favourable to dissatisfaction, to resistance, and to change, which, put plainly, means acquisition. Possession represents injustice and tyranny. Change represents reform and universal prosperity. The denunciation of the one and advocacy of the other formed the natural commercial rule of the printer, and the same influences operate to this day in various guises and in various degrees. [...]

We must always remember that the genius of a newspaper is to publish to the million what the individual desires to keep secret, and that it will always find an easier and more productive field of labour among the million than among the upper ten.[12] Nor can you controvert the principles here stated by pointing to the Radical papers published in towns that have always returned Conservatives, because there have always been, and will still continue to be, more readers than voters, just as the have-nots always outnumber the haves.

In addition to these considerations there is the personal reason. Because of the superabundance of Radical newspapers, the production of Radical journalists is in excess of Conservative. A young man joining the ranks without any well-defined political creed, naturally leans to the side that appears to him most likely to give him a good living. If he happens to live in a town where there are two papers, one thriving and the other weakly, he will aspire to join the more prosperous, without a thought of politics; moreover, he will aspire to join that side wherein he finds journalists are most thought of, and where the esteem in which their vocation is held is shown by the friendships they make and the politico-social status which is accorded to them. Thus the number and success of the Radical newspapers throughout the country create Radical journalists who will do their best to maintain the inequality from sheer force of habit. The majority of reporters are Radical, and though the inequality is less throughout the country than it was, the Conservatism of a reporter is always of the most shadowy character. As you ascend in the grades of journalism, the Conservative becomes more common, and this is to be accounted for from the fact that a writer cannot succeed without logic, and as soon as logic has sway the Radical theories become undermined. You will find many Radical papers that make a very good show of reason by evading all rules of logic, and working on the principles of declamation and general assertion on the base of false premises. When a journalist has reached the condition of mind necessary for this course, he is lost to the Conservative press, and can continue a Radical writer to the end of his course. [...]

As Conservative thought and opinion become more common throughout the country, the press will follow suit—gradually, and with hesitating steps, but it will follow. The few daily provincial journals of the first standing that are Conservative will increase in circulation and power. They are the growth of the last fifteen years, and their strides have been marvellous. In towns where there are two daily Radical journals, and no Conservative, the less Radical of the two will change. Commercial necessity will determine this, even if the inclination of the proprietor is against it. Fears of competition will precipitate the result, and the first sign of it is indicated by a desire to be known as independent of party ties. These influences, however, are slow, and the changes produced are gradual. It is not surprising that the more eager spirits in the Party are anxious for more rapid measures, and periodically demand the establishment of new journals. Whether or not this course is the best is a question that must be determined by the circumstances of each case; but it may be accepted as an indisputable fact that a limited company is the worst form of proprietorship, and individual ownership that most likely to result in success.

T. P. O'Connor, 'The New Journalism', *New Review*, 1 (1889), 423-34 [423-4, 428-34]

O'Connor (1848–1929) was the founder and first editor of the radical *Star*, which commenced in 1888 and which was arguably the first daily newspaper to practise New Journalism. In 1880, O'Connor was elected as an Irish Nationalist MP for Galway and enjoyed a long career as both journalist and parliamentarian. O'Connor's article in the *New Review*, itself launched only in 1889, forms part of its initial engagement of well-known writers to examine 'new' topical issues. It argues in favour of those very features of the New Journalism that made it notorious.

BEYOND doubt we are on the eve of a new departure in English journalism. All the new journals adopt the new methods, and even the oldest and the most staid, cautiously and tentatively, and with a certain air of self-reproach, admit some of the features of the New Journalism. Before the revolution is finally accomplished, it is well, perhaps, to argue the questions which lie at the root of the difference between the old style and the new.

The main point of difference is the more personal tone of the more modern methods. There was a day when any allusion to the personal appearance, the habits, the clothes, or the home and social life of any person, would have been resented as an impertinence and almost as an indecency. If you turned to the reporting columns of the Houses of Parliament you found full reports of all the speeches—fuller and better than those you can find now; but you had no information as to how the speech was delivered or how received. You were told nothing of the personality of the persons who made the speech. There the long, lifeless even columns were before you; the speech, delivered in the dread void of the dinner-hour to a select audience of the Speaker and the orator himself, filled the space in exactly the same kind of way as the speech that was punctuated by the ringing cheers of a crowded and deeply moved House. The words that came with the fierce fluency of an impassioned speaker were given in exactly the same way as the speech that was interrupted by hems and haws, or mumbled from an inarticulate throat. It was the same, of course, with public men throughout their whole life. You saw their names frequently in print; you read the speeches they made; the lengthy memorandums, the solemn protocols they wrote. But of the man behind these public utterances you were told nothing. And so it was with the other departments of human life with which a newspaper has to deal. If such a trial as that of Mrs. Maybrick had taken place fifty, or even twenty, years ago, the one thing which even the most sensational newspaper would publish would be the report of the evidence, and perhaps a report of the charge of the presiding judge.[13] This is the state of things which the *laudatores temporis acti*[14] regard as representing the halcyon period of British journalism; and this is the kind of thing to which many worthy persons would desire our newspapers to return.

Yet the very persons who make these exclamations are not consistent with themselves. If they were asked which history they prefer to read, history as written by Robertson and the older school of historians, or history as written by Macaulay and Carlyle and Green, there is little doubt as to the answer they would give.[15] But Macaulay devoted a considerable portion of his writing to destroying what was called 'the dignity of history.' He did not scorn any detail—however trifling apparently—which threw a light on the habits or character of the historical personages with whom he had to deal. It is for this reason that his portraits are life-like and immortal, and that we all read his history of dead-and-gone personages with the same breathless attention as though they were beings of still living flesh and blood with whom we ourselves were acquainted. [...]

But apart from the value of personal journalism as historical material, I hold that the desire for personal details with regard to public men is healthy, rational, and should be yielded to. Statesmen are not ciphers without form or blood or passion. Their utterances and acts are not pure intellectual secretions. If you want to know how such and such an act of weakness or folly is intelligible at some crisis in the history of a politician, you must have learned something more of the politician than you can get from the verbatim report of his speeches, or the colourless and dry language of his public documents. Behind every speech and every act there is the man—a weak man or a strong man, high or low, generous in purpose or base in intrigue. You cannot get rid of this background if you want to describe the event accurately. You cannot do so when you are listening to the man, though you should never have to describe him. What lends effect to the speeches of Mr. Parnell?[16] It is not oratorical fire, for he has none, and never attempts any. It is not great descriptive powers, great resources of wit. It is mainly the strong personality that one sees behind the words. With a few sentences apparently cold, the Irish leader is able to subdue and almost cow a House of Commons in which he is in a hopeless minority, and for the reason that words from him mean facts—are but the forecast of inevitable event. Suppose you were the historian of our times at the end of the twentieth century; how invaluable would it be to you to have a graphic account of some night of heat and passion in which Mr. Parnell made one of his historic utterances with clenched teeth and pale face! Three lines in the letter of a good London correspondent would give to such a historian a better idea of the scene than columns of reporting in *Hansard*, or in the journals of the following morning.

But then, it will be said, personal journalism goes further than the public man. No one's life is now private; the private dinner party, the intimate conversation, all are told. If this kind of thing go on, say the critics of modern journalism, we shall before long be in the same plight as the journalism of America. No doubt a real danger in the new school of journalism is here pointed out. I should be sorry, indeed, to see many things find their way into the columns of the pages of English journals which are admitted into the newspapers of America. Gossip of a personal character is good or bad according to its tone; and to the subjects with which it deals. Gossip should be always good-humoured, kindly, and free from political or other bias. One of the most common fallacies among those outside newspaper offices is that a paper is read solely for its politics. There could be no greater mistake; and, indeed, I may go further, and say that it would be highly undesirable that politics and politics alone should sell a journal. We should have come to a pretty pass indeed if all other departments of human life were shut out of our newspapers except those of party conflict. We, fortunately, are not always talking politics. In the domain of charity, philanthropic effort, amusement, and society, we find common ground, however bitterly we may be divided on political questions; and an editor will make a great mistake who does not recognise this fact and conduct his paper accordingly. Nothing could—to my mind—be greater folly than to introduce political controversy into all and every department of a newspaper. Every journal which is of any political value greatly delights its friends and bitterly exasperates its foes by its comments on political subjects; but equally every journal, which is a true journal, supplies news in those columns which are devoted to news, that can be read with equal interest and amusement by men of all parties.

And now as to gossip. The lines between that which is legitimate and that which is illegitimate are pretty clearly laid down. One of our judges very properly said once that it would be an odious thing if newspapers were to be a sort of lion's mouth into which every man could drop his charge against the enemy he wanted to secretly stab. With this view I entirely concur. A journal that lends itself to slander, to scandal, to personal attack, is unworthy of journalism, and nobody ought to have any sympathy with it. But between slander, scandal, and personal and pleasant detail, there is a wide gulf. Why should not the public be told of how the party of Mrs. Smith went off; of how Miss Robinson looked; of the dress Miss Jones wore? These are things which deeply interest a large number of people. They are the subjects about which we talk over the dinner-table; and it is the sound principle to which we shall all come at last in literature and journalism, that everything that can be talked about can also be written about.

With regard to private individuals: that there are restrictions which good taste and, if necessary, the law should put upon personal journalism, is clear. A different rule holds good with regard to public characters. There has recently grown up in the jury-box a spirit of savage hatred to journalism which has led to some very unjust verdicts and some scandalous damages. A portion of the public seem actually to imagine that it is the desire and also the interest of a certain class of journalists to libel everybody they can. There are newspapers open to this charge; but of the ordinary respectable journal no conception could be more incorrect. In every newspaper office there is a perfect horror—an almost morbid dread—of an action for libel. [...]

A point on which the journals of the new school differ among themselves is the attitude a newspaper should assume to political questions. A great many people are of opinion that newspapers should take up towards all party conflicts what is called an 'independent' position. So far as the interests of the journal itself is concerned, probably this is true. The journal whose course on any question can be foretold is not one that ever excites much enthusiasm. The journalist, on the other hand, who is able to keep his reader always in a state of suspense and curiosity as to the line he will adopt, undoubtedly does much to increase the interest and the number of his readers. It may further be argued that the newspaper has a responsibility of its own, and a function as a public teacher, and that it ceases to perform that function when it becomes allied with any political association. To all these things I have to reply that I like an 'independent' journal as little as the politician who assumes to himself the same adjective. In one case and the other I have found that independence was a euphemism for political vanity; personal interest, or mere crankiness of temper and opinion. [...]

Finally, I think a journal, whatever its views, should express them with the greatest lucidity and in the strongest and most striking manner it can command. We live in an age of hurry and of multitudinous newspapers. The newspaper is not read in the secrecy and silence of the closet as is the book. It is picked up at a railway station, hurried over in a railway carriage, dropped incontinently when read. To get your ideas through the hurried eyes into the whirling brains that are employed in the reading of a newspaper there must be no mistake about your meaning: to use a somewhat familiar phrase, you must strike your reader right between the eyes. The daily newspaper often appears to me to bear a certain resemblance to a street piano; its music is not classical, nor very melodious, and perhaps there is a certain absence of soul, but the notes should come out clear, crisp, sharp.

Evelyn March-Phillips, 'Women's Newspapers', *Fortnightly Review*, OS 62 NS 56 (1894), 661-70 [661-5, 667-8]

There was a tremendous growth of women's weekly newspapers in the 1880s and 1890s. This format broadened the very definition of a newspaper by combining two established forms, the illustrated newspaper and the women's magazine. March-Phillips, who contributed several articles to the *Fortnightly Review* on women's issues, here examines the characteristics of women's newspapers. As she suggests, while providing a welcome focus on women's lives, they were nevertheless inspired by consumer culture's promotion of an ideal femininity.

The career, the claims, the character of her whom *Punch*, with a lapse from his habitual gallantry, styles 'the irrepressible she,'[17] meets us at every turn in modern life, and perhaps the multiplication and development of newspapers devoted to her special interests, is not the least significant token of her vitality.

It is curious to turn over a pile of those which existed thirty years ago. Earlier still, in the days of our grandmothers, the *Repository*, or the *Ladies' Companion*, made its monthly appearance, adorned with a few coloured woodcuts, some bold descriptive remarks of what were believed to be Paris fashions, and supplied with inch-square patterns of new dress materials, pinned between the pages of a keep-sake poem, a sentimental tale, or a receipt for distilling lavender water. In 1861 the *Lady's Own Paper*, a feeble little publication, the only representative of its kind, was giving up a languid struggle for life, when it was bought up by Mr. Cox, the father of the present proprietors, and given a fresh start as the *Queen*.[18] The *Queen* was a spirited and novel departure compared to its predecessors. Its advent was an excitement in the feminine world, and it advanced steadily in public favour. The pages of reading matter were just half the present number (for the same price), while the advertisement sheets were three, instead of twenty-three. We find a great deal about the doings of Her Majesty, profusely illustrated; considerable space is given up to the latest murder, railway accidents and general news of all kinds. Women's tastes are catered for mainly by pages of needle-work designs, hideous as the early Victorian knew how to make them, and by cookery receipts.

Inadequate as we should now think it, it was all that was needed for a long time, and it was not till 1880 that a rival near the throne appeared in the *Lady's Pictorial*, with the features in embryo of the new journalism.[19] This obliged the *Queen* to sharpen its weapons, and to-day it is as 'up-to-date' as any of its younger competitors, and in some ways still holds the first place. The feminine reading public increased apace, but it was some years longer before the success of the two older journals encouraged the rush of 'weeklies' that has since taken place. In the last thirty years or so the following have started into existence:—

Queen	1861	*Woman*	1891
The Ladies	1872	*Health and Home*	1891
Lady's Pictorial	1880	*Winter's Weekly*	1891
Lady	1885	*Ladies' Review*	1892
Lady's World	1886	*Pioneer of Fashion*	1892
Women's Gazette	1888	*Shafts*	1892
Women's Herald	1888	*Homeland*	1892
Women's World	1888	*Fashions of To-Day*	1893
Gentlewoman	1890	*The Young Woman*	1893
Princess	1890	*Woman's Signal*	1894

I do not include a number of monthly publications, which come under the head of Magazines.

These papers are very much alive—full of enterprise and keenly competitive. One or two exist to advance a special purpose, but the ultimate object of the great majority is dress and fashion. Where one woman studied these subjects twenty years ago, a hundred do so to-day; and though the upper classes may be no more extravagant than of old, dress is of far more importance to women in general. Appearance is more constantly dwelt upon and its influence is more widely recognised. Even those who excel in other ways, cannot afford to neglect cultivating the art of dressing well. 'Mind you go well dressed,' is a common piece of advice to the seeker after employment. If a paper, then, is to be popular, it thinks it necessary to obtain the brightest and most varied news, on this topic, above all others. [...]

These papers live mainly by their advertisements. A shilling would scarcely cover the cost of production of those which are sold for sixpence, much less make them pay. It is from the high prices charged for advertising space that the harvest is reaped. We shall be within the mark if we put the advertisements of the *Queen* at £1,000 a week. Its importance to trade may be gauged by the fact that while, at the beginning of its career, the outside sheet was let out for £10, the price has crept up, till it now commands £40 or £50. The *Gentlewoman* and the *Lady's Pictorial* are not far behind. A paper must needs be enlisted to some extent in the service of its clients, and as long as this influence does not weigh unduly, the transaction, on the whole, is a fair one. The lady is lucky in getting her shilling's worth for sixpence. The proprietor and the trade strike a balance between the profit and cost of circulation. It is obvious that if a paper, which is sold under the cost of production, is made to pay by advertisements, every copy sold reduces the profits, so that circulation beyond a certain point would be fatal. On the other hand, if the trade is not satisfied that circulation is pushed sufficiently to recompense its outlay, the advertisements will fall off. Certain papers exist, and are well known, which are merely advertising touts, and need very sharp supervision on the part of those shops which consent to employ them. The smaller papers, which keep under weight, succeed in clearing some fraction on each copy. An immense postal trade is done by means of these advertisements, which sensibly aid the deliberations of the country maid or matron. As a girl, living in the depths of Devonshire, remarked: 'They are my walk down Bond Street.' In fact, where dress is concerned, the ladies' illustrated papers tend to constitute a species of perambulating shop, in which wares are set forth by means of print and picture.

Anybody who takes the trouble can easily trace the connection between shops whose goods are quoted over and over again in answers to correspondents and the *quid pro quo* in the advertisement sheets, and as long as the goods brought forward have been carefully examined and found to be worth recommending there seems nothing particular to cavil at, but there is small doubt that these tactics are carried to excess. Writers, who would be conscientious if they dared, are perpetually cautioned against neglecting the claims of Messrs. So & So, who threaten to withdraw their patronage unless they receive more glowing criticism, warmer recommendations, more frequent notices and illustrations. As a consequence, untrustworthy puffing prevails. Hopelessly worthless dressmakers and tailors are thrust upon our notice, furniture shops which advertise are exploited vigorously. Those who wish to furnish cheaply or artistically are crushed if they suggest the picking up of antiques or second-hand goods. At sales times the enthusiastic chroniclers of fashion surpass themselves in their efforts to clear off the stock of the shops, and real bargains and soiled rubbish are included in one indiscriminate paean of praise. In short, this custom, which is enormously on the increase, goes far to render all commendation valueless, it becoming impossible to distinguish that which is genuine from that which is due to interested motives and the coercion of tradespeople. [...]

It is a deplorable fact that almost all these journals are edited by men. One would think women should know best what will please women, but as editors we are told they are deficient in the capacity which grasps a business situation and comes to a quick and definite judgement on financial matters, while they seem wholly unable to master the intricacies of the law of libel. Many are sub-editors, and manage special departments, and on every paper, I think I may say, the bulk of the work is done by women. The woman journalist, to whom, cry her down as it may, the press of to-day owes much of its brightness and life, has been, in great measure, created by writing on subjects she understands, in journals for her own sex. [...]

I should be unwilling to leave the impression that women's newspapers have no higher ambition than that of chronicling modes of the moment, or fashions of the hour. Editors begin to show a more decided inclination to minister to wider and more intelligent tastes. The time is past when it was thought that anyone could write well enough for ladies. Now, every kind of account, comment, and criticism must be supplied in a fresh and finished manner. Not only are high prices paid for serial novels, but well-known pens contribute short articles more often than they used. Perhaps few things give us a better idea of the versatility of the average Englishwoman than a careful study of these papers. Dressmaking, cooking, and housewifery are dealt with exhaustively and intelligently, and in a practical, attractive, and scientific manner. Those who wish to make their own clothes and train their own cooks, are helped to do so well and efficiently. We are almost astonished at the constant successes chronicled, and the excellent standard attained in art, music, literature, medicine, and university degrees. The pages supplied on gardening and art needlework prove that here again something better than an amateur performance is aimed at. Very interesting accounts have appeared of experimental ventures in new trades and professions, showing the methods of the factory inspector, the lady laundress, the photographer, the co-operative store-keeper, &c., &c.

NOTES TO SECTION VIII

1. [Gibbons Merle], 'Newspaper Press', *Westminster* Review, 10 (1829), 216.
2. Edward G. Salmon, 'What the Working Classes Read', *Nineteenth Century*, 20 (1886), 110.
3. Lucy Brown, *Victorian News and Newspapers* (Oxford: Clarendon Press, 1985), 22.
4. Mathew Arnold, 'Up to Easter', *Nineteenth* Century, 123 (1887), 638–9.
5. [Walter Coulson], 'Newspapers', *Westminster Review*, 2 (July 1824), 194–212.
6. The *Manchester Examiner* was launched as a weekly liberal paper in January 1846. It commenced a daily edition in December 1854, the *Manchester Daily Times*.
7. See Section V n. 64.
8. John Walter II (1776–1847), proprietor of *The Times*, who inherited the newspaper from his father, also John Walter.
9. William Pitt (1759–1806), long-serving prime minister; although Pitt declared that he belonged to no party, one of his main political opponents was the Whig politician Charles James Fox (1749–1806).
10. Probably a composite of G. W. M Reynolds (see P. 2), and 'Alphabet' Bailey, the first editor of the *Illustrated London News* (so called because of his numerous Christian names).
11. A character from Dickens's *Martin Chuzzlewit* (1843–4).
12. i.e. the 'upper ten thousand' families who were supposed to control the country.

13. In 1889 Florence Maybrick was found guilty of using arsenic to murder her husband. She was sentenced to death, although this was later commuted.

14. 'Praisers of time past'.

15. Thomas Carlyle (1795–81), social critic, historian and philosopher; Thomas Babington Macaulay (1800–59), historian and essayist, achieved spectacular success with his *History of England* (1849–61); John Richard Green (1837–83), historian, best known for his *Short History of the English People* (1873).

16. Charles Parnell (1846–91), elected MP for Meath in 1875, was the leader of Irish constitutional nationalist party at the time of Gladstone's 1886 Home Rule Bill.

17. *Punch* was vociferous in its dislike of the liberated New Woman: the term was used in a cartoon of 3 February 1894.

18. The *Queen* was launched in 1861 by Isabella and Samuel Beeton; in 1863 it merged with the *Lady's Newspaper and Pictorial Times* (1847–63).

19. *Lady's Pictorial* (1881–1921), a 3*d.* illustrated journal containing a mixture of advertisements, fashion, serial fiction, and articles on 'woman's work'.

IX

GRAPHIC MEDIA

INTRODUCTION

This section examines the role played by illustration in the appeal of periodicals, newspapers, and novels. Its aim is to provoke questions concerning the usage and aesthetic status of different nineteenth-century graphic forms, as well as the synergy between text and image. The extracts included, however, inevitably constitute only a small part of the larger histories of photography, engraving, and the print trade: we have chosen to examine only those aspects of visual culture that relate to forms of print media. Thus, although photography established itself as a popular medium in the early 1860s, this section deals with photography only in so far as it was incorporated into illustrated newspapers and journals in the 1880s and 1890s.

Numerous images have been included in this section in order to demonstrate the changes that took place in graphic reproduction, and to provide a partner to the written extracts. Some of the images included were published as part of the original article, as is the case with several images from the *Bookseller*. Other engravings have been included because an article, despite being unillustrated, discusses specific images, as is the case with John Ruskin's essay. A third type of illustration is that which typifies general developments described by the extracts. Thus the pages from the *Strand*, together with an illustration of Queen Victoria's funeral from 1901, exemplify the integration of photography into the illustrated press. In the latter picture an engraving has been drawn over a background photograph of Windsor Castle (Fig. 21). Where is the 'realism' of this picture? What interaction between visual media does it suggest? The illustrations in this section have been chosen to provoke as much discussion as the articles: each contextualises the other.

The growth of cheap illustration was facilitated by a revival in wood-engraving that took place in the 1820s and 1830s. An engraved woodblock could supply many more prints than could a steel or copper-plate engraving, dramatically reducing the cost per item. Wood-engraving was also utilized because, as a form of relief printing, it had the advantage of being able to be printed alongside typeface. Probably the most prominent examples of the successful use of cheap illustration in the early nineteenth century are the radical graphic satires of William Hone and George Cruikshank, which include *The Political House that Jack Built* (1819), *The Queen's Matrimonial Ladder* (1820), and *The Political Showman—At Home* (1821). The 1820s subsequently saw the commencement of *The Portfolio* (1823–5) and the *Mirror of Literature, Amusement and Instruction* (1822–47). These 2*d.* illustrated miscellanies were the precursors to the *Penny Magazine* and the *Saturday Magazine*, whose high-quality yet inexpensive illustrations were an important element of their remarkable success. The tempting allure of illustration for a semi-literate audience is a belief expressed in several articles of this Reader (see Braddon, Brougham, Collins, Knight, Mayhew).

The proliferation of illustrated books and periodicals in the 1830s and 1840s created a new world of images that is described by both Catherine Gore's article and the opening address of the *Illustrated London News*. The examples discussed by Gore can be considered in conjunction with illustrations included in earlier sections. Section V showed that one of the most prominent forms to take advantage of the potential of illustration was the penny miscellany; most of them used an eye-catching engraving to head up their weekly serial fiction (see Fig. 5). Advances in book production also meant that colourful illustrations came to appear on the front of cheap books. The famous railway 'yellow-back' novel emerged in the mid-1850s; they were so called because they were bound using glazed yellow paper laid over boards, with a striking picture on the front and adverts on the rear (see Fig. 4). However, while the 'yellow-back' is another example of a cheap illustrated format, it was precisely such industrialization of art that motivated Ruskin to write a stinging critique of popular illustration in *Ariadne Florentina*, an extract of which we reproduce. Ruskin attacked specific illustrations from *Barnaby Rudge* and the *Cornhill Magazine*: we have included these illustrations so as to allow the reader to judge the validity of Ruskin's critique (Figs. 18 and 19).

Newspapers, like books and periodicals, were similarly affected by the rise of wood-engraving. In May 1842 the *Illustrated London News* became the first newspaper devoted to graphic news. Published weekly at 6*d.*, the *Illustrated London News* provided an extensive variety of image types, ranging from panoramic pullouts to small vignettes. Its success meant that it was soon imitated by publications like the *Pictorial Times* (1843–8), the *Illustrated Times* (1855–62), and, later in the century, the *Graphic* (1869–1932). Several illustrations have been included from the *Illustrated London News* (Figs. 10, 11, 12, 21). The comparison with the traditional woodcuts accompanying street ballads (Fig. 6) demonstrates their impressive scale and quality. The engravings from the *Illustrated London News* also pose a question: what relationship did pictorial journalism produce between the viewer and the event depicted?

The use of explicit engravings by penny-issue fiction and periodicals provoked anxiety over the immediate appeal of illustration. It is in this vein that the article from the *Bookseller* contrasts the illustrations of 'improving' religious and historical narratives with the sensationalism of the engravings accompanying cheap serial fiction: we similarly offer up for comparison illustrations from G. W. M. Reynolds's Mysteries series with those of *Good Words* and *Cassell's History of England* (Figs. 13, 14, 15, 16, 17). The *Bookseller* article also marks a significant shift in the status of book and journal illustration in the late 1850s and early 1860s. This was partly because a number of Pre-Raphaelite artists became involved in producing high-quality designs for engravings. Their work included illustrated editions of poems and books, as well as designs for the popular periodicals *Once a Week* (1859–80), *Good Words* (1860–1906), and the *Cornhill Magazine* (1860–1939). For example, Holman Hunt, Edward Burne-Jones, and Frederick Sandys executed designs for *Once a Week*, while John Everett Millais's work included illustrating Trollope's *Framley Parsonage* for the *Cornhill Magazine*, a short story by Mrs Craik for *Once a Week*, and an edition of Tennyson. The article from the *Bookseller* situates the illustrations published by *Once a Week* and *Good Words* in the context of the use of illustration for moral and aesthetic improvement.

Towards the end of the century, the prominence of illustration was one of the features of the New Journalism. Publications like the sixpenny *Strand Magazine*, founded by George Newnes in 1891, famously defined itself through the number of illustrations it included. Other illustrated titles amongst the many that commenced during this period include the *English Illustrated Magazine* (1883–1913), *Sketch*

(1893–1959), *Black and White* (1891–1912) and *The Gentlewomen* (1890–1926). Clement Shorter's article assesses the role that photography played in encouraging the expansion in the number of illustrated periodicals during the 1880s and 1890s. An illustrated article from the *Strand* correspondingly suggests the intersection between photography, New Journalism, and the construction of celebrity (Fig. 22).

FURTHER READING:

Altick, *Punch*; Anderson; Ashton; Beetham; Beetham and Boardman; Fox; Goldmann, *Victorian Illustrated Books, Victorian Illustration*; Jackson, Mason; King, '*Paradigm*', Maidment, *Reading Popular Prints*, *Into the 1830s*; Plunkett; Sinnema.

'Our Address', *Illustrated London News*, 1 (14 May 1842), 1

When the *Illustrated London News* was launched in May 1842, it was the first periodical to be explicitly devoted to pictorial journalism. In its initial address it attempted to define its position in the periodical market through promoting the aesthetic quality and realism of its engravings. The *Illustrated London News*'s assertions stemmed partly from its desire to disassociate itself from the crude and lurid woodcuts accompanying street ballads, penny fiction, and illustrated periodicals such as Edward Lloyd's *Penny Sunday Times and People's Police Gazette* (1840–2).

IN presenting the first number of the ILLUSTRATED LONDON NEWS to the British public, we would fain make a graceful entrée into the wide and grand arena, which will henceforth contain so many actors for our benefit, and so many spectators of our career. In plain language, we do not produce this illustrated newspaper without some vanity, much ambition, and a fond belief that we shall be pardoned the presumption of the first quality by realizing the aspirations of the last. For the past ten years we have watched with admiration and enthusiasm the progress of illustrative art, and the vast revolution which it has wrought in the world of publication, through all the length and breadth of this mighty empire. To the wonderful march of periodical literature it has given an impetus and rapidity almost coequal with the gigantic power of steam. It has converted blocks into wisdom, and given wings and spirit to ponderous and senseless wood. It has in its turn adorned, gilded, reflected, and interpreted nearly every form of thought. It has given to fancy a new dwelling-place, to imagination a more permanent throne. It has set up fresh land-marks of poetry, given sterner pungency to satire, and mapped out the geography of mind with clearer boundaries and more distinct and familiar intelligence than it ever bore alone. Art—as now fostered, and redundant in the peculiar and facile department of wood engraving—has, in fact, become the bride of literature; genius has taken her as its handmaid;

and popularity has crowned her with laurels that only seem to grow the greener the longer they are worn.

And there is now no staying the advance of this art into all the departments of our social system. It began in a few isolated volumes—stretched itself next over fields of natural history and science—penetrated the arcanæ of our own general literature—and made companionship with our household books. At one plunge it was in the depth of the stream of poetry—working with its every current—partaking of the glow, and adding to the sparkles of the glorious waters—and so refreshing the very soul of genius, that even Shakespeare came to us clothed with a new beauty,[1] while other kindred poets of our language seemed as it were to have put on festive garments to crown the marriage of their muses to the arts. Then it walked abroad among the people, went into the poorer cottages, and visited the humblest homes in cheap guises, and, perhaps, in roughish forms; but still with the illustrative and the instructive principle strongly worked upon, and admirably developed for the general improvement of the human race. Lastly, it took the merry aspect of fun, frolic, satire, and *badinage*; and the school of *Charivari* began to blend itself with the graver pabulum of Penny Cyclopœdias and Saturday Magazines.[2]

And now, when we find the art accepted in all its elements, and welcomed by every branch of reading into which it has diverged; now, when we see the spirit of the times everywhere associating with it, and heralding or recording its success; we do hold it as of somewhat triumphant omen, that WE are, by the publication of this very newspaper, launching the giant vessel of illustration into a channel the broadest and the widest that it has ever dared to stem. We bound at once over the billows of a new ocean—we sail into the very heart and focus of public life—we take the world of newspapers by storm, and flaunt a banner on which the words 'ILLUSTRATED NEWS' become symbols of a fresher purpose, and a more enlarged design, than was ever measured in that hemisphere till now.

The public will have henceforth under their glance, and within their grasp, the very form and presence of events as they transpire, in all their substantial reality, and with evidence visible as well as circumstantial. And whatever the broad and palpable delineations of wood engraving can be taught to achieve, will now be brought to bear upon every subject which attracts the attention of mankind, with a

FIG. 10. Front page, *Illustrated London News*, 12 (4 March 1848), 127.

spirit in unison with the character of such subject, whether it be serious or satirical, trivial or of purpose grave.

And, reader, let us open something of the detail of this great intention to your view. Begin, *par exemple*, with the highest region of newspaper literature—the Political. Why, what a field! If we are strong in the creed that we adopt—if we are honest as we pledge ourselves to be, in the purpose that we maintain—how may we lend muscle, bone, and sinew to the tone taken and the cause espoused, by bringing to bear upon our opinions, a whole battery of vigorous illustration. What 'H.B.'[3] does amid the vacillations of parties, without any prominent opinions of his own, *we* can do with double regularity and consistency, and therefore with more valuable effect. Moreover, regard the homely illustration which nearly every public measure will afford:—your Poor-laws—your Corn-laws—your Factory-bills—your Income-taxes! Look at the field of public portraiture presented in your Houses of Legislature alone, and interesting to every constituency in the land. Open your police-offices, your courts of law, your criminal tribunals—all the pith and marrow of the administration of justice— you can have it broadly before you, with points of force, of ridicule, of character, or of crime; and if the pen be ever led into fallacious argument, the pencil must at least be oracular with the spirit of truth.

In the world of diplomacy, in the architecture of foreign policy, we can give you every trick of the great Babel that other empires are seeking to level or to raise. Is there peace? then shall its arts, implements, and manufactures be spread upon our page. The literature— the customs—the dress—nay, the institutions and localities of other lands, shall be brought home to you with spirit, with fidelity, and, we hope, with discretion and taste. Is there war? then shall its seat and actions be laid naked before the eye. No estafette[4]—no telegraph—no steam-winged vessel—no overland mail, shall bring intelligence to our shores that shall not be sifted with industry, and illustrated with skill in the columns of this journal; and whether the cowardice of China or the treachery of Afghanistan be the theme of your abhorrence or resentment, you shall at least have as much historical detail of both as, while it gratifies general curiosity, shall minister to the natural anxieties at home of those who have friends and relations amid the scenes delineated and the events described.[5]

Take another fruitful branch of illustration, the pleasures of the people!—their theatres, their concerts, their galas, their races, and their fairs! Again, the pleasures of the aristocracy—their court festivals, their *bals masqués*, their levees, their drawing-rooms—the complexion of their grandeur, and the circumstance of all their pomp!

In literature, a truly beautiful arena will be entered upon; for we shall not only, in most instances, have the opportunity of illustrating our own reviews, but of borrowing selections from the illustrations of the numerous works which the press is daily pouring forth, so elaborately embellished with woodcuts in the highest style of art.

In the field of fine arts—but let the future speak, and let us clip promise in the wing. We have perhaps said enough without condescending to the littleness of too much detail to mark the general outline of our design; and we trust to the kindness and intelligence of our readers to imagine for us a great deal more than we have been able to crowd into the compass of an introductory leader. Moreover, we would strongly premise an expression of gratitude for all suggestions that may hereafter reach us, and assure our volunteers of this, that

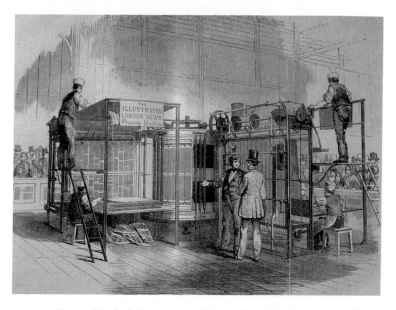

FIG. 11. 'Patent Vertical Printing Machine in the Great Exhibition—Class C, No. 122', *Illustrated London News*, 18 (31 May 1851), 502.

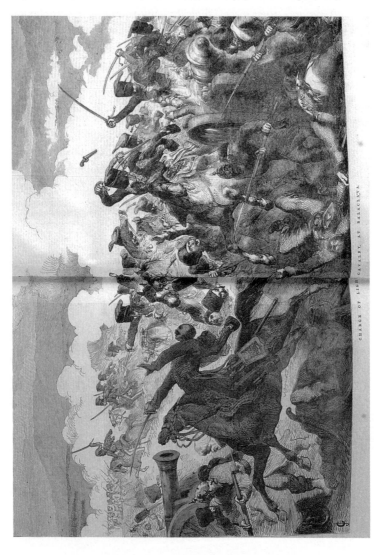

FIG. 12. John Gilbert, 'Charge of the Light Cavalry at Balaclava', *Illustrated London News*, 25 (23 December 1854), 675–6.

wherever there seems a possibility of acting upon them creditably, that course shall be taken with promptitude, vigour, and effect.

Here we make our bow, determined to pursue our great experiment with boldness; to associate its principle with a purity of tone that may secure and hold fast for our journal the fearless patronage of families; to seek in all things to uphold the great cause of public morality; to keep continually before the eye of the world a living and moving panorama of all its actions and influences; and to withhold from society no point that its literature can furnish or its art adorn, so long as the genius of that literature, and the spirit of that art, can be brought within the reach and compass of the Editors of the ILLUS-TRATED LONDON NEWS!

[Catherine Gore], 'The New Art of Printing', *Blackwood's Edinburgh Magazine*, 55 (January 1844), 45-9

Catherine Gore (1799–1861) is best known for the silver-fork novels of aristocratic life that she published during the 1830s and 1840s, though she also wrote plays, poetry, periodical articles, and music. Here, at the height of her career, she describes the excitement caused by the rapid growth of illustrated newspapers and novels. Gore's prophecies, which suggest a future threat to the unillustrated *Blackwood's*, are indicative of the way new print forms often became emblematic of 'the modern'.

It is more than probable that, at the first discovery of that mightiest of arts, which has so tended to facilitate every other—the art of printing—many old-fashioned people looked with a jealous eye on the innovation. Accustomed to a written character, their eyes became wearied by the crabbedness and formality of type. It was like travelling on the paved and rectilinear roads of France, after winding among the blooming hedgerows of England; and how dingy and graceless must have appeared the first printed copy of the Holy Bible, to those accustomed to luxuriate in emblazoned missals, amid all the pride, pomp, and vellum of glorious MS.!

Dangerous and democratic, too, must have appeared the new art, which, by plebeianizing knowledge and enlightening the mass, deprived the law and the prophets of half their terrors, and disrobed priestcraft and kingcraft of their mystery. We can imagine that, as soon as a printed book ceased to become a great rarity, it became an object of great abhorrence. [...]

A year or two hence, however, and all this will have become obsolete.—*Nous avons changé tout cela!* [6]—No more letter-press! Books, the *small* as well as the great, will have been voted a great evil. There will be no gentleman of the press. The press itself will have ceased to exist.

For several years past it has been frankly avowed by the trade that books have ceased to sell; that the best works are a drug in the market; that their shelves groan, until themselves are forced to follow the example. Descend to what shifts they may in order to lower their prices, by piracy from other booksellers, or clipping and coining of authors—no purchasers! [. . .]

For some time after books had ceased to find a market, the periodicals retained their vogue; and even till very lately, newspapers found readers. But the period at length arrived, when even the leisure requisite for the perusal of these lighter pages, is no longer forthcoming. People are busy ballooning or driving; shooting like stars along railroads; or migrating like swallows or wild-geese. It has been found, within the current year, impossible to read even a newspaper!

The march of intellect, however, luckily keeps pace with the necessities of the times; and no sooner was it ascertained, that reading-made-easy was difficult to accomplish, than a new art was invented for the more ready transmission of ideas. The fallacy of the proverb, that 'those who run may read,' being established, modern science set about the adoption of a medium, available to those sons of the century who are always on the run. Hence, the grand secret of ILLUSTRATION.—Hence, the new art of printing!

The pictorial printing-press is now your only wear! Everything is communicated by delineation. We are not *told*, but *shown* how the world is wagging. The magazines sketch us a lively article, the newspapers vignette us, step by step, a royal tour. The beauties of Shakespeare are imprinted on the minds of a rising generation, in woodcuts; and the poetry of Byron engraven in their hearts, by means of the graver. Not a boy in his teens has read a line of Don Quixote or Gil Blas,[7] though all have their adventures by heart; while Goldsmith's 'Deserted Village'[8] has been committed to memory by our daughters and wives, in a series of exquisite illustrations. Every body has La Fontaine by heart, thanks to the pencil of Granville, which requires neither grammar nor dictionary to aid its interpretations;[9] and even Defoe—even the unparalleled Robinson Crusoe—is devoured by our ingenious youth in cuts and come again.

At present, indeed, the new art of printing is in its infancy, but it is progressing so rapidly, that the devils of the old will soon have a cold birth of it! Views of the Holy Land are superseding even the Holy Scriptures; and a pictorial Blackstone is teaching the ideas of the sucking lawyers how to shoot.[10] Nay, Buchan's *Domestic Medicine* has (*proh pudor!*[11]) its illustrated edition.[12]

The time saved to an active public by all this, is beyond computation. All the world is now instructed by symbols, as formerly the deaf and dumb; and instead of having to peruse a tedious penny-a-line account of the postilion of the King of the French misdriving his Majesty, and his Majesty's august family, over a drawbridge into a moat at Tréport,[13] a single glance at a single woodcut places the whole disaster graphically before us; leaving us nine minutes and a half of the time we must otherwise have devoted to the study of the case, to dispose of at our own will and pleasure; to start, for instance, for Chelsea, and be back again by the steam-boat, before our mother knows we are out.

The application of the new art is of daily and hourly extension. The scandalous Sunday newspapers have announced an intention of evading Lord Campbell's Act, by veiling the libels in caricature.[14] Instead of *writing* slander and flat blasphemy, they propose to *draw* it, and not draw it mild. The daily prints will doubtless follow their example. No more Jenkinsisms in the *Morning Post*, concerning fashionable parties.[15] A view of the duchess's ball-room, or of the dining table of the earl, will supersede all occasion for lengthy fiddle-faddle. The opera of the night before will be described in a vignette—the ballet in a tail-piece; and we shall know at a glance whether Cerito and Elssler performed their *pas* meritoriously, by the number of bouquets depicted at their feet.[16]

On the other hand, instead of column after column of dry debates, we shall know sufficiently who were the speakers of the preceding night, by a series of portraits—each having an annexed trophy, indicative of the leading points of his oration. Members of both houses will be, of course, daguerreotyped for the use of the morning papers; and photographic likenesses of the leaders of *ton*[17] be supplied gratis to the leaders of the press.

How far more interesting a striking sketch of a banquet, containing portraits of undoubted authenticity, to the matter-of-fact announcements of the exploded letter-press—that 'yesterday his Grace the Duke of Wellington entertained, at dinner, at Apsley House, the Earls of Aberdeen and Liverpool, the Dukes of Richmond and Buccleuch, the Master of the Horse, the Lord Chancellor, Sir Robert Peel, Sir James Graham, Sir Frederick Trench, Colonel Gurwood, and M. Algernon Greville!' Who has patience for the repetition of a string of names, when a group of faces may be placed simultaneously before him?

And then, accounts of races! How admirably will they be concentrated into a delineation of the winner passing the post—the losers distanced; and what disgusting particulars of boxing matches shall we avoid by a spirited etching. [...]

We have little doubt of shortly seeing announcements—standing like tombstones in those literary cemeteries, the Saturday papers,—of 'A New Work upon America, from the graver of George Cruikshank;' or 'A new fashionable novel, (diamond edition,) from the accomplished pencil of H.B.' Kenny Meadows will become the Byron of the day, Leech the Scott, Forrester the Marryatt, Phiz the Trollope; Stanfield and Turner will be epic poets, Landseer preside over the belles-lettres, and Webster and Stone become the epigrammatists and madrigalists of the press.[18]

All this will, doubtless, throw a number of deserving persons out of employ. The writers, whose stock in trade consists of words rather than ideas, will find their way to Basinghall Street, prose will be at a discount, and long-windedness be accounted a distemper.[19] A great variety of small Sapphos[20] must turn semstresses, at three-halfpence a shirt instead of a penny a line; while the minor poets will have to earn a livelihood by writing invoice, instead of in verse. But this transposition of talent, and transition of gain, is no more than arose from the substitution of railroads for turnpike roads. By that innovation thousands of hard-working post-horses were left without rack or manger; and by the present arrangement, Clowes, Spottiswoode, and the authors who have served to afford matter for their types, will be driven from the field.[21]

But the world (no longer to be called of letters, but of emblems) will be the gainer. It will be no longer a form of speech to talk of having '*glanced* at the morning papers,' whose city article will, of course, be composed by artists skilled in drawing figures. The biographies of contemporary or deceased statesman will be limned, not by Lord Brougham or Macaulay, but by the impartial hand of the Royal Academy; and the catacombs at Kensal Green, like those discovered by Belzoni on the banks of the Nile, exhibit their eulogistic inscriptions in hieroglyphics.[22] By this new species of shorthand we might have embodied this very article in half a dozen sprightly etchings! But as the hapless inventor of the first great art of printing incurred, among his astounded contemporaries, the opprobrium of being in contact with the evil one, (whence, probably, the familiar appellation of printers' devils,[23]) it behoves the early practitioners of the new art to look to their reputations! By economizing the time of the public, they may squander their own good repute. It is not every printer who can afford, like Benjamin Franklin,[24] to be a reformer; and pending the moment when (the schoolmasters being all abroad) the grand causeway of the metropolis shall become, as it were, a moving diorama,[25] inflicting knowledge on the million whether it will or no—let us content ourselves with birds'-eye views of passing events, by way of exhibiting the first rudiments of THE NEW ART OF PRINTING!

'Illustrated Periodical Literature', *Bookseller*, 4 (30 November 1861), 681-9

The *Bookseller* (1858–) is a monthly magazine (and now virtual information source) detailing new publications for the book trade. In the nineteenth century its November issue was usually devoted to illustrated works in preparation for the lucrative Christmas trade in gift books. In 1861 two periodicals notable for their high-quality illustrations had also recently commenced, *Good Words* (1860–1906) and *Once a Week* (1859–80). The *Bookseller* applauds the recent growth of the use of illustration for improving rather than sensational purposes.

If the historian of nineteenth-century literature would present to the world a true picture of the sort of reading most in vogue—real evidence of the popular taste—undoubted proofs of the state of education in this year of grace eighteen hundred and sixty-one—fair digests of the methods employed by the purveyors of literary food for the million, in order to satisfy the universal craving for what is wonderful, new, true, political, historical, or exciting—he must needs study the broadside-covered walls, and the picture-filled windows, of our great centres of population. If he would learn the secret of the immense successes that have been achieved by modern publishers, he must go even further, and examine for himself the nature and particularities of the best-known works patronized by the poor, the half-educated, and the uneducated; he must carefully study the broad sheets issued in weekly and monthly portions at the cheapest possible rates, varying from a halfpenny to sixpence; he must look with unprejudiced eye upon the literary and pictorial candidates for popular favour, and hold the balance evenly between the valuable, the mediocre, and the worthless. [...]

Bearing these premises in view, our suppositious historian will calmly and impartially weigh the evidence in favour of and against the influence of illustrated periodical literature as a means of popular education. He cannot arrive at his conclusion without careful observation, or deliver his verdict without a thorough examination of the evidence before him. He must not only notice the contents of shop-windows and the placardings of hoarding and walls, but he must endeavour to ascertain the condition of the purchasers and readers of the thousands—nay, millions—of printed sheets periodically issued from the teeming press. [...]

Lying before us are several representatives of the most popular of the periodicals claiming wide acceptance by the people; and, when we examine them, we can easily understand the secret of their success. They are all well printed and admirably illustrated by wood-cut engravings in really good taste. The work of education begun some thirty years since by the *Mirror, Chambers's Edinburgh Journal,* the *Penny Magazine,* and the *Saturday Magazine,* has, in different degrees, though by somewhat like means, been ably carried on by Messrs. Chambers, Cassell, Routledge, and other well-known publishers. [...]

But standing at the head of all the periodical literature of the day, in its surpassing interest and its high value, is properly and naturally the Bible. It is not strange that amid all the exciting stories contained in the illustrated weeklies, the Holy Scriptures should secure an immense amount of circulation; for, at least, the English are a moral and religious people. Fathers and mothers may have indulged in exciting reading, but they would hardly choose that their children should seek to gratify their eyes and imaginations by the filth and atrocities of Holywell Street.[26] The day has passed away when the wretched 'Mysteries' of Reynolds, *Fanny Hill,* and similar works, sold in thousands.[27] In the place of such trash as these, made even more abhorrent by disgusting pictures, we have now, as we have said, respectable works issued in penny numbers, fitted for family reading, and by no means to be regarded as slight helps in the education of the rising generation.

In every bye-street, in towns and cities, and in almost every village throughout the country, the passer-by may see exposed in the windows of the booksellers and newsmen, copies of *Cassell's Illustrated Family Bible.*[28] This beautiful work is issued in weekly penny numbers, and in monthly parts. It is in all respects remarkable, for almost every other page contains an engraving, executed in bold style, besides vignettes, tail-pieces and initial letters. The large pictures—for so they may be fairly called—are all illustrative of events in sacred

FIG. 13. [Murder of her maid, Lydia, by Lady Ravensworth and the Resurrection Man] in G. W. M. Reynolds, *The Mysteries of London*, ii (London: John Dicks, 1867), 273.

history, or landscapes, natural productions, & c., explanatory of the manners, customs, or peculiarities of the East. Whether they be original—as in most instances in the two volumes before us—or taken from the works of the old painters, these pictures are valuable aids to the unlearned, often explaining the text in the most satisfactory matter, and always possessing a value beyond their mere pictorial merits.

We next come to the periodicals issued by the Religious Tract Society—the *Leisure Hour* and the *Sunday at Home*.[29] We are

FIG. 14. W. H. Thwaite, [Venetia Trelawney entertaining two suitors, Sir Douglas Huntington and the Earl of Curzon, in her boudoir] in G. W. M. Reynolds, *The Mysteries of the Court of London*, i (London: John Dicks, 1848–9), 281.

enabled to present two engravings—the first, a portrait of Count Cavour,[30] illustrative of what we may call the historico-educational aspect of the Society's works; while the other, from one of the capital tales to be found in the *Leisure Hour*, illustrates the moral and attractive feature. In both the *Leisure Hour* and the *Sunday at Home* there is a vast amount of excellent reading of an amusing, and, at the same time, highly-improving tendency. The sale achieved by these publications is, we understand, something astounding. And they well deserve their popularity; for they contain no line or sentence that may not be read aloud in the midst of the family—no small praise when we compare them with some of the weekly sheets we might name. To this questionable pabulum, the weekly literature issued by the Tract Society forms a valuable counterpoise. [...]

We may here be allowed to express a regret that the older Society, that for the Promotion of Christian Knowledge, has not, like the Religious Tract Society, issued a popular illustrated serial. One was announced, not long ago, under the title of *Our Daily Task*, but which, for some reason never made public, has been either suppressed or suspended. There are some works which may most appropriately be issued by Societies, and we think a journal to be circulated by the clergy is just such a work. The only Church periodical with illustrations, having any circulation, is the *Penny Post*; but this, being monthly, by no means supplies all that is

FIG. 15. J. D. Watson, 'The Toad', *Good Words*, 2 (1861), 33.

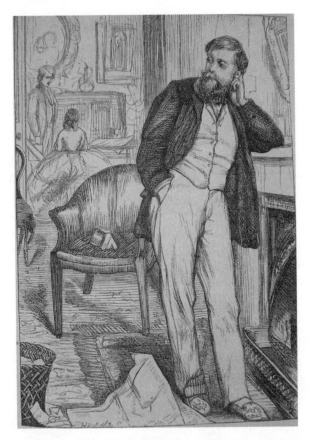

FIG. 16. Thomas Graham, 'He Never Told His Love', *Good Words*, 2
(1861), 681.

required.[31] *Good Words* is a periodical that may be warmly and
honestly commended. It is edited by Dr. Norman Macleod, than
whom it would be difficult to find a more painstaking and conscientious conductor for a popular periodical.[32] *Good Words* seeks, by the
aid of good writing and exquisite engravings, to elevate and improve
the public taste. It has an immense sale in Scotland, but it enjoys a
very large and daily-increasing degree of acceptance on this side
the border. Some of the best writers of the day are engaged in
contributing to its pages, and our most-celebrated artists are
employed in producing the illustrations. By the kindness of the

FIG. 17. 'Burial of John Moore', *Cassell's History of England*,
in *Bookseller*, 4 (30 November 1861), 687.

enterprising publishers, Messrs. Strahan and Co., of Edinburgh, we
are enabled to place two of these before our readers; the first, from the
pencil of Mr. J. D. Watson,[33] is the story of a toad which, after being
crushed by a reverend priest, having had an eye poked out by the
young lady's parasol, and been hunted by schoolboys, is eventually
spared by the friendly ass, which could find sympathy for a creature as
wretched as itself. Our second is a new illustration of the old, old
story, 'He never told me his Love,' and, consequently, allowed
another to step in. Can anything more feelingly tell the story than
the drawing in which the artist has depicted it? [...]

Cassell's History of England is carefully written by William Howitt, and excellently illustrated by some of our best draughtsmen on wood.[34] The style is popular; and as many thousands of our working men have been enabled, by this means, to provide themselves with a history of their country, we may fairly assume that the knowledge now possessed is one of the great reasons why the noisy demagogue now finds few willing listeners. We have been enabled at page 687 to offer an illustration from the work, which is highly creditable to the enterprise and public spirit of its publishers.[35]

John Ruskin, 'Notes on the Present State of Engraving in England', in *Ariadne Florentina* (London and Orpington: George Allen, 1876), 229-31, 235-41

Ariadne Florentina comprises a series of six lectures on wood and steel engraving first delivered by Ruskin (1819–1900) at the University of Oxford in 1872. The following is extracted from the appendix. Ruskin's hostility to popular illustration constitutes part of his long-standing critique of the industrialization of art. Ruskin's dislike of the ability of engraving to reproduce multiple copies was precisely the quality that made it the dominant graphic medium.

I have long deferred the completion of this book, because I had hoped to find time to show, in some fulness, the grounds for my conviction that engraving, and the study of it, since the development of the modern finished school, have been ruinous to European knowledge of art. [...]

It never seems to occur even to the most intelligent persons that an engraving also is 'only a copy,' and a copy done with refusal of colour, and with disadvantage of means in rendering shade. But just because this utterly inferior copy can be reduplicated, and introduces a different kind of skill, in another material, people are content to lose all the composition, and all the charm, of the original,—so far as these depend on the chief gift of a *painter*,—colour; while they are gradually misled into attributing to the painter himself qualities impertinently added by the engraver to make his plate popular: and, which is far worse, they are as gradually and subtly prevented from looking, in the original, for the qualities which engraving could never render. Further, it continually happens that the very best colour-compositions engrave worst; for they often extend colours over great spaces at equal pitch, and the green is as dark as the red, and the blue as the brown; so that the engraver can only distinguish them by lines in different directions, and his plate becomes a vague and dead mass of neutral tint; but a bad and forced piece of colour, or a piece of work of the Bolognese school,[36] which is everywhere black in the shadows, and colourless in the lights, will engrave with great ease, and appear spirited and forcible. Hence engravers, as a rule, are interested in reproducing the work of the worst schools of painting. [...]

Take up, for an average specimen of modern illustrated works, the volume of Dickens's *Master Humphrey's Clock*, containing *Barnaby Rudge*.

You have in that book an entirely profitless and monstrous story, in which the principal characters are a coxcomb, an idiot, a madman, a savage blackguard, a foolish tavern-keeper, a mean old maid, and a conceited apprentice,—mixed up with a certain quantity of ordinary operatic pastoral stuff, about a pretty Dolly in ribands, a lover with a wooden leg, and an heroic locksmith.[37] For these latter, the only elements of good, or life, in the filthy mass of the story, observe that the author must filch the wreck of those old times of which we fiercely and frantically destroy every living vestige, whenever it is possible. You cannot have your Dolly Varden brought up behind the counter of

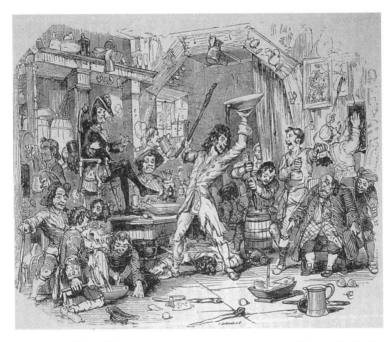

FIG. 18. George Cattermole, 'Sacrilege in the Sanctuary', *Barnaby Rudge* (London: Chapman and Hall, 1841), 398

a railway station; nor your jolly locksmith trained at a Birmingham brass-foundry. And of these materials, observe that you can only have the ugly ones illustrated. The cheap popular art cannot draw for you beauty, sense, or honesty; and for Dolly Varden, or the locksmith, you will look through the vignettes in vain. But every species of distorted folly and vice,—the idiot, the blackguard, the coxcomb, the paltry fool, the degraded woman,—are pictured for your honourable pleasure in every page, with clumsy caricature, struggling to render its dulness tolerable by insisting on defect,—if perchance a penny or two more may be coined out of the Cockney reader's itch for loathsomeness.[38]

Or take up, for instance of higher effort, the *Cornhill Magazine* for this month, July, 1876. It has a vignette of Venice for an illuminated letter. This is what your decorative art has become, by help of Kensington![39] The letter to be produced is a T. There is a gondola in the front of the design, with the canopy slipped back to the stern like a saddle over a horse's tail. There is another in the middle distance, all gone to seed at the prow, with its gondolier emaciated into an oar, at the stern; then there is a Church of the Salute, and a Ducal Palace,—in which I beg you to observe all the felicity and dexterity of modern cheap engraving; finally, over the Ducal Palace there is something, I know not in the least what meant for, like an umbrella dropping out of a balloon, which is the ornamental letter T. Opposite this ornamental design, there is an engraving of two young ladies and a parasol, between two trunks of trees. The white face and black feet of the principal young lady, being the points of the design, are done with as much care,—not with as much dexterity,—as an ordinary sketch of Du Maurier's in *Punch*.[40] The young lady's dress, the next attraction, is done in cheap white and black cutting, with considerably less skill than that of any ordinary tailor's or milliner's shop-book pattern drawing. For the other young lady, and the landscape, take your magnifying glass, and look at the hacked wood that forms the entire shaded surface—one mass of idiotic scrabble, without the remotest attempt to express a single leaf, flower, or clod of earth. It is such landscape as the public sees out of its railroad window at sixty miles of it in the hour—and good enough for such a public. [...]

These woodcuts, for *Barnaby Rudge* and the *Cornhill Magazine*, are favourably representative of the entire illustrative art industry of

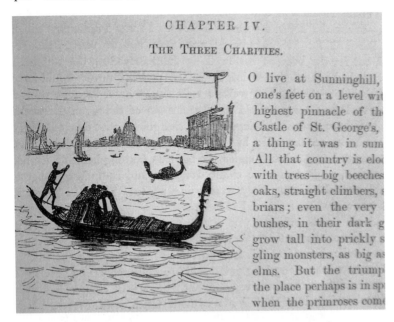

CHAPTER IV.

THE THREE CHARITIES.

O live at Sunninghill, one's feet on a level wit highest pinnacle of th Castle of St. George's, a thing it was in sum All that country is elo with trees—big beeches oaks, straight climbers, briars; even the very bushes, in their dark g grow tall into prickly s gling monsters, as big a elms. But the triump the place perhaps is in sp when the primroses com

FIG. 19. Illuminated letter, *Cornhill Magazine*, 34 (July 1876), 1.

the modern press,—industry enslaved to the ghastly service of catching the last gleams in the glued eyes of the daily more bestial English mob,—railroad born and bred, which drags itself about the black world it has withered under its breath, in one eternal grind and shriek,—gobbling,—staring,—chattering,—giggling,—trampling out every vestige of national honour and domestic peace, wherever it sets the staggering hoof of it; incapable of reading, of hearing, of thinking, of looking,—capable only of greed for money, lust for food, pride of dress, and the prurient itch of momentary curiosity for the politics last announced by the newsmonger, and the religion last rolled by the chemist into electuary for the dead.[41]

In the miserably competitive labour of finding new stimulus for the appetite—daily more gross—of this tyrannous mob, we count as lost, beyond any hope, the artists who are dull, docile, or distressed enough to submit to its demands; and we may count the dull and the distressed by myriads;—and among the docile, many of the best intellects we possess. The few who have sense and strength to assert their own supremacy, are driven into discouraged disease by their

FIG. 20. George Du Maurier, 'Carry in her White Frock, Erect as a Little Pillar', *Cornhill Magazine*, 34 (July 1876), p. i.

isolation, like Turner and Blake; the one abandoning the design of his *Liber Studiorum*[42] after imperfectly and sadly, against total public neglect, carrying it forward to what it is,—monumental, nevertheless, in landscape engraving; the other producing, with one only majestic series of designs from the Book of Job, nothing for his life's work but coarsely iridescent sketches of enigmatic dream.[43]

Clement Shorter, 'Illustrated Journalism: Its Past and Its Future', *Contemporary Review*, 75 (1899), 481–95 [481–2, 485–7, 489–93]

Illustrated journalism expanded rapidly during the 1880s and 1890s, encouraged in part by a newly discovered ability to reproduce photographs directly in periodicals. Previously engravings of photos had had to be made: the direct introduction of photography marked the commercial death of wood-engraving, the previously dominant graphic medium. Clement Shorter (1857–1926) started his career on the *Star* and became editor of the *Illustrated London News* in 1891; he also founded *Sketch* in 1893, *Tatler* in 1891, and the *Sphere* in 1900. In the extract below he assesses the future of the illustrated press.

THE century will close in a year or two, and we shall no doubt be made weary by the various contrasts between its beginning and its end. The abundance of pictures illustrative of news that marks the termination of the century, as compared with their paucity at its commencement, will assuredly not be lost sight of. Pictorial journalism, indeed, has this in common with many inventions, that in its history ten years is a lifetime, and to write in detail the story of the last decade would be to make a book.

When the present writer entered the editorial department of the *Illustrated London News* nine years ago, there were but five weekly journals, exclusive of the fashion papers, devoted to the illustration of news—the *Illustrated*, the *Graphic*, the *Penny Illustrated Paper*, the *Sporting and Dramatic News*, and the *Pall Mall Budget*.[44] Although the *Pall Mall Budget* is now dead, there are at this moment in London no less than thirteen illustrated journals competing week by week for the favour of the public. The fact may be tabulated thus:

1890	1899
The Illustrated London News.	The Illustrated London News.
The Graphic.	The Graphic.

The Pall Mall Budget.

The Sporting and Dramatic News.
The Penny Illustrated Paper.

The Sporting and Dramatic News.
The Penny Illustrated Paper.
Black and White.
The Sketch.
The Westminster Budget.
The St. James's Budget.
St. Paul's.
Country Life Illustrated.
Army and Navy Illustrated.
Lords and Commons.
The West-End.

Many factors have contributed to this result. Not only has there been a remarkable cheapening of all the materials of production, but there has been an increased appetite for the purchase of newspapers, and an increased faith on the part of the commercial classes in the newspaper as a medium for advertisements. The extraordinary profits that have been revealed to the world by the flotation as companies of the newspapers belonging to Sir George Newnes, Mr. Alfred Harmsworth, Mr. Arthur Pearson, and the proprietors of the *Illustrated London News*, have tempted, and will continue to tempt, many speculators, although a record of the money lost upon newspapers that have failed would also prove a startling revelation.[45] [...]

The *Illustrated London News* was the first systematic attempt to illustrate news, subordinating in a manner its letterpress to its pictures.

This remarkable venture, which opened on May 14, 1842, owed its origin to Mr Herbert Ingram.[46] [...] His monument is not alone that he founded the *Illustrated London News*, and that he assisted in the repeal of the newspaper tax and the paper duty—it is that he founded *the* illustrated paper, now of so world-wide a popularity. *L'Illustration* of Paris and the *Illustrirte Zeitung* of Leipzig appeared the year following that of the *Illustrated London News*.

It is not, of course, possible for me within the limits at my disposal to trace year by year the development of the *Illustrated London News*, or to record the rise of rival journals. In any case, there has been but one rival to the *Illustrated* that needs to be taken into account, for

Black and White is at present too young a journal, and in too tentative a stage, for us to be quite sure of its future.[47] It stands, as it were, midway between what I call the illustrated newspapers and the photographic journals. At the commencement of this article I gave a list of thirteen illustrated papers at present existing in England, but of these only two, or at most three, are seriously devoted to illustrating news. The others, of which the *Sketch* is a type, are restricted in their presentation of news by the limitations of the camera. To such journals there may come success or failure, as there may be 'ideas' in the editorial department, or lack of 'ideas,' capacity in the business department, or lack of capacity. But in a higher sense I am disinclined to call them illustrated newspapers. So large a part of life, and particularly of public life, cannot be depicted by the camera. It has, it is true, been seen in the battlefield, and now and again in the church; but I am inclined to believe that there will always be a place for the artist in illustrated journalism, for the war-artist who makes rough sketches at the seat of war, and for the elaborate black-and-white draughtsman who works at home. Not only on the battlefield is the artist indispensable, but the royal wedding, the royal christening, the public funeral in the Abbey, and a thousand other functions dear to the heart of the public, belong to him alone. Now, in my judgement, the *Illustrated London News* and the *Graphic* are the only two journals that adequately recognise this at present. The *Illustrated London News* has had at one moment its Mr. Melton Prior in South Africa, its Mr. Seppings Wright in China, and a third artist sketching in another distant part of the globe.[48] And side by side with this expenditure it has to face an equally great expenditure for artists at home, some of them men taking the highest rank in the Academy as painters, and in other cases well in the running for the honours of the Academy when that body throws open its ranks to black-and-white artists, as Lord Leighton advocated.[49] The public would be startled, indeed, were they aware of the enormous sums spent by the *Illustrated London News* and the *Graphic* on genuinely artistic illustration. They would then more clearly recognise the great gulf which separates the mere photographic journal from the journal of the order to which the *Graphic* and the *Illustrated London News* belong. [...]

A circumstance that must rapidly break down the old barrier between the art and literary department of an illustrated newspaper is the death of wood-engraving in journalism. The great changes that have come over illustrated journalism are the arrival of the photograph, and the substitution of mechanical processes for wood-engraving. The place now taken by the photograph, some half-dozen journals being entirely run by it, I have already hinted at. An analysis of the contents of a few of the journals of more ambitious character gives interesting results. I have taken one week in March this year:

	Photographs	Drawings
The Illustrated London News	28	19
The Graphic	17	29
Black and White	60	13
Harper's Weekly (New York)	35	8
Leslie's Weekly (New York)	44	3
L'Illustrazione Italiana (Rome)	6	9
Ueber Land und Meer (Stuttgart)	5	8
Illustrirte Zeitung (Leipzig)	8	14
L'Illustration (Paris)	10	12

The same week's issue of the *Sketch* contained eighty-five photographs and four drawings, three of these last being fashion-plates. The corresponding papers of twelve years ago had only two or three photographs apiece.

Even more remarkable has been the revolution as to wood-engraving. It seems only the other day that engraving reigned without a rival in the offices of the illustrated papers. To-day it is all but extinguished in the journalism of this country, although there is plenty of it in the illustrated papers of the Continent. The process engraving is, it is perhaps hardly necessary to state, of two kinds. Line-drawings are produced by line-process engraving, and wash drawings and photographs by what is called half-tone process. The first line-process block, I am informed by Mr. William Thomas, appeared in the *Graphic* on September 13, 1879, and the first half-tone process block on September 6, 1884.[50] These changes crept into the *Illustrated London News* a year or so earlier.

It is not within the limits of my space to treat at length of the invention of the various processes of automatic engraving, as they are best called to distinguish them from hand engraving. [...]

How momentous these changes from wood to zinc and copper were was not, perhaps, entirely recognised at the time, nor the extraordinary shifting of a very skilled labour that they implied. The *Illustrated London News* of fifteen years ago was a paper of twenty-four pages, whereas it now consists of at least forty pages. Now, as the drawings come into the office they are sent out again to be processed, and, without any other manipulation than the interposition of a specially prepared screen and the use of photography, they are returned, always absolutely unsoiled, to the office of the paper, and with them solid blocks with a zinc or copper reproduction of the drawing, ready for the printer, if need be, although electros of the original block are constantly being made.[51] Fifteen years ago, however, a double-page drawing, when sent in by the artist, was first photographed on a solid slab of boxwood, the wood alone costing as much as the whole process block does now. That was but the beginning of the task. The slab of boxwood had, to the uninitiated, unexpected bolts in the back of it. These bolts unscrewed, and twenty-four separate pieces of wood were the result—one containing nothing but sky, another sea, another a piece of a ship, another a sailor's head. Each piece went to a separate engraver, who worked all night upon it. One engraver had a special faculty for sky, another for the human face, another for house-work, and so on. In any case, some twelve hours later the pieces were brought together, screwed up once more, and behold a wood-engraving—a double-page of the *Illustrated London News*.

An innovation of twenty years ago may be mentioned here. Sir John Gilbert and his contemporaries drew their illustrations on the wood and sent the blocks direct to the engraver.[52] Thus it happens that, as Sir John Gilbert on one occasion told me with regret, not a single one of his beautiful drawings for the *Illustrated London News* is in existence. The innovation of photographing the drawing on the wood left the drawing intact for artist or newspaper-proprietor—a valuable asset in the case of a great artist.

Now, instead of the twenty-four men taking twelve hours apiece, the whole block is forthcoming by mechanical process in eight hours

FIG. 21. T. Walter Wilson, 'The Funeral Procession of Queen Victoria', *Illustrated London News Special Number*, 7 February 1901, 23.

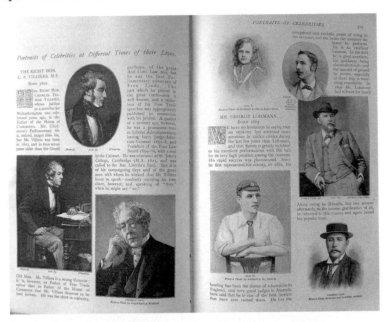

FIG. 22. 'Portraits of Celebrities at Different Times of their Lives,' *Strand*, 12 (July–Dec. 1896), 314–15.

or so, and at one-sixth the cost of the engraving. Small wonder that as far as illustrated journalism is concerned wood-engraving is all but dead—never to revive. It still has a field with the advertiser, to whom it is important that his blocks shall last a great many years, for process blocks are, alas! sadly ephemeral. And engraving may yet for many years command the magazines, when leisure is given to the engravers to turn out something really artistic. But in the hurried work that journalism compels the skilled handicraft can never again hold its own with mechanical processes, and among those who have seen it die without regret are many artists in black-and-white who have always considered that their work was falsified by the intervention of another mind. Fortunately for those engaged in it, it died slowly, thus giving the engravers the opportunity to quit the occupation gradually. Mr. G. F. Hammond, of the *Illustrated London News*—who, with his father before him, has guided the engraving department of the *Illustrated* for many years—informs me that he has known sixty men engaged at one time on the wood-blocks for the *Illustrated*. Now there is not a single wood-engraver employed in the production of the paper. Yet it may be presumed that this change has come without what is known as the 'general public' having in the least recognised that machinery here, as elsewhere, has dethroned hand labour. Here and there a correspondent will write to an editor making his plaint as to the destruction of the art in his favourite journal. One such complaint is before me as I write. But an analysis of two or three illustrated papers which formerly used the wood-engraving brings to light much the same result. I take up copies of the *Illustrated London News*, the *Graphic*, and *Black and White* for a given week (March 4, 1899). I find that the *Illustrated London News* contains forty-seven process blocks and one page engraving—evidently a block made some time ago. I find that the *Graphic* has forty-four process blocks and two small engravings— obviously portraits that had been used before in the pre-process days. *Black and White* also has but one engraving—obviously an electro purchased from a foreign source. Nor can the advocate for engraving have the consolation of a possible return to the old state of things. It is absolutely certain that a general return to wood-engraving would mean ruin to the journal that attempted it. As a matter of fact not one man in five hundred knows the difference between a wood-engraving and a process block. And the finer printing of to-day has far more than made up for any superiority that the old engraving enjoyed.

The future of illustrated journalism it is not easy to forecast. Will the public get tired of photographs? I think not—while they are able to convey with such intense reality many of the incidents of the hour. At the same time, however, the future of the black-and-white artist who illustrates current topics is absolutely assured. The thoroughly competent artist will always command even the somewhat high prices that in many people's eyes he now receives. One friend of mine—an accomplished journalist—does, indeed, insist that he prefers a photograph of a house to the most finished drawing by Mr. Pennell or Mr. Railton.[53] I do not, however, accept this as a normal state of mind. I believe there will always be a large public to whom good art will always appeal. The photograph, however, must have an even larger place in the journalism of the future than of the past, and the editor will prove himself most skilful who most perfectly realises the limits of the artist and the limits of the photographer.

The journalism of the future is probably to make its most important developments so far as concern the daily paper. Here, as in many aspects of the newspaper world, everything waits on the printing-press. Several of our daily papers more or less affect illustrations. The *Daily Graphic*, founded in 1889, of course takes the lead. Here we have in one issue some eight or ten pen-and-ink drawings, and some three or four half-tone process blocks from photographs. In the *Daily Chronicle* and *Daily Mail* we have a constant publication of pen-and-ink drawings, with occasional outbursts in their rivals. This is as far, in this country at least, as illustrated journalism would seem to have gone in the case of the daily paper. Now, I am quite satisfied that there is no overwhelming popularity attached to the pen-and-ink drawing, however intrinsically artistic, particularly when it is reproduced on somewhat common paper. The problem of printing half-tone drawings and photographs in large numbers has to be solved before illustrated daily papers will flourish in this country, a problem of which the principal parts are associated with the technicalities of the printing-machine. As an example of the gulf that separates illustrated from non-illustrated papers, I may mention that to produce from 1400 to 1600 copies an hour is considered a triumph for the best American printing-machines, whereas certain Austrian presses cannot attain more than 900 sheets an hour. As a contrast to this, it may be mentioned that a journal of the type of *Tit-Bits* is produced at the rate of 24,000 an hour.

NOTES TO SECTION IX

1. Charles Knight published an illustrated eight-volume *Pictorial Shakespeare* between 1838 and 1843

2. *Punch; or, the London Charivari* was launched in 1841; its name derived, in part, from a French satirical journal launched in 1832, *Le Charivari*. The *Penny Cyclopaedia* was issued in weekly parts by Charles Knight between 1833 and 1844.

3. H.B., pen name of John Doyle (1797–1868), painter, lithographer, and eminent political caricaturist.

4. Courier.

5. The *Illustrated London News* appeared in the final stages of the 'First Opium War' between Britain and China (1839–42) and of the First Anglo-Afghan War (also 1839–42).

6. 'We have changed all that.'

7. Two early examples of the picaresque adventure: Miguel de Cervantes, *Don Quixote* (1604–14), first translated into English 1612–20; and Alain-René Le Sage, *Histoire de Gil Blas de Santillane* (1715–35), first translated by Tobias Smollett in 1748.

8. 'The Deserted Village' (1770) by Oliver Goldsmith (*c.* 1730–74), a pastoral, nostalgic poem dealing with the effects of the enclosures.

9. Jean Jacques Grandville (1803–47) drew the illustrations for an edition of Jean de La Fontaine's *Fables* in 1838.

10. Gore is probably thinking of the lavish *Syria, the Holy Land, Asia Minor, &c., illustrated. In a series of views drawn from nature by W. H. Bartlett, William Purser (Thomas Allom), &c. With descriptions of the plates by J. Carne*, published by Fisher, Son and Co. in 3 volumes over 1836–8, and numerous times reprinted thereafter. Sir William Blackstone's *Commentaries on the Laws of England* had first appeared 1765–9; by the nineteenth century they were the essential reference book of every lawyer.

11. 'For shame!'

12. William Buchan, *Domestic Medicine; or Family Physician* (London: W. Strahan, 1769); Thomas Kelly published an illustrated edition in 1809 and 1827.

13. The King of France (1830–48), Louis Philippe, had just sailed from Le Tréport, a small town on the northern French coast where he had a villa, on his way to visit Queen Victoria.

14. Lord Campbell's Libel Act was passed in 1842; Campbell (1779–1861) was Attorney-General between 1834 and 1841, Lord Chief Justice 1850–9, and Lord Chancellor from 1859 until his death.

15. 'Jenkins', aka Rumsey Forster, was 'Society' journalist for the high Tory *Morning Post* during the 1840s and 1850s; he was notorious for his sycophantic prose.

16. Fanny Cerrito (1817–1909) and Fanny Elssler (1810–84), two of the most famous ballerinas of the period; they danced together in London in 1843.

17. The members of High Society who set the 'tone'.

18. George Cruikshank (1792–1878), leading British painter and draughtsman; on H.B., Section IX n. 3; Kenny Meadows (1790–1874), illustrator for *Punch, Illuminated Magazine*, and Knight's *Pictorial Shakespeare*; John Leech (1817–64), illustrator and

caricaturist, famous for his large sketches in *Punch*; Alfred Henry Forrester, aka Alfred Crowquill (1804–77), illustrator for *Punch*, the *Illustrated London News*, and numerous books; Captain Frederick Marryat (1792–1848), most famous for his maritime novels; Phiz, pen name of Hablot Knight Browne (1815–82), book illustrator who illustrated ten of Dickens's novels; Clarkson Stanfield (1793–1867), painter who also worked as scene-painter for several years at Theatre Royal, Drury Lane; J. M. W. Turner (1775–1851), innovative landscape painter; Frank Stone (1800–59), book illustrator and watercolourist; Edwin Landseer (1802–73), painter, best known for his animal paintings; Thomas Webster (1800–86), English genre painter.

19. The Bankruptcy Court was situated in Basinghall Street in the City of London.

20. i.e. women poets.

21. For Clowes see Section IV n. 7. Andrew Spottiswoode (1787–1866) became a partner in the printing firm Eyre and Spottiswoode in 1832. The firm held the title of Printers to the Queen.

22. Kensal Green is the site of a large cemetery, especially fashionable in the early 1840s. Giovanni Belzoni (1798–1823) is notorious today as a raider of Egyptian tombs who enabled the British Museum to begin its collection.

23. Printer's devils were apprentices in printing.

24. Benjamin Franklin (1706–90) worked as a printer before becoming an American statesman.

25. Enormous painted transparencies shown at the Diorama building in Regent's Park; the scene could be transformed by changing the play of light on the transparency.

26. Holywell Street, located by the Strand, was a well-known location for the sale of immoral publications.

27. John Cleland's *Fanny Hill, or, Memoirs of a Woman of Pleasure* (1749), remained notorious for its bawdiness.

28. Cassell's issued a serial *Illustrated Family Bible*, eventually in 4 volumes, published 1859–63.

29. On the Religious Tract Society, see Section II n. 3. Both the *Leisure Hour: A Family Journal of Instruction and Recreation* (1852–1905) and *Sunday at Home: A Family Magazine for Sabbath Reading* (1854–1940) were penny weeklies.

30. Count Camillo Benso di Cavour (1810–61), architect of a unified Italy and its first prime minister.

31. *Penny Post: A Church of England Illustrated Magazine of Healthy Reading, Suited for Old and Young, Rich and Poor* (1850–94).

32. Norman Macleod (1812–72) Scottish evangelical, writer and social reformer, most famous for editing *Good Words*.

33. John Dawson Watson (1832–92), British painter, watercolourist, and illustrator.

34. *Cassell's Illustrated History of England* (1857–64). Its initial volume was written by J. F. Smith (see Section V above) until Cassell realized that Smith was less concerned with facts than narrative drive. On Howitt, see Section VI n. 24.

35. Sir John Moore (1761–1809) was a distinguished general who achieved renown for his heroics at the battle of Corunna during the Peninsular War, during which he was killed. Moore's leadership of the British forces saved Spain and Portugal from the armies of Napoleon.

36. Late sixteenth-century school of Italian painting that advocated direct observation from life; Ruskin was a fierce critic of its paintings.

37. Dolly Varden was an inordinate success as the Catholic, coquettish heroine of Dickens's historical novel about the Gordon riots, *Barnaby Rudge* (*Master Humphrey's Clock*, 1841). Captured by haters of Catholicism, Dolly is rescued by the one-armed (not one-legged – *pace* Ruskin) Joe Willets whom she eventually marries. The locksmith refers to Gabriel Varden, Dolly's father. The later reference to a railway refreshment counter may be to Joe's father, an innkeeper.

38. Ruskin was always scathing of the 'cockney', but does not use it to refer simply to East Londoners: he used it to describe Christ Church, Oxford, and work by the painter Whistler.

39. The National Art Training Schools of South Kensington were set up in 1853 to provide training in art and design.

40. George Du Maurier (1834–96), English illustrator and writer; he produced many illustrations for *Punch*, *Cornhill Magazine*, *Good Words*, and *Leisure Hour*.

41. Electuaries were concoctions made up by chemists, often involving sugar.

42. J. M. W. Turner's *Liber Studiorum*, first issued in 1807, was a long series of landscape plates, drawn and etched by Turner; it appeared in fourteen parts until 1819.

43. William Blake (1757–1827), poet, painter, and printer, published a series of twenty-two engravings of the Book of Job in 1826; they were among the last works Blake completed.

44. *Penny Illustrated Paper* (1861–1913); *Illustrated Sporting and Dramatic News* (1874–1943); *Pall Mall Budget* (1868–94).

45. Sir George Newnes (1851–1910), newspaper and magazine proprietor, most famously of *Tit-Bits* (1881–1970); he incorporated his

business in 1891 with capital of £4,000. Alfred Harmsworth (1865–1922) launched the *Daily Mail* in 1896 at ½ *d*. Sir Arthur Pearson (1866–1921) initially started working for George Newnes but later founded the *Daily Express* in 1900 as a ½ *d*. newspaper.

46. Herbert Ingram (1811–60), publisher and proprietor of *Illustrated London News*.

47. *Black and White: A Weekly Illustrated Record and Review* (1891–1912).

48. Melton Prior (1845–1910), illustrator, started working for the *Illustrated London News* in 1868; known principally as a war artist. Henry Charles Seppings Wright (1850–1937), pictorial journalist and book illustrator, worked for *Illustrated London News* up until at least the First World War.

49. Fredric Leighton (1830–96), President of Royal Academy 1878–96; Leighton argued that illustrators should be able to have full Academy status.

50. William Thomas founded the *Graphic* in 1869; he had previously worked as an engraver for the *Illustrated London News*.

51. i.e. electro-type plates. Electro-etching had been around since the mid-1850s: see Charles Walker, *Electrotype Manipulation*, 1852.

52. Sir John Gilbert (1817–97), painter and illustrator. Gilbert was renowned for his pictorial work for the *Illustrated London News*; he provided illustrations from its inception over a thirty-year period.

53. Joseph Pennell (1857–1926), American illustrator, moved to London in 1884 and did work for the *Graphic* and *English Illustrated Magazine*, and illustrated numerous books. Herbert Railton (1858–1910), draughtsman and book illustrator, best known for his work in the *English Illustrated Magazine*.

FURTHER READING

Our further reading, in no way meant to be exhaustive, concentrates mainly but not exclusively on secondary works in book form that are widely available. Many of them will lead the reader on to more primary sources. For extensive indexes of primary materials, however, the reader should consult either the print or electronic versions of the *Wellesley Index to Victorian Periodicals 1824–1900*, 5 vols. (1966–89), *Poole's Index to Periodical Literature 1802–1906*, 7 vols. (1882–1906), and the ongoing *Waterloo* project, of which the latest *Directory of English Newspapers and Periodicals* (series 2, in 20 vols.) dates from 2003 (Directories of Irish and of Scottish Newspapers and Periodicals date from 1986 and 1989 respectively). Much useful material appears in the *Victorian Periodical Review* (1979– ; previously *Victorian Periodical Newsletter*, 1968–1978). Finally, an invaluable online resource comprises Rosemanry Van Arsdel's bibliography of Victorian periodicals at http://victorianresearch.org/periodicals.html.

ALTHUSSER, LOUIS, 'Ideology and Ideological State Apparatuses (Notes Towards an Investigation)', *Lenin and Philosophy and Other Essays*, trans. Ben Brewster (London: New Left Books, 1971), 127–86.

ALTICK, RICHARD, *The English Common Reader: A Social History of the Mass Reading Public, 1800–1900* (1957; Columbus, Oh.: Ohio University Press, 1998).

—— *Punch: The Lively Youth of a British Institution 1841–1851* (Columbus, Oh.: Ohio University Press, 1997).

ANDERSON, PATRICIA, *The Printed Image and the Transformation of Popular Culture 1790–1860* (Oxford: Oxford University Press, 1991).

ANDREWES, ALEXANDER, *The History of British Journalism, from the Foundation of the Newspaper Press in England to the Repeal of the Stamp Act in 1855, with Sketches of Press Celebrities*, 2 vols. (London: Richard Bentley, 1859).

ANG, IEN, 'The Nature of the Audience', in John Downing, Ali Mohammadi, and Annabelle Sreberny-Mohammadi (eds.), *Questioning the Media: A Critical Introduction* (London: Sage, 1995), 207–20.

ANG, IEN, *Living Room Wars: Rethinking Media Audiences for a Postmodern World* (London: Routledge, 1996).

ASHTON, JOHN (ed.), *Modern Street Ballads* (London: Chatto & Windus, 1888).

BARNES, JAMES, *Free Trade in Books: A Study of the London Book Trade since 1800* (Oxford: Clarendon Press, 1964).

—— *Authors, Publishers and Politicians* (London: Routledge, 1974).

BEETHAM, MARGARET, *A Magazine of Her Own?: Domesticity and Desire in the Woman's Magazine, 1800–1914* (London: Routledge, 1996).

—— and BOARDMAN, KAY (eds.), *Victorian Women's Magazines: An Anthology* (Manchester: Manchester University Press, 2001).

BELL, BILL, BRAKE, LAUREL, and FINKELSTEIN, DAVID (eds.), *Nineteenth-Century Media and the Construction of Identities* (Basingstoke: Palgrave, 2000).

BENNETT, SCOTT, 'Revolutions in Thought: Serial Publication and the Mass Market for Reading', in Joanne Shattock and Michael Woolf (eds.), *The Victorian Periodical Press: Samplings and Soundings* (Leicester: Leicester University Press, 1982), 225–57.

BESANT, ANNIE, *An Autobiography* (London: T. Fisher Unwin, 1893).

BESANT, WALTER, *The Society of Authors: A Record of Its Actions from its Foundations* (London: Society of Authors, 1893).

BLACK, JEREMY, *The English Press 1621–1861* (Stroud: Sutton, 2001).

BRAKE, LAUREL, *Subjugated Knowledges: Gender, Journalism and Literature in the Nineteenth Century* (Basingstoke: Macmillan, 1994).

—— *Print in Transition, 1850–1910: Studies in Media and Book History* (Basingstoke: Palgrave, 2001).

—— MADDEN, LIONEL, and JONES, ALED (eds.), *Investigating Victorian Journalism* (Basingstoke: Macmillan, 1990).

BRANTLINGER, PATRICK, *The Reading Lesson: the Threat of Mass Literacy in Nineteenth-Century British Fiction* (Bloomington, Ind: Indiana University Press, 1998).

BROWN, LUCY, *Victorian News and Newspapers* (Oxford: Clarendon Press, 1985).

CAMPBELL, KATE (ed.), *Journalism, Literature and Modernity* (Edinburgh: Edinburgh University Press, 2000).

CHANDLER, JOHN H., and DAGNALL, H., *The Newspaper and Almanac Stamps of Great Britain and Ireland* (Saffron Walden: Great Britain Philatelic Association, 1981).

CHANDRASEKHAR, SRIPATI (ed.), *Reproductive Physiology and Birth Control* (London: Transaction Publishers, 2002).

CHARTIER, ROGER, *The Order of Books*, trans. Lydia Cochrane (Cambridge: Polity Press, 1994).

COLBY, ROBERT, 'Harnessing Pegasus: Walter Besant, *The Author*, and the Profession of Authorship', *Victorian Periodicals Review*, 23.3 (1990), 111–20.

COLLET, COLLET DOBSON, *History of the Taxes on Knowledge* (London: T. Fisher Unwin, 1899).

COLLISON, ROBERT, *The Story of Street Literature: Forerunner of the Popular Press* (London: Dent, 1973).

COOVER, JAMES (ed.), *Music Publishing, Copyright and Piracy in Victorian England* (London: Mansell, 1985).

Copyright Commission, *Royal Commissions and the Report of the Copyright Commissioners* (London: HMSO, 1878).

CROSS, NIGEL, *The Common Writer: Life in Nineteenth-Century Grub Street* (Cambridge: Cambridge University Press, 1985).

DALZIEL, MARGARET, *Popular Fiction 100 Years Ago: An Unexplored Tract of Literary History* (London: Cohen & West, 1957).

DEANE, BRADLEY, *The Making of the Victorian Novelist: Anxieties of Authorship in the Mass Market* (New York: Routledge, 2002).

DODD, GEORGE, *Days at the Factories; or, The Manufacturing Industry of Great Britain Described* (London: Charles Knight, 1843).

DOUGHTY, TERRI (ed.), *Selections from the Girl's Own Paper* (Peterborough, Ontario: Broadview, 2004).

EDWARDS, PAUL, *Dickens's Young Men: George Augustus Sala, Edmund Yates and the World of Victorian Journalism* (Aldershot: Ashgate, 1998).

ELIOT, SIMON, *Some Patterns and Trends in British Publishing, 1800–1919* (London: Bibliographical Society, 1993).

FEATHER, JOHN, *A History of British Publishing* (London: Routledge, 1988).

FELTES, N. N., *Modes of Production of Victorian Novels* (Chicago: University of Chicago Press, 1986).

FETTERLY, JUDITH, *The Resisting Reader: A Feminist Approach to American Fiction* (Bloomington, Ind.: Indiana University Press, 1978).

FEBVRE, LUCIEN, and MARTIN, JEAN, *The Coming of the Book*, trans. David Gerrard (London: Verso, 1976).

FIDLER, ROGER, *Mediamorphosis: Understanding New Media* (London: Sage, 1999).

FINKELSTEIN, DAVID, *The House of Blackwood: Author–Publisher Relations in the Victorian Era* (University Park, Pa.: Penn State University Press, 2002).

FINKELSTEIN, DAVID, and MCCLEERY, ALISTAIR (eds.), *The Book History Reader* (London: Routledge, 2002).

FLINT, KATE, *The Woman Reader 1837–1914* (Oxford: Clarendon Press, 1993).

FOUCAULT, MICHEL, 'What is an Author?', in Paul Rabinow (ed.), *The Foucault Reader* (Harmondsworth: Penguin, 1986), 101–20.

FOX, CELINA, *Graphic Journalism in England during the 1830s and 1840s* (New York: Garland, 1988).

FRASER, HILARY, GREEN, STEPHANIE, and JOHNSTON, JUDITH, *Gender and the Victorian Periodical* (Cambridge: Cambridge University Press, 2003).

GILBERT, PAMELA, *Disease, Desire and the Body in Victorian Women's Popular Novels* (Cambridge: Cambridge University Press, 1997).

GILMARTIN, KEVIN, *The Press and Radical Opposition in Early Nineteenth-Century England* (Cambridge: Cambridge University Press, 1996).

GISSING, GEORGE, *New Grub Street* (London: Smith, Elder & Co., 1891).

GOLDMANN, PAUL, *Victorian Illustrated Books 1850–1870: The Heyday of Wood Engraving* (London: British Museum Press, 1994).

—— *Victorian Illustration: The Pre-Raphaelites, the Idyllic School and the High Victorians* (Aldershot: Scolar Press, 1996).

GRANT, JAMES, *The Newspaper Press: Its Origins—Progresses—and Present Position* (London: Tinsley Brothers, 1871).

GRIEST, GUINEVERE L., *Mudie's Circulating Library and the Victorian Novel* (Bloomington, Ind.: Indiana University Press, 1970).

HABERMAS, JÜRGEN, *The Structural Transformation of the Public Sphere: Inquiry into a Category of Bourgeois Society*, trans. Thomas Burger and Frederick Lawrence (Cambridge: Polity Press, 1992).

HATTON, JOSEPH, *Journalistic London* (London: Sampson Low, Searle and Rivington, 1882).

HAYWOOD, IAN, *The Revolution in Popular Literature: Print, Politics and the People 1790–1860* (Cambridge: Cambridge University Press, 2004).

HINDLEY, CHARLES, *Curiosities of Street Literature* (London: Reeves and Turner, 1871).

—— *The Life and Times of James Catnach* (London: Reeves and Turner, 1878).

HOLLIS, PATRICIA, *The Pauper Press: A Study in the Working-Class Radicalism of the 1830s* (London: Oxford University Press, 1970).

HOWE, ELLIC (ed.), *The London Compositor: Documents relating to Wages, Working Conditions and Customs of the London Printing Trade 1785–1900* (London: Bibliographical Society, 1947).

HUGHES, LINDA K., and LUND, MICHAEL, *The Victorian Serial* (Charlottesville, Va., University Press of Virginia, 1991).

HUNT, FREDERICK KNIGHT, *The Fourth Estate: Contributions towards a History of Newspapers and of the Liberty of the Press* (1850; London: Routledge/Thoemmes, 1998).

HYLAND, PAUL, and SAMMELLS, NEIL (eds.), *Writing and Censorship in Britain* (London: Routledge, 1992).

JACKSON, KATE, *George Newnes and the New Journalism in Britain, 1880–1910: Culture and Profit* (Aldershot: Ashgate, 2001).

JACKSON, MASON, *The Pictorial Press: Its Origin and Progress* (London: Hurst & Blackett, 1885).

JAMES, LOUIS, *Fiction for the Working Man 1830–1850: A Study of the Literature Produced for the Working Classes in Early Victorian Urban England* (London: Oxford University Press, 1963).

—— *Print and the People 1819–1851* (London: Allen Lane, 1976).

JARVIS, ROBIN, *The Romantic Period: The Intellectual & Cultural Context of English Literature 1789–1830* (London: Longman, 2004).

JONES, ALED, *Powers of the Press: Newspapers, Power and the Public in Nineteenth-Century England* (Aldershot: Scolar Press, 1996).

JORDAN, JOHN O., and PATTEN, ROBERT L. (eds.), *Literature in the Marketplace: Nineteenth-Century British Publishing and Reading Practices* (Cambridge: Cambridge University Press, 1995).

KEATING, PETER J., *The Haunted Study: A Social History of the English Novel 1875–1914* (London: Secker and Warburg, 1989).

KEEN, PAUL (ed.), *Revolutions in Romantic Literature: An Anthology of Print Culture, 1780–1832* (Peterborough, Ontario: Broadview, 2004).

KELLY, THOMAS, *A History of Public Libraries in Great Britain 1845–1975* (London: Library Association, 1977).

KING, ANDREW, 'A Paradigm of Reading the Victorian Penny Weekly: Education of the Gaze and *The London Journal*', in Bill Bell, Laurel Brake, and David Finkelstein (eds.), *Nineteenth-Century Media and the Construction of Identities* (Basingstoke: Palgrave, 2000), 77–92.

—— *The London Journal 1845–83: Periodicals, Production and Gender* (Aldershot: Ashgate, 2004).

—— and PLUNKETT, JOHN (eds.), *Popular Print Media 1820–1900*, 3 vols. (London: Routledge, 2004).

KLANCHER, JON P., *The Making of English Reading Audiences 1790–1832* (Madison: University of Wisconsin Press, 1987).

KNIGHT, CHARLES, *The Old Printer and the Modern Press* (London: John Murray, 1854).

KNIGHT, CHARLES *Passages of a Working Life during Half a Century, with a Prelude of Early Reminiscences* (London: Bradbury and Evans, 1864–5).

LAW, GRAHAM, *Serializing Fiction in the Victorian Press* (Basingstoke: Palgrave, 2000).

LEDGER, SALLY, *The New Woman: Fiction and Feminism at the Fin de Siècle* (Manchester: Manchester University Press, 1997).

LEE, ALAN, *The Origins of the Popular Press 1855–1914* (London: Croom Helm, 1976).

McCALMAN, IAIN, *Radical Underworld: Prophets, Revolutionaries and Pornographers 1795–1840* (1988; Clarendon Press: Oxford, 1993).

McGANN, JEROME, *Radiant Textuality: Literature after the World Wide Web* (New York: Palgrave, 2001).

McLUHAN, MARSHALL, *Understanding the Media* (London: Routledge, 1964).

MAIDMENT, BRIAN, *The Poorhouse Fugitives: Self-Taught Poets and Poetry in Victorian Britain* (Manchester: Carcanet, 1987).

—— *Into the 1830s: Some Origins of Victorian Illustrated Journalism* (Manchester: Manchester Polytechnic Library, 1992).

—— *Reading Popular Prints 1770–1870* (Manchester: Manchester University Press, 1996).

MILL, JOHN STUART, *Autobiography*, ed. Harold J. Laski (London: Oxford University Press, 1924).

MOORE, GEORGE, *Literature at Nurse: A Polemic on Victorian Censorship* (London: Vizetelly, 1885).

MYERS, ROBIN, and HARRIS, MICHAEL (eds.), *Censorship and the Control of Print in England and France 1600–1910* (Winchester: St Paul's Bibliographies, 1992).

NEUBERG, VICTOR, 'Literature of the Streets', in H. J. Dyos and Michael Wolff (eds.), *The Victorian City: Images and Realities*, i (London: Routledge and Kegan Paul, 1973), 191–209.

NOWELL-SMITH, SIMON, *International Copyright Law and the Publisher in the Age of Queen Victoria* (Oxford: Clarendon Press, 1968).

ONSLOW, BARBARA, *Women of the Press in Nineteenth-Century Britain* (Basingstoke: Macmillan, 2000).

PARKER, MARK, *Literary Magazines and British Romanticism* (Cambridge: Cambridge University Press, 2000).

PARSON, IAN, 'Copyright and Society', in Asa Briggs (ed.), *Essays in the History of Publishing* (London: Longman, 1974), 29–60.

PATTEN, ROBERT L., *Charles Dickens and his Publishers* (Oxford: Clarendon Press, 1978).

PLUNKETT, JOHN, *Queen Victoria: First Media Monarch* (Oxford: Oxford University Press, 2003).

PYKETT, LYN, *The 'Improper' Feminine: The Women's Sensation Novel and the New Woman Writing* (London: Routledge, 1992).

RADWAY, JANICE, 'Reading is not Eating: Mass-produced Literature and the Theoretical, Methodological and Political Consequences of a Metaphor', *Book Research Quarterly*, 2 (1986), 7–29.

RAUCH, ALAN, *Useful Knowledge: The Victorians, Morality, and the March of Intellect* (Durham, NC: Duke University Press, 2001).

REED, DONALD, *The Power of News: The History of Reuters 1849–1989* (Oxford: Oxford University Press, 1992).

REYNOLDS, G. W. M., *The Mysteries of London*, ed. Trefor Thomas (Keele: Keele University Press, 1996).

ROSE, JONATHAN. *The Intellectual Life of the British Working Classes* (New Haven: Yale University Press, 2001).

ST CLAIR, WILLIAM, *The Reading Nation in the Romantic Period* (Cambridge: Cambridge University Press, 2004).

SAUNDERS, DAVID, *Authorship and Copyright* (London: Routledge, 1992).

SEVILLE, CATHERINE, *Literary Copyright Reform in Early Victorian England: The Framing of the 1842 Copyright Act* (Cambridge: Cambridge University Press, 1999).

SHATTOCK, JOANNE, *Politics and Reviewers: The Edinburgh and the Quarterly in the Early Victorian Age* (Leicester: Leicester University Press, 1989).

—— and WOOLF, MICHAEL (eds.), *The Victorian Periodical Press: Samplings and Soundings* (Leicester: Leicester University Press, 1982).

SHERMAN, BRAD, and STROWEL, ALAIN (eds.), *Of Authors and Origins: Essays on Copyright Law* (Oxford: Clarendon Press, 1994).

SINNEMA, PETER, *Dynamics of the Pictured Page: Representing the Nation in the Illustrated London News* (Aldershot: Ashgate, 1998).

SULLIVAN, ALVIN (ed.), *British Literary Magazines*, 4 vols. (London: Greenwood Press, 1984).

SUTHERLAND, JOHN, *Victorian Novelists and their Publishers* (London: Athlone Press, 1976).

—— *Victorian Fiction: Writers, Publishers, Readers* (London: Macmillan, 1995).

TROLLOPE, ANTHONY, *An Autobiography* (London: W. Blackwood & Sons, 1883).

TURNER, MARK, *Trollope and the Magazines: Gendered Issues in Mid-Victorian Britain* (Basingstoke: Palgrave, 2000).

TWYMAN, MICHAEL, *Printing 1770–1970: An Illustrated History of its Development and Uses in England* (London: Eyre and Spottiswoode, 1970).

VANN, J. DON, and VANARSDEL, ROSEMARY T. (eds.), *Victorian Periodicals: a Guide to Research*, 2 vols. (New York, Modern Language Association, 1978, 1989).

—— *Victorian Pariodicals and Victorian Society* (Toronto, University of Toronto Press, 1994).

—— *Periodicals of Queen Victoria's Empire. An Exploration* (Toronto, University of Toronto Press, 1996).

VINCENT, DAVID, *Bread, Knowledge and Freedom: A Study of Nineteenth-Century Working-Class Autobiography* (London: Europa, 1981).

—— *Literacy and Popular Culture: England, 1750–1914* (Cambridge: Cambridge University Press, 1989).

WEEDON, ALEXIS, *Victorian Publishing: The Economics of Book Production for a Mass Market 1838–1916* (Aldershot: Ashgate, 2003).

WHEATLEY, KIM, *Romantic Periodicals and Print Culture* (London: Taylor & Francis, 2003).

WIENER, JOEL, *The War of the Unstamped. The Movement to Repeal the British Newspaper Tax, 1830–1836* (Ithaca, NY: Cornell University Press, 1969).

—— (ed.), *Innovators and Preachers: The Role of the Editor in Victorian England* (Westport, Conn.: Greenwood Press, 1985).

—— (ed.), *Papers for the Millions: The New Journalism in Britain* (Westport, Conn.: Greenwood Press, 1988).

WILLIAMS, RAYMOND, *Keywords: A Vocabulary of Culture and Society* (London: Fontana, 1976).

WILLIAMSON, JUDITH, *Decoding Advertisements: Ideology and Meaning in Advertisements* (London: Marion Boyars, 1978).

WOODMANSEE, MARTHA, and JASZI, PETER (eds.), *The Construction of Authorship: Textual Appropriation in Law and Literature* (Durham, NC: Duke University Press, 1994).

WYNNE, DEBORAH, *The Sensation Novel and the Victorian Family Magazines* (Basingstoke: Palgrave, 2001).

INDEX